THE MAROONS OF JAMAICA 1655–1796

Courtesy, Institute of Jamaica, Kingston

Jamaica in 1774

THE MAROONS OF JAMAICA 1655–1796

A History of Resistance, Collaboration & Betrayal

MAVIS C. CAMPBELL

Africa World Press, Inc.
P.O. Box 1892
Trenton, New Jersey 08607

Africa World Press, Inc.
15 Industry Court
Trenton, N.J. 08638

Cover design by Ife Nii Owoo

Library of Congress Catalog Card Number: 88-70992

ISBN: 0-86543-096-9

Acknowledgments

The research for this work of over ten years was done without the support of any grants from the great foundations. But I am grateful to Amherst College for the Faculty Grants that have been generously offered me. I am also grateful to many of my colleagues here in the History Department who gave me a great deal of encouragement: Theodore P. Greene (Ted), our Distinguished Winthrop H. Smith Professor of History, who read most of the earlier drafts and whose interest in the work was a great source of inspiration to me. Peter Czap, our Russian specialist, most generously translated two Russian texts on the Maroons for me, and John Petropoulos, our Middle Eastern specialist who also specializes in European resistance and collaboration, graciously pointed out to me some literature on collaboration generally. I am also grateful to Christopher Fyfe who read different versions of the entire manuscript, and, as is known in the scholarly community, his response was careful, conscientious, candid, and useful. To Edward Brathwaite of the University of the West Indies, I am always grateful for his sustained interest in the Maroon saga. To Ms. Jean Hughes of London, England, for her interest and support for the work and for her insightful comments.

The work was greatly facilitated by a year's sabbatic leave which I spent as a Visiting Fellow at the University of Edinburgh, where I refined the final draft of the manuscript. It was here that I met George Shepperson who read this final draft and, with his known historical flair, suggested a change of the title which was acted upon, and I am grateful to him for the suggestion.

I must also extend my profound gratitude to those Maroons who became my friends and advisors as I lived among them in their different communities: to Colonel Harris and Captain Smith and their families of Moore Town; to Colonel Latibeaudiere and his Major, Mrs. Mary Jonas, the first woman to be appointed major to this town; to Colonel Wright and his family of Accompong Town and to the indomitable Mann O. Rowe, an important official of this town, and a descendant of two former Colonels of the same name; but Rowe has claimed even more illustrious ancestry when he told me that he was a descendant of the great Nanny whose "real" name, he said, was Matilda Rowe (the text will reveal further obfuscation of this character); to old Robert Osborne (Tata) now dead, who was ninety-three years old when I interviewed him over twelve years ago. Secrecy to this old fox, whose faculties were razor-sharp, was second nature, reminiscent of the old Maroon fighting days when this trait was pivotal to their guerrilla strategies. He would tell me nothing save that which he considered unimportant but was generous in reciting lengthy poems, his favorite being Tennyson's "Charge of the Light Brigade."

A version of Chapter 2 has been published in the *Annals* of the New York Academy of Sciences (vol. 292), and I am grateful to the editor for permission to reprint it.

I consulted many repositories of learning on three continents for this work and the other volumes and articles connected with it: the National Archives of Jamaica in Spanish Town; the Institute of Jamaica, Kingston; the Library of the University of the West Indies at Mona; the Public Record Office, London; the University of London Library at the Senate House and its Manuscript Division; the Library of the London School of Economics and Political Science; the Institute of Commonwealth Studies; the Royal Commonwealth Society, London; the Library of the University of Bristol; the British Museum (the British Library) and its Manuscript Division; the Library of the University of Sierra Leone and its Archives Division; the Archives of the Gambia; the New York Public Library; the Columbia University Library; the Yale University Libraries, especially the Rare Books Collection Section; the John Carter Brown Library at Brown University; to the Frost Library at Amherst College, especially to Michael Kasper, of the Reference Department, who, like a ferret, would soon track down rare books within this country, but not found at Frost for me; and to all the small private collections I consulted but too numerous to mention here. To all of the officials of these institutions, I am grateful for their willingness and courtesy in service.

Finally, I must thank the secretary of the Department of Computer Science at the University of Edinburgh, Eleanor Kerse, who processed the manuscript on their ultra-modern LaTeX system; Betty Steele, director of the Academic Computer Center at Amherst College, who with professional swiftness and efficiency, arranged for technical assistance in transferring the Edinburgh computer work to the Amherst system; and Margaret Ferro, secretary of the Amherst College Academic Computer Center for final processing of the manuscript. I felt fortunate to have had the final stage of this manuscript done by the skilled and cool-headed Margaret Ferro, with her intelligent and sensitive concern for the work.

As is to be expected, I must state that any errors found in this book will be my responsibility.

Mavis C. Campbell
Amherst College

Contents

Chapter 1
Introduction

Resistance was an integral part of Caribbean slave society. Its pervasiveness demonstrated the slaves' consciousness of themselves as human beings with their own values and aspirations different from those of the slave owners. From the point of view of the slave masters, anxious to maximize their material wealth, slave resistance displayed the bothersome nature, and one of the inherent contradictions, of this peculiar species of property. Slaves resisted in myriad ways. These could range from the subtle and passive, constantly acted out on a routinized daily basis, to the violent, whether singly or collectively, planned or spontaneous. But perhaps the most vexing of the slaves' resistance techniques to the owners was the act of running away to establish their own habitations — Maroon societies. These were autonomous communities existing outside the purlieus of the territorial units of the slave plantations. These communities were the most vexing to the authorities, because they stood not only as a bad example to estate slaves, but were also a constant reminder of the slaves' rejection of the life-style the masters had designed for them. In so challenging the slave system, the Maroons were determined to defend their communities to the very end, ready to "moulder" before they would surrender.[1]

The word "Maroon" — *Marron* to the French — has come to be used as a generic term to designate fugitive slaves from plantations in the New World, although the Iberians had their own designations.[2] The etymology is uncertain, but consensus opinion would seem to accept the view that it derives from the Spanish word *cimarron*, which originally referred to domestic cattle that had escaped to a wild existence.[3] In the course of time, however, the term lost its faunal connotation to embrace runaway slaves almost exclusively. As *cimarron* would seem to be a peculiarly New

World term, first applied in Hispaniola, so also is its derivative, Maroon, when applied to runaway slaves. As far as Jamaica is concerned, the official documents, as well as early works on the island, did not make use of the term until well into the eighteenth century. This study, however, will apply the "proper" designation of Maroons, from their inception in 1655, under the British.

The history of Maroon societies in the New World is the history of guerrilla warfare. Guerrilla warfare is not new to history – nor are its techniques and tactics as well as its *raison d'etre*. Invariably guerrilla warfare is the choice of the weak against the strong — at least in material terms. Invariably, too, its *modus operandi* has been that of surprise attack and retreat and ingenious ambuscades, thereby avoiding direct confrontations. The Maroons in the New World were the first in this hemisphere to strike a blow for freedom — as far as recorded history goes. And it is in this sense that they can be seen as the first Americans.

Not surprisingly, marronage — the process of flight by slaves from servitude to establish their own hegemonies in inhospitable areas — had its beginnings in Hispaniola, the first European settlement in the New World. As early as 1503, two years after the start of the slave traffic to the Caribbean, the runaway problem had become so great that the governor of the island urged the Spanish government to suspend the trade — which, in fact, was actually done for a short time. By the middle of the sixteenth century bands of runaways — outnumbering the white male population seven to one — had established themselves in the mountains, descending at intervals to attack the settlements below.[4] This was to become the pattern throughout the Caribbean, and as the slave systems in the area developed, some of the harshest punishments were reserved for the "skulking runaways," or "sneaking and treacherous rouges," or "desperate villians" or "pernicious scum," among the many opprobrious terms used by one European power or another to describe the Maroons. Laws were passed in Jamaica and elsewhere giving every citizen the power to capture Maroons, dead or alive, and generous rewards were proffered. Even slaves would be granted freedom for capturing or killing Maroons. After all, in the purview of the capital accounting, a runaway — a Maroon — was both capital and labor, and a prime slave — the one more apt to run off — could fetch up to £350, especially in times of scarcity.

The Spaniards set the example in the region of instituting mechanisms for retrieving runaways. For the most part, these consisted of trained bloodhounds or hunting parties called *rancheadores*, comparable to the professional slave catchers of ancient Rome, the *fugitivarii*. The Portuguese in Brazil, fearing the example of Palmares, their largest Maroon settlement, organized units called *capitâos-do-mato* or bush captains to conduct their search. The Spanish Church also joined in, and the Inquisition, never backward in dispensing punishments, saw the attempt to escape from slavery as the equivalent of apostasy, for which such slaves should be made to atone either in this world or in the hereafter.[5] But the Africans, indifferent to the white man's punishments or to his ontological view of damnation, continued to run away from the indignity of slavery to set up their own communities in ways conformable to their view of things.

The ubiquity of Maroon societies in the New World plantation economy is now well documented by recent scholarship.[6] So far as their continuance into the present is concerned, Jamaica and Surinam stand unique. From the evidence, all Maroon communities were based on African sociopolitical and military formations, with creative adaptations to suit conditions applicable to the New World. This is not to imply that each was built on a homogeneous African culture block. It is more to say that they were not European based. For even where we are clear about the ethnicity of the leaders, we cannot be certain of the identity of the rank-and-file members. Indeed we have fragmentary evidence to suggest that there was ethnic plurality within most bands, although one group might be in a dominant position based on demography or on military capacity. We now know that most of the Maroon leaders, especially those of Jamaica, were of the Akan-speaking group. But this does not tell us that the Akans in each of these communities were also in the majority. Cudjoe of Jamaica, for instance — perhaps the best known Maroon leader in the hemisphere — in order to prevent ethnic cleavages that could be damaging to his authoritarian leadership, insisted that his people speak the enemy's language — English — in his community during the period before the Treaties that were signed between them and the colonial authorities later. This would seem to suggest ethnic heterogeneity in his midst. Ironically, the slave masters, too, were insisting on identical uniformity of language among the plantation slaves for the same security consideration.

Among the rich gleanings we have from a study of Maroon societies is the fact that despite ethnic plurality, the cultural commonalities would seem to have taken precedence over particularism. There appears to have existed a kind of "Africanness" that transcended regionalism, ethnic or linguistic affinities, on which these Maroons based their existence. Roger Bastide, in reference to the *Quilombos* (Maroon societies) of Brazil, said, rather engagingly, "[I]t would seem that in most cases, as in Palmares, we are dealing with 'tribal regression,' a kind of return to Africa." [7] The commonalities, for the most part, are reflected in sex roles, attitude to warfare, familial arrangements, attitude to hierarchy, but above all in religion, which was pivotal to all resistance in the area. More than any other single factor, African religious beliefs gave the unifying force, the conspiratorial locus, the rallying point to mobilize, to motivate, to inspire, and to design strategies: it gave the ideology, the mystique, and the pertinacious courage and leadership to Maroon societies to confront the mercantilist society with its awesome power. Maroon leaders were expected to be imbued with knowledge bearing on the supernatural forces. This, in their cosmology, was closely aligned not only to religion but also to military prowess, and such transcendental knowledge was to be manipulated for the benefit of the whole community.

The relationship between resistance and African religions is clearly demonstrated whether one looks at slave rebellions in general (the Haitian, for instance) or at Maroon societies. Regardless of ethnicity, the African — Yoruba, Ebo, Fon, or the Akan group — would invariably invoke the right *loa* (spirit) before going to war. And it is interesting to note that on these occasions, the *loa Ogun* (Yoruba god of war) was appealed to almost transethnically. Devotees, after taking oaths of allegiance and fidelity to the cause, thereafter would only need to rub themselves well with certain magical concoctions prepared by the religio-military leader, or to carry an assortment of charms or amulets on their persons to the place of war. This was perceived to render them impervious to the opponent's bullets, as was the belief among the native North Americans when fighting their wars against the "intruders." Such also was the belief of the Jamaican Maroon heroine Nanny and her followers, of Makandal of prerevolutionary St. Domingo (to the British; but St. Domingue to the French) and his followers, of Biassou, or Jean Francois and their followers, among others of revolutionary Haiti.

In Jamaican Maroon communities women played a multifaceted role. African fashion, they were the agriculturists, thus giving them nutritional power over the menfolk. What would happen should they go on strike? Well, the men would be engaged in hunting, so they did supply the meat-derived protein, although the women also raised domestic animals in their kitchen gardens. But some of the women were also great warriors. It is true that the very early Maroon societies did have a preponderance of men, reflecting not only the sexual imbalance on the plantations but also the hazardous nature of marronage and the peculiar dangers it held for females. But as marronage developed, some of these communities, especially those in the windward part of the island, had a parity of men and women, and, with children, by the 1730s the two latter would outnumber the men. This was the result of two main processes. First, early depredations on plantations by Maroons were not only for provisions, arms, powder and the like, but also for women. In some cases this was the primary purpose of raids. Then, there was natural procreation within the groups, which, surprisingly, from fragmentary evidence, was not without fecundity despite the precariousness of living. It appears that a few women did manage to run away singly to join one group or another, while some ran away in pairs with their lovers or "husbands." However, the incidence of female fugitives did not develop significantly until from around the first decade of the nineteenth century up to emancipation. There is no doubt that there existed priestesses and women warriors of great ferocity and leadership capability in Maroon communities in addition to the celebrated Nanny, now a national hero of Jamaica. Intriguingly, Nanny has also given patronymic significance to a child-care center in Cuba established in 1975 to accommodate some 180 children between the ages of six weeks and six years.[8] Unfortunately, most of the other women who fought side by side with the men, as mentioned in the documents, remain nameless to history.

Unfortunately, too, even some of the leaders — like Lubolo, Juan de Serras, Quao, and Accompong — can hardly be developed into well-rounded characters. We simply do not have the evidence. Juan de Serras, for instance, is not even known among the Maroons in Jamaica, as one discovers in field studies. In fact, from very fragmentary evidence, this work has attempted the first systematic treatment of de Serras, shadowy though the result may be. But we should be sensitive to the fact that a part of the frustration in dealing with certain aspects of Maroon affairs arises from the imperative of secrecy. Secrecy was a pivotal part of their strategy. This secrecy also precluded any intimate knowledge of their communities. The most we know came either from soldiers or from captured Maroons. But since the Maroons built their communities concentrically, with the outer towns serving as buffers, few, if any, soldiers ever reached the inner sanctum during the long period of hostility. Thus, the accounts we have from soldiers' diaries are not only perfunctory, describing evacuated settlements, but are also not representative of the strategic towns. It was not until the time of each treaty that we become privy to the strategic formation of these communities. A few of the captured Maroons have given us a glimpse of the internal organization of some of the towns. But this alone should not make us think that we have full and complete knowledge here. Even a captured Maroon under torture (as some were) could be relied on not to give away critical information. Most members of each community were bound by the awesome Akan oath, where secrecy was enjoined. We do not know if every member of each community took the oath, but we do know that all the ranking officials and the soldier class were participants. Some of the most insightful accounts we have of some of the Maroon settlements come from captured Maroon women. This may be telling us that the women were not generally under oath.

The history of the Maroons of Jamaica is not only a part of Jamaican military history, but also a part of the economic history of the island. Their hegemonies in the hills served as a model to the plantation slaves with the propensity to run away, either to join them or to set up similar communities. They preyed on plantations, advancing at intervals to inveigle away slaves, especially women, to carry off cattle and horses — or to kill or maim them on the spot, to help themselves to ammunition and other military accoutrement, or to kill or wound whites. Their depredations severely impeded the development of the plantation economy. The period of the greatest danger to the planting class was from the 1720s to 1738; the last ten years were viewed by the planters themselves as crisis years. Not only was there an exodus of planters from the island, who abandoned their estates because of Maroon intrusions, but, in addition, Maroon proximity to arable land either prevented owners with patents from settling or deterred the parceling out of lands in such vicinities — particularly in the northeastern sector of the country. And, in these years of crises, the slaves, always alert to detect any weakness in the social structure of the masters' world, deserted the plantations in large numbers — just as the slave masters themselves were abandoning their plantations.

It was at this period that one saw a clear parallel and a relationship between marronage and absenteeism. Like marronage, absenteeism was a flight — the flight of the master class, at times from the crudities of the slave society, and in this case definitely from the economic pressures derived from Maroon incursions. The relationship between these two flights, as we shall see, became dialectic in the early 1730s — with more masters fleeing home as more slaves took to the hills to become Maroons, and more masters again going off, and soon cause and effect became entangled. The process, as we said elsewhere,[9] might well have destroyed the plantation economy at this time, and the urgency of the deficiency laws of the plantocratic legislature aimed at increasing the number of whites on the island testifies to the whites' awareness of this. But, with the signing of peace Treaties with the "rebels" in 1738/9, the economic uncertainty disappeared, and the country became economically buoyant almost immediately.

The Maroons, too, must be seen as the first domestic-oriented agriculturists of the island, following the British occupation. The British planters were bent on the export-oriented monoculture of sugar, geared to the expanding markets of Europe. The Maroons, for their part, planted crops other than sugar, and their diversified surplus soon became accessible through the marketplaces for the larger population, especially during periods of droughts and other cataclysmic occurrences peculiar to the tropics. Long before the Treaties were signed, they would disguise themselves and pass as free blacks to enter the marketplaces both as buyers and as sellers.

By any standard, even when pushed to the irreducible minimum, the Maroon story is a heroic one. But it is a story that is also paradoxical, complex and puzzling — especially after the cessation of hostilities. The heroism, then, should be seen in terms of the courageous fight for freedom of a handful of bedraggled fugitives, whose numbers plantocratic fear had always inflated, against some of Britain's best trained soldiers. In recent times, perhaps, the Vietnam War comes a close parallel. Dallas quite clearly was also impressed by the almost absurdly one-sided nature of the balance of material power between contending parties. "Some may be inclined to think," he observed, "a Maroon insurrection a petty warfare of unskillful Negroes; but I believe that the officers who served in this campaign will allow that the events of it, and the tactics opposed to them, if not so grand as those that fill the Grecian and Roman pages of history, were at least as singular and embarassing .... Negroes defied the choicest troops of one of the greatest nations in the world, kept an extensive country in alarm,"[10] a country that was finally forced to sign a formal peace treaty with them, Dallas might have ended, had he been giving a conspectus of the Maroon wars in general and not just that of 1795–1796.

Many have made the error of citing the Jamaican eighteenth-century Maroon treaties as the first in the hemisphere, but this is not the case, although it would be correct to say that they were to be the primary influence on other such treaties. The Spaniards were in fact the first to conceive the policy of making treaties with Maroons — as well they might since they were the first in the area to have encountered this vexatious problem. As early as 1545, unable to defeat the major band in Hispaniola, they offered peace terms which were turned down by the Maroon leader, Diego de Campo. He was later captured, but talked his way out of execution by offering to lead expeditions against his former colleagues in the woods, and this was gladly accepted by the Spaniards.[11] This willingness on the part of the Maroons throughout the region to collaborate with the colonial slave regimes when resistance ended in "settlements" or treaties was as pervasive as was their resistance to such regimes.

It was in Panama that the *cimarrones* (Maroons) wreaked their greatest devastation on the Spanish Empire. In this case, their depredations were directed against the brutal slave portage (the *trajin*) of untold quantities of silver and gold, particularly between Nombre de Dios and Panama. The situation became even more alarming to the Spaniards when the *cimarrones* became "confederated" with the British pirates singly and in some cases with the French corsairs also. The period of the greatest harassment was between the 1540s and the 1570s. As the British were soon to complain in Jamaica that they feared the Maroons more than they did the Spaniards, so also was the complaint of the Spaniards at this time, fearing more the blacks than the British. The *cimarrones*, as the Maroons were to do in Jamaica, developed a superb system of espionage, and in Panama they were among the first to spot the arrival of the *flota*. The Spanish officials complained incessantly that the blacks, being so "thoroughly acquainted with the region and so expert in the bush," could thus show the British "methods and means to accomplish any evil design they may wish to carry out and execute."[12] One such demonstration was to show Drake how to cross the Isthmus of Panama, "a feat the English could not have performed alone."[13] After desperate, unsuccessful efforts to curb the power of the runaways, the Spaniards initiated peace negotiations with them. This was in 1579, some thirty-four years after similar overtures in Hispaniola. The net result yielded two separate treaties and the establishment of two free black communities close to Nombre de Dios.[14] So far as these communities are concerned, they soon became very useful to the Spaniards in fighting the British, their earlier allies. Upon his return to England, Drake had made much of his cooperation with the blacks, and he and his cronies were anticipating continued successful Anglo-*cimarrone* ventures. But their disappointment was acute when, in 1596, they returned to find the *cimarrones* now a part of the Spanish security system of Panama. "As for those symerouns [*cimarrones*] that were so much talked of before we left England, I protest I heard not so much as the name of them in the Indies," was the revealing complaint of one of Drake's men.[15] British perception of both the fighting prowess of these exrebels and their subsequent loyalty and collaboration with Spain as free communities was later to affect their policy toward the Jamaican Maroons.

But perhaps the most significant of these proto-treaties was that made in Mexico in 1609. We say significant simply because we know more about it, its terms, its leaders. Apparently this community maintained itself as an independent entity for a very long time. The Mexican treaty was made between the Spaniards and a sagacious old Maroon leader, Yanga (or Naga or Nanga), "an aging first generation African ... of the Bron nation, of whom it is said that if they had not captured him, he would have been king in his own land."[16] The term "Bron" should most probably be "Brong," a small branch of the Akan group, thus setting the precedent for Akan leadership in marronage in many parts of the region. There are certain comparisons that will be drawn later in this study between Yanga's treaty and that of Cudjoe. Even within Jamaica there were treaties made between rebels and the British in the seventeenth century. The Dutch, too, in 1684, made some form of peace settlement with some of their Maroons in Surinam, but "nothing more was heard [of it]."[17]

There are many misconceptions and misrepresentations regarding the Jamaican Maroons. This may well be due, in part, to the fact that the historical Maroons did not write their own story. Unfortunately we are not privy to any direct statements coming from them that could even approach the eloquence, the reasonableness, and the philosophical wisdom of the great Indian chiefs and warriors that have so illuminated and "lifted to high emotional and moral power," the narrative of Dee Brown's Indian history of the American West, for instance.[18] Hence we have no way of knowing what may have been in the minds of the leaders and how they perceived their goals. This is a handicap to the historians who must perforce lean heavily on official documents, eyewitnesses' accounts as well as on planter historians, almost all of whom were writing from the bias of their ethnocentricity and from the standpoint of their economic interests. But these sources are not without their uses. Apart from anything else, they serve to show contemporary attitudes toward the Maroons. The official documents provide the framework within which to reconstruct Maroon history, but from them we have nothing even close to ethnohistory.

Some of the misconceptions that have become common currency are due, no doubt, to the constant recourse to certain secondary sources that carried the contagion of inaccuracy and the neglect of primary source material, which, unfortunately, is not as accessible as the tertiary works. A most stubborn misconception, held even by some Maroons and other Jamaicans today, is that the Maroons are the descendants of the Arawak Indians — some adding the Miskito (Muskito or Moskito) Indians to the hybrid situation one would expect, without any evidence whatsoever.[19] The Miskito Indians were in fact used by the British as "mercenaries" to fight the Maroons on different occasions, but there is no evidence to show that there was ever any friendly relationship between these two groups. On the contrary, the evidence showed these Indians devoutly loyal to the British and by the eighteenth century they actually ceded their sovereignty to Britain, by having their monarchs approved of and crowned in Jamaica by the governor.[20] It does not seem likely that these Indians would have wished to join any enemy of Britain — not the Spaniards, whom they despised, not the Maroons, who would be deemed troublesome to their friends. As for the Arawak presence, we have no evidence that any had survived by the time of the British occupation. By 1655 Spanish ill treatment had decimated the race: "not a single descendant of either sex, being alive . . . nor, I believe, for a century before," declared Bryan Edwards, [21] writing in 1793; and he may well have been correct, for a census of 1611 had computed a remnant of seventy-four on the island. Dallas, writing in 1803, said, "To this day in the mountains of Jamaica caves are discovered in which human bones cover the ground: and the skulls being preternaturally compressed, it is evident they belonged to skeletons of the Indian race,"[22] which perished by famine. It appears that the Arawaks, who lived mainly on the flat lands along the coast — "even on the edge of the sea," according to Columbus — did not manage to conquer the environmental hazards of the mountains as the blacks were to do so

Miskito Indians "mercenaries"

successfully. But it is true that a few, being overburdened with the yoke of slavery, did escape to the mountains, and the skulls Dallas described may have included the remaining seventy-four of the 1611 census.

A most persistent misrepresentation is that which saw the Maroons fighting for their freedom not of their own volition, but upon the command of others. No Spaniard of Hispaniola or Panama, for instance, would have made such an egregious error. One source said that "[t]he Spanish taught the Maroons to fight the British as invaders,"[23] without giving any evidence. Another, committing a double error, said that "credit" should be given to the Spaniards for the early Maroon formation. For, "[j]ust before the Spaniards withdrew, they freed their negro slaves and armed them as guerrilla fighters against the English." The same source, in error again, said that "only in Jamaica . . . did these bands become anything more than gangs of depraved and skulking outlaws,"[24] thus denying Surinam of its heroic Maroon presence which exists to this day. All this is certainly not in congruence with Don Juan Ramirez's helplessness in writing to his Spanish monarch upon the British occupation, pointing out that his people, including "children, women and slaves," were "scattered about the mountains . . . without any hope of protection except from God . . . ."[25]

This study will not dwell on inquiries into the "causes" of marronage (as some have done),[26] based on the reckoning that, under ordinary circumstances, human beings will not tolerate their own subordination, and, given a chance, they will resist it in one way or another. We say "ordinary circumstances" since we know of at least one category of slaves, the *Machubes* of Northern Dahomey, who, we are told, would seem to have completely adjusted to their servile situation, viewing it as irreversible.[27] But throughout the work, we will examine the sociopolitical characteristics, the demographic and ethnic patterns, and certain ecological factors within a slave society that could be considered conducive to the formation of Maroon societies. There can be no doubt that ecology was of prime importance for the establishment of Maroon redoubts. And Jamaica, with its mountainous terrain, interspersed with countless hills, valleys, and rivers, with its deep ravines and its awesome cockpits with their narrow defiles and innumerable caves, is peculiarly suited for these establishments.

There has been no historical study of the Maroons of Jamaica tracing them through Nova Scotia to Sierra Leone since R. C. Dallas's *History of the Maroons* (1803). Although Dallas was not a trained historian, the work is not without merit, despite certain inaccuracies, and Dallas displayed less of the ethnocentricity — not to say racial bias — typical of the European attitude of the period to colonial people. His contemporary, Bryan Edwards, the planter historian of the Caribbean, is the very opposite of Dallas in his view of the Maroons. Edwards dealt with them in his two-volume *History*

... *of the British Colonies in the West Indies* (1793), and in his documentary on *The Proceedings of the Governor and Assembly of Jamaica in Regard to the Maroon* ... (1796). In both works Edwards displayed such a frenzied hostility to the Maroons that these works are hardly valuable except insofar as they exemplified the typical planter-class attitude toward a group that challenged the very existence of the plantation slave society. A relatively recent popular work worth noting is Carey Robinson's *The Fighting Maroons of Jamaica* (1969), which is almost wholly derived from Dallas's two-volume *History*. Robinson's work should be viewed in the light of that peculiar interest or romantic curiosity about the life of uneducated rebels that can engage the sophisticated, and within this genre, the work is most interesting. Most of the recent works, primarily theses, tend to be of a sociological or anthropological nature, and there is also a plethora of popular articles,[28] many of which are devoted to the inimitable Maroon leader Nanny. A large proportion of these articles should be seen as folkloric, and if every country needs its folklore, replete with mythology, then, in this sense, they have their value. Or, "To say it another way, when a story flourishes in the heart of a folklore, it is because in one way or another it expresses an aspect of 'the spirit of the group.'"[29]

An important landmark in recent works on the Maroons is Orlando Patterson's article, "Slavery and Slave Revolt: A Sociological Analysis of the First Maroon War 1655–1740," in *Social and Economic Studies* (1970). This work sets the stage for a systematic historical study on the Maroons. Patterson, a trained sociologist, laments that "no adequate historical analysis yet exists of this vital episode in West Indian history. Available accounts are either too inaccurate or superficial or ideologically biased, however, well meaning." The present work is an attempt to fill this gap.

The work was originally conceived of as a transatlantic history, under one cover, tracing the Maroons to Nova Scotia and from there to Sierra Leone. But the monumental proportion of the primary sources precluded this scheme as a one-volume proposition. Future works will deal with the Maroons in Nova Scotia and in Sierra Leone, and a comparison will be made with those remaining in Jamaica. Largely because of the misconceptions, the inaccuracies, and the misinterpretations connected with this subject, the author felt even a greater responsibility to search for the truth — "the only merit that gives dignity to history," in Acton's view. Materials of primary origin were therefore sought as far as they were available. This, of course, was both time consuming and expensive, but rewarding. The "facts" here marshaled can be subjected to empirical verification, but it is in the area of interpretation that dissent will more likely occur.

But a study of this subject could hardly have been done through documents alone. Other traces and clues leading, as much as possible, to the most exact reconstruction of this intriguing story were consulted. Old maps, surveyor's diagrams and notes, songs, folklore, taboos, and the like were all mobilized in the process, while a sense of Maroon *Weltanschauung* as well as their individual *Anschauung* was attempted by living among them at different periods. *In situ*, I have interviewed a number of people including the colonels, majors, and captains from all the existing Maroon communities (Accompong, Scotts Hall, Moore Town), in addition to disparate families from disintegrated former Maroon societies. One such is Hayfield (apparently donated to the Maroons after the 1865 Morant Bay "Rebellion," by one Harrison, whose life was saved by a Maroon in this local riot), and other settlements, especially those adjacent to Bath in St. Thomas. I have also spoken to a few who are living overseas. My interviews and conversations with the Maroon people, while living with them, were, above everything else, to ascertain a sense of their attitude to their history and to the other Jamaicans within the wider Jamaican polity. In current terms, many are particularly pleased about Marcus Garvey's Maroon heritage. Garvey, whose father is said to have been a Maroon, is seen as a continuation of the Maroon tradition of resistance to oppression. In terms of their perception of themselves as a community, they invariably and without any exception expressed a great appreciation for a historical work on them, primarily because they are aware that these communities would seem to be disintegrating. Where possible, their views have been incorporated in the text or in the notes of this work.

This work, therefore, marshaled a considerable body of data, presented not in a schematic or synthesized form but in the mode of narrative and analysis. The wealth of material lent itself to this approach. If it should be found "dense" in the historian's sense of the term, then it should never be forgotten that each detail has its meaning within the wider framework of this complex piece of human history, the Maroon saga. Furthermore, a focused study of this kind can permit us to arrive at the general from the particular. And this, to Peter Worsley,

> is one aspect of the scientific procedure .... The nineteenth-century distinction between "idiographic" and "nomothetic" studies, or the modern variant "descriptive *v.* theoretical" are not only logically fallacious, but practically-scientifically sterilizing .... "Nomothetic" work cannot be generated without empirical raw material in and from which patterns are derived. The ideal scientific desideratum, rather, is to abolish the distinction altogether. In lieu we should aim at analyses of limited situations — situations which may be very narrow or very large in scale — but *all* carried out, if not *sub specie aeternitas*, at least in the light of general theoretical problems, to which the research is always related and in the light of which it is always designed

> .... Equally, our theorising activities should always be anchored to, and located within, empirical inquiry.[30]

The work has also attempted to be free from technical jargon, which can often serve to obscure, in order to make it more accessible to a wide range of readers. Indeed, it is the hope that the descendants of the men and women whose history is treated herein will find it well within their range of comprehension, and it is largely with this view in mind that this work is dedicated to them.

I have also resisted any temptation, which would probably have been fashionable, to cast the Maroon resistance to plantocratic control in any theoretical construct, whether Marxist, Fanonian, "archaic," "primitive," "millenarian," or even Freudian, replete with psychoanalytic explanations. The Maroon saga would not fit neatly into any one of these categories. This may anger those who come to this subject with, for instance, a Marxist thesis. However, from the moment it was discovered that most Maroon societies kept slaves themselves, and that after the treaties and under the treaties, they were — and this is a most pervasive feature — willing to return runaways and to police the woods diligently in search of others, then we must, however reluctantly, yield theory to the reality of the case. We respect them for their fierce independent spirit, but we cannot see them as true revolutionaries or even as reformers, seeking to transform the society from one of servitude to freedom, as happened in Haiti between 1791 and 1804. Yet it is a story that has attracted many minds, including that of A. D. Dridzo, the Russian anthropologist from the Leningrad Academy of Sciences.[31] For the most part the Maroon communities had a "restorationist or isolationist, rather than a revolutionary content."[32]

But the fact is, their fight for freedom, however prepolitical, represents another chapter in the history of the human struggle for the extension of freedom — with all the contradictions. And, in this respect, a study of this kind is not, in the words of Hobsbawm, "merely curious, or interesting, or moving for anyone who cares about the fate of men, but also of practical importance."[33]

Chapter 2

Seventeenth-Century Marronage

Slaves in Jamaica were always on the lookout for propitious moments to throw off their chains. Such an opportunity presented itself when the British captured Jamaica from the Spaniards in 1655. The Spaniards of Jamaica, computed at "twelve or fourteen hundred," about 500 of whom were in arms,[1] from all accounts did not appear to have done much to develop the island. Although they had occupied Jamaica for nearly a century and a half (since 1509), the country remained underdeveloped and underpopulated. One source said that "not one hundredth part of the plantable land was in cultivation"[2] when the British took possession. Yet, determined not to dirty their hands with planting, they enslaved the native Arawaks, estimated variously at between six and sixty thousand, when Columbus "discovered" the island in 1494. But by 1655, Spanish ill treatment, European diseases, and the introduction of cattle, which destabilized native agriculture — among the objective factors — depopulated the island so that not a single descendant remained. Thus their most reliable source of slave labor, even before the Arawak population was decimated, was from Africa, in line with the inexorable pattern of the enslavement process of the New World.

The Spaniards lived, from the evidence, just above subsistence level, growing foodstuff for domestic consumption and supplying a few European-bound vessels with cocoa, lard, hides, fustic, ebony, and a sprinkling of other tropical commodities. It appears that they did not come to terms with the fact that Jamaica was not laden with gold, and the expectations, from silver and copper mines instead, equally were not realized. Nevertheless, for the relatively few activities they were engaged in, they needed slaves. Had they been in Europe, these activities would have been carried out by peasant or yeoman farmers. But the Spaniards and Portuguese who occupied the island brought with them a cultural heritage of slavery, not only as practiced in Iberia, but, more important, they also brought the model of the institutional complex of the slave-run sugar plantation of Madeira — Columbus himself having lived in Madeira for nearly ten years. Some of the slaves were, naturally, domestics, but those engaged in hunting wild cattle and hogs appeared to have been in the majority and "these hunters in the course of their work would have become masters of woodcraft and have known all the trails through the woods and mountains."[3] These skills were later to prove invaluable to them in their guerrilla activities. Edwards felt that the Spaniards, who had been for many years in "a State of progressive degeneracy, would probably, in a short time, have expiated the guilt of their ancestors, by falling victims themselves to the vengeance of their slaves."[4] The British conquest preempted Edwards's prophecy in the sense in which he meant it, although as will be shown later, the Spaniards did fall victims at least to some of their slaves.

The exact number of the black slaves at the time of the conquest is not clear, but the census of the island taken by the Spaniards in 1611 accounted for 107 free blacks and 558 slaves, while Edwards said "the number of Negroes" in 1655 "nearly equalled that of the whites,"[5] twelve to fifteen hundred, without making any distinction between the freed and the enslaved.

As victors, the British were hard taskmasters. They commanded the Spanish colonists to deliver up all their slaves and goods and leave the country altogether. But the Spaniards resented leaving. They pleaded that it was the only country they knew; they had been born and brought up on the island; they had neither relations nor friends elsewhere — therefore, they were determined to perish in the woods rather than leave! While a few finally left the island, chiefly for Cuba, Don Christoval Ysassi Arnaldo, who was later appointed governor of Jamaica by the Spanish king in acknowledgment of his strong stand against the British, with the rest of his countrymen and some slaves retreated to the hills on the north coast. From here they made frequent raids on the British on the south side, expecting to receive some help from Cuba, Puerto Rico, Cartagena, and New Spain. When this was not forthcoming, Ysassi was finally forced to give up his guerrilla activities and to leave the island in 1660.[6]

It was the black slaves of the Spaniards who took to the hills at the time of the British conquest who were to form the nucleus of the first Maroon society in Jamaica under the British. The question may be asked whether these Spanish blacks in the hills could properly be called runaway slaves. Given the definition of slaves as property, despite the inherent contradictions, then the Spanish blacks were by the conquest now British property and, as such, runaway slaves. This species of property in perpetuity was also heritable by itself and through its progeny. Thus descendants to be born in the hills would also be slaves, legally subject to be reconsigned to slavery in the event of capture, whatever their perception of themselves or their notion of their freedom might be, so long as a slave society existed on the island.

There is also a sense in which the Spanish Maroons could be seen as separate from and not a part of the continuum of Maroon society in Jamaica as developed from the turn of the seventeenth century to the first three decades of the eighteenth. The nature of their marronage, for instance, as arising from a historical event and not from the usual runaway situation — whether singly or in groups — was not typical. But despite the lack of unity among the different bands and despite the open hostility of the Spanish creole blacks toward the newly arrived African runaways considered in this study, the Spanish Maroons did set the stage for resistance; they created a precedent of defiance of the slave master's authority and their presence in the woods gave the inspiration to the plantation slaves either to run away or to rebel. In more concrete terms, when by the beginning of the eighteenth century they began to cooperate with the other groups, they contributed to the other groups their skill and expertise in guerrilla warfare and in adapting to their surroundings.

Another direct contribution of the Spanish Maroons — negative, perhaps, depending on one's point of view — is that they set the model for designating their leaders with Western titles, such as "governor," "serjeant major," and the like, and not with African ones as appeared prevalent in Maroon societies of the area in the seventeenth century.[7] This was of course due to the fact that the Spanish Maroons were creoles, again departing from the historical paradigm of newly arrived slaves taking the initiative and leadership position in slave revolts and marronage, although Haiti's Boukman and Toussaint Louverture were also exceptions to this rule.

The ethnic background of the Spanish slaves is imprecise. But if Curtin[8] is correct, then they were mostly from the northern part of West Africa and from Angola, encompassing numerous tribal groups, and not likely to be of the Akan speaking group at this time, as some would say.[9] The Akan presence among the Maroons began with the coefficient of correlation between Britain's capture of Jamaica and the Gold Coast's becoming a sphere of interest for British slave traders. Thus there is a clear ethnic difference between the seventeenth-century Maroons and their eighteenth-century counterparts, the former being mainly Spanish creoles of multiethnicity, some of whom were Christians, the latter mostly of the Akan — at least so far as the leaders were concerned.

The Spanish slaves saw their opportunity, in the fluid situation that followed the British capture of the island, to make a dash for freedom, and it would certainly be a gross distortion to suggest that they sat by idly and waited for instructions from others.[10] In the uncertain situation that followed, different black groups perceived their means of obtaining freedom in different ways. Thus some of the mulattos, whether free or bonded is not clear, and a few "Negroes" of unspecified number whose fidelity the Spaniards thought they could depend on, were left with strict charge to harass the British while the main body of the Spaniards went to Cuba for reinforcement. But as soon as these mulattos and the few blacks conceived the Spanish case to be hopeless they defected to the British, and the Spaniards returned to find them their staunchest enemies.[11] These fought courageously on the side of the British, and Governor Edward D'Oyley is said to have rewarded them mostly with formal freedom and lands for settlement. Among these was an exslave with his own private and personal grudge against his former Spanish master.[12] Interestingly, the slaves did not avail themselves of the British offer of general freedom. Upon capturing the island, Article Eleven of the Terms of Capitulation said, in paraphrase, that "[a]ll slaves and negroes were to appear on the savanna near the town on the 26th when Venables would inform them of the favours and acts of grace concerning their freedom to be granted to them."[13] Apparently none responded, quite possibly on the reckoning that they had had enough of white overlordship, be the nationality what it may. The majority took spontaneously to the hills, "separating themselves from their late masters."[14] Indeed, in the guerrilla-warfare situation that was to follow, the Spaniards themselves became the victims of some of their exslaves. But there is also some evidence to suggest that some of the black guerrilla groups may have worked in cooperation with the Spaniards when it was in their interest to do so. It appears also that a few remained with the Spaniards; from the evidence, it is clear that some were cajoled with promises of money, clothing, and freedom to do so.[15] Apparently the other mulattos, who were probably the domestics and house slaves, remained faithful to the Spaniards to the end, escaping with them eventually to Cuba.[16]

From fragmentary data it would seem that at least three main black groups with recognized leaders were later formed out of the early uncertainty and confusion. The best known of these groups settled in the hills above Guanaboa Vale under the leadership of Juan de Bolas, who has given his name to this place to this day. It is possible that the members of this group consisted of some free blacks, and the others may have been largely agricultural slaves. The second group, much less known to history, was established at Los Vermejales, an area which was more isolated and more secluded than that of the first group, and their locations were to affect the relative strategies of the two bands. This group was led in the 1660s by Juan de Serras, undoubtedly one of the most astute Maroon leaders of the island; his band may well have consisted largely of the redoubtable hunting class — the samurai of the early Maroons — who were to apply their hunting skills to guerrilla warfare. The location of the third settlement is uncertain, but it is generally thought to have existed somewhere in the valley between the Mocho Mountains and Porus, touching on the parishes of Manchester and Clarendon.

The Spanish-designated governor, Ysassi, may have helped to generate the notion that the blacks were his loyal slaves, completely under his control. In August 1657, for instance, from his mountainous hegemony he wrote to Spain to say that "all the fugitive Negroes are under my obedience."[17] This was either wishful thinking or ignorance of the large numbers of blacks on their own in the mountains, forming their own independent communities and descending, on occasion, to attack the British.

While it is easy to understand Ysassi's pathetic attempt to keep up the appearance of being a governor in control of his "Negroes" in very ambiguous circumstances, it is certainly not easy to understand S. A. G. Taylor's attitude. Writing in 1965 with the relevant document to hand, he consistently supported Ysassi's claim of "Negro" loyalty to him, the evidence to the contrary notwithstanding. Throughout Taylor's work he either explicitly or by implication made it appear that the blacks were mere ciphers acting mindlessly on behalf of and upon the command of the Spaniards. But this was decidedly not the case. Apparently Taylor so absorbed the colonial master's value system that he may have been quite unaware of the distorted picture he was presenting of the blacks, so bent was he on writing European history — thereby treating the people of the island, especially the blacks, rather incidentally or as mere auxilliaries.

As early as January 1656, for instance, Vice Admiral Goodson and Major Sedgwicke wrote to Cromwell, "As for the Negroes, we understand, and to satisfaction, that they, for the most part of them, are at distance from the Spaniards, and live by themselves in several parties, and near our quarters, and do very often, as our men go into the woods to seek provisions, destroy and kill them with their lances. We now and then find one or two of our men killed, stripped, and naked; and these rogues begin to be bold, our English rarely, or seldom, killing any of them."[18] Indeed, a few of the blacks who did not escape to the hills, but were apprehended by the British, were running away, and to prevent the escape of the "seven or eight" who were left behind, the British kept them in "shackles." Two months later the same officers again wrote to Cromwell to repeat the same story about the blacks: "Of the Negroes we have no certain intelligence, only this, that they are separated from the Spaniards, and live scattered in parties in the woods and mountains, as we have reason to believe, very near our quarters; for of late we find some of our men daily killed by them, and they were so bold one night not long since to fire a house in the headquarters of St. Jago de la Vega."[19]

It is important here to stress that within a year of the British conquest, the Maroons, "the rebellious slaves" in the hills, had made themselves so formidable — the word of the authorities — that, like the Spanish officials of Panama, the British soon conceived that they were a greater danger than were the Spaniards. The Maroons' boldness, their prowess in guerrilla warfare, their knowledge of the terrain of the country, were all soon noted with apprehension. "Concerning the state of the enemy on shore here," wrote Sedgwicke to Thurloe, "the Spaniard is not considerable, but of the Blacks there are many, who are like to prove as thorns and pricks in our sides, living in the mountains and woods, a kind of life both natural, and I believe, acceptable to them . . . ."[20] It was neither acceptable nor natural to them, but necessity forced them to adapt to their surroundings in a manner that soon seemed natural.

Reports of Maroon successes in plundering and burning plantations, capturing slaves, and killing British soldiers who ventured out too far into the woods continued to reach the British governor, D'Oyley. Yet there is only one instance on record where the British gained some trifling victory over them at this period. D'Oyley reported that "it hath pleased God to give us some success against the Negroes. A plantation of theirs beeinge found out, wee fell on them, slew some, and totally spoiled one of their chief quarters."[21] Another letter at the end of the same month, April 1656, said the British killed "seven or eight" of them. But Maroon retaliation to this was swift. Sedgwicke reported, "In two daies more than forty of our soldiers, were cut off by Negroes, as they were carelessly going about their quarters."[22]

Meanwhile, Don Quixote-like, Ysassi continued to convince himself that the blacks were under his obedience. He wrote to the Spanish king in August 1658 to say that he had been doing all he could to conserve them, and to keep them under his power, adding that he had "promised their Chiefs freedom in your Majesty's name but have not given it until I receive an order for it."[23] The Spanish lieutenant general of Jamaica (for so he continued to call himself), Don Francisco de Leyba, seemed rather more realistic when he testified in Madrid a year later that there were black settlements in the hills, consisting of men and women "who govern themselves." But no doubt in order not to offend royal sentiments or possibly not to appear to be contradicting Ysassi, he went on to say that they were obedient to the governor, "who keeps them in this way so that they may not separate themselves from His Majesty's service."[24] A year later, however, Ysassi received news that some of his "obedient" blacks had joined the enemy, the British.

This was the *palenque* or "pelinco" of British designation, "of Negroes, about one hundred and fifty, under one Boulo, which are lanciers and archers and many of the private men of war men [*sic*]."[25] Exactly what is meant by "private men of war men" is not clear, but this is probably the first British official report on Juan de Bola, variously called Juan de Bola, de Bolas, Lubola by the British, but called Juan Lubolo (possibly an African name without the Juan, and he may well have been of Angolan extract) by the Spaniards. Juan Lubolo's *palenque* of one hundred and fifty was stationed, as mentioned above, on the south side of the island in the Clarendon Mountains, and this settlement was among those cooperating for mutual benefits with Ysassi and his people. It also appears that the British had, from very early, made overtures to this group. In Sedgwicke's dispatch to Cromwell in March 1655/6 for instance, he admitted that he did not know how to capture any of the runaways but rather obliquely intimated some arrangement when he said, "[T]here is a work we are now striving to effect for be assured they must either be destroyed or brought in upon some terms or other or else they will be a great discouragement to the settling of a people here."[26] Further, in Ysassi's communication of August 1658 to the Spanish king, he mentioned that the fugitive blacks were being "sought after with papers from the enemy,"[27] while Dallas said that the British governor "found means to conciliate" them.[28] The strongest evidence of official overtures comes from D'Oyley's instruction, 1660, paragraph eleven stating, "You are to give such encouragement as securely you may to such Negroes, natives and others, as shall submit to live peaceably under his majesty's obedience, and in the due submission to the government of the island."[29]

In contrast to the Spaniards, the British were quick to see the economic potential of the island in terms of sugar plantations. In his first encounter with the Spaniards, when asked the purpose of his visit, Venables rather laconically replied that he came "not to pillage, but to plant."[30] Also, in his first account of Jamaica he gave some rather perspicacious observations on the possibilities of sugar culture and even looked ahead enough to have suggested the erection of sugar engines in areas contiguous to a plentiful supply of water. All the early dispatches from Whitehall to D'Oyley and other governors emphasized the encouragement of plantations.

Thus D'Oyley's overtures to Lubolo and other overtures to be dealt with later had this aim in view. D'Oyley's method in approaching Lubolo is not clear, but it is certain that the wily governor of aristocratic lineage, "descended of a very Ancient Family in Oxfordshire, who were Barons of D'Oyler or D'oyley, in the Dutchy [*sic*] of Normanby and came out with

William the Conqueror,"[31] would have had recourse to a combination of cajolery and terror. There is evidence to show that he employed the daredevil Buccaneers, as the French in St. Domingue were to do in 1679 when their slaves revolted. Perhaps the Buccaneers were the only whites of the area who could be a match for the Maroons, for they too knew the art of guerrilla warfare, and they too had some knowledge of the island's interior. The Buccaneers were to be used against the Maroons later in the 1670s and 1680s, with the intrepid Henry Morgan (not yet knighted) in command on these occasions. It is clear that D'Oyley would not wish to have any open conflict with the blacks whose skill in guerrilla strategy had already been established. First, even with the aid of the Buccaneers, the governor could not be certain that open confrontation with the Maroons would not be protracted and therefore deleterious to the development of the plantation economy. Second, the shrewd governor would also have seen good policy in incorporating the blacks on his side to be used against outside enemies such as the Spaniards or the French — as all governors up to Emancipation were to do when battling with their perceived enemies. Conceivably, therefore, the Buccaneers were employed to treat with, if possible, and not to fight Lubolo, promising him amnesty, freedom, and lands for settlement if he would submit to the British authority. The Buccaneer presence would thus have added the ingredient of terror to the promises and cajolery of the governor.

Exactly when Lubolo agreed to the British overtures is imprecise. The formal proclamation announcing the *rapprochement* was not issued until February 1662/3. But there is evidence to show that Lubolo had been working with the British against the Spaniards and apparently even against other Maroons in the hills, at least since 1660. One piece of such evidence is to be found from the communication of a British officer, which said in part that "the enemy in our bowels, to whom our lives have been a prey, and many men have been subjected to their mercy (I mean the Negroes) are now become *our bloodhounds* ... and they are *in our behalf* more violent and fierce against their fellows than we possibly can be"[32] (emphasis added). The last paragraph holds an ambiguity, as "their fellows" could either mean other runaways or the Spaniards or both groups together. Given white ethnocentrism, it is more likely that the term was intended to embrace other blacks. Another piece of evidence is to be found in the records of a council of war (dealt with below) held by the Spanish "governor" and his military officers "in the mountains of Jamaica" on February 27, 1660, when news reached them that Lubolo had joined the enemy. But the strongest evidence is to be found in the charter, which mentioned in part that Lubolo and his *palenque* had demonstrated their loyalty and affection to the British "upon severall occasions."[33]

The degree to which the Spaniards depended on the blacks not only symbolically but also in terms of their security is demonstrated in Ysassi's reaction to what he considered Lubolo's defection. The council of war was specifically called to determine what should be done in view of his action. Here they decided to leave the island not out of fear of the British so much as fear of the Maroons — the "rebellious blacks." They argued that the "Negroes" were "so experienced and acquainted with the mountains" that they could not hope to succeed against them; they were thus exposed "to the known risk of being murdered without escape" by their former slaves. The Spanish governor then issued an order commanding the remnants of his army to remove from the spot quickly, pointing out that the blacks were bound to disclose to the British their rendezvous. Three days after leaving, as the governor predicted, their settlement was reached and routed by the enemy, accompanied by Lubolo and his men. Ysassi himself managed to escape to Cuba.[34] Thus it is quite clear that the Spaniards finally left the island because they could no longer hope for loyalty or help from their exslaves.

Yet Edward Long and Bryan Edwards said quite the contrary. Edwards, who borrowed almost word for word from Long, said the "Negroes" were being "hard pressed" upon the final overthrow of the Spaniards by D'Oyley, and this took "from them all hope of future succor from their ancient masters ['ancient Friends,' — Long], they became very much streightened for want of provisions and ammunition. The main body ... at length solicited for peace, and surrendered to the English on terms of pardon and freedom."[35] Here Edwards contradicted himself, for in the *History*, he wrote correctly that the blacks had separated themselves from the Spaniards and had formed their own communities, attacking the British intermittently.[36] In maintaining that Lubolo surrendered *because* of the Spanish defeat, he was putting the cart before the horse, for the very opposite was the case. Here again Edwards, following Long slavishly, contradicted himself. In the above edition he stated the facts as they were — that Sasi, as the British called him, and his men were routed by D'Oyley with the aid of a body of "fugitive negroes," "these wretches" informing D'Oyley where their late masters were sheltered.[37] The hostility of Edwards particularly to the Maroons bristled throughout his works. He, like Long, was a planter historian whose economic existence depended on slave-run plantations, therefore marronage represented a great threat to his economic livelihood. Furthermore, these two eighteenth century English gentlemen/slave masters may have found it difficult to accept the fact that the white Spaniards were dependent on their black exslaves at a time when the spirit of the "white man's burden" was being conveniently promulged to redefine the interrelationship between whites and blacks.[38]

The "Declaration" or proclamation by the Jamaica governor and Council, officially called "a charter to the said Negroes," issued February 1, 1662/3 is among the first of these inchoate treaties, following those of Panama in the New World and anticipating those with the leeward and windward groups on the island by some seventy-odd years. And outside the island, it anticipated those with the Djukas, the Saramakas, and the Matawais of Surinam by between ninety-eight and over a hundred years.

In summary, the charter acknowledged the fidelity and affection of Lubolo to the British, in return for which he and his people were to receive their freedom, with thirty acres of land to those eighteen years of age and over. Lubolo's title of Governor of the Negroes was to be terminated, and instead he was "honored with the title of Coll. of the Black Regiment" in the island's militia. In addition, he and others of his men who were qualified were made magistrates to determine all ordinary matters against the blacks, "but all cases of great consequences and all of Life and Death shall be decided by ye English." They were to bring up their children "to the English tongue" and the adults should also endeavor to do the same. Those who fled to the mountains were offered freedom and similar benefits if they gave themselves up and yielded obedience to the government within fourteen days of the charter; otherwise they would be "proceeded against as Outlaws and Traitors."[39]

Unlike the 1738/9 treaties, to be dealt with later, Lubolo's charter was not drawn up as a treaty arising out of the termination of bellicosity between two contending groups. Rather, in this charter or treaty, every effort was made to emphasize their cooperation with and loyalty to the British, which was deserving of some recognition and reward, underplaying any rebelliousness on their part. In this sense, therefore, Lubolo's charter was more like manumission on a grand scale to a group of slaves who had rendered some heroic service to the state. The grant of thirty acres of land for everyone eighteen years and over, for "his pticular affection and service to the English," is indicative of this attitude. In depriving Lubolo of his original title, "Governor of the Negroes," and conferring on him the new one, "Colonel of the Black Militia," the British demonstrated their sovereignty over all on the island; equally, in appointing Lubolo, and others among his group who were qualified, magistrates the conquerors established their sole authority to make appointments and to integrate them within the rubric of the new polity. Furthermore, to recommend that Lubolo's people and their children endeavor to speak the "English tongue" was perhaps the most effective way of ensuring loyalty through acculturation, having regard to the fact that language is a weapon of imperialism. But the granting of quasi-juridical authority to them in all cases excepting life and death — to be repeated in the 1738/9 treaties — may well have been a concession, the only concession, to existing practices among Lubolo and his people.

It would be interesting to reflect on the possible factors that determined Lubolo's *rapprochement* with the British. To begin with, his position being on the south side of the island, was strategically precarious: it was too close to the area the British occupied, too easily accessible and much too close to Spanish Town. His band was thus somewhat isolated from the other bands who were further in the interior, some already moving toward and settling on the north coast, where the main guerrilla activities were to take place from the 1670s onward. Second, there is some suggestive evidence that Lubolo and his people, at least some of them, were free. The Spanish census of 1611, already mentioned, had accounted for 107 free blacks, and this category has been ignored or forgotten by most works on the island written since 1655. If they were indeed free without the necessary papers to prove their freedom, then they could be apprehended and reconsigned to slavery by the British, despite the offer of general freedom mentioned above. Lubolo may thus have felt that a treaty under the circumstances was the best policy, since it appears his group were not averse to integration within the system. The condition of their settlement also shows a great degree of stability. Even if Taylor's figure of 200 acres of cultivated crops[40] is exaggerated, it still was considered the largest single source of locally grown food, and the Spanish guerrilla bands appear to have depended on them for supplies of foodstuff. But perhaps the most important evidence to show that at least some were free is found in the charter, a part of the first paragraph of which said, "Bola and all the free Negroes . . . ."

Apparently the other bands of black guerrillas in the hills did not view Lubolo's new alliance with satisfaction; they rather saw him as a renegade who sullied their image by capitulating to the enemy. And perhaps, as if to demonstrate their disapproval of the *rapprochement*, various attacks on the plantations were soon reported to the authorities. In October of the same year as the charter, for instance, news reached the governor and Council that murder and other "[e]normities were done to severall good people of this Island by Negroes that have had too much of their Libertie."[41] But in keeping with the policy of blandishment, in order to hasten the development of the plantation economy, the Council tried to contain rebelliousness by instituting regular trials consisting of two justices of the peace with the power to examine offences such as the above. The punishment was to be either transportation or a recommendation to the master or mistress to sell the recalcitrant black.[42] This of course had no effect whatsoever either on the Maroons enjoying their freedom in the hills or on the slaves on the plantations who were determined to run away or rebel.

In line with the policy of blandishment with the view of integrating the rebels into the plantation economy, the governor tried to sue for peace with Juan de Serras' group, the Carmahaly or Karmahaly or Vermaholis or Vermahalles[43] as they were variously called, by issuing a proclamation in 1663 offering to grant twenty acres of land per head, and "freedom" to those who would turn themselves in to live as peaceful members of the community. But none responded: "On the contrary, they were better pleased with the more ample range they possessed in the woods where their hunting ground was not yet limited by settlement."[44] Indeed, the overture proved counterproductive, for the Maroons read from this that they were feared and this made them display greater opposition to the system. Realizing the Karmahaly's contempt for official blandishment, the governor therefore sent Lubolo, now the official bloodhound of the British, or Colonel of the Black militia, whether to treat with or to fight against his black brethren is not clear. Long said that he "was sent to endeavor their reduction."[45] Whatever the nature of the mission, the Maroons apparently felt that this was their chance to wreak vengeance on the black general.

Unlike Lubolo's victories over the Spaniards, in this instance he was up against more than his match. He fell into an ingenious Karmahaly ambuscade and was slain. It is reported that he was "cut into pieces," and this is not difficult to understand considering the supreme contempt they must have had for Lubolo's defection to the enemy.[46]

According to Dallas, after Lubolo's death his group decreased in number and morale and thus "sought quiet and protection in the vicinity of towns and settlements; nor were any of them ever known to return to their former haunts in the mountains in Clarendon," [47] where evidently a new cluster of Maroons was being formed. Nothing more has been heard of them as a collective.

The Karmahaly band under Juan de Serras is a Maroon group that deserves special attention, not only because they have nowhere else been systematically treated, nor because of their great skill in guerrilla warfare, but also because of their particular skill in negotiation and their diplomatic subtlety. From scanty data, Juan de Serras appears to have been a man of extraordinary ability, strongly seated in his leadership position, with a vigorous, disciplined organization based on a hierarchical ordering typical of Maroon communities. He himself carried the title of governor while the next in command was designated sergeant major, where ranking was based not on African monarchical tradition but on military discipline of a European model. He governed his people with consensual authority, recognizing those with particular skills in his group and delegating functions accordingly. Thus some were used as emissaries, the specific qualifications for these delicate positions being tact, finesse, and bilingualism in Spanish and English.

In simple arithmetical terms, the capitulation of Lubolo and his band meant fewer Maroon guerrillas fighting the British. The Karmahalys, therefore, clearly saw that their security more than ever lay in placing themselves in strategic positions, which by the very nature of Maroon societies meant inaccessible areas, which, fortunately for them, Jamaica did not lack. Although it is most difficult to reconstruct their movements, it is clear that their chief objectives were at least threefold: first, to gain access to the as yet impenetrable north and northeastern interior of the island, second, to augment their numbers in the process by capturing slaves from plantations, and third, to increase their military strength by pilfering arms and other supplies from planters or hunters carelessly wandering about in the woods.

By June 1664 their harassment of plantations became so alarming to the planters that Captain Rutter and a party of volunteers were sent out against them, but with no success.[48] By the following year reports of their plundering plantations, killing whites, and taking off with slaves reached alarming proportions; and in response to this the country was "put in a posture of Warr." Every regiment was given the power to raise and command parties either to pursue the "said Negroes" or to lie in ambush for them.

The Article of War, drawn up by the governor, Sir Thomas Modyford, and his Council, 15 August 1665, occasioned by "the Rebellion of the Carmahaly Negroes and other Outlying Negroes," was a formal document consisting of some three pages and ten clauses. This is the first formal declaration of war against any Maroon group in Jamaica, just ten years after the British conquest. Others were to follow. Thus it does not seem accurate to speak of the "First Maroon War" — as so many do — meaning the war of the 1730s, and the "Second Maroon War," in reference to the 1795 Trelawny Town war. One would rather say the series of "wars" from mid-seventeenth century to the period of the treaties and the "Trelawny Town War." These are the formulations used in this study. The Article outlined in banal terms the rigor of warfare, the necessity of loyalty and obedience from private soldiers to their officers, and the overriding duty of the army to commit itself to the suppression of the rebellious Negroes: "If any officer," clause 3 said, "do grossly let slipp any opportunity — wherein he might have done service on the said Rebels such officers shall be censured also by the discretion of a Court Marshall; not extending to Life and Limb."[49]

The resolutions emanating from the council of war were much more interesting and revealing. Here the nature and extent of the activities of the Karmahalys as well as the plantocracy's attitude to them was painted in vivid colors. The first resolution set the tone:

> Whereas the Rebellious Negroes, commonly called ye Karmahalys,

> do dayly under notion of freindshipp and fair Correspondence beguile many Hunters and commit divers Murders, and outragious upon them and others, which Negroes for their number and Condition are so contemptable and base that no way for the persecution of such perfidious villaines can be ill accounted of, and whereas the Assembly now in being did pass an Act for their Suppression and that the Monyes ... should be levyed on the Country by an equal Tax for the encouragement thereof, all the Inhabitants of this Island to surprise and kill those sneaking and treacherous Rogues ....[50]

Clearly the period of blandishment with the Maroons was over, and under pressure the Karmahalys' superb sense of strategy, implied in the first lines of the resolution, would soon be put to the utmost effect.

The other resolutions set forth the rewards for capturing or killing any of them: "any person or persons jointly or severally who killed or took alive the Karmahaly Negro called the Serjeant Major" (governor was the correct title) would receive £30 sterling; for any other officer among them then the reward would be £20, while £10 would be given for the killing or apprehending of any of the "common Negroes of the Said Gang." To the slave and the white indenture on the plantation, freedom was offered: Resolution 7 said, "If the said person so killing and takeing any of the said villaines be it Servant or Slave, he shall from thence forth be free and the value of him paid to his Master or right Owner."[51]

The attempt was also made, in keeping with British colonial practice, to divide the rebels among themselves, by promising pardon to potential renegades. Resolution 6 stated that "if any of the Karmahaly Negroes repenting of their lewd Course of Life shall bring in alive or dead any of their officers or fellows, such Negroes shall have pardon from what is past, and have his freedom any resolution to the contrary Notwithstanding." But the most interesting resolution was the last which gave license to the soldiers to possess the women of the Negro *palenque*: It stated that "if any number of pson. shall find out the Pallenque of the said Negroes, they shall have and enjoy to their uses all the Women and Children, and all the plunder they can find there for their reward."[52]

It may be that the British at this time were well aware of the acute shortage of women among the Maroon bands in their early formations in Jamaica, as was indeed the case elsewhere in the area. The capture of women was often the primary objective of many of their raids on plantations. This resolution was therefore intended to affect them on a most critical issue. But so far as the whites were concerned, it was counterproductive because any abuse of Maroon women was invariably met with the most serious consequences to the perpetrators.

It appears that the state of war and the general preparedness of the island placed the Karmahaly on the defensive for a while, although the parties sent out against them were almost totally ineffective.

But about a year and a half after the posture of war we find a Karmahaly black, Demingo Henriques, suing for "peace." This peace overture, however, was nothing more than a ploy to gain time in order to consolidate their position, to select strategically new positions, and to lull the whites into a state of security. And the ruse could not have been more successful.

The astute Karmahaly chief, Juan de Serras, arranged to have Demingo Henriques "captured" by one of the parties sent out against them; and accordingly, Demingo was duly "captured," apparently by one Captain Colbeck of the white militia, around the vicinity of the British military regiment at Guanaboa, and brought before the governor, Sir Thomas Modyford. Here Demingo told Modyford that the black general of the Karmahaly, his chief, if granted a charter of freedom, would submit to the King of England. The war-weary island, anxious to pursue its plantation economy, which was greatly jeopardized by the "rebellious Negroes," went for the bait and accepted the deceitful Demingo's olive branch. Thus it was instantly ordered "that the Carmahaly Negro Demingo Henriques be pardoned of all his Crimes and have a Charter of freedom for himself, Wife and two children, and that he presently take the Oath of allegiance,"[53] and this was done immediately.

It was further ordered that Demingo be sent with two other blacks, Paul and another Demingo, and "that he carry a Charter of pardon and freedom to all the Carmahaly Negroes to be enjoyed by them on their submission to his Majties Authority." The governor and Council also ordered that all rights of the said rebellious Negroes were now restored to them by pardon from His Majesty's government, and therefore no person was "to disturb them, or demand any of them as Slaves." It was also ordered that the expenses of the two blacks accompanying Henriques, Paul and Demingo, be paid out of the island's treasury.[54]

Paul and Demingo, the "two other Negroes," whether free or bonded is not clear (but the probabilities are that they were of Lubolo's band and bilingual, speaking Spanish and English), were now the official ambassadors to treat with Juan de Serras. This is an interesting commentary on the role of blacks in the Caribbean. They were not merely the sinews of the plantation. They fought in battles as soldiers either against external or domestic enemies; they built fortifications, bridges, barracks, and roads; they were used as explorers and on more than one occasion as emissaries of governments, as indeed the Maroons who eventually went to Sierra Leone were to be used as soldiers for the British on the very first day of their arrival, and were later to treat with African kings and chiefs in the interior of the country.

The report of the two black emissaries, recorded in the Council minutes of 28 March 1668 just about a year after their "accreditation," is clearly the most insightful Jamaican record we have of Maroon skill at diplomacy. Paul, the chief spokesman, reported to the governor and Council with skill and clarity. He told his audience that upon arrival at the *palenque* of the Karmahaly Negroes, he and Demingo were escorted to the black governor, who wanted to know the reason for their visit, whereupon Paul explained that it was to bring them a charter of freedom if they submitted to British authority. He explained that one of his Karmahaly people, Demingo Henriques, had already received his "Life and Liberty" from that source. The black governor, with calculated duplicity, replied that he and all his people did acknowledge themselves "subjects and soldiers" of the King of England, that they would be obedient to the British, and that he desired "thankfully" to accept the charter of pardon and liberty. He further observed that it was never his intention to do any mischief to the British, but would certainly acknowledge responsibility for the killing of five white hunters, which they were provoked into doing: the reason being that these hunters, "under colour of fair trading" stole away "divers of their Women," whereupon they pursued them and had the upper hand in a fair fight. In taking pains to narrate this particular episode, the black governor may well have been issuing a diplomatic caveat calculated to reflect on the Council of War's resolution, giving license to soldiers or volunteers to "have and enjoy to their uses all the women and children" captured from the Karmahalys. As for the party of his men who went to Guanaboa (where Demingo was "captured"), the black chief said he had given them strict orders to proceed to the north side of the island only to obtain salt. It was therefore contrary to his orders that they disturbed the British at Guanaboa, and for this they were justly punished, he himself imprisoning four of them.

But the most calculated part of the black leader's diplomacy was yet to come. He now bade the two emissaries, Paul and Demingo, "humbly" to ask His Excellency to issue a proclamation declaring their submission to the British authority, and granting them "freedom to go and come amongst the English to trade and traffique." In order to gain more time the black chief cleverly recommended sending some of his men to conclude the treaty with the British governor (it is not clear whether these were sent or not). He would wish to ascertain, for instance, in what part of the island he and his people were to be settled, what rules and regulations were to be imposed upon them, and so forth. Then the Karmahaly leader went on to denigrate "the other Negroes about town" — he could not agree with them; they were false to the English and he would not wish to associate with them. This was probably the only true statement of the black leader, for there was much disunity among the different bands of Maroon groups at this period.

Paul listened carefully to all this and informed the Karmahaly that his message would be faithfully conveyed to the British governor, but if he did not satisfy his side of the bargain, then the general of the British army would hang him. (A good diplomat knows when bluntness is necessary.) To this the black governor made serious protestations, declaring his faithfulness and honesty and promising to do any service to the British as soon as he and his people were settled, and for good measure supplied the two black emissaries with a guard and a "gang of doggs" to escort them out of his *palenque.*[55]

The governor and Council were delighted with Paul's deposition, and on the same day they ordered a proclamation to be issued "in every Precinct of this Island that the Karmahaly Negroes may pass quietly about their business throughout this Island." The proclamation gave notice to "all the Inhabitants" of Jamaica

> that the psons commonly called ye Karmahaly Negroes, have submitted themselves to his Maj*ties* Government here, and have ... received his Majesties gracious Charter of pardon and freedom, granted to themselves, their Wives and children, and therefore all officers both military and civil, and other his Maj*ties* loveing subjects, are hereby strictly charged and commanded to take notice hereof and quietly and peaceably to permitt the said Karmahaly Negroes to pass and repass about their affaires in any part of this Island, without any trouble, Lett or Molestation, and in all things, and on all occasions to treat and use them as other his Majesties loveing Subjects are treated and used, as they will answer to the contrary at their utmost peril.[56]

Thus time, which was of the essence to the Karmahalys, was now gained; also freedom of movement to trade for necessary provisions and to deploy their people at strategic positions on the island was now legally ensured. The Karmahalys gained everything and lost nothing, and they could well have taught the Maroons of 1738/9 how to make a treaty.

Richard Price has put forward a tentative suggestion that the most valuable Maroon leader was the one "skilled at understanding whites, as well as his fellow Maroons,"[57] and there may well be much in this suggestion, not only with respect to the Surinam Maroons but also the Jamaicans. Although not much is known of Juan de Serras, it is at least clear that he was a Spanish creole — or perhaps a creolized black — and would thus have most certainly interacted with whites in one capacity or another and could therefore hoist them by their own petard. His skill in leadership and his ability at delegating functions to his fellow Maroons suggested understanding of his people and their acceptance of his position.

If one may make a furtive comparison here with Cudjoe, the leader of the 1738/9 Treaty, then de Serras had certain advantages. He was not as straitened by warfare as was Cudjoe at the time of his Treaty; de Serras had his strategems well planned and was, in fact, using the British as instruments toward their implementation. Cudjoe, on the other hand, was at the mercy of British strategems. The British had, by mid-eighteenth century, changed their attitude toward treaty making with exrebel slaves. The aim was no longer to integrate them in the society with as much dispatch as possible, as was the case with Lubolo's Treaty of 1662/3 or with the Proclamations of 1663 and 1670 — now the aim was to use the Maroons as a part of their defense system. They were to be a kind of glorified Plato's auxiliaries at hand to track down internal enemies — runaway slaves — or to assist in fighting external ones like the French and the Spaniards, as the Buccaneers had done before. Indeed the use made of the Buccaneers may have suggested this policy of collaboration to the authorities.

The result of de Serras's ingenuity was that the whites were lulled into a state of false security, and as soon as the Maroons found themselves in a secure position, some took the offensive and resumed open hostilities just two years after the charter. Apparently, during the respite, some fanned themselves out into the Clarendon area, possibly using the old settlement of Lubolo, and further along the Mocho Mountain range, but the main body, as events were to show, proceeded further toward the north and northeast sections of the island. But their first great "outrage" was in Clarendon. Here the governor and Council heard that the "outlying Negroes commonly called ye Karmahaly ... committed divers Murders, Robberyes and other outrages on his Majesties Subjects," the most recent of which were the murders of John Piper, Pallisando Robin, John Townsend, Thomas Mason and Bloody Dick, all inhabitants of Clarendon.[58]

It was from this time (1670) that the most energetic measures were adopted against them. The two primary objectives were, first, "for the prevention of such Mischiefs for the future," and, second, "for the due and speedy punishment of those perfidious Villaines," and the usual resolutions, on this occasion ten, were passed with these ends in view.[59] The island was placed on a war footing for the second time. It became an offence for any person, whether soldier, officer, or hunter, to venture out alone two miles and beyond, without being armed; all persons on the island were to be ready with their arms to assist any officer of horse or foot or any justice of the peace or constable in the service of apprehending or killing the "traiterous Villaines," and anyone refusing to assist would be tried and fined at the discretion of the justices and liable to appear before a special court martial; everyone was "strictly charged and forbidden to give or suffer to be given any Cloths, Victualls or other things whatsoever, or treat, talk, or parly with ye said Traitors upon pain of being prosecuted as Ayders, Assisters,

Comforters, to the Said Rebells whereof all people are to take notice at their Perills, and that contrarywise they fire at them, endeavouring by all means possible to destroy them." Rewards were again offered; in this case the correct hierarchization of the Karmahalys' politico-military structure was ascertained when £30 was offered, not for the sergeant major as before, but for the killing or taking of the "governor," £20 for the sergeant major, and for any common one among them £10; again, as in the first war against them, indenture or slave would be freed for taking or killing a Karmahaly, the master or owner of such servants or slaves to be reimbursed according to their true value; voluntary parties were again encouraged to search "for the said villaine's palenque," and if success attended a party, it would be lawful for them to have "all their [the Karmahalys'] Wives and Children for slaves, also the respective Summs of money above provided." (The significant change in the wording here may have been the authorities' response to the now known attitude of the Maroons to their women.) An alarm should be sounded, day or night, on sight of the rebellious Negroes, and upon hearing it, all should repair "to the usual place of rendezvous there to await further orders"; failure to sound the alarm if a rebel was sighted, or to respond to the alarm would lead to a trial before a court martial to be conducted according to the "Articles of Warr."[60]

This kind of preparedness is indeed indicative of the authorities' perceived seriousness of the Maroon threat, which was no longer considered localized around the Clarendon area, but was now a general problem, and the orders were to be "publiquely read every exerciseing day in the head of every Company and that every Commander in chief of every Regiment have a true Copy hereof sent him, and he is commanded hereby to distribute the same to his ffeild officers and Captaines within his Regiment, chargeing them with the due publication thereof as aforesaid."[61]

There is much that is hazy about the fate of the Karmahaly after these vigorous measures were adopted against them. This is most frustrating. One source said that about 1670 "their number being about forty — when they retreated to the north-eastern section of the island and for the next thirty years remained relatively secluded."[62] This is partly correct, in the sense that some did settle in Clarendon, as we have already seen, and as will be intimated during the 1795 Trelawny War.[63] From the evidence it is certain that some retreated to the northeastern section of the country. It does not appear that they remained secluded or quiet for the next thirty years, but rather for not more than about fourteen or fifteen years, as we shall discuss below.

If they ceased their harassment of the British, there is some evidence to suggest that this may have been partly due to the influence of the Buccaneers, now under the leadership of the daring Henry Morgan, but more so to the fact that in their north and northeastern settlements they remained isolated and unmolested, their chief aim being "not to offend, or even to appear to the white inhabitants."[64] They felt settled, until a few British frontiersmen began to open up plantations contiguous to their settlements.

The Buccaneers,[65] who became firmly rooted in Jamaica soon after the British conquest, were countenanced and even encouraged and made allies of by D'Oyley and succeeding governors. No doubt alliance with such a lawless set of daredevil pirates was a risky business, but to have made enemies of them at such a precarious period of the island's history would probably have been much more dangerous. They were especially useful to the British in fighting first the Dutch and then the Spaniards, who even after leaving the island in 1660 never gave up hope of recapturing it. Edward Long stated quite categorically that "it is to the Buccaneers that we owe the possession of Jamaica"[66] at this period. In 1670, for instance, at the height of the Karmahaly problem, the Spanish forays on the north coast increased to an alarming extent; news reached the governor that they were marching inland, burning houses, killing and taking prisoners, while three Spanish ships were actually sighted on the south side of the island. Here the planters complained that while they attended to the foreign enemy, not only did their cattle and other stock run wild but their slaves also took "to the woods"[67] — which continues to show that the slaves were always on the alert for the right opportunity to seize their freedom. It was at times like these that the services of the Buccaneers were sought, and accordingly, the governor and Council appointed Henry Morgan, now admiral, to take control of the foreign enemy June 29, 1670. By August of the same year, Morgan reported much success, and by the end of the year the Treaty of Madrid was signed with Spain; ironically, a condition of the treaty was the British promise to curb the activities of the Buccaneers.[68]

Under the treaty, Spanish prisoners from Cuba and their slaves, among whom were Indians, Negroes, and mulattos, were to be released. But the Jamaican Council found these latter categories "useless and dangerous persons" who would be a security problem to the inhabitants; thus they were ordered to be sold (possibly to a foreign colony) for the purpose of increasing the revenue of the island, which was in a pretty desperate condition. Eighty pieces-of-eight for each Spanish "Negro" above the age of twelve, and twenty doubloons each for those under twelve was the going price; the price lists for the Indians and mulattos were not given.[69] A survey of each parish was thus made for such persons to be taken up by "military men" in each area.

It appears therefore that the activities of Morgan and his Buccaneers, as well as the rounding up and sale of the Spanish blacks and mulattos, may have had some inhibiting effect on the Maroon bands, whether Karmahaly or others in their mountainous retreats. For most of 1670, therefore, there are hardly any records of slave rebellions on plantations or of Maroon harassments, but by the end of 1671 sporadic attacks on certain plantations began and developed into a general pattern throughout the 1680s and 1690s.[70]

It seems important here to review the different types of resistance groups now operating on the island. To start with, a new dimension was added to the Maroon society with the influx of newly arrived runaway slaves from the plantations. Like the French, the British planters in Jamaica distinguished between *grand* and *petit marronage*, and passed laws attempting to define these categories. One such law said that all "Negroes" absent from their owners for six months "shall be accounted as in actual Rebellion." [71] The Slave Act of 1696 made finer distinctions, linking punishment to the duration of flight and the number of years spent on the plantation before flight. Thus, a slave who absconded for less than a year but who resided on the island for more than three years would be considered a runaway, punishable by severe flogging if caught; one who absconded for more than a year would be considered a rebel, and the punishment, if caught, would be death or transportation, while those on the island for less than three years who ran away were less severely dealt with.[72] The underlying assumptions behind these laws are not clear, but it would seem that the seasoned slaves were considered to be so sufficiently acculturated within the rigor of the plantation system that they were expected to settle down quietly and perform the bidding of their masters.

It is important to examine the relationship between the newly arrived runaways and the old established Maroon gangs like the Karmahalys. There is sufficient evidence to show that the Spanish creole Maroons, especially the Karmahalys under Juan de Serras's leadership, not only held themselves aloof from the other established Maroon groups but also displayed open hostility toward the newly arrived Africans, the *bozales*. From about the 1670s the fate of the *bozales* who took flight to the hills was intolerable because of the bad treatment meted out to them by the Spanish creole Maroons. It is said that some of these newly arrived runaways actually returned to their former plantations (whether to face trial as rebels or as runaways would depend on the duration of the flight) as a result of the Spanish creoles' brutality to them. It appears that the British exploited this hostility to the *bozales* by recruiting Spanish blacks among the parties sent out to subjugate them.[73]

Not all, however, returned to the plantations. Some apparently lurked among the woods, in some cases forming their own bands or joining larger groups already existing in the hills.[74] One such large, homogeneous community functioning in the woods was the Madagascar band.

These, according to one source, were said to have been the survivors of a slave ship, with mostly Madagascar blacks, which was wrecked off the coast of Jamaica in 1670, numbered at between forty and one hundred.[75] Dallas, however, describing their skin as being "of a deeper jet than that of any other Negro" with features resembling those of Europeans, but giving no date of their possible arrival in Jamaica, said that they ran away from certain settlements around Lacovia in St. Elizabeth soon after the planters had bought them.[76] Whatever their origin, in the eyes of the creole blacks the Madagascans were *bozales*, and must have acted as a magnet to the newly arrived runaways who were not being welcomed in the camp of the Spanish creoles.

The *bozales* therefore did not remain underdogs for long. With the large importation of Africans into the island to satisfy the pressing labor demand of the plantation slave economy, more and more of these resorted to rebellion and flight. Slave rebellions on the plantations served as a conduit by which means some joined Maroon communities or formed their own. The result is that these newly arrived Africans soon gained ascendancy in the hills in terms of sheer numbers, and by the beginning of the eighteenth century they were decidedly in a leadership position.

Meanwhile, cultivation on the south side of the island was experiencing ecological difficulties. The whites had established some sugar plantations along the low-lying plains around St. Catherine, St. Dorothy, and Vere, but these areas, once the "choicest and richest spots in the whole island,"[77] soon began to suffer not only from soil exhaustion occasioned by overutilization, but also from severe droughts, increased by excessive woodcutting, which adversely affected the rainfall. Thus the most hardy and determined of the planters — the frontiersmen — began to push toward the north, an area which "was one entire desert from east to west, totally uncultivated,"[78] to establish plantations. But these inland northern areas, the no-man's-land with their terrifying mountain ranges, had become the habitat of most of the Karmahalys and other runaways and were to become the most important Maroon territories on the island. These lofty, precipitous rocks — the Blue Mountains and the John Crow summit — provided the natural setting in which the Maroons acted out their saga. The Maroons in these retreats saw themselves as the autochthons of the area, since no one before, as far as is known — certainly not the Arawaks — had inhabited these pristine places. It is no wonder, therefore, that marronage from the 1670s onwards took on a more serious quality. Surrogate autochthons they may have been, but they were nevertheless determined to fight to the last ditch to defend their freedom and their territoriality.

Thus the relative quiet of the Karmahalys and other less distinctive bands was, as said earlier, due mainly to the fact of their seclusion, and if the British planters had not begun plantations in the north, we might never have heard of them again. But the establishment of plantations contiguous to their mountainous domains was considered an infringement on their territorial rights in terms of the lands they occupied and planted and in terms of what they conceived as the purlieus of their hunting grounds, and so they made it known to the white hunters that they would not countenance intruders in their environs. A contemporary account said, "[I]f a colonist had the temerity to commence a plantation at all within their reach, they were sure to take advantage of the night, or some unguarded hour, and murder his family, carrying off in their retreat, both negroes and cattle. So that for a long time, the plantations were necessarily confined to the coast and neighbourhood of the towns."[79] Even the efforts of the British to establish a watering resort at the Bath in St. Thomas-in-the-East in imitation of Tunbridge Wells and Bath in England, were thwarted by the proximity of the Maroon settlements.[80]

Some of the frontier planters, however, were apparently not deterred by Maroon hostility. These succeeded in establishing a few plantations in the north and northeastern parishes such as St. Mary, St. George, and St. Thomas-in-the-East — and even in Portland around Manchioneal — apparently around the end of the 1670s, during the period of quiet. But by September 1686 they were alarmed by the sustained and successful activities of the Maroons who had become so "imboldened" that they had already succeeded in driving out the planters and other inhabitants who had settled in St. Thomas-in-the-East; these settlers had "been destroyed, and wholly driven from their Settlements from Manchinele [Manchioneal] Bay to Fort Antonio." [81] The St. George planters, frightened that they might suffer the same fate from the "murderous and Rebellious Negroes" who for "several years past" had gathered together from diverse parts of this island into their parish and adjoining ones, petitioned the governor, Council, and Assembly for "speedy" relief in combatting the enemies. They pointed out that their plantations were yet small, that they were too poor and too weak to repress the rebellious Negroes who had grown strong from their great numbers as well from the firearms and ammunition they confiscated from hunters or planters or from purchase.[82]

The legislature acted promptly by calling together the field officers and mayors of the affected parishes to advise on the best means "for reducing and destroying ye rebellious and Runaway Negroes" of the northeastern parishes, those "most infested" with the rebels. The governor thought these parishes in "imminent danger," and if the inhabitants were not defended, then other parts of the island would soon be in a similar situation. Captain Orgile, who presented the petition for St. George, also testified before the governor in Council. He explained that the Maroons were in two gangs, the

Windward and the "Cove," and from the large tracts they found, as well as from the cultivated grounds, they appeared to be very numerous. To his knowledge, they had been gathering in these parishes for the past fourteen or fifteen years, though not so mischievous in the early years as of late. (This certainly coincided with the time the Karmahalys deployed themselves into strategic positions after the 1670 "treaty" discussed above.) Orgile testified that the planters in the area had attempted to repel them, but that all their efforts were ineffectual, while the Maroons grew in strength, "stealing great quantity of Provisions, and doing other mischiefs, and being imboldened by their strength often came to one and the same place, so that parties might the most easily know where to come up with them."[83]

The actions that were adopted to crush the "rebellious Negroes" were to be repeated throughout the period of the Maroon wars, and indeed the pattern was not confined to Jamaica, but was applied to almost every other Maroon society in the Americas: parties of white volunteers, often headed by professional soldiers or militiamen, were sent out against them. Invariably these volunteers were insufficient, ill equipped or wrongly equipped, undisciplined, and in many cases inebriated and downright incompetent. In Jamaica as elsewhere in the Caribbean, the most effective parties against them were the blacks, whether slaves or free, named the "Black Shots" in Jamaica, "Chasseurs" in Haiti and Surinam. Indians, too, as already described, the Miskito from Honduras, were employed against them in Jamaica. Rewards were offered by the authorities to the free or bonded for taking or killing Maroons, and from about the first decade of the eighteenth century the "choisest" British soldiers were sent against them with little or no success. Finally, forts and barracks were erected at strategic positions,

> sufficiently manned, as near their settlement as possible, that at convenient seasons and opportunities they may make Excursions on them, and attack them to the best Advantage, and in the Marches root up, burn, and destroy their provisions each Barrack be duly provided with a sufficient Gang of Dogs, which the Commissioners are hereby directed and impowered to buy, or impress to be paid for by the Church-wardens of the respective Parishes out of the Parish Stock, or money they are obliged to levy and raise for the several Uses and Purposes by virtue of this present Act, which the Justices and Vestries are hereby obliged and required to do, on the penalty of Twenty Pounds on each Justice and Vestryman neglecting his Duty herein.[84]

The first party against the "Rebels," after the St. George's petition, is representative of the inefficiency and bungling of the British, not to mention their misunderstanding of the nature of Maroon guerrilla warfare throughout the 1680s and 1690s. It was only from the beginning of the eighteenth century that a more sustained effort was made against them.

Following Orgile's testimony, Major Henry Archbold proposed to lead a volunteer party of thirty persons, while one Barnet Risby volunteered to lead another party of twenty, and both men undertook to be ready in ten days. Empowered with executive orders from the governor and Council, it was left to their discretion to destroy and subdue "the sayd Runaways and Rebels." Two other officers, Captain William Bragg and Captain Drax, offered to assist Major Archbold, promising about sixteen and fourteen men respectively, but neither was certain of mustering the desired number of white men: Drax, however, promised to supplement his army "with Indians and Trusty Negroes."[85]

Two months later, we have an account of their adventures. Major Archbold fell ill close to one of the Maroon settlements and although he did not encounter any of them, this did not prevent him from pronouncing that the Maroons could easily be destroyed by a party of not more than twelve men and that the reports about their strength were "but imaginary danger." The major displayed his ignorance of the very essence of Maroon warfare, which was to be perfected in the eighteenth century, by stating that he did not encounter any of them in his whole march and that he returned to headquarters without so much as hearing where they were.[86] This was precisely the strength of the Maroons. They mastered, and by subtle disguises became such a part of their surroundings that detection was difficult. Incredibly, the governor accepted Archbold's report, reiterating that Orgile's petition from St. George was the "mere contrivance" of the petitioner.[87] This naturally infuriated the inhabitants of St. George, who at a neighborhood meeting pointed out that they were still in "dayley feare of being murthered" by the blacks, and that the white hunters who made their living from hunting were discouraged from going out because of the terror of the "rebellious Negroes"; they repeated that their poverty and the long distances between their plantations made it impossible for them to defend themselves, while the enemies were growing daily in strength from the addition of runaway slaves and from their increased arms.[88]

A few of the parties at least, unlike Archbold's, did encounter some well-established settlements and therefore could give a more realistic account of the situation. Lieutenant Pitts discovered "divers plantations," about twenty acres altogether, filled with provisions, and he himself had fought them there on several occasions. Commenting on their ethnic background, he thought they were of several parties, "each being of a different country." (It is possible that the Madagascans were among these, as well as the new additions from plantations embracing different tribal groups.) They were apparently well established, with their snares laid out for about twenty miles in length for catching wild hogs; one of the communities had fifteen huts with four or six "cabins" in each.[89]

Another party came within hearing and sight of the "houses" of the rebels, and reported that the houses were built on "inaccessible" precipices. The white captain of this party, unable to scale the rocks, gave his "launce" to a member of the Black Shot corps, commanding him to do so and to "launce" the "enemies." But a Maroon, possibly reconnoitering, soon spotted him, and after firing a few shots to alert the others, they all ran away. In line with official instructions, they burnt the houses of the settlement and destroyed their meat and other provisions — a practice which Stewart[90] considered unnecessary, but no doubt the prevailing philosophy was that all's fair in war. The captain of this party rode away and returned to headquarters, leaving the others to shift for themselves and to return home as they could.[91] But to have dislodged the Maroons without pursuing them was to exacerbate the situation for the St. George planters. To avenge themselves on the whites became the immediate concern of the Maroons, and the people of St. George became "more apprehensive of Danger than ever, unless care be taken by the Government for them." The first victim was one Serjeant Cooke, who was "dangerously wounded" by a Maroon, shortly after they were dislodged.[92]

The performance of the parties was indeed shoddy, especially when it is recalled that the "rebels" had previously displayed their strength by audaciously returning to the same place for confrontations with the white parties of the area. Some of the more efficient officers complained of the "ungovernableness" of their parties and recommended that martial law be proclaimed on subsequent marches to insure better discipline. Also, more realistically, these saw the necessity for a standing party (in addition to the ad-hoc volunteer parties) to maintain constant vigilance.[93]

The Council, no longer guided by Archbold's myopic report, now saw the necessity to relieve the people of St. George "with all possible expedition," and after much debate they tried to effect some improvement on the deployment of and on the strategies of the previous parties. For one thing, they agreed to implement the recommended standing party, which was to consist of about sixteen to eighteen woodmen and hunters, who obviously would have more knowledge of the interior of the island; these were to be paid for every day that they marched and not otherwise. Further, they agreed on a base as the rendezvous from which the different parties were to be sent out. From this central position an army officer would be in charge and the governor could then send instructions to him, giving directions when to march upon the intelligence he might receive of the enemies. Major Langley and Captain Orgile, by virtue of their proximity to the "infested" areas, were both appointed to alternate in their duties, one of which was to be constantly at a bivouac at Swift River in St. George. Another innovation was that instead of desultory parties going out singly, the "total extirpation of the Rebellious Negroes" would be better effected, the Council decided, if many parties were sent out simultaneously. Thus six parties were raised: one each from St. Thomas, St. David, St. Andrews, two from Port Royal, and one from St. Mary and St. George together, each party consisting of a commissioned officer, a sergeant, and twelve men.[94]

From this period too, more consideration was given to the modalities of guerrilla warfare. The governor took it upon himself to instruct the commanding officers of the necessity for strict discipline among the volunteers, and above all, of the need to observe silence during the march in the interior.[95] It was well that the governor gave such instructions to his officers, who were men trained in the iron-clad logistics of open combat warfare in Europe, with no knowledge of guerrilla tactics and strategems. Stewart has left us a good account of the early troops who marched in "pomp and circumstances of war . . . in their proper regimentals, as if they were going to fight a regular and civilized enemy, and sometimes had even the absurdity to traverse the mountainous roads with drums beating."[96] The noise of the drums assisted immensely the Maroon espionage system in warning the bands of the approach of the enemy. Equally, Stewart observed that "the customary accoutrements were too clumsy and burdensome for traversing the woods and clambering over the rocks, and the red coats were too conspicuous an object to the Maroon marksmen, who seldom missed their aim."[97] By the turn of the century, however, the red coats of the British soldiers were changed for light green or blue, and the customary accoutrement were also lightened.

The financing of the new measures was of primary concern to the authorities of the island, who were operating a treasury that was almost depleted. The volunteers of the standing party, as well as those of the parties on the march, in addition to the regular soldier, were all to be paid on a per-diem basis. The going rates were between 5/– and 5/8 for a commissioned officer, 2/6–2/8 for a sergeant, and 18^{d} a day for the ordinary soldier or for a volunteer. In addition, supplies of arms, ammunition, food, clothes, shoes, and the like were sent to each party. The rendezvous party, for instance, had for its first installment of supplies, one hogshead of good dry fish, one hogshead of "briskitt," one hogshead of salt, 50 lb. of fine pistol powder, 4–500 good French flint, 200 lb. of bullets and proportionate cartridge paper, and a good supply of shoes.[98] Exactly how long this was intended to suffice is not clear. Furthermore, rewards for "further encouragement" were given for every rebellious Negro taken or killed. The price varied, apparently according to the danger potential of the black as perceived by the whites. Thus for the killing or taking of Peter the reward was £20. Peter was clearly a British slave and therefore designated only by a first, Christian, or practical name — unlike the blacks under the Spaniards, who, from all accounts, although also renamed, seem to have been given the full complement of Christian names and surnames. For another black named Scanderberg, the reward was £15. These awards are closer to those offered for Juan de Serras and his serjeant major, while the rewards throughout the last decade of the seventeenth century were much less, varying from a range of £5 to 20/– in a decreasing order which may have reflected more the bankruptcy of the treasury than the need to catch the runaway. Other payments were also made variously to the hangmen of "Negroes," and it appears, in many cases, to those also who could prove that they had pursued "rebellious Negroes" — even apparently if they had not caught them. Thus one George Bayley was paid £43/10 "for executing the Rebellious Negroes," while one Nicholas Scarlett tendered a bill (amount not stated) to the Council for the pursuit of rebellious blacks.[99]

Since the treasury was empty, voluntary contributions from the different parishes were again sought, as had been done in the 1670s. To this end the governor in Council sent out circular letters to the vestries of each parish with strong emotional appeal, urging the "relief and defence of the poor inhabitants of St. George against the said Runaway and Rebellious Negroes." The letter said, in part, that without speedy relief from the public, more planters would "be forced to desert their settlements" since they were not in a condition to defend themselves, and "the volunteer parties who went to their reliefs were more generous than successful in their undertaking." The seriousness of the matter was stressed, "but having noe money in the Treasury," they approached the several justices and vestries of the island for some "charitable benevolence" toward the payment of a standing party "for the Reliefs of those poor and necessitous Peoples." Without relief, "the major part of the Settlements of that parish must be inevitably lost, neighboring parts brought into danger, and those places become Receptacles for other Runaway and Rebellious Negroes, that may be apt to joyne unto them, which will be vastly prejudicial to the General Interest of the Island."[100]

Meanwhile, the appeals of 1676 to the different parishes had borne some favorable responses from the following parishes:

St. Catherine	pledged	£50
Pt. Royal	pledged	£150
St. David	pledged	£50
St. Thomas in the East	pledged	£30
St. Mary	pledged	£25
St. Dorothy	pledged	£25

while St. Andrews promised to maintain four men at the cost of the parish, possibly on surveillance duty, for as long as they were required.[101] Thus the attack on the Maroons was beginning to be more systematic and sustained than hitherto.

But the general effect of this more energetic effort was another matter. The most positive "victories" the white parties could claim were the destruction of Maroon provision grounds and huts, the spoliation of their meat and other supplies, and the cutting of the springs they had set up to ensnare wild hogs. And even this kind of victory was of doubtful benefit, because the destruction of their property and foodstuff invariably roused the angry passion of the Maroons, and retaliation against the whites was always swift and bloody. Again, although we know that many white soldiers and volunteers were killed it was "never positively ascertained that any Maroon had been slain in action,"[102] and apparently those Maroon deaths that were reported were usually of recent runaways, who may have been lurking around the periphery of the Maroon communities. Major Langley's party of May 1697 appears to have had some unusually good fortunsce from the planters' point of view. He reported that after seven days' march he killed "two Negroes" and wounded "others" — this latter fact he knew from the large tract of blood he saw; he also burnt down huts with about twenty-two cabins in them, and after some pursuit he and his party lost the track, and abandoned the chase, because his men had become "sick and in great want."[103]

The seventeenth century, therefore, came to a close without any appreciable victory against the Maroons, and the morale of the whites was low indeed. This was exacerbated by the disastrous earthquake of 1692, which in the space of two minutes laid to the ground all buildings — dwelling houses, churches, and sugar works — in Port Royal. Following in its wake were violent rains and epidemics, which took the lives of many of the whites and left others in a state of great physical weakness.[104] Apparently the Maroons in the mountains did not suffer from the effects of the earthquake and the epidemics, and they as well as the slaves on the plantations saw the plight of the whites as their opportunity. The Council reported that large numbers of blacks were running away from the plantations either to join already established Maroon groups or to set up their own communities.[105] In addition, the Maroons were boldly descending on plantations to pillage supplies, and there appears to have been at some point a confluence of Maroons converging on plantations and runaways diverging from them; between the two movements the whites seemed helpless. A letter from the Council to the Lords of the Committee for Trade and Foreign Plantations in England stated flatly that the whites were not in a position to defend themselves from the insurrection of the slaves.[106] Port Royal, the richest of the parishes, which could supply the largest money contributions, as listed above, could also supply the largest force — some two thousand "effectual men" — was reduced, after the earthquake, to some two hundred men, and the parish would now need monetary contributions for its rebuilding.

Thus the eve of the eighteenth century saw the position of the Maroons stronger, perhaps, than at any other time since they had established their communities after the British conquest. Although it is not possible to give an exact number of their population, a contemporary manuscript source said that it became "considerable"[107] through additions from runaways, while Dallas said that the Madagascans were "remarkably prolific,"[108] and Robert Renny considered the women in general very "prolific,"[109] enjoying, as they did, the delectable highland climate of Jamaica, with clean, fresh air and a plentiful supply of fruit and vegetables. Fruit and vegetables were to be found in every band, for the first thing every Maroon group did, as a prerequisite of survival, was to plant provision grounds.

Yet despite their strength, or possibly because of it, and notwithstanding the ineffectuality of the parties against them, the Maroons were shrewd enough to have responded to the systematic attack against them by consolidating their position (Toynbee's theory of challenge and response is perhaps applicable here). Since the days of Lubolo and de Serras, it appears that the Maroon method of fighting, from scanty evidence, was rather of a free-lance nature, with small bands attacking plantations and retreating under no recognized or permanent leadership, "but now finding that the colonists had determined to suffer themselves to be annoyed no longer by a lawless band of plunderers, and that parties were fitted out to attack them wherever they could be found, they concentered [concentrated?] their force and elected a chief, whose name was Cudjoe, a bold, skillful and enterprizing man, who, on assuming the command, appointed his brothers Accompong and Johnny leaders under him, and Cuffee and Quao subordinate Captains."[110]

Chapter 3

The Critical Years

The wild Maroons, impregnable and free
Among the mountain-holds of liberty
Sudden as lightning darted on their foe
Seen like the flash, remembered like the blow.[1]

Dallas's summing up of the situation, given in the preceding chapter, is much too neat and too precise. It is true that the leeward groups did respond to official attack by seeking to consolidate themselves. But Cudjoe's eventual commanding position did not arise from different groups voluntarily surrendering their "sovereignty" to his rule for the common good. Rather, from the evidence, it appears that Cudjoe's ascendancy arose from the bitter power struggles that manifested themselves in battles for leadership among different clans, based, to a large extent, on ethnic particularities consisting of "different countries and of different manners and customs in Guinea and often very opposite and at great Variance with one another . . . ."[2]

It is now generally established that Cudjoe was of the Akan-speaking group from Ghana, but numerous contemporary sources referred to the Akans loosely as "Coromantes," "Koromantee," or "Coromantine" — designations derived from the name of the Fante town, Koromantyn, a port from which many Africans were exported to the New World. But it is erroneous to suppose that all the Africans who came through this port were of the Akan-speaking group. It was the British practice to trade along the windward coast before entering the Gold Coast for new shipments, but the entire cargo of the two areas would be listed as from Koromantyn. The slaves bought at the Gold Coast were generally of the Akan-speaking group; most of these were war captives. Their skill in warfare was to stand them in good stead for the guerrilla warfare they were to conduct as Maroons in Jamaica and elsewhere in the region. Recent studies have shown that of the Akans transported to the Caribbean, the majority went to Jamaica,[3] because they were most sought after by the British planters in this colony. Indeed no other African group has received from the British so many encomiums as the Akans. Christopher Codrington, governor of the Leeward Islands, wrote in 1701 to the Lords of Trade and Plantations, "They are not only the best and most faithful of our slaves, but are really all born Heroes. There is a difference between them and all other Negroes beyond what 'tis possible for Your Lordships to conceive. There never was a rascal or a coward of yt nation, intrepid to the last degree, not a man of them but will stand to be cut to pieces without a sigh or groan, grateful and obedient to a kind master and implacably revengeful when ill-treated."[4] Bryan Edwards, writing nearly a hundred years later, felt that the "circumstances which distinguish[ed] the Koromantyn, or Gold Coast Negroes, from all others, are firmness both of body and mind; a ferociousness of disposition; but withal, activity, courage, and a stubbornness, or what an ancient Roman would have deemed an elevation of soul which prompts them to enterprizes of difficulty and danger and enables them to meet death, in its most horrible shape, with fortitude or indifference."[5]

But this group was also feared by the planters because they were the most rebellious of any African group in the region. Edward Long, for one, did not share Codrington's or Edwards's views, but rather that of the factor, Bosman, who saw them as "bold, hardy, and stick[ing] at nothing, where revenge or interest is concerned ... vain and haughty in their carriage; envious and malicious in the highest degree, dissembling their resentments, for many years, until a fit opportunity offers of gratifying their thirst of revenge; they are the most treacherous villians and consummate knaves, yet known on that continent."[6] The fear of the planters was not unfounded, for almost all of the major rebellions on plantations in Jamaica, from the seventeenth century to the nineteenth, were led by Africans of Akan ethnicity. And the courage, ferociousness, and tenacity praised by the slave masters were to be used against the plantation society with devastating effect. The result was that both in Jamaica and in Barbados attempts were made at different times to bar their importation into the islands. That the attempts in Jamaica were unavailing, despite the Akans' history of resistance throughout the hemisphere, showed that their qualities of leadership, industry, and agricultural capabilities — which served well the needs of the plantation society — must have outweighed the planters' fear of their propensity to rebel.

Among the groups that did battle with Cudjoe was the Madagascan clan, now led by a "resolute, cunning fellow,"[7] and it appears that Cudjoe had the most strenuous opposition from him. As mentioned before, the Madagascans were, from the very beginning, receptive to runaways and soon made it their business to inveigle away discontented slaves from plantations, and by the first two decades of the eighteenth century they had become "considerable." When, however, their leader was slain in battle, they opted for Cudjoe's leadership, thus helping to form the great body of the leeward Maroons, whose number was constantly increased by the frequent addition of runaways.

Cudjoe's defeat of the Madagascan is thought to have occurred around 1720. But the exact date of Cudjoe's ascendancy is wrapped in doubt, as are his place and date of birth. Dallas seems to place him among the Gold Coast slaves who rebelled on Colonel Sutton's estate in Clarendon in 1690, some of whom fled to the hills in the leeward part of the island.[8] These were soon joined by another group from St. Elizabeth who also revolted; these two groups are considered to have constituted the very core of the leeward gang. Cudjoe's place in these rebellions is not clear. One source said that "Captain Cudjoe ... is the son of one of Colonel Sutton's Negroes, who was at the head of the conspiracy and governed the gang until the time of his death."[9] If this is correct, then Cudjoe was probably born in the rebel camp and therefore would not have experienced slavery — or he may have escaped as a young man with his father, who probably trained his son to succeed him. We have no way of knowing Cudjoe's age despite certain undocumented and imprecise assertions claiming that he was "certainly more than 60 years old,"[10] having spent forty-eight years of strenuous living, at the time of the treaty. But there is at least one piece of evidence to show that some of Colonel Sutton's slaves were still active guerrillas during the late 1720s. In June 1729 a flying volunteer party commanded by Simon Booth in Clarendon succeeded in killing five Maroons, among whom were one man and two women "who were marked T.S., with a heart, which was old Colonel Sutton's mark, [were] supposed to be in Sutton's rebellion, which happened about forty years ago, and out ever since."[11] As far as we know, Cudjoe had no such marks.

There is sufficient evidence to show that Cudjoe or Kwadwo — "a male born on a Monday," according to Akan tradition — described by Dallas as "rather a short man, uncommonly stout, with very strong African features,"[12] was a man of great courage, and once in power, he ruled his people with an iron hand. He first divided his gang into politico-military companies under the loyal command of two of his "brothers," Accompong, a name of Akan derivation, and Johnny — which may have been another Akan name, *Gyani*, having suffered from Anglo-Saxon orthography. It is of interest to note that Accompong is the name of a Maroon community still found in Jamaica. The use of the term "brother" here may have been a direct transfer of Ashanti tradition in which chiefs and others belonging to the same clan may address one another as "brother," though there may be no blood tie. In Africa this fraternal relationship insured unity, as it did among Cudjoe and his two "brothers."[13] Further loyalty was insured by a stratification system based on ability, especially in military skills. This made for a strong competitive spirit, each Maroon "ambitious to excel in whatever might contribute to the good of the whole."[14]

As in a Spartan camp, the chief employment of the men was warfare, in which they used lances and small arms "after the manner of the Negroes on the Coast of Guinea." There appears to have been a rather careful division of labor pattern, some becoming proficient in attacking plantations for provisions, others for slaves, especially women; still others were of the hunting class, hunting wild hogs. Those not skilled in warfare helped to clear the ground for the women to plant; this group of men was held in very low esteem indeed. Following African custom it was the women who planted, which outraged Bryan Edwards who regarded this as a sure sign of Maroon brutality to their women. They planted crops such as plantains, sweet corn, bananas, cocoa, pineapples, cassava, and in some cases even sugar cane; some of the men would be engaged in turtle catching and in the shooting of wild birds that abounded on the island, some noted for their delicacy. Salt making was also a most important occupation. When not derived from the sea, it is said—and this was said specifically of the windward group—that they would supply their great need for salt "by making a strong *Liscivium* of wood ashes (which they accidentally) observed to be salt and dipt their Hogg for some time in this pickle and thereafter strongly smoke it."[15] But this may not have been accidental since it was a common practice of salt making in Africa.

The formation of the Maroon "towns," as they were called by the island's authorities, was based on strict security consideration. These were to be found in the mountains, with the outer towns relatively accessible at a lower declivity, the others becoming increasingly less so until the most strategic one, which was usually at an almost inaccessible point, was reached. Hardly any whites ever reached such a town. Each town was planted with provisions and should the colonists' parties capture one, the Maroons would simply retire to another, equally well supplied with food. The high elevation of these towns gave them a commanding view of the lowlands from whence the parties would approach. And at every approach to these towns, sentries were constantly posted to watch for the enemies. Upon the approach of the British, the sentries would alert the communities by blowing the *abeng*, the horn of a cow used as a trumpet, as was and is the practice in parts of West Africa.

The *abeng*, still used today in Maroon communities, can be heard at a considerable distance. Its sound would immediately alert other Maroons. For they must listen. This instrument can utilize a wide range of notes; thus it was capable of transmitting complicated messages, intelligible only to the Maroons, informing them of the size of the approaching troops, the amount of armaments they possessed, the path they were using, and the like. Similarly, directions regarding Maroon strategies would be given on the *abeng* by their chief of operations. Once the alarm was sounded everyone knew what to do. Immediately, the soldiers would repair to their posts under their respective captains, almost always in a defensive position to ambush the unsuspecting enemy; simultaneously, the women and children, their clothes already packed, would fly to a prearranged rendezvous. This African instrument, the *abeng*, was a source of terror to the enemies, in itself and by itself. The Maroons soon became aware that the British parties found its sound "hideous and terrible," and they exploited its use to the fullest extent, by blowing on it continuously when the parties were close to their towns, thus creating confusion and in some instances flight among the soldiers.[16]

Cudjoe also took drastic steps to insure that no other language but English was spoken among his people. Possibly based on his experience of ethnic rivalries before his ascendancy, he punished them severely for the least transgression of the laws he instituted among them. One of these was that "on pain of Death, they are to use no other language but the English and they are not to be found conversing in small companies."[17] A reflection of the efficacy of this rule is that every Maroon captured from this town could converse in English. But it is certain that what they called the Coromantee language was used for rituals, as indeed it is used (at least smatterings of the Ashanti language) today among certain Maroon communities in the Jamaican hills, particularly those of Scotts Hall. Equally, Cudjoe and his captains may have kept up its use only among themselves for the purpose of secrecy based on security considerations.

Information on family structures among Maroon communities is rather fragmentary and not infrequently contradictory, but there is sufficient evidence to show that following African custom, polygamy was practiced. In Cudjoe's camp, for example, it is said that each man was allowed as many wives as possible, while adultery among the women was severely punished. One source, a white officer who claimed to be well acquainted with Maroon customs, has mentioned wife sharing among Cudjoe's people.[18] This is not African practice, and this singular piece of doubtful evidence should not be used to demonstrate Maroon social behavior.

Much has been said of the other major group, the windward Maroons; their original cluster was predominantly Spanish creole blacks, among them the Karmahalys, inhabiting mainly the parishes of St. George, St. Thomas, and Portland. It appears that from the last decade of the seventeenth century into the first decades of the eighteenth, the policy of this community, having gained its territorial objectives, was to be as unobtrusive as possible, avoiding all confrontation with the planters. But circumstances soon forced them into greater activities. For instance, they often found their neighborhoods occupied by small gangs of runaways, most of whom were, in all probability, *bozales*; but the Spanish creole bands from about the turn of the eighteenth century had perforce to change their attitudes toward them, showing a greater willingness to treat with them and to coopt them into their communities. This was due partly to the concerted official action against them, partly to the extreme scarcity of provisions, especially salt and ammunition, from which they were suffering in their isolation. Besides, the small gangs were growing in number and could combine to overpower them in the event of a battle, so uniting with them soon became expedient. But they also found the new arrivals of service to them in terms of accessibility to provisions — as indeed the new arrivals would find them useful in terms of their experience in adapting to hostile surroundings. The newcomers were able to make guided raids to different plantations, from which some had only recently fled; they had intimate knowledge "of every road, every lurking place, as well as of the strength of their masters, their customs, places of lodgings, so they generally came in the nights and surprised masters or overseers in bed, and knowing where the arms etc., were kept, seized them and anything else of use to them and then retire."[19] These were mostly the remote and marginal estates whose defenses were relatively weak, but as the Maroons grew more successful in their raids they became more audacious and by the 1730s, they were attacking and even taking over larger estates.

From all accounts, it appears that the windward groups did not coalesce under any one strong leader as did the leeward under Cudjoe. Instead, they formed different communities under different leaders in contiguity and in cooperation, reminiscent of a loose federation. Some of these communities took the names of their leaders, the most famous of which was Nanny Town. But there were others, such as Guy's Town, Molly's Town, Diana's Town, and the like, ready to cooperate with each other in the face of danger.[20]

We do not know why the windwards did not have a monolithic organization under a strong leader like the leewards. It may be that they did not choose to have such a system, or no one strong leader appeared. But these communities — with their separate identities, yet cooperating when necessary — show a marked resemblance to the Akan migrants into what is now modern Ghana, where the internal group dynamics saw them settling into different areas, and even after being established, some would still splinter off into other locations. With adaptations and different historical experiences each group viewed itself as distinct, but each was also conscious of its shared cultural frame of reference and kinship affinity with the others.[21]

From the deposition of a captured Maroon we have some inside knowledge of the windward communities, the two most important being Nanny Town and Guy's Town. And in line with the Akan structure just described, these two towns were markedly different, but cooperated with each other when necessary. Each of these towns had a headman, who, by the 1730s, "order[ed] everything."[22] In Nanny Town, for instance, if a man committed any crime he was instantly shot to death. But the crimes, apart from treasons, were relatively few, the most important being "the lying with one another's wives." Even the headman here, unlike what prevailed under Cudjoe's autocratic leadership, was not above equally severe punishment for wrongdoing. Should he be "guilty of any Great Crime," he would be shot by the soldiers, and another would be appointed. The headman in 1733 was Cuffee but at the time of the treaty he was Quao, a creole. Cuffee was distinguished from the rest of his people by wearing a "Silver- laid Hatt and a small Sword — no other daring to wear the like."[23]

Guy's Town, said to have been named after a headman called Guy or Gay, was at the top of the Carrion Crow Hill, and in 1733 the number of men here was 200. These, like the Nanny Town men, chose to arm themselves with lances and cutlasses rather than with guns. These would not normally go to meet the parties unless to defend the paths that led to their town,[24] for the active fighting was done by the greater warriors from Nanny Town. Guy's Town was the food basket for these communities. It had a wide open area well planted with sugar cane, cocoa, plantains, yams, melon, and corn, and the hogs, poultry, and grazing cows gave the impression of a ranch with a great degree of permanency.

The runaways who joined both these groups had to show their loyalty by taking an oath, African fashion, which was held "very sacred," and those refusing the oath, whether prisoners or runaways, were instantly put to death. Severe indeed are such treatments, but it must be noted that nothing constituted so much security risk to Maroon communities as the casual runaway — the truant who would wish to be with them today and gone tomorrow. Such a runaway might divulge to the authorities the locations of these communities, and in some cases they were actually used as guides to parties, with fatal consequences to the Maroons.

Nanny Town, with its estimated 300 fighting men, was esteemed for possessing the greatest warriors among the windward clans. This town, set in the very center of the awesome and seemingly inaccessible Blue Mountains, received its name from the redoubtable Nanny, around whom is woven such an intricate network of myth and legend that it is impossible to get at the real facts about her. This has been made more complicated by the recent romantic panegyrics on her purporting to be "history."

Her exploits include sorcery or witchcraft, in the terminology of the authorities — *Obia* or *Obeah*, in the African cosmology; oracular wisdom, and the possession of so much supernatural powers that she could spirit away, apparently without being seen, the best slaves from the plantations around. Apparently she also fought in battles; one of the most popular stories about her describes her prowess in catching the bullets of the British soldiers directed against her, returning them in a manner not usually mentioned in polite circles. Nanny allegedly kept a huge cauldron that boiled continuously without any visible fire, which was a bane to any soldier or militiaman of the parties who went too close, for they would fall in and die of suffocation. (The unromantic — those killjoys imbued with a strong sense of causal relationships – have looked into the matter and have discovered that the cauldron was a basin formed from the confluence of the Macungo River flowing over a precipice of some nine hundred feet, into the swift-running waters of the Stony River, thus creating froth and bubbling, and giving the appearance of a boiling cauldron.)[25]

But there is one thing though that the historian must note in dealing with a subject of this kind: it is that legends are not built around nonentities. Today the area that is considered Nanny's old town is regarded as sacred, and few outsiders would be allowed to visit it. Old Granny Nanny, as she is called in all the existing Maroon communities, is revered by all; and even Maroons with little or no knowledge of their history can become rather articulate when it comes to recounting the great deeds of "Granny Nanny," as this author found while conducting field work in the communities. This by itself should be of importance to the social scientist, irrespective of the "truth" of the belief, since it serves as an important indicator of the probability domain of their belief system, representing a cosmology that is undoubtedly a reflection of their African roots.

What is certain about Nanny is that she was a freedom fighter of the first order, reminiscent of the great African queen, Nzinga (c. 1580–1663), the death-defying "Black Terror," who stoutly repulsed Portuguese rule in her country, Angola, and who was feared by them as "the greatest military strategist that ever confronted the armed forces of Portugal."[26] As we shall see, there is some shadowy evidence to show that Nanny was against Cudjoe's treaty with the slave regime.

These, then, were the two main groups operating during the first three decades of the eighteenth century up to the time of the treaties: the leewards under the uncompromising and autocratic Cudjoe, with his iron discipline, utilizing his "absolute power" to set the rules and to mete out punishment to those who transgressed — punishments which invariably carried the sentence of death — and the windwards with their quasi-autonomous towns under different leadership and apparently having a politico-military structure that made for more democratic inter- and intragroup relationships. In between these two main groups, small gangs with varying degrees of permanency and size lurked about through the length and breadth of the island.

The question may be asked whether these two main groups knew of each other's existence. One source said that Cudjoe "had established a general interest with the windward, or original Spanish Maroons, who, encouraged by the example of his activities and success, had become bolder and more enterprising in their hostilities,"[27] which certainly does not coincide with the evidence. It is not clear that these groups knew of each other's existence in their formative stage, but by the 1730s there is much evidence to show such knowledge, with Cudjoe's band none too friendly to the windwards and the other groups when they sought help from him.

From all accounts, the windward group demonstrated a greater aggressiveness toward the slavocracy than did the leewards. This was almost certainly due to their location, situated as they were in the east and northeast, and known to the plantocracy, which was bent on developing these fertile areas with sugar plantations. As said above, location was a very strong factor in determining the policy of a Maroon community. The more isolated and the more settled they were in their mountainous strongholds, the greater the tendency to relax activities and to consolidate. This was precisely the case with Cudjoe's clan, which was virtually unknown until the 1730s, except to a few planters around St. Elizabeth and St. James. But perhaps even more important was the aggressiveness of Nanny, who, from sketchy accounts, seems to have been uncompromising in her stand against the slave system. Her reportedly powerful and pervasive influence must have helped to shape the policy of the windwards.

The Maroon question, which certainly taxed the energy of the plantocracy from the middle of the seventeenth century, became much more critical from the 1700s up to the time of the treaty. This period can be roughly divided into the time spans of 1700–1730 and 1730–1738, when the situation — from the planters' point of view — deteriorated alarmingly. The concern of the plantocracy, almost to the exclusion of everything else, is reflected in governors' speeches and memoranda, in acts of the Assembly, in official correspondence from the island to the home government, and through the correspondence of citizens and soldiers on the island to private citizens in England.

Yet, incredible as it may seem, the measures adopted to deal with the problem were hardly more than a tedious repetition of those already tried, unavailingly, throughout the 1680s and the 1690s. The Acts of the Assembly between 1700 and 1720 are like a lengthy shopping list for the "extirpation of the Negroes in rebellion." That of 1702 was an "Act for the more effectual raising of Parties to pursue and destroy rebellious and runaway slaves"; that of 1705 was "an Act for the further Encouragement of Parties, and more speedy Reduction of rebellious and runaway slaves"; that of 1718 reflected, first, the ineffectuality of the previous Acts, and second, the growth in strength of the Maroon bands in numbers, in better coordination, in better organization, and more efficient deployment of men, arms, and ammunition. The Maroons were more provident of their ammunition, "seldom throwing a shot away ineffectually."[28] The preamble of this act set forth the problem: "Whereas divers rebellious and runaway slaves have formed themselves into several bodies; and of late have very much increased, by the Neglect of keeping up standing parties for the entire suppressing of them: And whereas the several Laws for the Purpose have hitherto proved ineffectual, be it therefore enacted ... that it shall and may be lawful to and for His Majesty's present Governor ... to commission such Person or Persons ... to command any Party or Parties that will voluntarily inlist themselves to go out in the Pursuit of the said rebellious and runaway slaves."[29]

As in earlier enactments, rewards were offered for every rebel taken dead or alive. In this case the increment was not based on the rank of the rebel, as with Juan de Serras and his band, but on the age of the Maroon: thus, the sum of £50 would be paid for every rebellious slave above the age of fourteen; further, parties should also "take to themselves and their Heirs, every Boy, or Girl, or Pickaninny which they shall so take under the age of Fourteen, together with all such plunder as they shall take from such rebellious slaves."[30] It may be noted here that no mention of "possessing" the women was made, as had been the case back in the 1660s, with the Karmahaly group.

It is certain that during the 1720s Maroon activities against the plantations increased — not only among the windward, but also among the erstwhile quiet leewards — largely because of the government's aggressive campaign against them. Both groups raided plantations for ammunition, powder, arms, and supplies of different kinds and abducted plantation slaves, particularly women. It appears that the capture of women was so successful that by the 1730s, in both Nanny Town and Guy's Town, the number of women and children exceeded that of the men, and these women, although guarded "day and night," for their defense each carried two or three knives.[31] Perhaps indicative of the success of these raids is the case of planter George Manning. In 1728, Manning purchased twenty-six slaves for his estate, but by the end of the year, after the usual "seasoning" deaths and Maroon raids, in addition to a few who ran away singly, only four remained.[32]

But marronage was not confined to the island. From this period a large number of slaves escaped to Cuba from north-coast parishes such as St. Ann and St. Mary. Major John Richardson wrote from the north "that it became of late so frequent for Negroes to go off for the island of Cuba, that for some weeks last, several had stole off in canoes."[33] This was not difficult to do, because of the trade, chiefly for mules and cattle, which St. Ann conducted with Cuba in open boats. Long blamed the slaves' desertion on this "pedling intercourse," and claimed, at the time he was writing (1774), that "several hundred ... within a few years past," had withdrawn to Cuba in hopes of obtaining their freedom.[34] Apparently some of these were inveigled away "by the flattering assurances of ... strolling Spanish traders," and, on occasion, representations were made by Jamaica to the Cuban government for the return of British "property," but invariably they were rejected.[35]

As on other occasions, the successful activities of the Maroons increased the confidence of the slaves and concomitantly their rebelliousness. And from this period the authorities of the island expressed their fear repeatedly of an all-island slave insurrection inspired by the Maroons. More parties were sent out against them, but with little or no success. Each party consisted of white volunteers from the civilian population, white officers and soldiers, militiamen (whites who were mostly indentured servants), armed black slaves, the Black Shots, and slave baggage carriers. Slave owners were obliged by law to send these slaves with the volunteer parties, but they were first priced, so that their owners could be compensated for those lost in battle. But as the situation became more difficult for the government, other means were employed. In June 1720, for instance, Governor Lawes employed the services of the Miskito Indians under King Jeremy to fight against the Maroons. These Indians, who resided off the Honduras coast, had such a robust antipathy for the Spaniards who would wish to colonize them that they soon perceived friendship with the British as a means of protection, since the British and Spanish were at loggerheads in the region. Lawes entered an agreement with King Jeremy to have fifty Indians and their officers transported to Jamaica to be engaged in a six-month campaign. Immediately upon their arrival, they were to go out into the woods "to pursue and destroy the rebellious Negroes lurking in the mountains." They were paid forty shillings per month for every common soldier; sixty shillings for every officer, and eighty shillings for their chief captain; they were also provided with arms, ammunition, and the necessary provisions. After six months of service, the Indians were given the choice either to remain in Jamaica as planters, with "all the liberty that any of the subjects [whites?] of this island now have or here after may have," or free transportation home. Apparently they all returned home.[36]

When the Duke of Portland, "a Nobleman of the Greatest worth and abilities, and of the first rank in England," arrived in Jamaica as governor in June 1722, like every other governor throughout this period, his first speech to the Assembly reflected the colony's anxiety over the rebellious and runaway slaves. He reiterated that the rebels had at last appeared in many parts of the country in great numbers and had "taken away several arms and some ammunition: so we may justly apprehend Danger from them and none of us know whose lot it may be they'll fall upon next. I ordered out Parties in Pursuit of them, but the want of money to pay the men, who ventured their lives for our Safety is a great Discouragement and Obstruction to the service."[37] Nevertheless, in 1723 the Assembly requested Portland to send for more Miskito Indians to suppress the "continual insults and many depredations on the settlers and inhabitants of this island,"[38] though how they were paid is not known. They were used again in the 1730s, although there are mixed views about their effectiveness. It has been pointed out, for instance, that they were more experienced in fighting in swamps on flat terrain than in a mountainous situation. In 1731, Governor Hunter thought that "they were utterly unfit for such Service in the Rocks and Mountains, their own country consisting of Marshes and Boggs."[39] But according to Edward Long, they did at least give excellent advice to the British soldiers, pointing out to them, for instance, not to use their rifles to kill game on a march but to use arrows or lances, which were silent and thus would not alert the Maroons.[40] Bryan Edwards echoed Long on their understanding of the importance of silence in marching to the "enemy's quarters," and also went on to praise them: they had "effected considerable service, and were indeed the most proper troops to be employed in that species of action."[41]

Land reform schemes were also introduced by the island's authorities as a counter to Maroon activities. Large tracts of uncultivated lands served as a magnet for the establishment of Maroon communities. To counteract latifundism — the disadvantage of having only large plantations, but especially of having "the greatest part of the Valuable Lands Unsettled [and] in hands who neither Cultivate nor care to dispose of it"[42] — land reform schemes were initiated by the planters and merchants of the island, with the full support of the different governors of the period. It was proposed that all tracts of land exceeding one hundred acres, uncultivated and uninhabited by whites, be taxed or surrendered to the Crown, and then regranted to the landless within a specified time. The aim was to reestablish a class of small farmers, which the inexorable process of capital-intensive sugar production had wiped out. This would increase the number of whites on the island, as their population in relation to the blacks had become alarmingly small. In dealing in this way with the racial imbalance of the island, the authorities felt that both the colony's security and economic needs would be met.

A memorial from planters of the island to the Board of Trade as early as 1715 stated explicitly that such settlements would secure the "Island against the Insurrections of Negroes and invasion of Enemys."[43] Realizing that the expense of settlement had greatly increased, another memorial to the Board of Trade suggested that Britain should supply a part of the initial capital to prospective settlers as the French were doing in Hispaniola. Here, by an order of the French monarch, every merchant ship going to Hispaniola was obliged to carry a "proportionable number of white people according to their tonnage," and upon arrival the government would allot them a quantity of land according to the size of their families, and would give them credit for a number of slaves and other requirements for plantations until they could support themselves. They were then required to repay the debt accrued. "By this means that colony is mightily settled and improved."[44] But the British government, soon to be envious of Hispaniola's enormous sugar production, nevertheless was not prepared to expend any capital on this venture, and the scheme was not implemented at this time, although it was to be recommended again.

Proposals were also made to settle the island in those parts that were "very thin and weakly settled for want of people" with some of the poor whites of the Virgin Islands and their slaves.[45] Governor Lawes envisaged 200 families availing themselves of the scheme, under which each family was to receive ten acres of Crown land and other encouragements along the northeastern section of the colony. This way, in the governor's view, some of the uncultivated lands would be utilized, which would greatly aid the "future prevention of those disorders and Incursions of the Rebellious Negroes upon the Inhabitants." To the legislature, an act to settle the island from the Virgin Islands was seen as "a means to wholly Extirpate and Destroy those Rebellious Negroes and their Settlements."[46] In addressing the Assembly, the governor pointed out the great importance of the bill, as it dealt with the security of the country against "Foreign Enemies and Domestic Rebels." He argued that benefit and public advantage would further accrue in settling that part of the island — some 60,000 acres which had "lain useless in the hands of about one hundred and fifty tenants" who had neither paid rents "nor planted any part of it for more than 45 years."[47] The governor probably had not realized that most of these settlers were the original victims of the Karmahaly Maroons, who brooked no settlement around their territory. The greater part of these lands had become escheatable, and all this contributed to the miserable economic condition of the country, at a time when revenue from the quitrents of these lands was desperately needed to help to defray the expenses contracted for the suppression of the "rebellious Negroes," as the authorities continued to call them.

There is no evidence to show that the Virgin Islanders availed themselves of the offer — partly because many of the Jamaican planters, probably those guilty of hoarding lands, were against the measure — but also because of the Virgin Islanders' great fear of the much-reported Maroon activities in Jamaica, for immediately after the Treaties of 1738/9 some Virgin Islanders and others from the Leewards did settle in the colony.

Meanwhile, the Maroons had become so bold and "impudent" that in addition to their usual plundering, burning, purloining of supplies from plantations, inveigling away slaves, and the like, they now also resorted to the finer technique of holding hostages as a means of control and of achieving their objectives. In the early 1720s, for instance, after killing one white on a plantation and wounding another, they held the wounded man as a hostage to bargain for passes to send some of their own people to market towns and also to obtain passes for blacks on plantations to visit them. It is not clear how prevalent this practice was, but a contemporary writer said, "By this practice they hold a correspondence throughout the island."[48] Situations of this kind, transmitted by grapevine within the island, increased the anxiety of the planters. They could no longer be certain that the free blacks of the marketplaces were not from among the rebels. "Nay," wrote Dallas, "a Maroon himself might by carrying a few fowls and a basket of provisions on his head, pass unnoticed and unknown through the numerous crowds of Negroes in the large towns."[49]

Every contemporary account of the Jamaican Maroons concurred that by 1730 they had grown "formidable" in strength, and that the island was in a state of crisis. The administration of Governor Robert Hunter from 1729 to 1734 was thus one of the most critical in the history of Maroon affairs. Hunter, born in 1667 at Ayrshire, Scotland, distinguished himself as a soldier both in the Wars of the Spanish Succession and in the Battle of Blenheim and was soon promoted to lieutenant colonel. From 1710 to 1719 he was appointed captain general and governor of New York and New Jersey, where he was characterized as "a man of good temper and discernment, the best and ablest of the royal Governors of New York."[50]

Hunter's stint in New York and New Jersey certainly prepared him for the governorship of Jamaica — then as now a turbulent place with glaring social and economic problems. A brilliant administrator, Hunter encountered the same kinds of problems — factionalism in the Assembly, the struggle between the governor and the legislature, the constitutional problem of the control of finance — in Jamaica that he had just successfully dealt with in North America. He was not as successful in Jamaica, although his policies were perfectly sound — that is, from the planters' point of view. This was largely because to the Jamaican brand of factionalism and dissensions were added a lamentable lack of public-spirited men, generally, and this in the face of the heightened successes of the "intestine" enemies and the very real external threats from the French and the Spaniards. Relations were so strained between Britain and these two powers that one of Hunter's first instructions from the Duke of Newcastle was to put the island in a posture of defense against a Spanish invasion from the north, where the island was at its weakest.[51] The invasion did not materialize, but it remained a constant source of anxiety in the Colonial Office and among the colonists, and the Spanish question was not confronted until after the Treaty.

Hunter conducted the most energetic and sustained campaign yet against the Maroons. From very early in his administration he very clearsightedly saw that given the Maroons' superb skill in guerrilla warfare and given their virtually impenetrable strongholds, the overall strategy should be to aim at reducing them to such extremities that they would be induced to embrace any terms that might be offered to them.

Hunter was thus the first governor to have conceived the possibility of a treaty with the Maroons.

A greater concentration on the building of barracks at strategic places from Maroon communities, Hunter saw as of the first importance. In combination with this, he saw the settling of the island with more whites and, of course, the sending out of parties, as critical to government success. The construction of barracks, which began in the 1690s, was greatly handicapped by lack of money and sheer lack of will among the colonists. Hunter spent his own money on parties — a practice that was becoming a habit, since he had also spent his own funds while governor of New York, in helping to settle some three thousand refugees from the Rhenish Palatinate on the banks of the Hudson River in New York.[52] He also further procured credit from private individuals to pay for parties that had refused to march, not having been paid for some time. He enjoined cooperation and harmony in the legislature, which was constantly squabbling over petty and personal matters. So enthusiastic was he for the success of the island, that when his leave of absence was due, he postponed it indefinitely, though his health was failing, arguing that at such critical times he did not wish his absence to jeopardize the country.

But even with Hunter's energy and intelligence all the schemes failed. The parties sent out were almost always unsuccessful, and the governor had the depressing task of reporting to the Assembly what he intriguingly called their "bad success," against the "intestine enemies."

His settlement scheme was much more successful, at least in the initial stage. Indeed, its very success was to be its eventual downfall. As has been said, the settling of the island with whites was seen to serve the dual purposes of security and economy. But by the time Hunter began his administration, despite the earlier attempts at settlement, a great part of the north and northeastern sectors of the island was entirely possessed by the windward Maroons. Here, again, many of the marginal planters had perforce to abandon their estates, either from being too poor or too inefficient to defend themselves; others found that they had been too greedy in enclosing more lands than they could effectively cultivate.[53] Hunter encouraged whites to settle these lands, even affixing his children's names to certain land titles with a view to encouraging others to do likewise.[54] He was well aware, though, of the fear of the planters even to go near these areas. He responded by employing the services of the navy, then under Admiral Charles Stewart, soon to be replaced by Sir Chaloner Ogle in 1732. Stewart was made to careen the Port Antonio coast with a well-manned squadron, much as Commander Barnet, "a Known and Experienced Stout, Brisk man" had done in the early 1720s, and the presence of His Majesty's squadron not only facilitated Hunter's settling scheme greatly, but also served as a deterrent to any invasion attempts of the Spaniards or other foreign pirates and other "Pickerooning Rogues."[55]

Coffee growing was also encouraged, and in 1732 several planters and merchants petitioned Parliament for an act to encourage coffee raising as a means of settling more whites, to be "carried on by the Midling sort of People, who are not able to bear the great Expense necessary for Erecting and Carrying on a Sugar Plantation ...."[56] This request was to be repeated again, for the same reason, in the early years of the nineteenth century, when the whites perceived that they were threatened — in this instance not by their slaves, but by the "free" mulattos.[57] The coffee raising drive of this period was partially successful for a few small planters, since the overhead costs were relatively small. It was generally felt that a planter with only two slaves could profitably carry on the production of coffee. For encouragement, a reduction of the duty in England from 2/– to 18^{d} per pound was granted, which helped the industry. However, foreign coffee, especially from Hispaniola and from the French-run coffee culture in Dominica, soon competed adversely with the Jamaican-grown product, thus making it very difficult for the marginal estates.[58]

The success or near success of Hunter's settlement plan rankled with the Maroons. The unsettled lands taken up by the new planters were in the parishes of St. George and Portland, along the Titchfield and Manchioneal Bays. These areas were of the greatest strategic importance to the Maroons, serving as their outlets to the sea, their chief source not only of fish and turtle but it also of salt, the lack of which they thought would impair their health. Salt was also vital to them for the curing of their meat. The new plantations therefore hemmed the Maroons in, cutting off their communication to and from the sea.[59]

These plantations also cut off the Maroons' access to the towns from which they could buy other supplies, as well as sell their produce: "It is well known that many of them resorted every Sunday amongst the vast crowds that assemble there from all parts of the country to sell their fruits, Fowls, and other produce of their grounds and buy what they want."[60] It was also thought that this easy congruence with the outside world enabled the Maroons to purchase powder, a commodity which, as will be seen, they had in plenty, despite the many stringent laws against its sale to any but a few specified persons.

Thus from the very beginning, the Maroons attacked these settlements; "they daily came down in bodies" to rob and annoy the new settlers — again reminiscent of the Juan de Serras era — and Hunter would respond by having more fortifications built (not always successfully, for lack of money and public-spirited men) and by sending out parties against them. But invariably the Maroons had the upper hand. They would ensnare the parties into ingenious ambuscades, killing many and destroying settlements so that settlers had to retire, leaving the rebels "as before possessed of that part of the island."[61] By 1734, the Assembly reported that "twenty seven settlers were obliged to abandon and desert such their settlement [because] a large number of rebellious Negroes in those parts have . . . made frequent attacks on the settlement there, plundering and burning the houses, wounding some of the inhabitants and killing others."[62]

The situation worsened alarmingly for the plantocracy, despite Hunter's efforts. Even the erstwhile apathetic large planters felt bound to involve themselves in the crisis situation that developed. All too often the opulent planters had connived at Maroon activities — at times inadvertently, but often quite consciously. There is evidence that some of these planters paid certain Maroons a kind of retainer's fee that served two purposes: first, to insure that they would not attack their plantations, and second, to use them as a defense force to police their estates from attacks by other gangs.[63] Other great landowners, "being generally men of power and often commanders of the militia," possessed on their estates auxiliary whites, employed as overseers, bookkeepers, artisans, and the like. Thus they could muster volunteer parties against any Maroon incursion.[64] The Maroons, with their effective methods of communication with the plantations, would generally keep clear of such estates. Owners of these plantations were therefore not overly concerned with the Maroon problem. By localizing the situation and not seeing it as a national one, they inadvertently helped in the growth and the strength of the rebels. This apathy was one of Hunter's main problems on the island, but by the end of his administration even these planters knew that they could no longer sit on the fence. Their greatest fear came from the slaves who were leaving plantations most freely at this time to join the Maroons — and what if there should be a general insurrection of the slaves, with the Maroons joining them?

The governor responded to the situation by sending to England for more troops. Hunter was prepared to use all the forces at his disposal — volunteers, the militia, slaves, the army, the navy — to deal with the situation. Free blacks and mulattos were also mandated to serve. Men of these categories between the ages of fifteen and sixty were obliged to answer the Custos' warrant to serve in parties. For the first offense of failing to do so, the punishment was six months' imprisonment without bail. For the second it was twelve months' imprisonment; and for the third, loss of freedom.[65] Before the expected troops arrived, parties were sent out, but each ended in one debacle after another, and in charges and counter-charges. In one instance this led to the arrest of one of the commanding officers, who, while in custody, was "barbarously murdered."[66]

In reporting these events to the island's legislature, Hunter again stressed the need for peopling the island with more whites and the need for more effective means of reducing the slaves in rebellion, "who, by some late depredations and Barbarities, and the bad success of our ordinary Parties, seem to be increasing in Numbers and Audacity by which your Inland Settlements must either be abandoned or kept in perpetual Alarm and the danger in all Probability spread further."[67]

The danger to Hunter was real, especially because he was further convinced that the "Runaway Negroes" had a secret correspondence with the Spaniards, in cooperation with whom they intended to take over the island.

The legislature was at a loss to know what to do to protect themselves from "the Insults of those slaves who begin to grow both numerous and powerfull"[68]; but this did not prevent dissensions and wranglings between the Council and Assembly. Hunter was fortunate to have had the support of the Council and in November 1730, before the troops arrived, the governor and Council felt the situation critical enough to send a "Humble Address and Representation" to the Crown, representing, *inter alia*, the frequency of the rebels' incursions and the great ravages they committed on the new settlements: "They are now grown to a greater head than ever, and Wee have less power to Quell them, having neither means nor power to help ourselves. We are more Convinced of the Weak and Defenceless Condition of the Island by the defeat of Several partys which have been lately fitted out at a great expense of Men and Money in order to reduce those Rebels, but by the want of Experience in the officers, and of Discipline in the Men, they have always Miscarried or met with little or no Success, which hath Encouraged our Slaves to that Degree that we are under the greatest Apprehension of a General Insurrection, which may be the Entire Ruin of this Colony there being so great a disproportion in the number of

Whites and Blacks." A month later the Assembly also sent its own address to the king.[69]

The two regiments from Gibraltar under the command of Colonel Robert Hayes finally reached Jamaica in January 1730/1, but little or no provisions were made for them, to the extent that for the first few days they could not disembark; when they finally did, the barracks were not completed. This lack of preparation was partly due to the Assembly's irritation that Hunter had not consulted with them before asking for the troops, and partly to lack of revenue in the colony. The soldiers were finally divided into small groups and posted to certain parishes contiguous to plantations, where malaria, yellow fever, and intemperate living soon took their toll, and they complained bitterly.

"We are now come to a Country, where I believe Nobody Expected us, because no provision was made for our Reception,"[70] wrote Colonel Townsend to Walmesley, in one of the many valuable private letters these soldiers wrote home, representing a condition that was expressed in all the letters. They complained also of inaction; of debts, diseases and deaths, and altogether Jamaica received a poor rating from their pens. The inaction resulted from the guerrilla-warfare tactics of the Maroons, a form of combat completely alien to them. They were constantly bemused by fighting an enemy not visible to them, and they all jumped to the conclusion that the Maroon threat was much exaggerated and their presence was therefore unnecessary — in fact, it was degrading to them as soldiers to be called in to fight savages unworthy of their disciplined training. "The affair of the Blacks I look upon to be quite a Bam [?] for I can find no Body that has either seen or felt them in a Wrathful Manner," wrote Colonel Hayes. He also complained of the lack of accommodation, the sickness, and the increasing mortality among them, and he was convinced that "no Oven sure was ever so Hot" as Jamaica. For his part, his only business here was to sacrifice his health (a true prophecy, for he died a month later) and impoverish his fortune, for twice his income could not maintain him here in a manner befitting a colonel. (His salary, as an officer, was 20/- per week, while that of an ordinary soldier was 5/- per week.) He would consider himself fortunate if this expedition cost him only £1,000 extra; he rented a house at "Ligony" for £200 per annum, which was "no better than an English barn," paying £50 per annum for an indifferent cook — and everything else was expensive in proportion. His friend in England might well judge "what a pleasant situation I am in."[71]

Colonel Townsend was equally exasperated about the lack of provisions and accommodation, and he doubted the necessity of the entire operation: "I am very sure that at the present there is no Occasion for us: the Affair of the Rebellious Negroes is a Trifle, they have force sufficient of their own twenty times told, to put an End to that whenever they have a Mind to Exert themselves . . . in the meantime we are a Burthren to the Island," costing some £15,000 per annuum. And even if the Rebels were as "Troublesome" as the authorities reported, it would seem "impracticable to destroy them . . . as they have 120 miles of Mountain to range in." His later letters complained of the sicknesses and the fevers, and as for the expense, everything here was "twice dearer than they were at Gibraltar."

Colonel Cornwallis was an avid writer of letters to his brother, Lord Cornwallis, and his letters became more shrill and irascible with the duration of his stay in Jamaica. By March 5, 1730/1 he was beginning to be truly sorry to be in Jamaica, "the most Expensive disagreeable place under the sun." It vexed him to think that so many young men were sent here with nothing to do except sacrifice their health and accumulate debts, especially when it is remembered that there was no enemy to be seen: "in many places . . . there never was a Rebellious Negro heard of." He was intrigued by a report from a party sent out against the rebels, some of the soldiers being among the party. They went to the Maroon settlements, fought for several hours, and burnt some of their towns; but, wrote the exasperated officer, in the "terrible engagement" they neither killed nor did they take one, which led him to presume that "those that they pretend to have fought with so long were men in Buckram, otherwise they surely must have killed some of them," while two of the party were killed. "In short, I believe there is very little in it, and if there is, in the Manner we are dispersed, we cannot be of much service," for they were sent to places where the planters would not send their slaves — not even the new ones not yet seasoned. He spoke of the daily death among the officers and even more so among the soldiers. "I'm sure there is not an officer here but with pleasure would go to the most desperate Siege rather than stay in this damned unwholesome place, for there one should have a chance to gain some credit or die honorably, here no Reputation to be gained and no service to be done." In all his letters he asked his brother to represent most strongly to the right authorities in England the plight of His Majesty's troops in Jamaica, while he undertook to write directly to the secretary of war, to represent "the Barbarous Usage we here Suffer"; not even the "New Negroes were [ever] used in so ill a Manner as we are," and all this, "for the sake of, I fear, a few people."[72] When Colonel Hayes died March 19, the command fell to Cornwallis, who was next in rank, but by this time he was so feeble and demoralized that we find no more letters from him. But a private, most probably in Cornwallis's corps, wrote engagingly of the shock created by the death of Colonel Hayes. The regiment was in a most "mallancholy" posture, hardly a man but in tears; the officers, those alive, "have lost all their spirits," and as for "poor Coll. Cornwallis," he must be kept alive; "we are resolved to cheer him up;

this is a mallancholy subject for you, but was you to see the many we have where ... we dye daily, you would pity the two Regiments who will Soon fall." He gave a list of seven of the officers who were dead by March 19 — that is, after arriving on the island January 1730/1. And as for the privates, "they are passed by and for the number, I cannot mention."[73]

Cornwallis's complaints most probably bore results, for by July of the same year we find Newcastle writing to the Lords Commissioner of Trade to say that it was represented to the king that the officers and privates of the two regiments in Jamaica "suffer[ed] greatly from the badness of the climate," and that the regiments were "of little or no use for Suppressing the Rebellious Negroes." He asked to have the matter reviewed to ascertain how far the troops were necessary toward reducing the rebels and for the defense and security of the island and requested a report "with all Expedition."[74] Apparently the report (which is not traced) found the presence of the troops unnecessary, and within six months of arriving in Jamaica they were ordered back home. Governor Hunter, taken unawares, called an emergency session of the Assembly to announce this and to reflect on "the bad success of the party sent out against the slaves in rebellion on the north side of the island." This piece of news, in combination with widely circulated reports that the rebels on the north side of the island had formed themselves into "formidable bodies," plunged the colony into a state of extreme anxiety.

This is not to suggest that the regiments had any effect whatsoever in the battles with the Maroons — enemies in the first place they could not even see as their letters attested. The troops' impact was far greater on the slaves on plantations. Their presence — and some were actually posted on certain plantations — acted as a deterrent to slaves intending to run away or to rebel against their owners, thus preventing a "General Secession of Negroes in Plantations."[75] Hunter with his acute sense of the problem had written before the troops were recalled that it was the opinion of "the men of substance and sense here, [that] the arrival of these two regiments at that time was so Seasonable, that it was looked upon as a Special Stroke of Providence in their favour for their plantation Negroes were grown to that Degree of Insolence that they durst hardly order them out to work, and have been very tractable ever since; altho' the regular Forces have been of little use hitherto in their reduction ... yet their removal from the island as it is industriously given out to be intended, must be attended with fatal Consequences by the Incouragement it would give to the slaves in Rebellion, and to others to rebel" and the militia could not be depended on. The Council, too, soon regretted the recall of the troops at "this time of Imminent danger."[76]

Nevertheless, the regiments were recalled, but in view of His Majesty's "great regard for the Safety and better peopling" of the island, he ordered that any private soldier wishing to remain should be discharged with his arms,[77] thus fulfilling Colonel Cornwallis's fear, stated in one of his letters, that "they have a mind to make planters of us," adding that the locals were glad of their presence because they wanted "white people and not for fear of the Blacks." But the Colonel has missed the point, since it was precisely for fear of the blacks and fear of their inflated population vis-a-vis the whites that the planters saw the need to increase their own population. Apparently the scheme was none too successful, despite the encouragement to the soldiers: the Assembly enacted that every soldier who wished to remain should receive a certain lump sum of money according to rank, as well as a monthly salary or grant and lands, but there is no mention of the duration of time for the continuing grant; to every sergeant was given £20 (Jamaican currency) and £10 per month when made a captain, £8 per month when made a lieutenant, and £6/10 per month without promotion; to every captain, £5 and £6 per month; to every soldier, £5 and £4 per month. In addition, each was to receive one hundred acres of land and two slaves not exceeding the value of £50. One acre of every soldier's lot was to be cleared and planted and a house was to be built on this site at the country's expense. The official source gave the number of soldiers who remained under this scheme as "about 150," while a more recent secondary account said 126 soldiers and two sergeants remained,[78] but by the 1740s it appears that few, if any, stuck to their new life style. This was reflected in Governor Trelawny's reply in 1741 to the Lords Commissioner of Trade's enquiry of the extent of the soldiers' settlement, when Trelawny said that "soldiers seldom reconcile themselves to a life of labor and industry."[79]

After the withdrawal of the troops, Hunter was acutely aware of the perilous situation of the island and continued to remind the legislature of the stark facts: the slaves in rebellion were animated by their successes, and those on the plantations were ready to join them at the first favorable opportunity; the militia was insignificant and inept, and indeed constituted in itself a security problem; he noted the lethargy of the men of substance and the decreasing number of whites on the island; the decline in the colony's trade; and the scarcity of goods and supplies which led to exorbitant prices. Jamaica, as the soldiers' letters demonstrated, had become one of the most expensive areas of the period. In addition, neither the quitrents nor the deficiency taxes were yielding revenues enough to defray the heavy expenses accrued by the Maroon wars. Furthermore, the external enemies, the French and the Spaniards, but particularly the latter, who allegedly had designs of retaking Jamaica, were making incursions on the north side of Jamaica.[80] This entailed extra expenses with the presence of the Navy along the areas vulnerable to attack. There appears to have been no area of Jamaica's life which seemed favorable at this point, and this general malaise was due, whether directly or indirectly, to the Maroon problem.

In these circumstances Hunter felt that the Maroon situation demanded a new perspective, and for the second time, broached the subject of a treaty with the Assembly. Again the Assembly did not respond favorably to any terms with the Maroons, but repeated the same ritual of sending more parties out to "extirpate the Negroes in rebellion." A glance at some of these parties will help to demonstrate the nature of the warfare, the skill and overall strategy and tactics of the Maroons, the many real hardships the parties had to endure — but also their incompetence, the lack of discipline among the soldiers, their drunkenness, the lack of experience among most of the officers, and their downright cowardice in many instances. Between 1730 and 1732 about four major parties were sent out in addition to the smaller "flying" ones.

In March 1730 after the Maroons had attacked an out-settlement in Port Antonio, carrying off six women and a boy and wounding an overseer, a party of thirty-eight armed whites and nine baggage slaves were sent out against them; they were soon ambushed by the rebels and put in confusion, with "several wounded" and "about a dozen either killed or lost in the woods."[81] It is this type of situation one writer had in mind when he said, "to send out men that are not used to the Fatigue of Travelling in the Mountains and Lying out in the Woods, Crossing Rivers, and Lying Wet you had as good Cut their Throats . . . ."[82]

A larger force, called the "Grand Party," was again sent out in July in response to this defeat. This party consisted of ninety-five shots and twenty-five baggage "Negroes." They were again surrounded and routed, and the heavy rains on this occasion, as on so many others, also contributed to the downfall of the party. The rebels in the meantime attacked a settlement windward of Port Antonio, plundered and burnt it, carrying off a slave woman and her child. All these failures made for despair among the whites, as they gave the Maroons a heightened sense of their importance and their audacity grew. The governor complained that despite the great care and pain taken in fitting out the Grand Party to dislodge or destroy the "slaves in rebellion," yet "they have returned without any manner of success, having lost themselves in the Woods, supposed to be by the Mismanagement of some of their officers or Guides, by which some of them have been famished, others drowned in crossing the rivers, and many thro' sickness have dyed, so that it's computed one fourth part of them are destroyed."[83]

But in November 1731 a party under Captain Peters had some small success with the rebels. Here the party surprised them in one of their "Chief Towns" — apparently the historic Nanny Town[84] — and captured it and kept possession of it for three days. But contrary to the governor's instructions, the soldiers left the town after having set fire to it, on the pretext that they could not hold out any longer. Others sent out were retarded by the heavy tropical rains — a critical part of the Maroon saga which worked in their favor, if only negatively, in that the parties in these flood rains were greatly handicapped in their pursuits. As said elsewhere, what was termed success by the authorities almost invariably boomeranged against them. To burn a Maroon town is comparable to destroying the boxes of a beehive without destroying the bees. The Maroons were dispersed, thus becoming more desperate for food and provisions, and therefore the attacks at this time became more diversified and certainly more savage. Immediately after this "success," reports of rebel forays came from as far apart as St. David in the east and St. James in the north. One report mentioned that small groups of the rebels attacked an area close to the barracks which were built along the road toward their chief settlement at Port Antonio, although there was a party of soldiers and other armed men stationed there. They killed one black guard, wounded three others, and took a "Negro" woman prisoner. Then news of attacks came from St. David, where they again killed one black, wounded three, and carried off one, possibly a guard; and again news came from St. James where the rebels were said to have killed two soldiers who were "straggling" from their barracks. These were savagely dealt with, one having his head cut off, while the body of the other was found in the woods. The dispersed rebels, as usual, influenced the slaves on the plantations, for at this time there were reports that "several Negroes have deserted their masters lately." Among these, twenty were from Colonel Nedham's estate from the north side, and it later became clear that these had joined the Maroons and had assumed leadership positions.[85] This correlation betweeen the "success" of the parties and diversified and savage attacks was to manifest itself over and over again.

Another large party, surpassing almost all others, was sent out March 1732. In this instance, ninety-three armed blacks, five overseers (whites), four soldiers, "including officers," and twenty baggage slaves marched from Liguenae in the south, while another party of eighty-six whites, 131 blacks, and sixty-one baggage slaves marched from the north side. Both parties attacked almost simultaneously, and this was the most important "success" yet the authorities had ever had against the Maroons. For, in this case, they surprised and ousted them from three of their settlements at windward; among them Nanny Town was again captured.

Governor Hunter was jubilant. He told Newcastle, "We are now possessed of the 3 chief settlements of the Rebels, and may keep possession if the Assembly . . . will do their duty."[86] In the meantime he gave orders for their reinforcement, and supplies were sent out; but heavy rains and floods in the river meant great difficulties and such parties had to return without reaching the "captured" settlements. In his address to the Council and Assembly, he reminded the members of the importance of this meeting, "aris[ing] from an Incident very different from that of the former session, I mean the Success your Partys have had against the Slaves in Rebellion, which if supported or pursued, may be improved to the future Security and better peopling this Island."[87] Despite the success though, the governor pointed out that there was much "desertion and backwardness of baggage slaves," insisting that "there must be some immediate remedy for that Evil, lest the whole affair should from so slender a Cause prove abortive."[88] He again stressed the importance of the construction of barracks at strategic points from the rebel towns now held and again pointed out the need for settlements in the unsettled northeast. The legislature was heartened and plans were made to act upon Hunter's suggestion of building more defensive barracks. It was also decided that in view of the rebels' dispersion from their towns, flying parties should be sent out against them.

But the nature of the success soon began to boomerang on the plantocracy. The dispersed Maroons were desperate, and their attacks were reported from different parts of the island. Again slaves were abducted, cattle slaughtered, and outlying plantations raided and set on fire. The first example of this came when a gang of rebels attacked the plantation of one Mr. Barclay in St. Elizabeth, killing six of his slaves, and carrying off eight and a child, whom they dashed against a rock and left for dead, but who was later found barely alive. A flying party pursued this gang but without any success. Another Maroon gang fell on Woodstock's plantation, in the same parish, killing two slaves and carrying away eight. St. Elizabeth, a southern parish, had been relatively free of Maroon incursions up to this period, and this accounted for its thirty-two plantations producing some 2745 hogsheads of sugar. Then news spread that the rebels were attacking more plantations to leeward and were doing much "Mischief." Clarendon, for instance, "the richest and largest parish on this side," was attacked. This parish — which, since Lubolo's Treaty, had steadily increased its sugar production unmolested (with sixty-six plantations producing 5480 hogsheads of sugar) was certainly the largest producer of sugar on the island.[89]

The sterling planters of this parish, knowing of the ineffectuality of the regular parties, organized their own force of planters and their slaves to "pursue the rebellious Negroes,"[90] in addition to that obliged by law; there is no record to show how they fared. The situation soon became fluid and uncertain even in Clarendon, and as we have repeatedly seen, the plantation slaves were always alert to any opportunity to make their forward thrust for freedom. This time, thirty-one slaves belonging to John Morant of this parish left their master, taking with them their field implements, declaring they would be followed by many others, and defying any to come out against them. By this time they had already reached the other side of the river Minho, but seeing the small number of pursuers, the rebels recrossed the river to confront them — certainly with more bravado than discretion or experience, because successful running away was a very skilled activity. They were met with brisk fire from the party, which killed five of them and wounded eight; the rest finally surrendered and were returned to their owner for whatever arbitrary and brutal reprisal he might think fit. Their surrender brought joy to the planters of the area, for they were apprehensive of a general insurrection of slaves.[91]

Meanwhile, the flying parties sent out against the dispersed rebels were faring very badly indeed, and there were reports of "shameful retreats" of several parties, and the desertion of armed blacks continued unabated. On this occasion it was reported that 100 Black Shots and baggage slaves deserted, and Hunter again called for more serious penalties for desertions. The militia, too, at this critical period was even more hopeless, the exasperated governor complaining that they were more a "drawback ... than an addition to our strength." Equally, the Spanish threat was uppermost at this period; there were rumors that the Cuban militia was about to attack the British ports at Campeachy. In addition to these and all the other difficulties, there was the constant financial pressure. Not only was there an empty treasury but there was also a languishing state of credit, not to be revived, in fact, until immediately after the Treaty — and there was also an acute shortage of coins on the island.[92]

The euphoria over the success of a year earlier soon gave place to gloom and genuine alarm from all over the colony. In an emergency session of the Assembly in March 1733, the governor enumerated the problems, reminding the legislators of the late "bad success" of the parties against the rebels and the defeat of some of them, by their own negligence more than by the force of the enemy. Again he stressed the necessity for greater efforts, "lest, encouraged by success, they should disturb the frontier settlements, and be joined by other slaves of the same disposition." He further mentioned that with some difficulty he had managed to fit out a fresh party, consisting of "about 250 men, completely armed and victualled," to march in different routes, and he was expecting "every hour an account of what success they have had." He did not have to wait long for, upon uttering these words, a note was received from Lieutenant-Colonel Ashworth of the party, giving an account of this party's "bad success." Indeed the "Great Negro Town," which had been captured by the parties a year ago, was now retaken by the Maroons. The governor said that the note gave a rather sad prospect of any hope of success from the parties, therefore the legislature would need to take concerted action for some speedy and effectual means of defeating the enemy. And, strange as it may seem, the house met in committee and proceeded to pass the same futile resolutions for the extirpation of the rebels and "to consider the properest methods for rendering parties more serviceable for the future, and for preventing mutiny and desertion."[93]

One may pause here to examine the situation of the rebels since the "success" against them. At this period the documents became enriched from two sources: diaries kept by some soldiers of different parties and the confessions of captured Maroons. As diaries are to the Maroon saga what slave traders' journals are to the slave trade, captured Maroon testimonies and depositions are to Maroon history what slave narratives are to a study of slavery. One of the first depositions we have from a Maroon came after the capture of the "Great Negro Town," when the soldiers came upon the beginnings of a new settlement started by a party of dispossessed rebels. Here they captured one woman and six children, the rest escaping in the woods, and to this woman we are indebted for some of the knowledge we have of Maroon settlements. She herself had been born in one of the settlements and spoke "good English," which would seem to suggest that the rebels of this gang might have been creoles — or at least they may have spent long enough periods on the plantations to have acquired a knowledge of English before running away. But it has already been noted that for security reasons Cudjoe saw to it that his people conversed in English, assuming that to allow different tribal groups to speak their own tongues could well lead to convenient plots against his hegemony.

The woman told her captors that after the chief towns were taken, the Maroons were in great need for provisions and there arose a heated dispute among them, deciding whether to keep together as a body or to divide into different gangs. They decided on the latter, forming "3 Partys," and taking as many routes, and "I believe some of them have found a way thro' the mountains to the westward of the island, for there has lately been discovered a large Settlement with a very considerable body of those Rebels in it in the parish of St. James, which has alarmed the people in those parts very much."[94] This testimony is vital in view of the fact that this is the first clear evidence we have of the existence of Cudjoe's group in the Cockpit Mountains between St. James and Trelawny. But her testimony is unclear on whether the windward group had any prior knowledge of Cudjoe's band, or merely came upon it unawares. From her we have, naturally, no further knowledge of the leewards, and it is from other deponents that we gain valuable facts and insights into Cudjoe's settlement — his character, his form of government, and the like.

No sooner had the authorities received the deponents' testimony than they sent out three different parties against the rebels, but they were soon forced to return without any success.[95] The governor, however, promised to send out a stronger party with the hope of destroying this newly discovered gang, which, from all accounts, he computed as "of at least a hundred bould resolute fellows."[96] The authorities were determined to take advantage of the rebels' plight — their distressed condition, the lack of provisions, and above all their being constantly hounded out of new settlements, running from place to place — and it was at this crucial point that Hunter postponed his well-deserved leave. The woman's deposition has been more than corroborated by the parties who came frequently upon new haunts lately deserted, often so suddenly that they left "their arms and other things behind them." And in line with good tactics, the Maroons knew they were on the defensive and would only attack if surprised by the parties or if the guard slaves on plantations tried to thwart their purposes. But the parties were hampered by the heavy rains and floods to the windward at this time — longer than had been known in "the memory of man."[97]

In the meantime, the parties under Lambe and Williams were faring no better than the others, and their diaries give us some interesting accounts of some of the guerrilla tactics of the Maroons. They recounted how they "took" the "Negro Towns," but soon discovered that the (women) rebels had burnt it before evacuating, leaving behind some pots and crockery before escaping to the top of the Carrion Crow Hill, pursued by fifty-two men from the party. But this was a snare, and the party was cleanly ambushed. In this instance, the rebels piled up a vast heap of huge stones against which they set up props, then, as the soldiers came close enough to this excessively steep hill, they pulled the props away and the stones, like the walls of Jericho, came tumbling down with great force and violence, putting the party into much confusion. "Many" were killed, and three were taken alive, others running away, leaving their arms and ammunition behind, for which the rebels were always most grateful. This battle gives us a good practical demonstration of the strategic formation of the windward towns, where the Carrion Crow Hill was the location of Guy's Town.[98]

During this time, the party from its bivouac — or what was left of it — sent for more provisions and ammunition, and the Maroons were so bold that some approached the troops, close enough, most probably camouflaged, to talk with them, as was to happen on other occasions. They showered insults on the party, threatening, too, that they were going to starve them out because they would intercept the detachment for provisions and ammunition they knew had been sent for. They promised that the men who had left the town before they burnt it would return to attack them, and this promise was soon kept with devastating results. One of their leaders was said to have been one of the twenty who escaped from Colonel Nedham's plantation. This audacious man, whose name was Cudjoe — almost certainly from the Akan-speaking group of Ghana, thus following the pattern of Akan leadership in Maroon societies — inquired of the party

"Negroes" if they remembered him and bade them give his regards to those he and his men had left behind — their wives and acquaintances. But he implored them to quit being slaves and to join him. He boasted about how well they were living in freedom, repeating that the party blacks should cease fighting the white man's battles. Again they repeated that they had more strength coming, most certainly from the other towns. Saturday and Sunday they "lay by," and their silence was probably even more ominous to the soldiers than their insults and parleys. Then came Monday morning, by which time the rebels had surrounded the towns the party thought they had taken, and from 8 a.m. they began brisk firing from their ambushes, no one really seeing them, until 3 p.m., when the party could hold out no longer. So they fled, pleading insufficient arms and ammunition, taking into consideration what they had lost to the rebels on the Carrion Crow Hill. [99]

Apart from the obvious ignominy of being so clearly defeated by the Maroons even after they had the temerity to inform the party that they were returning to attack them, there were other features of this engagement that puzzled the soldiers. One was the amount of powder and ammunition the rebels had. Lieutenant-Colonel Ashworth, writing of the battle, said clumsily, "It's a Mistery that so much Ammunition i.e. 16 cartridges at least each man some more and more powder in their horns." The bemused Ashworth found it difficult to accept the fact that the party should take "three of their towns and be drove out with the loss of 4 white men taken alive and 4 killed, and not the ear of a Rebel brought in," especially when it was remembered that they came "so nigh our party" as to speak to them.[100] It should be noted that when a soldier killed a Maroon he would cut off both ears, and in some instances, the head, while the Dutch in Surinam, fighting their Maroons at about the same time, would cut off the right hands of dead Maroons for similar reasons. This grisly practice served both as a trophy of the soldier's valor and as evidence by which he could collect his reward. The Maroons abhorred this practice of mutilating their dead, and for this reason they would take the bodies of those who fell in battles with them, even under the most straitened circumstances. In this particular battle the Maroons lost a few of their men to the party under Williams, who sent "a body of men for their ears," but the Maroons, lying concealed, would not allow it, and fired on them, forcing them to retreat without obtaining their trophies. In the event, Lambe, another soldier leading another party, was more fortunate. He had his reward of £90 for the three pairs of ears he retrieved. Another soldier in his account also dwelt on the quantity of powder in the possession of the rebels. In fact the rebels boasted of it, asking the party if they wanted any powder, if so, they could supply them. Several called to Captain Williams by name, and this soldier as well as Ashworth felt that many of these eloquent rebels may have been some of the deserters from the parties.[101]

Powder was of high security consideration, and the Assembly passed numerous laws with stringent penalties to insure that it did not fall into the wrong hands — the rebels', for instance. But the authorities soon found their efforts ineffective. How then did the Maroons come by powder? The first and most obvious source was the parties themselves, when they, on many occasions, had of necessity to run away from the Maroons, leaving powder, ammunition, provisions, and the like behind. And soon the rebels came to look upon this as a regular source.

Then there were the Black Shots and baggage slaves. These, in deserting from parties, would take with them whatever powder and other supplies they could lay their hands on, and mostly they would join other Maroon gangs. Again, slaves, on escaping from plantations — especially those who left in groups, after previous planning, and often in collusion with established Maroon communities — would take with them powder and ammunition if possible, and invariably that awe-inspiring agro-military implement, the machete.

But there was yet another source, fraught with much secrecy and danger, and requiring skillful diplomacy. The rebels could actually purchase powder from certain whites, considered to be mainly Jews, from the main towns such as Kingston and Port Antonio. In one of the windward groups, possibly Nanny Town, they captured two white boys, one named "Done" or "Dun" and the other, Charles. These soon became the local scribes, made to write passes in Colonel Nedham's name for the Maroon couriers bent on the dangerous business of buying powder from one "Master Isaac" or "Jacob," a Jew of "Church Street" or "Jew Alley" who "belonged" to a sloop in Kingston. On one occasion they bought "2 long horns full" and a bag of balls from the "Judian." With all these sources available to them, it is little wonder that the Maroons were always amply supplied.[102]

The soldiers also marvelled at the number of the rebels. They felt they had increased to "several hundred," and Ashworth for one was of the opinion that the leeward gang must have joined them. The leeward gang did not join them, but it is true that all Maroon communities at this time gained in numbers and supplies from the many plantation slaves who joined them. The official reports said that no plantation was without its runaways during this period, and the authorities repeatedly talked of the demographic growth, giving it as "excessive," as "formidable," or in the "hundreds of thousands,"[103] without much precision. In fact, their number, as we see after the Treaty, did not amount to a thousand between the two major communities. But, as noted, a part of Maroon guerrilla strategy was that they should not be seen by the enemies (thus, demographic computation was next to impossible), their method being that of attack and ambush, using elaborate camouflage, imitating the woods and shrubs around them. Furthermore, their gun-fire was always reported as very fast and brisk, coming from different directions but representing, in fact, their dexterity in swift gyrations on the ground as they fired, so that a single Maroon, turning and skipping from place to place while in action, might be thought to have been at least half a dozen men. It need hardly be said that this added to the difficulty of the parties in shooting down a Maroon.

What is certain, though, is that the additions from the plantations, especially those from Colonel Nedham's, represented a new dynamic dimension to marronage. These men and women, fresh from slavery, had a more poignant memory of this brutal system — unlike Cudjoe's, for instance, "free" since the 1690s — and like the Spartans their philosophy seems to have been either to return from battle *with* or *on* their swords. This new spirit did help to improve morale, especially among the windwards, and the new style of verbal abuse as well as the boasting regarding their strength was encouraged and developed by the new recruits.

It certainly appears to have been good policy on the part of the windwards to have worked in concert with the new blood, and it soon paid high dividends for them. After their latest victory with the party, as would be expected, the rebels became much bolder, more contemptuous of the authorities, and decidedly more enterprising in their operations. Some, in small groups, would make hit-and-run raids on plantations, carrying off "a great number of cattle and other provisions,"[104] also slaves, to increase their numbers. But their most audacious act at this time was the taking over of plantations. One such which they took over and occupied, after first ravaging adjoining ones, was Hobby's within sight of Titchfield near Port Antonio. This was done after a well-organized and systematic plan where Colonel Nedham's Cudjoe was in a leadership position. He concerted his action with two other commanders, Scipio and Pompey — whether from Nedham's group or not is not clear. But their names would certainly indicate that they were former plantation slaves where, out of whimsy, owners would name some of their slaves from the classics, from the Bible, or from given dispositions (Charity, Faith, Felicity, Love, and the like). Cudjoe himself led the attack on Hobby's plantation with one hundred men and "several women," while Pompey led another gang with the same number of men. Apparently Scipio was in charge of the most strategic town with the greatest ascent, and he was to take his cue from the "Drummer," who was placed on the ridge overlooking the town to watch for the advancing parties.[105] As mentioned before, Titchfield Bay was of great importance to the Maroons, and they may well have resented the new fortifications being built there.

Hunter had hoped that the dangerous situation would make for unity in the legislature. But this was not so; the old squabbling between the Council and the Assembly continued. This time the petty arguments had a most deleterious effect on the revenue bills necessary for defraying the costs of the party. Hunter pleaded for harmony, reminding the legislators of the encouragement given to the rebels because of their many successes over the parties. The "one common interest" of the colony was the Maroon affair, and the colonists would "Sink or Swim together ... All Seems to be at Stake."[106] Writing to the Lords Commissioners of Trade, August 1733, the governor said that it must seem surprising to them that "in such a clime of danger just at our Doors," which usually unites the most divided people, there should be such divisions in the legislature: "Nothing can account for this but the frailty of mankind."[107] In the face of what he perceived as "Imminent Danger," the governor sent a party of volunteers to Port Antonio against the rebels. But incredible as it may seem, the legislature was unable to agree on a tax bill to finance the venture. The party was thus straitened for provisions and refused to march without advance pay, and again Hunter solved the problem, by advancing his own private credit — along with "some friends" — before the party would march. The governor felt convinced that the conduct of the war should have been left to the executive; then, "with God's blessing," he would in a short time put an end to the present danger from the rebels; but their growing power might be "too great for any Remedy within [our] power."[108]

The assemblymen deplored the "unhappy miscarriage" of the party, and then went on to make the extraordinary statement that they had always used the utmost of their endeavors to "Suppress and Destroy our Intestine Enemy" and would continue to pursue such methods as were conducive to the reduction of the rebels.[109]

However, apparently realizing the danger even more than the Assembly, the Council sent an address to the Lords Commissioners of Trade enumerating the distressed state of trade and credit, "but our chief and our greatest arises from the trouble and danger which our Rebellious Slaves have created for us, We have been at very great Expense of men and money to suppress them, but our constant ill-success has only convinced us of our own Weakness, and their strength. The Evil is become too great for any cure we can apply, And we are in daily Apprehensions of a General Defection of our Slaves, To whom without some speedy relief we must fall a sacrifice, And this once valuable Colony to be made useless to His Majesty. This we have often represented but have not had the good fortune to be believed."[110]

A great effort was now made, in July 1733, to send out what the Council and Assembly considered the "strongest force" yet against the rebels. In preparation for this, the two chambers held a joint conference to examine the crisis situation, and it was resolved that the services of the navy should also be employed. Rear Admiral Sir Chaloner Ogle was thus requested to send all the ships in harbor, as well as seamen volunteers, to subdue the "rebellious Negroes." The result was a very impressive outfit, with a high proportion of professional men — one hundred soldiers from the two independent companies of the colony, with their officers, and one hundred volunteers — fifty whites and fifty free blacks. In addition to this, 200 trusted slaves were included. The strategy of this great force was to attack the "Negro Towns" from three sides, coordinating the matter so as to fall in at the same precise point of time.[111] Yet this was to be the most humiliating defeat the government parties yet had from the Maroons.

The soldiers' reports and their diaries give the result of this "most promising effort." By August they were ready to march, and within two miles of the settlement, at 4 p.m., the advance guard was fired on by an ambush that attacked them "with the utmost fury," where "several" were killed on both sides, and "many" were wounded, including Captain John Swanton, an exceptionally courageous officer, whose reports and journal have given us much information. Another encounter took place and "most officers" were killed. With night approaching, Swanton, though wounded in the breast, was apparently still in command, so he ordered the baggage slaves to "fly," which they did — gladly, it would seem, for many deserted, not to be seen by the party again. Then the officers had the presence of mind to destroy every bag and box with powder and balls, and the medicine, throwing away the surgeon's instruments, the beef and bread, down precipices, and drinking as much liquor as they could before throwing away this commodity. Only about eleven of Swanton's men were left after death and desertions had taken their toll, and of these eleven, only seven had "serviceable pieces"; this group was in the middle of an ambush. And the rebels, who could see them, knew this, but displayed their great experience by not attacking in the dark. Also, the Maroons, always careful with their dead, were on this occasion taking care of the body of one of their leaders who had fallen in battle. Ashworth's report reflected on the bravery of Swanton, the superior skill of the rebels, and he gave it that eight of the officers of the party were killed. In his view, nightfall and heavy showers of rain saved the rest of the party. The island's gentlemen, he said, "must (I think) admit that unhappy Jamaica is in a Tottering State and requires nothing less than the most vigorous and Expedient Means to save us from the Impending Danger which now seems to be ripe for every Body believes their numbers are greatly Increased." Another soldier, J. Draper, also commented on the bravery of Swanton in the midst of his soldiers running away on all sides. He mentioned that five rebels were killed, and their ears were taken. He, for one, had seen four pairs of ears; the other pair must have been in possession of some of the soldiers: he estimated the dead of the party to have been "6 or 7" and "about 16 wounded."[112]

In the post mortem of the battle it was discovered that things went well up to the time when the ambush fired on them; the seamen returned the fire for about an hour, and the situation was pretty much under control until, it was alleged, a pilot announced that they should all retreat as they would otherwise be surrounded by the Maroons. But as we have seen, the Maroons had no inclination to do so, and pandemonium reigned. Soldiers, sailors, and baggage men began to run away, leaving the wounded Swanton and the few faithful soldiers. Soon all began to blame the fiasco on the "villainy" of this unfortunate pilot, who was considered "the sole cause of the misconduct" of the party and was accordingly later shot by order of a court martial. There was also much drunkenness and disorderliness on the part of the soldiers. In fact they mutinied even before they left Port Antonio for the march and were only subdued when they were drawn up in a body against the sailors, who were ordered to shoot if they did not submit — which they finally did "with much difficulty."[113] Hunter, in commenting on the drunkenness of the soldiers, which was endemic in the army, had opined that "rum the ruin of this island, is easier to come at here than small beer in England."[114]

The extent to which the island's inhabitants had placed their faith in this Grand Party is amply demonstrated by the number of anguished private letters written by colonists to friends in England. All these letters spoke of the growing strength of the enemies and the helplessness of the island, and all solicited help from Britain. One writer would not trouble his friend with any other news than that "we are in terrible Circumstances, in respect of ye Rebellious Negroes, they gott the better of all our partys, our Men are quite Despirited, and dare not look them in ye face in ye open Ground or in Equal Numbers." He then mentioned how their last resort was to apply to Sir Chaloner Ogle and "we imagined this Force would have done ye Business Effectually" — but the men ran away and were defeated. "This account will Surprise and Effect you and everybody who hath any regard for this Country. Its certain we cannot send a stronger or more promising Force than that was and wee have now nothing to do but to be on our Defence. Its Gods Mercy they are not joyned by our own Slaves; if that should happen this country must be cutt off." Britain, therefore, must intercede. The letter ended by asking his friend to "make our case known to ye Government," hoping that they will "take all ye care of us in their power." Another thought the "Expedition" would have answered their "Design," and felt that if the others of the party had had the bravery and fidelity of Swanton, then the affair would have ended differently. Now "God only knows what will be the Event of this Miscarriage," but

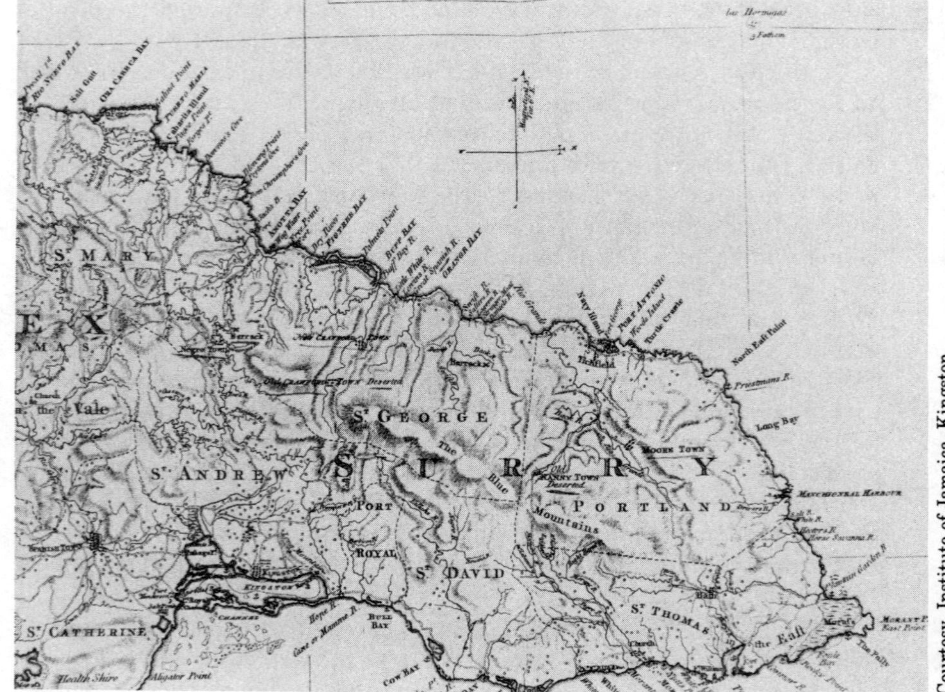

Courtesy, Institute of Jamaica, Kingston

Windward Maroons, as shown on map of 1774

he was certain that without assistance from Great Britain, the colony was in danger of being lost. Still another, replete with information, said that twenty-two plantation slaves and some of the deserters from the party had joined the rebels; also about forty able Coromantines from St. Thomas-in-the-East had run away to join them. He predicted that because of the daily alarms and apprehensions, martial law would have to be declared, without which he could only see fatal consequences. He touched upon the rebels' great increase in strength, their "Insolence" especially since they defeated this last Great Party, and ended that without assistance from Britain the colony was powerless.[115]

Again, Spanish collaboration with the Maroons was suggested. One writer was convinced that "the Spaniards of Cuba have given assistance to, or Countenanced these People." He thought that if some effectual means were not employed against the Maroons, then, from the encouragement of this, their "late and former successes," they might well take over the island.[116]

Meanwhile, as would be expected, the Maroons were literally strutting. As for the planters of the northeastern parishes — frontiersmen who had remained there largely because of Hunter's endeavors and encouragement, because of the barracks that were built adjacent to them, and also because of the presence of His Majesty's squadron at the harbor of Port Antonio, ready for any eventuality — these were now completely chased away by the rebels. "From the Insults of the Rebellious Negroes, who have done much Mischief among the Neighboring Plantations, ... most of the people are flown to this place for Shelter."[117] Thus the barracks adjacent to Port Antonio and the breastwork near Titchfield served as veritable shelters for the casualties — or refugees — of Maroon successes. And when these were proved inadequate the Assembly prepared two bills to construct more barracks "in order to secure the settlers."[118]

Not only did the Maroons confine themselves to those areas they considered their own purlieus, but now they "kept no bounds." They came down openly to make incursions on plantations all over the island. In the event, the island's main roads became so infested with them, as in the days of Robin Hood, that travel, even in broad daylight, became a most hazardous undertaking to the slavocracy: "[T]he insecurity of our country," wrote a Jamaican assemblyman, "occasioned by our slaves in Rebellion against us whose insolence is grown so great that we cannot say we are sure of another day and Robbings and Murders so common in our capital Roads, that it is with the utmost hazard we Travel them ...."[119]

Two weeks after the last defeat, about eighty or ninety Maroons took possession of a plantation and two penns (mixed farms consisting of crops and livestock, its usage dating from the seventeenth century in Jamaica) in the northeast. Fifty soldiers were sent out against them but they were beaten, after killing only one rebel. Even after being reinforced with fifty more soldiers, they refused to attack, pleading insufficient strength, but the authorities were unable to spare more soldiers from those guarding Port Antonio. Thus the "Enemy" was left in possession of "great plenty of cattle and other provisions."[120]

Maroon power grew, and their attitude to the authorities could be summed up in one word — contempt. "These constant successes," complained the Council and Assembly, "have Emboldened the Rebels to that degree that they now despise our power and instead of hideing themselves as they formerly did in those mountains and Covered places, they openly appear in Arms, and are daily Increasing by the desertion of other slaves whom they incourage and Intice over to them and have actually taken over 3 plantations within 8 miles of Port Antonio and the Sea, by which means they may at any time cutt off Communications by land with that harbour and Town and the new Settlers in that Neighborhood have been obliged to retire thither with their families for protection."[121]

The situation had reached the point where "No man at [the] North side" could be said to be master of a slave — many of them not doing half the work they used to do "nor dare their master punish them for the least Disgust will probably cause them to make their Escape and join the Rebels as many from several plantations frequently do . . . ,"[122] was the opinion of an eyewitness. The legislature was well aware of the difficulty of computing Maroon population, but nevertheless thought they were "not less than 2,000" in the several parts of the island, and should defection of slaves become widespread, "You will see, we could not defend ourselves."[123] The planters found that they could no longer depend on their most faithful slaves because "the hopes of freedom . . . has shaken the fidelity of our most Trusty Slaves," and they admitted that they were "at a loss what measures to take." They were convinced that even those slaves who remained with them "in seeming subjection to us wish well to their [the Maroons'] Cause, and only wait for an opportunity of joining them." Under these deplorable circumstances, they told the Lords Commissioners, they must address His Majesty for aid and assistance, without which, since they were already under the greatest extremity, they would either have to abandon the island, or become "Victims to those Merciless People."[124]

The planter legislators certainly knew what was in the minds of most slaves. Indeed the behavioral pattern and the cognition of the Jamaican slaves — especially during the period 1730 to 1738 — would seem to make any precise definition of the word "slave" rather bothersome. Consider Sam, for instance: Sam belonged to Colonel Nedham of Port Antonio, from whose plantation we have already met many — among them the impudent Cudjoe, who had proved his mettle as a guerrilla leader on many occasions. As far as can be ascertained, Sam remained on the best of terms with Cudjoe, visiting him on occasion, especially when Cudjoe was holding Hobby's estates. On one of these visits, Sam was on his way to town, whether on his master's errand or not, is not clear, but what is clear is that Sam had a great deal of time — and indeed a choice. An eyewitness gave us an account of the enthusiastic greeting Sam had from Cudjoe and Pompey, who inquired of Sam why he did not join them, whereupon Sam's reply reflected his consciousness of his choice: "Master uses us goodee yet, but when he uses us ugly we'll come," and the plural pronoun should not be seen as just a royal formality, for it can be surmised that a man like Sam would command respect and therefore leadership position among his fellow slaves. It was also said that "one of" Sam's wives was residing at Hobby's.[125]

It appears that Sam was also connected with the dangerous business of powder buying, for he played host to two famous Maroon spies, Cudjoe and Quashee, engaged in this business. Sam made it his business to entertain them on Colonel Nedham's plantation, though without the colonel's knowledge. Indeed it was reported to the Assembly "that several of the rebellious Negroes have been sheltered at Port Antonio, and amongst Colonel Nedham's and Newland's negro-kind, but without the masters' knowledge."[126] It is not doing damage to historical "facts" at all to imagine the jaunty Maroons entertained by the quietly efficient Sam on the best of the colonel's venison and quenching their thirst on the choicest of the gentleman's port, becoming sybaritic and boastful of their successes and their exploits as the entertainment progressed.

Behavior of this type depicts the heroic audaciousness of the Maroons, perhaps even more than their actual attacks on plantations. From the point of view of the slaves, it also shows a lack of that necessary sense of fear for the masters, so important for the proper regulation of the slave system. This easy and regular congress between Maroons and slaves was also another side of the weakness and the failures of the planters' efforts against the rebels. The communication systems and the espionage of the rebels were so efficient that almost always they knew of government plans to send out parties against them, even when only discussed in the legislature. This was a source of despair and frustration to the plantocracy, and a committee of the Assembly complained in 1733 that the Maroons "are as well acquainted with our designs as we ourselves."[127]

The desertion rate among the slave soldiers, as mentioned already, was another constant source of frustration to the slavocracy. From the records, no party that went out against the Maroons escaped its quota of desertions. Some reported ten, some thirty, fifty, or one hundred Black Shots or baggage slaves taking off into the woods, either to join the Maroons or to establish small communities among themselves. Their worst "treachery" to the authorities was that they were thought to have been supplying the rebels with powder and ammunition — and, what was more, with useful information. In one of the private letters mentioned above, the writer felt that a major contribution to the "ill-success" of the Grand Party was the treachery of the baggage slaves who were suspected of having a correspondence with the rebels "and, I fear, there are too good grounds for it."[128] It would seem that while the slave masters were arming their Black Shots with guns and loading their baggage slaves with supplies, they had one thought and one thought alone in their minds and that was how to get these accoutrement and supplies to their brethren in the woods.

The case of the baggage slave Cuffee is instructive. Cuffee marched dutifully and assiduously with his party, led by Edward Creswell and Ebenezer Lambe, through some of the most hazardous mountain conditions; then after about a week, when by this time the whites were suffering from the most harrowing fatigue, he "threw down his baggage, took a Calabash of rum out and run from the party"[129] — perhaps, like Patrick Henry, arguing for liberty or death.

Hunter disapproved increasingly of the large number of baggage slaves accompanying each party, not only on grounds of security but also because he thought it rather expensive. But he probably was well aware of the dependence of the soldiers and the volunteers on their "baggage Negroes," when he observed that "he is a bad soldier who cannot carry four days' provisions for himself."[130]

Numerous means were devised by Hunter to combat desertion, ranging from suggestions of the most severe treatment to seductive inducements. Flogging was recommended, but whether this could have been applied or not is not clear, because mostly the deserters made a clean break and might never be *seen* again by the authorities — but might later be *heard* in some abusive sessions with the parties. Special guards were also set up at strategic points to cut them off should they attempt to run away during a march. When all these proved ineffectual, more leniency was recommended: instead of more punishment, "extra inducements should be held out to them to remain loyal;" money was offered to those who served well; a storehouse was established at Manchioneal for their benefit, for "all plunder taken or to be taken;" also a more generous leave-of-absence scheme was devised for those "who have given of the most service."[131]

But there was certainly another side to the soldier slave question. Some gave intrepid and loyal service to the slave masters. And it is no exaggeration to say that the few successes the government had against the Maroons in Jamaica — as was also the case in Surinam — were due almost wholly to the skill of the black soldiers or to the black guides who divulged the secret of Maroon communities to certain parties, in which case such parties could take them by surprise.

One of the most outstanding of the government slave soldiers was the Black Shot with the unfortunate — some would say appropriate — name of Sambo. Sambo was so outstanding as a soldier that he was soon promoted to the rank of captain. He led many parties, was apparently good at shooting wild boars too, and invariably it was reported that whatever victory the parties had depended "more on him and the little Successful Party under his Command than on Peters" (a white commanding officer who was later recalled for incompetence and misbehavior). The same comparison could be made between Sambo and just about any other commanding officer between 1731 and 1734. The records show that while the whites of the parties would often wish to halt from the fatigue of long, arduous marches in impossible situations, Sambo, on the contrary, would "use his utmost endeavour to get them to go forward and all to no purpose."[132] Apparently Sambo was freed before his family, for his devoted service, but by 1733 there appeared an act for the manumission of the wife and children of "a free Negro man, Sambo," and for the compensation of their owners.[133] It is not to be assumed that all the black slaves who fought the slave masters' wars were freed, in contrast to the situation in Surinam. [134] The few who were freed in Jamaica were like Sambo — outstanding. Others, after their discharge from the parties, must return to their masters to resume their lives as plantation slaves in perpetuity.

Meanwhile, the leewards too were on the offensive. In the parish of Hanover "where we least expected it, they have destroyed a plantation belonging to one Knowles, a minor, burnt the work and the Canes, but the plantation slaves escaped by flight,"[135] thus following the same pattern of the windwards — successful attacks on plantations and slaves taking off in groups. Considering the length of the island, 144 miles long from east to west, with its rugged mountainous terrain, it was certainly no easy task to deploy troops to fight the rebels when their activities were now extended to the west, even if the militia had been efficient. The situation was even more difficult, given the few straggling plantations scattered throughout the island, with large tracts of woodland in between. The Assembly initiated a seemingly wise measure to meet this situation, by passing a new barracking act in October 1733. This divided the island into two military and administrative sections, the Eastern and the Western Divisions, each having its own barracks. Lands were to be cleared and roads cut to facilitate easy movements of parties, all for the "more speedy and effectual suppressing the rebellious and runaway negroes."[136]

The Act, the preamble said, was necessary because of the great increase of the rebels within the past few years, and because they had become "formidable in the North-east, North-west, and South-west parts of this Island, to the great Terror of His Majesty's Subjects in those parts, who have greatly suffered by the frequent Robberies, Murders, and Depredations committed by them." The Act spoke of the difficulty of a force in the east coming to the aid of the west, and vice versa, and with "the great Number of Slaves lately run away," and joining those ine rebellion, "the Western parts of the island will soon become the Seat of an intestine War, as well as the Eastern;" this prediction was soon realized.[137]

Just seven days after this act was passed, other depressing news arrived which greatly hampered its implementation. One Lieutenant Allan of the party sent out to Port Antonio had been killed; Lieutenant Robinson was forced to leave because of ill health, and the soldiers of the independent companies were all in very poor health; above all, there was much desertion, in this case from some of the white party men as well as fifty baggage slaves. All this made it difficult to proceed with the cutting of roads and the building of barracks, without reinforcement, and as for the breastwork at Port Antonio and the few settlements around this area, these were in the "utmost danger."[138]

In the midst of all this the conscientious Governor Hunter died (March 31, 1734). Hunter's administration, 1729–1734, represents a critical period in the island's history. It is the period which saw the most sustained, and the most energetic, government activities against the Maroons. Yet it is a period that experienced some of the most humiliating "bad successes" against them, making it a time of the greatest danger to the authorities. The plantocracy's fear of a Maroon-slave insurrection was not farfetched, and the island might well have witnessed a situation with parallels to what was to happen in Haiti later.

What then went wrong with Hunter's courageous policies? There can be little doubt that the economic situation of the colony contributed to the administration's failure in dealing with the Maroon threat. The period of greatest danger from the Maroons, 1730–1738, coincided with the economic decline of the island. The loss of profits from sugar made the financial burden of defending themselves from their intestine enemies almost impossible. The economic decline also made for the exodus of most of the poor and marginal whites. Others yearned to leave but could find no purchasers for their estates in this Maroon-infested land. A nephew commenting on his uncle's letter from Jamaica in 1734 expressed what was not peculiar to his relative:

> I find by Uncle's letter he wd. be willing to dispossess of his estate now, wch. in my opinion wd. be the best thing he could do. But fear which shd. be the strongest Motives to induce him to sell will likewise be an objection to the Purchaser .... The Methods hitherto taken to suppress them, have been attempted with unsuccess, and so vast an expense that I can safely Say two thirds of the inhabitants are already ruined, and Taxes from this Calamity so high that it is impossible that we can long stand under them.[139]

The taxes were indeed heavy and many. The administration constantly cast its net about for supplementary revenue to meet the heavy financial demands on the country. In April 1731 Hunter sent a series of new bills to the Board of Trade for the raising of taxes. New taxes were laid on slaves, young and old, already in the colony; on all cattle, horses, mules, mares, computed to bring in about £6,000 to be used "entirely" for additional subsistence for the soldier class. But the highest rates were reserved for every slave to be imported into the island, 15/– per head, and 30/– per head on each exported.[140] This was too much for the slave merchants in the great trading ports in England — London, Bristol, Liverpool — who all protested. They argued that such taxes would not only lessen production on the island, but would also depress the trade with the Spanish, lessen the exports to Africa, and curtail the entire navigation system. These were powerful voices and the measures were disallowed by the home government. Hunter himself received a stern rebuke on pain of removal from office never to give his assent to any such acts.[141] The acute shortage of revenue and of credit remained, and the governor was soon complaining that the country knew not "where to find money for Immediate exigencies."[142] It is fortunate that the governor was a wealthy man because, with an empty treasury and with debts outstanding, it is conceivable that on occasion he went without a salary; at least we know that there were times when his salary was very much behind.[143]

Taxes were further laid on free blacks, free mulattos, free Indians; on houses, storehouses, wharves, and the like; but a later imposition of 1735/6 that created much protest was the tax on Jews. The act for raising several sums of money, all to be used against the "rebellious Negroes," taxed the Jews (by how much is not clear) in addition to the uniform tax laid on the other whites. The Jews rightly protested, and after a difficult struggle the Assembly finally accepted the principle of equal taxation.[144] It is not clear whether the taxes on free blacks, free mulattos, and free Indians were additional taxes, as with the case of the Jews, or whether these categories were for the first time being taxed; there is no record to indicate their attitude to the new taxation.

Some of the opulent planters, responding to Maroon threats, did flee the country. A few went to the North American colonies but for the most part they went to Britain, leaving their plantations in the hands of overseers and other surrogates. The decreasing number of whites gave the slaves greater opportunity to escape to the woods or to rebel, and the dialectic relationship between marronage and absenteeism became again most pronounced. Unfortunately, the whites left behind were constantly engaged in petty wranglings and dissensions among themselves, in and out of the legislature, and Hunter complained incessantly. "I must in duty observe," he wrote home on one occasion, "that the great Source of all our Evils on this side is the Indolence and Inactivity of the men of figure and Substance."[145] And it is clear that the officials of the Board of Trade would not disagree with the governor. In evaluating the situation in Jamaica in a memorandum, they had derisively remarked on "how little judgement the people of Jamaica have in running their affairs ...."[146]

Another of the governor's vexing problems was the militia. This was composed mainly of white indentured servants, generally Irish Catholics, and their number was always considered inadequate. But inadequacy of numbers was the least of the governor's problems. These people were hired servants of a very lowly status and treated in many respects just a degree above the slave. They thus had very little stake in the system. Hunter complained repeatedly, representing them as more a security risk than an aid in solving the country's internal security problem. Moreover, the governor, aware of the constant French and Spanish threat to the island, impugned their loyalty when he reflected that he could not be certain that they would not fight on the side of the enemies out of religious sentiments, if the circumstances arose. "You'll think it strange but it is true, my Chief Dependence in Case of an Attempt was upon the trusty Slaves for whom I had prepared Arms,"[147] he wrote upon one of his first Spanish invasion alarms. After every debacle against the Maroons, Hunter commented scathingly on the militia, and eventually he supported a bill known as the "Protestant Act" against them. This required that all importers and buyers of indentured servants must guarantee that the indented personalities were Protestants or forfeit £50. Hunter felt the bill would deter "the native Irish Papist of which our Servants and Lower Rank of People chiefly consist from pouring in upon us in such Sholes, as they have done of late years; they are a lazy useless sort of people who come cheap and serve for Deficiencys and their hearts are not with us."[148] The bill was finally repealed by the local Assembly on the grounds that it would have been difficult of implementation, but intriguingly enough, it was supported by the Board of Trade in the hope that "it [would] be a seasonable check on the Growth of Popery in Jamaica."[149]

Hunter's frenzied hostility against the white militia does not seem unfounded, in the light of the lack of discipline, the misconduct, the carelessness, and, worst of all, the drunkenness on the part of militia parties, generally.[150]

Not least of the governor's failures was the desertion of the Black Shots and the baggage slaves already described.

Apparently the free blacks, too, obliged by an act of the Assembly to fight against the Maroons, deserted and devised all kinds of strategems to avoid fighting them. A colonist complained that "It is always to be observed that when We fit out our parties the Free Negroes generally skulk and abscond to prevent their being sent out against the Rebells, nor are they, when sometimes sent out, of any use, pretending fear of Something else to excuse themselves."[151]

The Duke of Newcastle's ineptitude must also be mentioned as a part of Hunter's problem. A niggardly and obstinate man, he refused to send the troops Hunter incessantly asked for, realizing that the navy and the militia together were not sufficient. Then when he did send troops in 1731, they remained for only six months, much to the chagrin of Hunter. It is also known that Newcastle had a great antipathy for militias generally, equating them with standing armies, reminiscent to him of continental absolutism; he stoutly refused to support a strong and reorganized militia in England in 1756.[152]

These then, were some of the problems, structural and otherwise, that Hunter had to contend with: acute monetary shortages; apathy of the men of standing; bickerings from the legislative body, especially the Assembly, which made him yearn — as so many colonial governors had done before him and were to do after him — for a strong executive; absenteeism among the most influential, thus increasing the racial imbalance between the rebellion-prone blacks and the whites; the unnecessary dependence of the soldiers on baggage blacks; desertion of black military support personnel; the ineptitude of the militia; and the seeming insensitivity of the Board of Trade to the dangerous state of the island. In addition to all this, of course, was the formidable intestine enemy whose skill in guerrilla warfare had by this time developed into a fine art.

It is ironic, perhaps tragic, that only a few months after Hunter's death a sizable troop, more commensurate with the situation as he had perceived it, arrived in Jamaica. Newcastle ordered a complete regiment, consisting of six independent companies of one hundred men each, sent to Jamaica. With the 200 already on the island, this would make 800 regular soldiers, and the navy would be alerted to give all the assistance necessary. Newcastle, not missing the opportunity to be unpleasant, wrote that when the two regiments went to Jamaica in 1731, the colony did not seem to require their service. However, he hoped the island would now make provisions for them.[153] It is clear that Newcastle had taken those soldiers' letters very seriously.

Thus with the added force and with martial law soon to be instituted where even the militia could be more efficient, the Maroon situation seemed to be entering a new phase.

Chapter 4

Prolegomenon to the Treaties

Governor Hunter's death brought about the kind of administrative instability that represented to one author "the weakness involved in not having a permanent lieutenant-governor"[1] in the colony. Upon his death, the office devolved upon John Ayscough, president of the Council, until the expected arrival of John Cunningham, who was appointed to succeed Hunter even before his death. Ayscough died within a year and a half after taking office and was succeeded by Chief Justice John Gregory, another local man, until Cunningham's arrival in 1735. He, in turn, died barely seven weeks after entering the colony, whereupon Gregory was again called upon to act until Edward Trelawny's arrival in 1738.

John Ayscough, born in Jamaica "about 1675," was the eldest son of Major Thomas Ayscough, a prominent proprietor and member of the Assembly who had accompanied Penn and Venables to the Caribbean in 1655 to execute a part of Cromwell's Western Design. The son himself soon became a powerful and experienced member of the legislature, having served as member of the Assembly from 1702 to 1706, and on the Council from this latter date until 1735, during which time he acted as governor for a short period in 1726 upon the sudden death of the Duke of Portland. [2] Being a local man had the advantage in that it placed him in touch with the prevailing sentiments of the planter class. But this is countered by the likelihood that such a person would almost always be identified with a certain faction or with an "ideology," and this could create problems of divisiveness in government. Hunter, aware of this, had warned against the government devolving on Ayscough, who "is far from being in any manner qualify'd for such a trust and is strictly linked with that perverse Faction who are apparently for running matters Into Confusion here."[3] Furthermore, although the colonists, at the rhetorical level, would voice resentment against the British government's practice of filling the highest offices of the island with imported Englishmen, these same men would invariably find it difficult to give due respect to a local person. The net result, therefore, was that a local man as chief executive could generate an even greater amount of dissensions and factionalism than that which was characteristic of the Jamaican legislature, even at the best of times.

In this instance, despite Ayscough's undoubted political bias, his administration saw relatively little political strife because of the critical Maroon situation. Yet it cannot be overemphasized that, as bad as the situation was for the colony, it could have been much worse without Hunter's firm stand against the rebels. One major difference in Ayscough's administration was that he succeeded in instituting martial law, which Hunter had attempted unsuccessfully. Martial law was never a welcome measure for the plantocracy but it was under this system that the island saw some of the most important successes against the Maroons. The system made for a heightened sense of danger, which Hunter had been stressing all along, and this helped to strengthen Ayscough's hand. After mentioning the melancholy news of Hunter's death in his first dispatch home, he turned his attention to the Maroon situation — as had every other governor in his first communication since the 1720s. He pointed out the weak state of the colony and requested relief against the enemies "who have infested" recently some settlements towards the northeast. "The Security of the Island," he later wrote, "against the Rebellious Negroes being, upon my coming into Government, the first object of my care."[4]

Ayscough's ordering out of a party may not seem revolutionary, but in this case it was under the auspices of martial law, which encouraged men of property and substance with a stake in the system to venture forth. He deployed 200 men under Captain Swanton, with his known courage, and Colonel Thomas Brooks, one "who was before drove and burnt out of one Estate which he hade in St. George." The whole outfit consisted of "men of experience and known valor," and gentlemen's sons and volunteers whose interest it was to crush the growing "mischief." The second force consisted of the same number of men, and the design was to destroy the windwards and to march on to Nanny Town, "their chief place of residence," by two different routes, one party from the Blue Mountain valley and the other from Port Antonio. Ayscough and most of the council members left the seat of government in Spanish Town to an adjacent parish, St. Thomas-in-the-East, to issue any order that might be necessary, with a view to preventing delays.[5]

The party — led by Captain John Swanton, according to the official records, and by Captain Stoddard, according to certain secondary sources — gained a major victory against the Maroons. After a most arduous and difficult march where many perished, they came within sight of Nanny Town, and after some resistance, the rebels evacuated it but "hovered about it in separate bodies," behind trees and bushes, and fought the party for five days, killing eight and wounding thirteen soldiers. The party reported that they in turn killed "a great many," and among these was a "Head Captain." Were it not for the rains and floods which prevented the second party from joining Swanton, who had to retire when ammunition was in short supply, the situation might have been very serious for the Maroons. Swanton's report gave it that the party drove the rebels out of 127 huts and rather imprecisely said that these huts "at most could not hold 400 men, women and children"; about 100 of them were arms-bearing men.[6]

The secret of the party's success was, according to official report, that Swanton's party found a new route to the "Negro Town," at the back of the mountain on which the town stood, and they scaled the awesome heights — a feat which a recent source felt could not be done "without being spotted somewhere along the way."[7]

The party was tired but exultant, and Swanton sent a "list of Arms and things taken out of the Negro Town" to Ayscough. These were:

38 Bills [most probably billhooks or machetes]
48 Iron Polls [?]
3 large Kettles
1 large Saucepan
1 large Tea kettle
1 quart Pot
19 Pewter plates
1 Pewter basin
26 Muscheats
12 Gunpowder
18 Gunns
13 large Powder Horns
A great no. of Bullets
1 China bowl
4 Drums
12 Knives
About 100 Negro men's loads of Linnen [8]

Although Nanny Town had been passing between the Maroons and government parties since March 1731, this attack was the beginning of its downfall. It was soon recaptured by the Maroons but a year later was again taken by the government, after which time it appears that the rebels never again resettled this town to restore it to its former glory. Apparently they built another,[9] which was the only sensible thing to do, considering that the government was now boasting of having access to the town and plans were being made for building feeder roads to serve the area, and defensive barracks were also soon built.

The victory cheered the country, and morale was high. The arrival of the six independent companies sent by Newcastle from Gibraltar early in 1735 also added spirit to the plantocracy. It was from this force that Ayscough was to choose an emissary to treat with the rebels later. It was generally agreed that the institution of martial law contributed to the parties' successes. Ayscough wrote home about the better discipline among the parties, their willingness to serve, their cheerfulness, and, even more gratifying to the acting governor, he reported on the greater cooperation from private citizens who had become more interested in acting together in the public service.[10] Even assemblymen were volunteering to go out with parties. In these circumstances the chief executive felt emboldened to approach the legislature to recommend an extension of martial law. Martial law was anathema to the plantocracy because these slave owners valued their freedom passionately — an ironical, universal constant among slave masters from antiquity to the modern system. Ayscough, himself a local man, sharing this penchant for freedom with his fellow slaveholders, introduced the motion rather apologetically. "Although martial law may be disagreeable to a free people (which I should have been as Unwilling to put in force as any person in my station, had not necessity required it), yet I am persuaded that the country is by this time convinced, that, under the circumstances we were then in, this was the best method that could be taken to put a stop to the executions of the rebels and to deliver us from the apprehension of their gathering into too great and powerful a body." Although the expenses of martial law had been considerable, nevertheless it answered the ends in routing and dislodging the rebels from their "strongest hold," and in so distressing them they were forced to disperse into several bodies. The extension was granted grudgingly, May 8, 1735, for not more than three months, amid "great clamour" from the Assembly, but Ayscough felt the disagreement in this case came mostly from men with no property to protect.[11]

Parties were sent out, and it was at this time that Nanny Town, or the "Negro Town," was finally retaken by a large party, consisting of some 600 men and their officers. Again the story of 1732 was to repeat itself. The dispersed rebels were extremely harassed by the flying parties. They were driven from one place to another, short of provisions and ammunition, and many were said to have perished this way from sheer fatigue, hunger, and sickness, while the parties relentlessly "hunted them out in their Fastnesses as so many wild beasts," destroying and burning any of their provision grounds they came across.[12] Numerous accounts were sent in to Ayscough variously reporting rebels being captured, wounded, or killed or having to evacuate new settlements precipitously, leaving behind supplies including kitchen utensils, clothes, cutlasses, guns, powder, and the like. Those rebels taken alive were of great importance to the parties. In their depositions under questioning some would reveal secret hiding places or would tell of the strength of the different groups. A "Sensible Woman" so captured said about thirty rebels were killed during the encounter between her group and a government party, and among those killed was a captain. Another rebel found in the woods and taken alive was discovered to have been their "Obia Man or Conjuror."[13] He was tried and executed. The acting governor could cheerfully report to the home government that since the extension of martial law, the parties had killed, wounded or taken altogether "above 50."[14]

Again the Maroons, in desperation, were to repeat their great march to leeward, as they did around 1732 when Nanny Town was first "captured." History is not without its many examples of ominous marches — Alexander's from Europe to Asia, Napoleon's into Russia, and perhaps more apropos to this study, Hannibal's across the Alps — and the Maroons certainly contributed their quota.

The official documents stated that they were so distressed that they separated "into several bodies, one of which consisting of about 140 men, women and children — now making way to St. Elizabeth to find some remote places to settle, or to join one John Cuffee, Captain of another Gang of Rebells, that way; this account I had from a young Negro man, who after he had kept them company for two days . . . made his Escape from them"[15] — thus demonstrating the danger of the truants among the Maroons. Parties were accordingly sent out against them, unavailingly; "tho' they were attacked twice or thrice."[16]

Another official account gave a slight variation on the general theme. Here it is said that the rebels divided themselves into two bodies, one consisting of about 300 men, women, and children, who marched from the eastern to the western region, "near 150 miles," while the size of the other group was not stated. But the report warned against taking the number of 300 too seriously because "Negroes [from whom he received this information] dont know how to express themselves by Numbers."[17] But the writer may well have been nearer the mark had he said that even a captured Maroon should not always be relied on for giving the "truth" of their communities. As said, this constitutes another problem in reconstructing Maroon history, when the sole source is the depositions of captured rebels, in some cases taken under torture — possibly following Roman practice, where slaves' testimonies were always taken under torture on the assumption that such torture would induce the truth!

We are left with a very vivid account of Cudjoe's reception of the windwards, but the source of this information is not clear though it would appear to have emanated from a captured Maroon. From a manuscript account, which so far has proved most reliable when tested against official minutes of the Council and Assembly, we learn that those who went to leeward, whether on the first or second march is not clear, were met with "a very indifferent reception from Captain Çojoe who was unwilling to receive them on three accots": first, Cudjoe would scarcely have provisions for them and his people besides; second, Cudjoe blamed them for great indiscretions in their conduct before the parties were sent out against them, telling them that it was a rule with him never to provoke the whites unless forced to it, and showing them — rather ominously — several graves where he said people were buried whom he had executed for murdering white men against his orders. Expanding on the theme, he said their "Barbarous and unreasonable cruelty and Insolence to the white people was the cause of their fitting out parties who would in time destroy them all"; third, that Cudjoe was an absolute and despotic master of his group, and was therefore unwilling to receive an army of independent people, subject to their own chief, who might not submit to him.[18] One may doubt the phraseology as Cudjoe's but the spirit of the account is certainly in keeping with what extant material there is on the man — his autocratic regime and his accommodationist policy towards the whites, when it served his interests.

This account on Cudjoe is in line with the testimonies of "2 Negro Men, both named Cudjoe" who were party shots; whether these were deserters or not is not clear. The Cudjoes testified that Captain Gummor, or Goomer (to be dealt with later), who commanded a gang of about forty or fifty in the woods somewhere in the leewards, lived in constant fear of Captain Cudjoe and his gang, who "troubled him very much, and for fear of him and the Backarara partys, he, the said Gummor, could not sitt down in one place but was forced to goe Every day to a New one."[19]

Cudjoe, however, allowed the windwards to remain with his group until things quietened. This was a decision based more on security consideration than on any kindliness toward them. Cudjoe was well aware that a return journey for them at this time would most certainly bring them in contact with the flying parties that were scouring the woods, and should they be defeated or any be captured, they would in all probability divulge his hiding place. So they were housed among Cudjoe's gang until the parties withdrew and then they returned to windward, whether voluntarily or not is not clear. But the manuscript source said that "they were sent or drove back again by Cudjoes men and lived to windward as before and in a little time began their

Roberys and Crueltys" and repeatedly appeared at Nanny Town, which was now held by the parties.[20]

But, as usual, the Maroons were not beaten. Despite the better morale among the parties, their greater efficiency, and their "successes" under martial law, the Maroons, for their part, were refurbishing their ranks. These were men and women — especially the windwards — with a strong propensity for survival. These were people of iron will nurtured in survival tactics; cruel, courageous, resourceful, and scornful of danger. These are the pioneers of the island, the first Jamaicans that the slavocracy could not defeat.

Even the leewards under Cudjoe, the accommodationist, were on the offensive. And it appears that at this period he divided his community into sections, sending out different groups to attack plantations and government parties. These attacks were designed not only for the purpose of obtaining new recruitments from plantations, but were also calculated to decoy parties into successful ambuscades. In addition — and perhaps even more important — from the point of view of strategy, they were meant to keep the parties from Cudjoe's main towns, secure in their mountainous strongholds.

With both the leewards and the windwards on the offensive, the entire island was in a state of anxiety. The planters of St. James, for instance, complained that the harassment from the rebels made them "despondent." Many were making preparations to leave the island, middling planters with 300 or more slaves, as well as poorer ones; and "God knows what will be the consequence of such things,"[21] a colonist reported to Ayscough. Parties were sent out against the leewards only to make the discovery of "several Negro towns and several settlements," hitherto unknown to the authorities. These were most probably some of the strategic outer settlements of Cudjoe's, and others were most certainly some of the more recently formed communities arising from the widespread flight from plantations. The government parties soon discovered that "for several years past," some of these were making attacks on plantations, plundering and burning houses, wounding and killing residents, and setting fire to cane fields, and that twenty-seven such plantations were abandoned. Some of these planters declared their willingness to return to their estates if they could be guaranteed protection "against such barbarous insults and depredations for the future."[22] But in the crisis situation their chances of receiving effective security on the island were negligible, and it is highly probable that they did not return until after the Treaty.

Meanwhile, the situation in the northeast sector of the island was moving toward a state of anarchy. The rebels, for example, attacked a plantation in St. George, about twenty miles from Port Antonio, and the slave master and his two white male servants ran away, the master leaving his wife behind. But the wife secured herself "into a little fort," and with the assistance of two of the slaves, so "manfully defend herself," that the Maroons were beaten off — after burning a part of the house, setting fire to the growing cane, carrying off some of the slaves, and threatening to return.[23]

There was also an attempted coup. The inhabitants of Titchfield in October 1734 felt that they had had enough of the "Insolent behaviour of our own slaves" and of the threatening messages sent them from the Maroons. They were apprehensive of being attacked daily; and what was more, they had no expectation of getting any help from Ayscough. Indeed, they had heard that the latter had openly declared his intention of giving up Titchfield to the rebels. In view of this, the inhabitants of this place renounced all connections with the government and applied to the naval commander, Sir Chaloner Ogle, for assistance and to be under his command: "We must humbly beg leave to put ourselves under your protection, and desire You will be pleased to let us have a Ship of War, to Defend us, We being not sufficient to withstand so numerous a Body, we are Informed the Rebells Consist of . . . ."[24]

Ayscough considered their behavior seditious, and their allegation that he intended to abandon Titchfield to the Maroons, he saw as a "scandalous libel." He therefore instructed the attorney general to proceed with a case against them. Apparently there were eight signatories to the letter to Ogle.[25] It is not clear what the outcome of this case was, but it is a classic example of the type of problem that a local man in the capacity of a chief executive could encounter.

The presence of the six independent companies from Gibraltar was to have similar effects to those who were on the island in 1732. Although they landed in "good health," they soon fell prey to tropical diseases, intestinal disorders, and fatigue occasioned by the excessive heat and the long hazardous marches — but perhaps above all by an excess of alcoholic intake. Again, they were no match for the Maroons in combat, but they did have a stabilizing effect on the slaves on plantations, some actually being posted on certain estates.[26]

Ayscough died in September 1735, and although Nanny Town was still held by the government, it is difficult to say whether the Maroon issue, from the planters' point of view, had improved. He was succeeded by Chief Justice John Gregory, another local man, until December of the same year, when Cunningham arrived.

The situation at this time could best be characterized as ambiguous. The Maroons were quiet, and this was perhaps even more ominous to the authorities than their attacks. The quietus began around June 1735 and continued up until the time when the windwards made their second great march back to their own haunts, around 1737. The march was described as silent and expeditious. Gregory confessed that he "had some intelligence of their design" and although he "took all the precautions ... to prevent it, [he] did not succeed" because his orders were badly executed. The Maroons were in fact attacked "twice or thrice" on the march, unsuccessfully, by government parties, and the acting governor also blamed the mountainous terrain for their failure.[27] The authorities were certainly not deceived by the surcease of the Maroons, which continued to puzzle them until the beginning of Governor Trelawny's administration. Gregory saw the quiet as comparable to the proverbial calm before the storm. In reporting it to the Lords Commissioners he conjectured that they might have joined another "large town" in the west and were probably settling down to plant provisions until after which time, the "irruptions" would follow, and he was very "apprehensive" of this.[28]

When John Cunningham arrived as governor in December 1735, as was now the pattern, his first address to the Council and Assembly dealt with the Maroon question. Cunningham was well apprised of the Maroon affairs by the Board of Trade while in England and it would seem that he was not unaware of the contemplated new approach to settling the Maroon war. He was disappointed that despite all the attempts against them, not "above 10 of them" had been taken or slain these past two years. He reiterated Gregory's concern that their surcease was no more than preparation to attack with "greater savagery" later. Like Hunter he saw the necessity of erecting more barracks, and, with too much energy in unaccustomed tropical heat, he soon made a tour of the western parishes, noting with concern the lack of progress in the construction of barracks and the building of roads. He heard of one Dr. Barber from St. Elizabeth whose outlying settlement was plundered by the rebels, but who had since "drawn off his Negroes," and left the island. More barracks, the governor felt, should be built to cover others like him.[29]

Cunningham's energetic and popular governorship came to a sudden end with his death in February 1735/36, not quite two months after arriving on the island, and Gregory was once more acting governor. John Gregory, said to have been born "about 1696" in Jamaica, was the son of Matthew Gregory, who had also been active in the island's affairs. The son came into the administration by way of the Council when in 1717 Governor Lawes appointed him to that body. Gregory was to sit here, as "a formidable man, for over forty years." As a local man, he had the same kind of factional problems Ayscough had, even with respect to his very appointment, but apparently a skillful politician, he overcame that, and was soon to have much cooperation from both the Council and the Assembly — an unusual feat.[30]

By this period the rebels were beginning to be in "motion" in several places and in "considerable" bodies and had done some "mischief,"[31] but by June 1736 Gregory was again alarmed by their "quiet." Despite a few excursions "now and then," he felt that it all made the colonists very uneasy, putting them at great expense for being constantly upon their guard. November of the same year, and still no disturbances, and the authorities could not figure this out. They knew, as Gregory observed, that this quiet did not proceed from any "great successes against them."[32] A "Negro" reported that several died from the smallpox, thus lessening their numbers, but Gregory did not think this report reliable. Then again he was disconcerted that the government party had not discovered Captain Cudjoe's Town. Still, if they continued to be quiet, it would be prudent to let sleeping dogs lie, unless the parties could go out and destroy them completely — but the acting governor knew this was mere wishful thinking. There is no doubt that Gregory had spent some time thinking through the Maroon situation and, in the process, had become quite convinced that parties of whites were no match for them; thus he was foremost in encouraging a treaty with them. Indeed, Gregory's very substantial contribution to the peace treaty, which has not been dealt with before, will be discussed later. Gregory saw that if the Maroons were to be crushed, "It must be done by their own Colour if we could safely trust such a Body ... with Arms." If His Majesty could assist them with some money to purchase the freedom of two hundred slaves, to be placed under a British establishment on the island, then this would not only be effective against the Maroons but also against external enemies, thereby obviating the necessity of sending British soldiers to defend the island.[33] This idea of forming an independent black corps for the island's defense was again to be recommended, much more explicitly, by other governors throughout the eighteenth century and into the first two decades of the nineteenth.

The depressed economic situation did not disappear and the country's legislators expressed their perplexity to the King, in an emotional address from both houses, in November 1736. They pointed out the distressed state of the colony arising from the "Rebellious Negroes," the loss of trade and credit, the great expenses arising from the Maroon wars, and the legislators saw no other hope but from His Majesty: "Take our unhappy Case into your Compassionate and Gracious Consideration and ... Stretch out your Royal Arm to Succor and relieve us and rescue this island from the ruin and Misery that must otherwise inevitably fall upon it."[34] Yet the wrangling among the local politicians continued, this time, chiefly within the Council, and Gregory saw five of them resigning *en bloc*. It was at this critical period, April 1738, that Edward Trelawny arrived in Jamaica as governor, when "the island seemed in many ways in worse condition than ten years before."[35]

Edward Trelawny (1699–1754) was the son of Sir Jonathan Trelawny, bishop of Winchester. He was educated at Westminster School and Christ Church, Oxford, and was returned to Parliament as member for West Looe, Cornwall, between 1723–1724 and 1732–1733.[36] His appointment as governor of Jamaica to succeed John Cunningham was from August 1736 but he did not arrive on the island until more than two years later. Trelawny's administration of Jamaica, 1738–1751, represented the second longest in the colony's history, the Duke of Manchester's, 1807–1827, being the longest.

It is one of the quirks of history that it is Edward Trelawny's name, more than that of any other governor's of the period, that has come to be associated with the Maroon Treaties of 1738/9. Trelawny inherited rather fortuitously — one may even say gratuitously — the fruition of the bold and imaginative plan of treating with the Maroons that Hunter initiated in 1730, but which was also recommended by the Board of Trade four years later.[37] It is not clear whether Hunter's plan had influenced the latter, but he was certainly apprised of the Board of Trade's new thinking on the subject, and his successors Ayscough and Gregory were to work assiduously on the policy of trying to effect a treaty with the Maroons.

Lacking the disinterestedness of a Hunter, who expended his own money and much energy, sacrificing his health — "careful of the people's health and destroyed his own,"[38] as his epitaph said — Trelawny was largely concerned with his own self-interest. Indeed, his attitude to the Maroon question was rather matter-of-fact, and from the beginning of his administration he was inordinately preoccupied with his promotion, spurring the colonial office to appoint him colonel. A recent assessment of him felt that he "owed his appointment solely to Parliamentary interests and influential connections," and was "totally unqualified for his new position," being without administrative experience, "and was in all probability completely ignorant as to the state of affairs in Jamaica."[39]

After the Treaty was signed, Trelawny's bellicosity toward the Spaniards was clearly as much motivated by winning laurels for himself and to satisfy his unfulfilled desire for a military career, which was thwarted by his cleric father, as to gain kudos for the British empire. Admittedly, credit must be given to Trelawny for falling in line with the plans afoot to treat with the Maroons when he arrived on the island. But even here his own personal rewards were never far from his mind, and, being ambitious, he did not let slip the slightest opportunity of dramatizing his participation in the Treaty, as his communications to Whitehall on this matter demonstrate. But it is his private letter to the Earl of Wilmington, written one month after the Treaty and no longer under the constraints of the bland language required of a formal dispatch, which gave him away: "I am sure you will be so good to use your good offices that I may be made Colonel and that you will make all the kind use you can of our late success against the rebels, which may be made to appear a greater thing than it really is. May we not lawfully set ourselves off more than we deserve, to get what we want, and which it would be for his Majesty's service to grant? Surely it is a lawfull boasting, and but an honest deceit?"[40]

Here a comparison with the Earl of Balcarres is irresistible. In dealing with the Maroon crisis in the 1790s, he had not only the restoration of his family fortune in mind, but also a penchant for a sword which he had failed to receive from Louis XVII of France when he tried unsuccessfully to restore this monarch to the French throne, but which the Jamaican government was to grant him after he "saved" the island from the Maroon threat.[41]

Hunter's part in the Treaty has been mentioned on several occasions but here it will be dealt with more systematically. Hunter first articulated the idea of a treaty with the Maroons in 1730 when the Maroon situation had reached its worst stage since the first Spanish blacks took to the hills in 1655 in Jamaica. As the situation deteriorated at this critical period, the government's propensity to treat with the Maroons became more pronounced, only to be subdued during the few intervals of government "successes." It was thus after the "bad success" of Ashworth's party in June 1730 that Hunter first gave voice to what he perceived as the best policy toward the Maroons and what appeared to have been his well-considered opinion on the matter. In an emergency session of the legislature, he said that he had no reason to alter his opinion, "which is, and always was, that the sure way to destroy these rebels, or distress them or at least so as to make them embrace any terms you may think fit to offer them,"[42] was — and this was a reiteration of his policy — to hem them into their mountain fortresses by building barracks at the several passes to their communities. A mere hint at terms, but nevertheless it is the first on record from an official. Hunter was to repeat this much more explicitly, two years later after still another debacle against the Maroons. In this case Hunter was acting on instructions from home; there is no evidence to show whether his first intimation was on his own initiative or whether he was acting under instructions.

Commenting again January 4, 1731/2 on yet another party fiasco, the governor pointed out that since all measures so far had failed, a new directive against the intestine enemy would seem to be required. He then mentioned that it had "been suggested at home to His Majesty's minister and the Lords Commissioners of Trade, that a treaty with the rebels, by which they are to agree to be transported to some of the Bahama Islands, or the employing again the Mosquito Indians against them, may be of use . . . ."[43] The Bahamas, which Charles I had, with reckless largesse, granted to his attorney general, Sir Robert Heath, in 1629, was already known by the Spaniards, and soon to be confirmed by the British, to possess neither gold nor any other precious stones, nor fertile soil for cultivation, and could thus be readily dispensed with.

The recommendation of a peace treaty *or* the employment of Miskito Indians proceeded to stalk together, the suggestion to be made again in 1736 and 1738. The services of the Miskito Indians seemed to have been more greatly appreciated by the authorities when they were employed against the Maroons in the late 1600s but, as already noted, Hunter for one did not think much of them as soldiers. The legislature did not take these peace recommendations seriously enough even to vote on them, but proceeded on both occasions to pass the same farcical resolutions to send out parties to extirpate the rebellious Negroes.

Peace overtures were also made to the Maroons during Ayscough's administration, 1734/1735. Ayscough was well apprised of the Board of Trade's new interest in treating with the Maroons, and he pursued the policy to the utmost. The Board of Trade's interest in Jamaica was wholly economic. When it was discovered that the Maroon activities had a deleterious effect on the island's economy, then a very serious appraisal of the situation was made towards this colony, which was of "so great Importance to the Trade and Navigation of His Maj^{tys} Dominions."[44]

The most thorough appraisal came from a well-researched, unsigned memorandum — a position paper, in modern parlance — dated October 26, 1734, entitled, "Some Consideration Relating to the Present State of Jamaica with respect to their Runaway Negroes." This paper is conjectured to have originated from Martin Bladen, "the ablest and most energetic member of the Board of Trade and the one with the greatest knowledge of West Indian affairs."[45] The paper acknowledged the latest reports from Jamaica, which saw the slaves deserting to the Maroons "daily" and recognized that their reduction was now a matter of the utmost importance. It deplored the great expenses to the Crown in sending out troops, and was aware that the miscarriages of the parties rendered the colonists "contemptible" to the rebels, "who now begin to think themselves equal to any undertaking." It saw the importance of well-organized expeditions against them "for the fate of the island may in some measure depend upon their Success." The causes of the many failures against them should be carefully analyzed and the necessary precautions taken; high-ranking field officers should be sent out to command the troops and they should be allowed to sit and vote in the Council when matters pertaining to the troops were debated. It saw the necessity for good communication and recommended that a road system be built from one end of the island to the other, as General Wade had done in Scotland; defensive barracks, too, should be constructed (apparently the writer was unaware that this was already being done), and it would be good if the troops were attended by Miskito Indians, who were good for the woods and used to be most loyal to Britain. So, if there were misunderstandings between them and Jamaica, "It would be of great consequence to reconcile them to our Interests." The numerous desertions of the blacks may well have prompted the writer to concentrate on the Indians as the troops' attendants.

But the most important recommendation was that terms should be offered to the Maroons. Certainly, the paper emphasized, this should not be done before "some advantage [was] obtained over them" which would serve to render them "more humble." Displaying his sound knowledge of the situation on the island, the writer admitted the difficulty of his proposal, noting that by the most moderate account, the Maroons were at least 600 men able to bear arms — and what if they should receive support from the French and/or the Spaniards with whom "it is supposed they have some correspondence?" Jamaica would be in danger of being lost. Terms could be offered to them, and, after granting them general amnesty, some remote corner of the island, distant from the French and Spanish settlements, could be allotted to them. In return, they should submit to His Majesty's "Mercy," acknowledge his government, deliver up their arms, promise to live peaceably and not receive any more fugitive slaves, but return them to their owners for a reasonable reward.

The author of the paper revealed that he had his model from the Spaniards, who had practiced this "method" with great success, throughout the "whole Continent of the West Indies." There was hardly a great town in New Spain, he contended, that had not a place of refuge of this sort, called *"Polankys."* By this means their old runaway blacks, through process of time, had become as good subjects to the king of Spain as any in Mexico or Peru.[46] The British were determined to be equally served.

This allusion to Spanish treaty making with *palenques* (Maroon societies) led to a feverish search for evidence. The search bore fruit and found the treaties in Panama and Mexico mentioned earlier in this volume. There is no doubt that Drake, both verbally and through his *Memoir*, had made much of the advantages he gained from his alliance with the *cimarrones*,[47] and the colonial officials were not unaware of this.

The home government accepted the recommendations in substance. But there was also an earlier position paper to which Hunter referred in 1732. This was first sent to the Duke of Newcastle, Secretary of State for the Colonies, by the Board of Trade, when in October 1730 this body circulated a "paper" relating to the affairs of Jamaica. Here, in a covering letter, they saw clearly the potential danger of the rebels to the island, pointing out that when the whites were out in parties the colony was most vulnerable, and the rebels, with the slaves, could well exploit this weakness. But the writer dismissed the proposition on the grounds that the rebels had not the "Understanding" sufficient to plan such an operation, otherwise "they might come down in a Body and destroy a whole Precinct before they could be stopped (if at all) for one such alarm, thousands of slaves would joyn the Victors, All equally fond of Liberty!"[48]

These two papers, in the main, became the basis of the first Maroon Treaty, and energetic efforts were accordingly made to effect it.

Initially, Ayscough, who had gained some successes over the Maroons under martial law, had some problems in putting the plan into execution, for want of a "proper Person" to treat with the Maroons, so "that they may be made Either usefull to the Country or shipped off to some other of His Majesty's Dominions."[49] But upon the arrival of the troops from Gibraltar he dispatched one Bevil Granville, or Bevill Grenville, apparently a private, whom Ayscough appointed lieutenant till His Majesty's pleasure be known. Granville undertook to carry in person "Ye Terms of Peace and ffredom to the Rebells," with proper instructions from the acting governor. He felt that if the mission succeeded it would be "a great service to the King and Country" and would save the country many thousand pounds. Ayscough then promised to send "[his] Lordship a better account of this Intended Treaty."[50]

It should be remembered that this particular effort was made at a time when the parties had succeeded in dislodging the Maroons from Nanny Town, and they were thus dispersed and under some extremities for food and provisions — but their spirit was not crushed and they soon refurbished their ranks.

A month later Ayscough reported that the mission was not a success; Granville's letter to him, dated February 6, 1735, with its original spelling, will inform us of the details of the mission:

> Sir, After an indefatigable pursuitt of my Scheme, and after many obstructions thrown in my way (that are only to be told not writ), after having seen and been seen by the wild Negroes, without being able to come to a parl [parley?], and after everything was done, that could be thought on my part, but goeing to Hobbeys, which was the next thing I proposed, I met with a party of the Wild Negroes the 5th of this month, one of them was so ingenious, as to tell me that some small parties were determined to kill me if they mett me, that my business was well known, But that they were determined never to believe a Baccara [white person]. The Negro that spoke to me seemed to bear great authority. He dismissed the rest (about seven in Number) before he spoke to me; He had a Comely genteel and good Natured aspect, He seemed to pity me and look'd in a manner upon me which spoke his Sentiments before he gave birth to his words and after asking some Questions and answering others he advised me to make haste back with a caution not

> to come out again after them, for if I should, I should certainly be killed.
>
> I thought this was sufficient Reason for my desisting even from a thing, upon the Success of which I had Sett my heart, and humbly hope that you and the Gentlemen of the Council will believe that I have been strictly diligent in the Execution of it, and altho' I did not succeed, yet it was not for want of anything that man could do and I hope the next time I have the Honour to be Employed by you and the Country I shall have better success ....[51]

He ended by repeating that he would give the rest by word of mouth — tantalizingly lost to history.

"Fools tread where angels fear to walk" may very well characterize poor Granville, and it is clear that the Maroons understood this when, with compassion, they spared his life but advised him not to return. But his letter is an important signpost in the processes leading up to the treaty. Its importance lay in the fact that it is the first concrete evidence beyond mere articulation we have of the efforts made to effect a treaty with the Maroons. Granville's experience could also highlight the foolhardiness of sending a single white person into Maroon territory to treat with them, and Guthrie's well-organized plans later, backed up with the powerful party of volunteers and the independents under Sadler, may well have profited from the insanity of Granville's mission. Or, it may be that by then the British knowledge of the Spanish model in Mexico was made perfect. For, in sending their emissary, Captain Pedro Gonzalo de Herrera, the Spanish Viceroy had seen to it that Herrera was accompanied by a sizable force.[52]

Granville's mission, like that of Herrera, was known to the Maroons through their very effective grapevine, a constant feature of all Maroon societies in the New World. Ayscough reported that since Granville's return, a rebellious Negro man, lately captured, informed him that one of their captains named Goomer or Gummor, born in the woods "and a very stout fellow," was willing to come in with his forty to fifty men if they could be assured of pardon.[53] The acting governor was quick to act on the request by sending out a negotiator for he was well aware that the time was propitious, the rebels being greatly distressed from being dislodged from their chief towns. "I am not without hope," he wrote, "in a short time Either to oblige them to submitt, or reduce them. Several of them have lately been killed and some taken alive," and he was further informed that a party had taken a spy near Port Antonio. This spy, upon being offered pardon, was made to guide the party to a rebel community consisting of about fifty shots and a "great number" of women and children, but the result of the mission is not clear.[54]

Captain Goomer's story was later confirmed by the captured Maroon mentioned above, who said that Goomer was much troubled by Captain Cudjoe and his gang and by the "Backarara partys," and would therefore be willing to come in with his men if pardoned. Despite Ayscough's quick response to Goomer's overture, nothing more has been heard of this encounter, and it is not at all clear what ensued. In any event, efforts continued through the soldiers of the parties to take every opportunity offered to acquaint the Maroons of the government's intention to treat with them. They did this. But the rebels were disdainful of any offer, and particularly those coming from soldiers; they countered with abusive and threatening language, declaring that they could not trust any *Bacara.*[55] Governor Cunningham too, was well apprised of the new policy toward the Maroons. In London he had immersed himself in Jamaican affairs, consulting with the home ministers and officials from the Board of Trade, and, with his known energy and concern, it is highly probable he would have been the governor to effect the treaty with the Maroons had he lived.

But it is John Gregory, who acted as governor after Ayscough's death and after Cunningham's, who played a most pivotal role in the processes of the treaty — a fact, as said before, that is little known to history. Convinced that the whites — soldiers or volunteers — could not fight the Maroons successfully, Gregory recommended the establishment of a black corps consisting of freed slaves. But he was also in full agreement with the plans to treat with the Maroons, and he pursued a vigorous policy toward this end. Gregory was not as fortunate initially as Ayscough in finding some foolhardy soldier to convey the olive branch to the rebels: "I have used my Endeavour," he complained, "to propose a Treaty to such as have been out for the space of 5 years promising them Liberty and Lands to Cultivate if they would submit upon Condition that they would clear the Woods of such as resolve to stand out, and entertain no more amongst them, But I have not been able to procure any that would venture to carry the Message to them, tho' upon Promise of Reward."[56] But Gregory was soon to find his Guthrie.

Like Hunter, Gregory introduced in the Assembly the twin proposal of a treaty with the rebels or the introduction of Miskito Indians to be employed against them (March 1735/6). These proposals were recommended by "His Majesty" and were brought over by Cunningham. At least in this case, the proposals were discussed in committees and voted upon. The committees saw the proposal to employ warrior Indians against the Maroons as "reasonable and practicable" and therefore deserving of encouragement. But as for that which called for a treaty with the rebels the committees resolved that it would be "dangerous to enter into any treaty with the slaves in rebellion, and may be a motive to encourage the slaves in the plantations to join them, in hopes of obtaining their freedom by the same means."[57]

But they further resolved to grant pardon to those rebels born in the woods and to those who had been runaways since April 1731 and who surrendered themselves voluntarily; to these would be given their freedom and lands to settle, when they agreed to conform with the laws of the country.[58] Nothing more is heard of this, apart from the rebels' rejection of peace overtures at this point. But these recommendations certainly foreshadowed the peace treaties three years later.

Nevertheless, Gregory did not allow matters to stand still, and from some very valuable private letters of Guthrie's we now know that the acting governor had employed instead a more secret and diplomatic approach. Gregory was heartily sick of the Maroon situation and was convinced that a showdown was necessary. For his part, he knew of two ways of dealing with an enemy: "either by force, or by treaty; the first we have often unsuccessfully tried."[59] And it was his instructions that were being acted upon and that were eventually implemented under Trelawny's administration.

By the time Trelawny arrived in Jamaica the Maroons were no longer quiet, and both major groups had renewed activities, especially against outlying plantations. The cessation of pursuit by the government parties allowed them to consolidate their positions. Cudjoe was probably feeling relatively secure in his new town, as we have reason to believe that he was forced to change his location. Equally, some of the windwards who had retraced their march were probably resettled in old haunts, while others definitely formed new settlements, as we shall see later. Altogether, from the evidence, it appears that the windwards were again more aggressive in their offensive against the slave regime, possessing what Trelawny would designate a "dangerous Spirit of Liberty," when he characterized the general nature of the "Negroes" of the British plantations.[60]

In recognition of the Maroons' new offensive, Gregory had requested — and Trelawny reiterated in a memorial to Newcastle — that the troops sent from Gibraltar remain on the island. Trelawny then repeated his favorite theme: that Jamaica, next to Ireland, was the most important possession of Great Britain, therefore, "the supplying Georgia with Forces can be no reason for stripping the most valuable of our Colonies of its Defence . . . ,"[61] and the island was allowed to keep the troops up to the time of the Treaty.

By July 1737, when the Maroons were active again, Trelawny told the legislature that he was informed of "several complaints from different quarters of Insults committed by the Rebellious Negroes. They have long infested the country, and still continue to endanger the Lives and damage the Fortunes of many Inhabitants. The attempts made to Reduce them have been burthensome to the Publick in General and to several Persons in particular but I hope your Wisdom may suggest some effectual Measures to put an End to this Intestine Evil."[62]

Not surprisingly, the legislators had nothing new to suggest beyond the sending out of parties, and by December of the same year, Trelawny, after importuning Newcastle again to be appointed colonel, reported that the "Rebellious Negroes" were a "growing Evil, their wants render[ing] them audacious and enterprising, and they are daily reinforct by the desertion of Slaves."[63] The government parties were once again ineffectual, and the same pattern was repeating itself. The rebels were now spread out through the island, and "almost daily, fall on one settlement or another, many of which are forced to keep continual guard, many who cannot bear that expense are forced to be thrown up."[64] Upon application for assistance from such planters, the governor sent from four to twelve soldiers to individual plantations and deployed them in general in small detachments to cover the most exposed settlements, with the hope that those who were about to quit would remain and those who had already done so would return. But he was none too hopeful. He had little confidence in the soldiers, and he felt disappointment that the gentlemen of the country did not exert themselves more. As for the militia, they consisted of servants who behaved "most wretchedly," but he rather generously observed that it was "hardly equitable to punish these creatures according to the rules of war, as they never dreamt of such service when they indented themselves at home."[65] And this should be seen in juxtaposition with the lethargy of the proprietors even in their own interest. It was only during Ayscough's administration, when martial law was declared, that the men of property did become more active in Maroon affairs. Trelawny ended his dispatch by repeating his famous request: "If I was Colonel, I could make the soldiers do their duty"; and the planters, being encouraged, would therefore exert themselves more,[66] said the governor, although the logic is not altogether self-evident. The following January he reported mutinies among the soldiers and again repeated his request to be colonel, arguing that this would give the soldiers more confidence in him.[67]

But all the while, as Trelawny was asking to be made colonel, Colonel Guthrie of the militia and Lieutenant Sadler were performing yeoman service to the colony — from the planters' point of view. They were trying to effect a peace treaty with the Maroons, with Gregory as the *primum mobile.* This is a most complicated period to deal with, largely because of the necessary secrecy that attended the preparations for the Treaty and because the earliest extant work on the matter, Dallas's *History* (which has become common currency), is not altogether substantiated by the official documents. The strictest secrecy would be required for whatever the nature of the plans and preparation leading up to the Treaty. Should the legislature learn that the army officers were attempting secret negotiations with the rebels, without their consent, this would have put them up in arms to defend their much-flaunted constitutional rights; nor would it have been wise to raise the hopes of the war-weary colonists too precipitously. Nor would it have been politic to give the slaves on the plantations time to savor the implications of a treaty with rebel slaves, having regard to their own situation; they were the "loyal" ones who remained with their masters, only to continue in their state of slavery, while the "prodigals" were pardoned (as indeed they were to complain later), treated as "equals," and allowed their "freedom."

Thus it is that most of the writing on this period glossed over what really led up to the Treaty, because the evidence is not readily available, not even from the minutes of the Council and Assembly. The best evidence extant is to be found in those private letters written by Colonel Guthrie,[68] mentioned above. Colonel Guthrie of the militia, a local planter himself, was obviously a most discreet and well-respected person and was most atypical of militia men. All accounts of Guthrie characterized him as a man of courage, good conduct, and ability, and these qualities made him well suited to carry out the delicate negotiations with the Maroons. Gregory's choice of Guthrie, as well as the method of approaching the Maroons, was clearly superior to Ayscough's choice of Beville Granville and his solo mission and more reminiscent of Herrera's mission to Yanga's camp in Mexico.

In one of Guthrie's letters, sent from Trelawny Town, February 21, 1738/9, we are made aware, most explicitly, that he was acting under the instructions of Gregory, who had alerted him to the Maroon problem. "It was you Sir," he wrote, "that first put a sword in my hand to fight the Rebells, and also the Scheme in my head to treat with them; I own I have done little as to the former, but as [to] the latter, I must be so vain to say, that I have gone a great length, but in whatever Respect I am lyable to Censure, I hope Sir you will be my Advocate."[69] It is clear that after Guthrie received his instructions "verbally," for the purpose of the strictest security, he planned his strategy systematically.

Guthrie first established a reliable espionage system on the leewards, he himself being a planter from those parts, spying on the movement of the rebels as much as possible and as safety would allow. To assist him in this as well as to guide him on his eventual and eventful march to Cudjoe's compound he employed the services of "loyal" slaves — in line with these slave masters' ironic, Hegelian dependence on their slaves. These black guides, some nameless to history, were in fact the very pivot of Guthrie's success, without whom he could hardly have discovered the strategically situated towns with their awesome acclivity. And the country acknowledged this when the Assembly later voted these traitors their freedom. Some may have been exrunaways who had previously lurked around the periphery of Cudjoe's band thus possessing not only the skill required for marching through thick woods, craggy mountains, and great precipices, but also — and even more important — knowledge of Cudjoe's Town, since this was still undiscovered, as Gregory had complained. Lurking truants around a Maroon community constituted a security risk to the Maroons, as Cudjoe well knew. There were also those who were but recently incorporated into Cudjoe's group with no grounded sense of loyalty forged out of common experience through the accretion of time. Some of these reneged on Cudjoe, and Colonel Guthrie was proud of Venus, who belonged originally to Mr. Lamport in Clarendon, fled to Accompong Town, and now turned traitor. Venus informed Colonel Blake that most of the rebels were out hunting or robbing and therefore it was a most propitious time to take the town. She then led a party successfully to the town. Then there was Assiba. She had belonged, not more than six years earlier, to Mr. Garbrand's estate, but had joined the rebels during this time and of "her own Accord deserted the Rebels" — for what reasons we do not know; she guided Colonel D'warris to a rebel town, which he took. Guthrie recommended freedom to these, and they were accordingly manumitted by law to be "for ever absolutely set free" and their owners were to be indemnified to the tune of £30 each, while to the male traitors the sum of £40 each was made the reimbursement fee. These were Cuffee, Sambo, and Zuashey, all of whom were lately "taken by the Rebels," but deserted them and soon became "engaged in the Service of the Country, by going out as Guides with the ... Party and led them to the Negroe Town."[70]

Guthrie, from the evidence, took meticulous care to execute Gregory's instructions. He wrote to Gregory, August 20, 1737, a year before the Treaty, to recapitulate his instructions and to report on what he had already done. He said that to those parties he had already sent out, he gave such instructions, that to the best of his memory, were "received verbally from Your Honor but lest I should have made any Mistake, I beg leave to transcribe one or two of them; if they meet with Your Honor's Approbation, I shall be convinced that I understood you right, If otherwise, I shall stand corrected:

"If you come up with the Settlements of any Negroes in Rebellion, you are, if possible to take one or more alive, and when taken to use them kindly, but in such manner as they shall be well secured in your return."[71]

By the time Guthrie was empowered by Trelawny to march with his party and to treat with the Maroons, he had a pretty good notion, thanks to his guides, not only of Cudjoe's location, but also of the strength of the rebels. At this stage, it was Guthrie's task to convince Trelawny of the feasibility of the plan. Apart from everything else, Guthrie could also tell the governor that he could muster a good number of the gentlemen of worth, with a stake in the society, to go out with him in a party. The analogy with the Mexican pacification commission continues. Herrera, a "man of valor, wealth, experience and providence" — characteristics equally applicable to Guthrie — first recruited an army of one hundred Spanish troops, then another "100 or so irregulars" and 150 Indian archers and with this expeditionary force, accompanied also by a Jesuit priest, they marched out in search of the Maroons.[72] It was left to the governor and Council to make the decision by granting Guthrie the necessary commission to march out and to endeavor a ratification with the rebels. Trelawny, in response to this, said, "I . . . dreaded, I must own, the sending out this Party, nor should I have done it if I had not been well informed and entirely satisfied by the Courage, Conduct, and Ability of Colonel Guthrie, who as well as Mr. Sadler has entirely answered my utmost expectations," but he was nevertheless most apprehensive of offering the Maroons any terms.[73] This is in contrast to Gregory, who was convinced of the advisability of offering them pardon and terms. (By Jamaica's law, all the Maroons were under the sentence of death if taken, with the exception of children who were not to be allowed to reside on the island but were to be sold as slaves elsewhere.)

Gregory's instruction to Guthrie, as he remembered it, was:

> If you come to the [illegible] of any Negroes more especially those under the command of Cudjoe, offer them in his Honor the President's name [that is, Gregory's] terms of Accomodation, and propose a time, and place to treat of the said terms that time not to be less than 10 or 12 days.
>
> If you come up with any Town belonging to Cudjoe, on his offering to treat you are not to burn or destroy such Town or suffer the same to be plundered, that thereby you may give the Rebells a Testimony of his Honor's good intentions touching the said Treaty.[74]

Guthrie's first official letter to Trelawny, after his commission to march with his party, reported success. "It is with some pleasure," he wrote from Cudjoe's Town, which he had now named Trelawny Town after the governor, "that I am to acquaint Your Excellency that we are now Masters of Cudjoe's Town."[75] He then gave an account of his march, which is given in detail here as it also serves to describe the formation of a typical Maroon community.

They left Montego Bay with their guides and soon came upon an open ground where several rebels were at work, obviously taken by surprise. But on being discovered they created a great alarm and retired to an ambush, the party taking a woman and a child, while another child was killed in the general confusion. The party with its excellent knowledge of Cudjoe's Town, through the Maroon guides, knew they had to pass through this ambush to get there, and in the encounter, only one soldier was killed, and two were wounded. Having successfully passed through, they continued their march until they came upon another spacious opening where they halted within a mile of the rebel compound. But the next stage of the march to reach the innermost town was the most difficult — typical of the strategic arrangement of all Maroon communities. The outer towns served as buffers, and not many parties did get beyond them. "It is impossible," wrote Guthrie, "for me to describe to Your Excellency the difficult access to it, but being resolved to make ourselves Masters of it we made our way thro' a strong ambush where 3 more of the soldiers were wounded and I am afraid, one of them mortally." They remained for about two hours in the town and then burned it. In burning Cudjoe's Town, Guthrie certainly went against Gregory's instructions. In burning the town Guthrie might have been making concessions to Trelawny who, with his energetic thrust for promotion, desired a quick victory over the rebels at any cost. Guthrie might also have reckoned that a show of strength was necessary to bring Cudjoe to the negotiation "table," especially considering the degree of suspicion the Maroon had for him and his overtures of peace.

Guthrie ended his letter almost apologetically when he said that he was well aware that the governor would be surprised to see that "We have done so little as to the affair of taking or killing the Negroes, but if ever Your Excellency visits this Town which now bears your name you will not attribute it to any remissness in us."[76]

The following day he wrote again to the governor to say they had sustained a few shots from Cudjoe and a "second conference" was arranged with him, and then he made the famous statement in the most cautious manner, "Now Sir, let me assure you that I dread telling you that it ended in Peace. I have had him by the hand altho' by so doing Mr. Sadler and myself ran some small risk, as did one or two other Gentlemen." Guthrie reported that at the first conference Cudjoe and his officials "offered" to assist against any foreign enemies and "to take up for the future all Runaway Negroes, and I on my part have promised in Your Excellency's name that they shall live unmolested in this place with all that they now enjoy. It is likewise stipulated that I shall stay here in a peaceable manner with them for 10 days by which time I hope to receive Your Excellency's command; but as this affair requires a better head than mine I pray Your Excellency will make choice of a person to transact the whole with them." He also pointed out that since the Maroons lived in such places that are "almost inaccessible," to reduce them entirely would certainly cost much blood and treasure.[77]

Sadler's letter of February 18, 1738/9 to Trelawny also reported the Treaty, stating that they had found the Maroons

> inclinable to peace ... [and] very well disposed to acknowledge Your Excellency with all the deference due to your character, to hold a perfect harmony with the Country and to render themselves as useful

> ›ossible by taking up our Runaways and returning them, eir own accord offered to be assisting on the first command e Spaniards or any other foreign Enemy on condition that t have free possession of this place and be free from Slavery, be disturbed by Parties and might have a commerce with we undertook to answer for as far as possible we could it would be agreeable to Your Excellency's pleasure and l of the Country.[78]

appears that Guthrie and Sadler did everything in their ith Gregory's instructions, to allay the fears and suspi- ›ons and to bring about an amicable peace. A manuscript how through the difficult passes to Cudjoe's Town, the le of the narrow valleys, firing on occasion, would, as was practice, parley with the troops. They knew some of the men of the party and would call to them by name, using much "abusive language." But Guthrie, in accordance with his instructions from Gregory, pressed to speak with their commander, telling them of the plan of truce; this they received with skepticism, charging the whites as perfidious and not worthy of trust. This continued for a day or two, after which time they became more "familiar," and agreed to send one of their people to meet one from the party.[79] This may have been the "first conference" Guthrie and Sadler wrote about in their letters. The person sent was Dr. William Russell, surgeon to Guthrie's party, described as "very ready and brisk in his march." He was to remove all "jealousies, suspicions, and diffidence" from Cudjoe and his people, which he certainly succeeded in doing. Russell was later awarded £200 for his bravery, the house reminding itself that he volunteered to go among the "rebels ... when no one else cared to run so great a risk."[80]

Upon receipt of Guthrie's and Sadler's letters, Trelawny called the Council and Assembly together to report on the matter and to solicit their counsel. Emerging from this caucus was a report titled, "His Excellency's Thoughts upon Cudjoe's proposal of submission" (referred to hereinafter as "Thoughts"). Cudjoe did not propose submission. In "Thoughts," the governor in caucus made certain recommendations, but insisted that such recommendations should be seen as guidelines and not as restrictions. The most delicate question, as reflected in Hunter's and Gregory's treaty proposals earlier, was the status of Maroons who were relative newcomers to Maroon societies. Here Trelawny saw no problem with giving those born in the woods their freedom, but had difficulties with those who fled from their masters; he recommended their return; or, should they object, then they probably should be employed "as slaves in the publick service." He advised Guthrie and Sadler to handle this difficult point "tenderly."[81]

In dealing with the issue, the Council was even more cautious when it met in its official capacity to empower the two men to offer terms to the Maroons. The substance of their recommendations was not dissimilar from Trelawny's, only they were even more circumspect and tentative, resolving that the "said John Guthrie and Francis Sadler be instructed to *hint* to the said Rebels *in the most tender manner* an Article in relation to the giving up those Negroes to their Masters who have not been in the Woods above two years" (emphasis added). Gregory had recommended that those who were out less than five years be returned to their masters.[82]

But Trelawny's language in reporting the event to the Council and Assembly does not seem to be in consonance with the processes of the Treaty. He said that

> A party of the militia, under the command of Colonel Guthrie, together with a detachement of soldiers under that of Lieutenant Sadler, having drove the rebellious negroes, that were situated in the leeward parts of the island, out of their Town, *and obliged them to sue for terms*, I impowered those gentlemen to grant them such as should be reasonable, and for the welfare and tranquility of this island ... The reduction of the rebels is now brought into so fair and sure a way, that, if we follow it closely and with spirit, it cannot fail of being happily accomplished. But it becomes us to follow it closely and to lose no time, but to exert ourselves more than ever in opening roads, and scouring woods with parties, till every rebel is brought under [emphasis added].[83]

In reporting the matter to the British government, Trelawny repeated it that the rebels sued for terms, "which considering the difficulty and almost impossibility of getting the better of them by force, by advice of the Council I impowered Colonel Guthrie and Mr. Sadler to grant them." Trelawny then repeated what Hunter, Gregory, Guthrie, and most of the planters had long known: that "the universal opinion of those that have been the oftenest out upon Parties and the most acquainted with it, is that it is impossible to reduce the Rebels by force,"[84] giving an account of the treacherous nature of the areas the rebels occupied and the difficulty of even reaching their location.

It is nowhere clear that the rebels sued for peace. There is no doubt that peace terms were offered to them, and after much suspicion on the part of the Maroons, Guthrie, with tact and cajolery reminiscent of Governor D'Oyley in the 1660s, gained the confidence of the Maroons enough to have sent Dr. Russell in their midst to explain the terms of the treaty. Guthrie was bent on a treaty with the Maroons. In one of his private letters to Gregory from Trelawny Town, dated February 21, 1738/9, he asserted his commitment to a peace treaty with Cudjoe, declaring that "it would be of great Service to the Island ..." In pointing out the "greath length" he had gone in trying to effect such a treaty, he wrote: "Before I could bring it to bear in any Respect, I was obliged to tye myself up, by a Solemn Oath, not to Fight against them until he [Cudjoe] should Infringe the same, the which if he should do (especially soon) I think I should be Master of Resolution enough to give him another Tryall ...."[85]

All this is not in keeping with Trelawny's language or with the wary approach of the Council that had instructed Guthrie and Sadler to make compromises, if they could not obtain the points this body had recommended: "[I]f the said John Guthrie and Francis Sadler cannot obtain all or any one of these points that they make a Treaty with them [the Maroons] notwithstanding upon the best Terms they can ... they are of Opinion it be left to [Guthrie and Sadler] to make it upon the best terms they can for the good of the Country and if any other matter not mentioned should occur to them which they think advantageous that they may be impowered to negotiate the same."[86]

Another curious aspect in the reporting of this Treaty is Dallas's famous account of Cudjoe's behavior in the presence of Colonel Guthrie when they finally met to effect the Treaty. Dallas wrote:

> Cudjoe, after some hesitation, consented to their coming forward and persuaded his people to come down from the rocks, which a few did, but not without their arms. As the gentlemen approach Cudjoe, he appeared to be in great trepidation, but whether caused by joy or fear was doubtful; though he was certainly under the protecting fire of his own men, and the negotiators were unarmed. Colonel Guthrie advanced to him holding out his hand, which Cudjoe seized and kissed. He then threw himself on the ground, embracing Guthrie's legs, kissing his feet, and asking his pardon. He seemed to have lost all his ferocity, and to have become humble, penitent and abject. The rest of the Maroons, following the example of their chief, prostrated themselves, and expressed the most unbounded joy at the sincerity shown on the side of the white people. Colonel Guthrie and Captain Sadler repeated the offers that had been communicated by Dr. Russell, which was accepted with joy; and confidence being established on both sides, the parties intermixed, exchanged hats, and other tokens of congratulations, and reciprocally testified their satisfaction.[87]

This passage — or at least the part about Cudjoe's kissing Guthrie's feet and asking for pardon — has aroused much controversy, especially in recent times when the approach to black history is to stress the triumphs and the heroic side of a people who perhaps have had more than their share of oppression. The revisionist attitude to Dallas's account ranges from total rejection to a type of psychophilosophical explanation that would probably leave Cudjoe perfectly bewildered. The Maroons of Jamaica today uniformly reject the account — understandably — and with spirit deny — or rather refuse to believe — that Cudjoe, the mighty warrior, would have behaved so ignobly. This was the unanimous response this author had when conducting fieldwork among the Maroons of Jamaica in their different communities.

Without exhausting all the interpretations, what is certain is that there is no known official recording of Cudjoe's behavior as portrayed by Dallas. It seems strange that Sadler, for instance — who was much more expansive in his reporting on the Treaty than was Guthrie — did not record it. All the same, Guthrie had more than ample opportunity to have reported such an incident. Apart from his official letters to Trelawny, he also wrote many private letters on the Treaty, commenting in many instances on Cudjoe, who seemed to him "a person of much Humanity and I . . . Believe will punctually observe on his part those terms of peace that he submitts himself to, as to his Captains, they pay him the greatest Defference imaginable, they are entirely under his subjection, And his Word is a Law to them,"[88] but never mentioning any grovelling behavior on Cudjoe's part — which would certainly contradict the humanity and authority he noted. The closest intimation of this behavior could be *interpreted* from a sentence in Sadler's letter, quoted above, when he said that Cudjoe and his officers "seemed well disposed to acknowledge Your Excellency with all the deference due to your Character." It is also strange that the manuscript sources are silent on this "interesting" piece of information. Most of these manuscripts are most obviously written by enthusiastic amateurs, in a fluid, racy style suggestive of journalism and withal short of analysis, long on details, especially if they are "interesting." It does not seem likely that they would have lost out on this piece of information, a veritable vignette.

Carey Robinson's interpretation seems interesting. Robinson does not appear to question the authenticity of Dallas's account, as this author does. His assertion that he could not accept the account "any more than historians like Dallas could accept the biased account of the Maroons by men like his fellow-historian Brian [sic] Edwards," [89] has no logical connection. This is no reasoning for his rejection — although it is a fact that Bryan Edwards's account of the Maroons *is* biased. And it is also true that Dallas rejected Edwards's biased rendering repeatedly, by supplying countervailing accounts — in most instances successfully — to prove Edwards "wrong."

But Robinson shifted his position when he observed that "Great emotional stress sometimes leads to strange reactions in people . . . ." Here, he would seem to be, in effect, accepting Dallas's account. If we could "prove" that Cudjoe did behave according to Dallas's description, then Robinson's emotional-stress thesis might be a valid proposition. But we simply do not know. History, though, is not without at least a parallel example. General George Monck (1608–1670), later Duke of Albemarle, described by consensus opinion as the fiercest of warriors in battle, did become overwhelmed with emotion upon seeing Charles II, fell on his knees, as if he had come to ask the monarch's pardon and not to receive his thanks — although in this case Monck had been fighting for the restoration of the monarchy. Nevertheless, eyewitnesses who knew Monck's character were amazed at his seemingly grovelling behavior.[90]

More apropos, if Edward Long is correct, then at the time of the Treaty, Cudjoe and his people were enduring the greatest extremities. Long, a resident planter historian of Jamaica, told us that he "conversed with [Cudjoe] many years" after the Treaty, and Cudjoe declared to him that "if peace had not been offered to them," they would have had no choice "but either to be starved, lay violent hands on one another, or surrender to the English at discretion."[91] To be under such constraints and at the same time to have had offers of peace from one's adversary is the type of situation that could certainly generate emotional reactions from even the most phlegmatic. But as Long pointed out, the white inhabitants were unaware of the straitened condition of the Maroons at the time. They were equally "wearied out from the tedious conflict [desiring] relief from the horrors of continual alarms, the hardships of military duty, and the intolerable burthen of maintaining an army on foot."[92] It is worthy of note that neither Edward Long nor Bryan Edwards made any mention of Cudjoe's grovelling behavior before Guthrie.

All the evidence seems to suggest that Cudjoe kept a cool head during the negotiations, pressing adamantly for what he considered important to him and his people — although, as we shall argue later, the long-term and the overall effects of the Treaty certainly favored the British. We recall that in one of his private letters, Guthrie told us that before he could bring about a treaty, on which he had set his heart, he was obliged to "tye [himself] up by a Solemn Oath" not to fight against the Maroons. This was Cudjoe's overriding consideration at the moment of the Treaty, and it is understandable, perhaps, considering the great hardships he and his people were experiencing. The oath in question is the famous Ashanti oath — also performed during the Dutch treaties with their Maroons in Surinam later. It involved the drawing of blood from both the white officers and the Maroon leaders, into which rum was poured, and this mixture was drunk by both parties. It is for this reason that the Maroons to this day refer to their Treaty as the "blood treaty." It seems unlikely that a man who was busily engaged in kissing white people's feet would also have dared to superimpose his folkways onto them. To impose one's sense of difference — one's cultural heritage — on another is an act of power, or at least of self-confidence. It is not the act of the timid. It would be difficult to assume that Guthrie and his officers relished the mixture they had perforce to consume.

The last component of Robinson's interpretation would seem to have a great deal of validity: he feels that "the old accounts [Dallas's?] were greatly exaggerated in order to restore the morale of the English colony and repair its damaged concept of racial superiority."[93] We have already seen for instance how Trelawny distorted the processes of the Treaty, reporting home and constantly reiterating that the Maroons capitulated or sued for peace. Edward Long said Cudjoe told him that, if peace *had not been offered to them*, their situation would have become unbearable. And even Bryan Edwards, who held no brief for the Maroons, in the preface (xiii) to his *Proceedings* ..., said unequivocally that Trelawny, "by the advice of the principal gentlemen of the island, proposed overtures of peace with the Maroon chiefs." Nevertheless, as we shall see, Trelawny was not the only one distorting the processes of the Treaty, but also the Council and Assembly of the island, the Board of Trade in England, the British government generally, and intriguingly, even the manuscript sources we have relied on for this study. We have already noted (in Chapter 1), too, how both Edward Long and Bryan Edwards refused to accept the fact that the Spaniards under Ysassi finally left Jamaica in 1660 when they could no longer rely on the help of the blacks in the mountains, writing instead that the opposite was the case. Another aspect of this phenomenon was the carelessness of the whites, generally, in the face of Maroon successes. They refused to accept a social reality that did not conform to their view of things, even when it was costing them their lives. The idea of recognizing that an amorphous assemblage of untrained, "uncivilized," bedraggled, and motley group of blacks could defeat and befuddle the best trained of British soldiers, with their superior equipment, was beyond comprehension. The Maroon story is the first Vietnam.

But Dallas himself requires some consideration. An Englishman born in Jamaica who lived there only for short periods, he wrote his *History of the Maroons* in London in 1803. There is no doubt that he dealt fairly with his subject. If then, he is responsible for reporting an episode which does not appear to be authentic and which could be interpreted negatively, or even as racist, then there may be an explanation. Dallas dedicated his work to William Dawes Quarrell, who figured prominently in the 1795 Maroon war, at times in ambiguous circumstances. The author acknowledged his indebtedness to Quarrell, who furnished him with "so large a portion of [his] materials."[94] He also acknowledged receiving information from other officers who served in the Maroon wars and from relatives and friends of participants, as well as from the acts of the legislature and from the journals of the House of Assembly. If the bulk of his information came from exsoldiers of the Maroon wars, then Carey Robinson's suspicion of fabrication — by them and not necessarily by Dallas — to restore morale and to preserve racial superiority may well be close to the truth. Dallas was not a trained historian and may thus have been too uncritical in accepting information from friends without what ought to be "due process" of every true historian — checking, weighing the probabilities, testing, and double checking the material.[95] Ralph Korngold has also noted this exigency for white superiority when dealing with the Haitian revolution. Here the black general, Toussaint Louverture, with consummate skill defeated the best of the British, the Spanish, and the French armies: nevertheless, a certain class of historians will insist on dealing out credit to yellow fever and climate for these defeats.[96]

However it may be, the event of the Treaty was greeted on all sides with enthusiasm. The planter class was jubilant with the Treaty and the colonial department and the trading interests in Britain were delighted: the plantation slave economy could now proceed. It was with "a great deal of pleasure" that the Assembly received the news, and no praise was too great for Trelawny: "The completion of an Affair of so much consequence to the well being of this Country must remain a most distinguishing monument of Your Excellency's prudent administration of the government of this island and always endear it to the memory of those who have experienced the dismal effects of so dangerous and stubborn a rebellion." [97]

The Council met the news with "utmost satisfaction," welcomed the terms of the Treaty, and hoped that it would soon enable them either to oblige the windwards to accept the same conditions or to suppress them entirely. They recounted how they had labored for many years "under the greatest Calamities from this our intestine Enemy," their best lands remaining uncultivated, their houses burnt, and so on, and despite their many and expensive efforts they had scarcely been able to "protect the larger while the smaller Settlements became their Prey." But owing to Trelawny's honor they were now not only free of their "mortal enemies," but could now make them their "Friends and Assistants."[98]

The Council and Assembly also sent an address to the King, praising the monarch for his goodness and care toward them, among which they included the appointment of Edward Trelawny as governor to Jamaica, "whose Vigilance, Prudence and Impartiality give us the strongest Hopes of becoming once more a contented and flourishing people." This, because he has "***brought to submission***" (emphasis added) a considerable body of the slaves in rebellion, and they doubted not that he would do likewise with the others.[99]

Newcastle, in a private letter, soon made Trelawny aware that he had His Majesty's "entire approbation of your Zeal and attention to His Service and of your Care for the Good of the Island under your Government." He congratulated the governor upon his "Good success" in "reducing the Rebellious Negroes to reasonable Terms" and hoped that it would be attended with great advantage to the island. But, like Trelawny, Newcastle's mind was on another matter which was, however, certainly connected with the Maroon affairs. This was the Spanish threat to the British islands in the Caribbean, hence the private dispatch. He told Trelawny — repeated in stronger terms later — to do his "best to revenge the Injuries your Countrymen have suffered from the Spaniards, now that you have full power to do it."[100] The island's full force, no longer required to fight the Maroons, could now be deployed against the external enemies, and Cudjoe, as we shall see, was ready to assist in this.

Meanwhile, what of the windwards, who, as noted, had a much more aggressive attitude toward the slave regime than did the leewards? Furthermore, they were trained practitioners in the art of survival, their life-style being always characterized by dislodgment and the refurbishing of their ranks. The strength and resilience of this group seemed to have derived from this, an argument that would give point to those theorists of revolutions who would say that the only successful revolution is a constant one, inactivity and consolidation being ruinous to the spirit of revolution.

But whatever the attitude of the windward groups — and there is some evidence suggesting that the women particularly were against the Treaty — their fate was sealed. So long as Cudjoe and his people, now the "Friends and Assistants" of the plantocracy, were prepared to collaborate with the whites to force the terms of the Treaty on them, they hardly had any choice. In the event of a war, for the first time they would have had to fight against their match.

The official documents on the processes of the Peace Treaty with the windwards are rather scanty, but fortunately we have the *Memoirs* of Philip Thicknesse, a lieutenant of the militia, who was one of the party sent out against them. We find Trelawny writing to Newcastle, June 30, 1739, some three months after the first treaty, to say, "I have the pleasure now to acquaint your Grace, that the Rebels to the Windward, upon our party's being in possession of their provision ground, submitted likewise on the 23rd, inst. upon pretty much the same terms as those which the other lately agreed upon," with a few differences. He did not believe they "will ever revolt, as it cannot be their interest to do it, they receiving greater advantages than we do by the agreement, tho' those we receive are very great." The governor reminded Newcastle of the many-faceted advantages of the Treaty to the island: the colony was not only rid of an enemy within almost impregnable fastnesses, but these areas were also places of refuge to the slaves on plantations, who continually helped to increase the numbers of the rebels — but now, they were "a great addition of strength and the most useful people we can have in going after any slaves that may rise in rebellion hereafter."[101]

Their population, the governor reported, was obtained by the account of their captain, "by notches[102] on a stick, amount to 470 persons, men, women, and children," while those of the leeward, "by a Register taken of them are about the same number." In addition to this there were a few "skulkers" in small bodies of ten or twelve which, the governor felt, would soon be defeated.[103] Again this dispatch reflected the correlation between the Maroon situation — the internal enemies — and the Spanish threat. Trelawny happily wrote that it would be "very fortunate if there should be a war to have got rid beforehand of the intestine enemy." Nevertheless he warned that they should not entirely put their trust in the agreement with the Maroons; the authorities should be on their guard against any treachery.[104]

It is certain that by this time Trelawny was thoroughly bored with the Maroons, and his mind was wholly tuned to the Spanish situation. Thus it is to other sources we must turn for accounts on the preliminaries leading up to the Peace Treaty with the windwards, since Trelawny's official report is so incomplete. The manuscript sources have again come to our assistance. These sources made it clear that after Cudjoe's treaty the government saw only two options for the windwards: they could either accept the conditions as did the leewards or be reduced by force, and Colonel Guthrie was again asked to treat with them. Guthrie accepted reluctantly, pleading lack of knowledge of the ambience of the windwards, he himself being from the leewards, but with his known zeal for the public good, he was prevailed upon. In this instance, Guthrie had at his command a new ally, Cudjoe, who sent fifty of his men, under one of his captains, to assist in the venture against the windward rebels. The account gave it that Guthrie soon became violently ill with a "gripping [?] griping [?] pain in his bowels" just one day after his departure from Spanish Town, and died shortly after reaching St. George, a windward parish. It is alleged that he was poisoned by discontented slaves — presumably instigated by runaways who had been returned by Cudjoe. These, naturally, were adamantly opposed to another treaty with the windwards — their only remaining haven for future runaways. But alluring as is this allegation, we have no proof for or against it. During his illness, Guthrie is said to have sent on ahead some of Cudjoe's men who were supposed to have been acquainted with the leeward rebels, to inform them of the new development in Maroon affairs, and to encourage them to accept similar terms to Cudjoe's.[105]

There are certain discrepancies between these manuscript sources and Thicknesse's *Memoirs*. Thicknesse was an adventurous Briton, newly arrived in Jamaica, when he was drafted for militia service to fight the Maroons. Apparently Thicknesse was on the island for only a short period previous to the first Treaty, and thus saw most of his service against the windwards. It appears that immediately after the first Treaty, Trelawny had sent out parties against the remaining rebel group, even before that of Colonel Guthrie, and Thicknesse was second-in-command in one of these early parties, with Lieutenant Concannen as the leader.

With fifty militia men, seventy baggage slaves, and black and white shots, they were ordered to march along the Spanish river until they came upon the windward community. This march, reminiscent of Guthrie's to the leewards, again demonstrates the strategic formation of Maroon towns. They first made "two or three days" strenuous march, when they came upon a spot with impressions of human feet on the sand, but, it being nightfall, they bivouacked, and early next morning they saw "Smoak" emerging from the Maroons' "little Hamlet." This, of course, was not the main strategic town, but rather an outer one serving as a buffer to the interior town — or the one with the steepest ascent. Yet it was positioned strategically enough for the inhabitants to have seen quite clearly the party advancing toward them, and everything thereafter was carefully planned and orchestrated according to the strategic imperatives of the rebels. Their "hamlet" consisted of seventy-four huts with a fire burning in each, but there was no one in them. As was the practice with government parties, they burnt the town down and began to pursue what they conceived as a people who had perforce to make a very hasty departure indeed. But all this was according to what the rebels would have the party believe. "At every half mile, they found cocoes, Yams, Plantains etc. left artfully by the Negroes, to induce us to believe, they were in fear of our overtaking them, and at length we found a fire, before which they had left several grills of wild hog, *probably well seasoned for us*, we continued the pursuit, till near night, and then, hearing their dogs bark, we concluded they had heard us also, and we gave over all hope of seeing or hearing anything more of them." Thicknesse is writing from the hindsight of time, because when all this was happening they did not know that it was a trap. On the contrary, they were congratulating themselves on their good fortune in having such an easy route to follow to the inner town. Thus encouraged, they marched rather expeditiously and were thoroughly fatigued by the end of the day. But the Maroons were perfectly in control throughout, seeing every one of the party, yet not being seen, noting rank and numbers, and were well satisfied with what they saw.

At their planned ambush location, they waited for the advance sergeant to pass clear through the ambush. Then, as Concannen and Thicknesse, "us Grande-men," as Thicknesse would have it, were well into the ambush, a volley of shots came down upon them. Although the Maroons did not aim, "several" soldiers were mortally wounded, and Thicknesse thought all would have been killed, had they aimed. At this point, the baggage slaves, seventy in all, threw down their loads and ran for it, the militia men following "to a man," leaving only the officers, Thicknesse included, behind. The Maroons were delighted; and it may well have been for the purpose of seeing this anticipated phenomenon that they did not aim to kill all the soldiers in the perfect ambush: "Becara run away, Becara run away," they sang in unison, and still not one of them was seen by the party. Thicknesse, with charming candor, said, "It is probable too, that we should have followed, but fortunately, there were some large masses of the mountain which had caved down, and which lay in the middle of the stream, just under the foot of the ambush," and here they went under cover. By this time only "about sixteen" soldiers were still alive out of the original number of "about" fifty. These continued to aim at the "smoke only" of the enemies, because they still had not seen anyone, until they had not a single cartridge left. The situation seemed hopeless and "to say the truth, we durst not run away," for the rebels only fired when they saw movement from frightened soldiers, so "there we staid, more out of fear than from any hopes of victory, up to our waist in water for four hours and a half, with a burning sun upon our heads." Finally, fearful of being taken alive (for they had heard horrendous stories of what would happen to them, should the rebels capture them), they did what they thought was a suicidal act by running away, believing that they would be mercifully shot in the process. A few of these including Thicknesse escaped successfully and returned to their base in St. George. [106]

Thicknesse wrote that about three months after this runaway business, the governor "honoured me with a second tryal." [107] This was to be the crucial march under Captain Adair, which ended in the second Peace Treaty. Tantalizingly, Thicknesse mentioned rather casually that their party of 300 regular troops was in possession of a prisoner, a hornman, from Quao's — which he variously rendered as Quoha, Quaba, Quoba — group. Exactly how and when they captured him has not been explained. However, this hornman knew of Cudjoe's treaty, but his community still did not know of it. With a Maroon prisoner as their guide, then, like Guthrie, they could now be certain of reaching the most strategic towns. After "two or three' fatiguing days' march, the hornman conducted them to the foot of a very steep mountain, well planted with ground provisions and, on the other side, with its awesome acclivity, stood the town. The only accessible way to this town was up a very narrow path, along which holes about four feet deep were dug at intervals, with crutch sticks before them, receptacles for the guns of the Maroons. Thus, should a party attempt to climb, which could only be done in single file because of the narrowness of the path, then the Maroon sentries would gun each one down, before any advance could be made.

The hornman told the party that it was impossible to take the town: "no Body of men, or scarce an individual could approach it," he explained, without giving the Maroons five or six hours' notice, because their eagle-eyed sentinels were on the lookout all the time. Adair understood what he saw and heard and thus bade the hornman to send a message on his horn (the *abeng*) to inform Quao that they "were come to agree; not to fight"; that Cudjoe had signed a treaty and the same was offered them. They responded to the hornman, knowing him to be from their camp, but when they heard that they were dealing with soldierss and not with the militia, a complication developed. The Maroons apparently had an enormous antipathy to soldiers: "soldiers had no tatta, no mamma, and ... one soldier dead t'other tread upon him" (soldiers have no fathers, no mothers, and if one soldier dies the others will walk over him, in translation and reflecting their attitude to their dead) was just about their view of soldiers. However, after a lengthy parley, reminiscent of the leeward situation, hostages were exchanged, and Thicknesse was chosen for this purpose. He accordingly took up his abode at "Captain Quaba's habitation" and was soon to note the response of the Maroon women and children to him. Although the children "saw their father in civil conversation with me, they could not refrain from striking their pointed fingers, as they would knives if they had been permitted, against my breast, saying in derision, *a becara — becara* — that is, white man."[108]

From this experience, Thicknesse has recounted some rather gruesome but questionable details. He saw, for instance, the underjaw of a lost soldier, "the poor laird of Laharrets ... fixed as an ornament" to the *abeng* of one of the hornmen. He found that "the upper teeth of our men slain in Spanish River," during the debacle three months ago, "were drilled through and worn as ankle and wrist bracelets by their *Obea* women, and some of the ladies of the first fashion in town"; but upon informing "Quaba" that such objects were very painful to them, "they did not appear the next day."[109] These accounts do beg certain questions. To begin with, it is not clear how Thicknesse could have identified the "underjaw" and the upper teeth "drilled through" of human skeletons — unless of course he was Hamlet addressing Yorick's skull, and even here Hamlet was assisted by the experience of the gravediggers. Thicknesse apparently anticipated this kind of question when, in a footnote, he explained that "the laird's teeth were so very particular, that some of our men, *could have sworn* [emphasis added] to the identity of the jaw bone." Doubtless, Thicknesse's men were no Hamlet's gravediggers. Thicknesse reported that he inquired of Quao how the laird had fallen into their hands and was told that he, singly, had brought the news of Cudjoe's treaty to them and that Quao might have agreed then and there to a similar situation had he not consulted their obeah woman. But she opposed any dealings with the laird, declaring that "him bring becara for take the town, so cut him head off," whereupon her fiat was summarily carried out.[110] This made for an obvious discrepancy in a part of Thicknesse's story. Earlier he had written that Quao's group did not know of the Treaty, although the captured hornman knew of it. Yet later we read that the laird had visited them with the news of Cudjoe's treaty. The explanation could be that the hornman was out reconnoitering and did not know of the laird's visit.

The *Obeah* woman of the summary fiat is described by Thicknesse as wearing "a girdle round the waste and (I speak within compass) nine or ten different knives hanging in sheaths to it, many of which I have no doubt, had been plunged in human flesh and blood."[111] Some of these exotic details should be taken with the proverbial grain of salt especially because Thicknesse was obviously a collector of exotica, which found a ready market in England at that period. (He also visited the United States and collected vignettes on the "Red Indians.") Nevertheless, there are those who arrived at the conclusion, on the basis of Thicknesse's description of the "old Hagg," that this was the great but elusive Maroon leader, Nanny. But one cannot be certain. The precise date when Nanny figured is nowhere clear. The only conclusion that one can arrive at regarding this *obeah* woman, from Thicknesse's account, is that whoever she was, she was a very influential figure, superseding Quao's inclination to treat with the laird, for instance.

Thicknesse's *Memoirs* also demonstrated a point about Maroon leadership we noted when dealing with Juan de Serras. We indicated there that the most effective Maroon leader was the one skilled at understanding whites as well as his own Maroon people, and Quao apparently exemplified this paradigm. Thicknesse recounted a quaint incident, which, he said, nearly lost them the honor of making peace with the windwards. Just about when confidence was achieved between the Maroons and the soldiers, the terms of the Treaty discussed and agreed upon, Colonel Robert Bennet of the militia showed up. Hearing that Captain Adair was about to sign a treaty with Quao, he marched up to the town with his men and, being of superior rank to Adair, insisted he should sign the document. Quite an affray developed between the officers of the two groups, the militia soon ordering its men under arms; fortunately, the colonel, perhaps realizing the absurdity of the situation, abandoned his claim, and a battle was avoided, although the official Treaty did receive Bennet's signature. During all this the Maroons became agitated and could not be certain that they were not going to be attacked, but Quao calmed his people, assuring them that there was nothing to fear. Quao the creole, once a plantation slave, "spoke tolerable good English, and seemed a reasonable man" to Thicknesse; he also knew "something of the customs, and manners of the white people [otherwise] all had been lost."[112] He thus saved the peace with his understanding both of his people and the whites. But whether or not the situation would have ended differently were Quao a newly arrived African with no knowledge of white people, we will never know. Thicknesse's *Memoirs* also show some of the devastation on certain eastern plantations caused by the exploits of the Maroons.[113] As with the leewards and with Adair and his hornman, Bennet also had his black traitor guides. Mark and Caesar "distinguished themselves, and behaved well as Guides to the Party under the Command of Colonel Robert Bennet, and also have on other publick Services behaved well," and as recompense they were "manumised and for ever set free and made free."[114] Nothing is said here of cash awards as was the case with the leewards — perhaps indicating a diminishing return of gratitude on the part of the authorities.

Once again, we note the wording of Trelawny to Newcastle, that the windwards *submitted* "upon our Party's being in possession of their provision ground . . . ,"[115] does not synchronize with Thicknesse's account. In fact Thicknesse, from experience, had written, "Such who are unacquainted with that island will be surprised when they are told, that all the regular troops in Europe, could not have conquered the wild Negroes, by force of arms; and if Mr. Trelawny had not wisely given them, what they contended for, LIBERTY, they would in all probability have been, at this day, masters of the whole country."[116] In so declaring, Thicknesse adduced a wisdom to Trelawny the latter did not merit since he did not initiate the Treaty, and Trelawny, by his false reporting, repudiated the wisdom.[117]

Once more the colonial department was extremely pleased with the governor's "good success" against the windwards, and with — one is tempted to say indecent — haste, Newcastle hurried on to give instructions, as he did upon the occasion of the first Treaty, on how to deal with the Spaniards now that the Maroon problem was solved. The governor was to "encourage the people under (his) Government to take out [Letters of Marque and Reprisal] and to make use of this opportunity to revenge the Insults, which His Majesty's subjects in America have received from the Spaniards." Then in the strongest terms yet, Newcastle represented to Trelawny that he saw it as a most "practicable thing to make Descents upon some of the Spanish settlements in America," and the governor should encourage the colonists of Jamaica to undertake such enterprises — enterprises which would greatly "annoy the Spaniards, and [would] probably be attended with great Benefit to the adventurers."[118] Needless to say Trelawny was ready. Since "the Rebels are now brought to terms" he for one would be prepared to make a descent upon Havana. Havana seemed to the governor the only place of any consequence to take, it being so situated that it would give the British the command of the West Indian Seas. With the help of the Northern Colonies,

Periclean-like, the governor said they could, with their superiority in shipping "take it [Havana] and keep it .... It is the only conquest in these parts worthy [of] the English Nation and I wish your Grace would Move His Majesty to command it. I should be ambitious to have a share in such an undertaking ...."[119] Once more he reminded Newcastle that he would be glad to be made a colonel, which was finally granted to him in 1743. But interesting though the Anglo-Spanish relations may be at this point – which soon led to the War of Jenkin's Ear – we must return to the Treaties and their implications in the next chapter.

Chapter 5

The Leeward and Windward Treaties

The leeward treaty, formally concluded March 1, 1738/9, is as follows:

> In the Name of God, Amen. Whereas Captain Cudjoe, Captain Accompong, Captain Johnny, Captain Cuffee, Captain Quaw, and several other Negroes their Dependants and Adherents, have been in a State of War and Hostility for several Years past against our Sovereign Lord the King, and the Inhabitants of this Island: And whereas Peace and Friendship amongst Mankind, and the preventing the Effusion of Blood, is agreeable to God, consonant to Reason, and desired by every good Man; and whereas his Majesty George the Second, King of Great Britain, France and Ireland, and of Jamaica Lord, Defender of the Faith, etc. has by Letters Patent, dated February the Twenty-fourth, One thousand seven hundred and thirty-eight, in the Twelfth Year of his Reign, granted full Power and Authority to John Guthrie and Francis Sadler, Esquires, to negotiate and finally conclude a Treaty of Peace and Friendship with the aforesaid Captain Cudjoe, the rest of his Captains, Adherents, and others his Men, they mutually, sincerely, and amicably have agreed to the following Articles,
>
> 1st, That all Hostilities shall cease on both Sides for ever.
>
> 2dly, That the said Captain Cudjoe, the rest of his Captains, Adherents and Men, shall be for ever hereafter in a perfect State of Freedom and Liberty, excepting those who have been taken by them, or fled to them within two Years last past, if such are willing to return to their said Masters and Owners, with full Pardon and Indemnity from their said Masters or Owners for what is past. Provided always, That

if they are not willing to return, they shall remain in Subjection to Captain Cudjoe, and in Friendship with us, according to the Form and Tenor of this Treaty.

3dly, That they shall enjoy and possess for themselves and Posterity for ever, all the Lands situate and lying between Trelawney Town and the Cockpits, to the Amount of Fifteen hundred Acres, bearing North-west from the said Trelawney Town.

4thly, That they shall have Liberty to plant the said Lands with Coffee, Cocoa, Ginger, Tobacco and Cotton, and to breed Cattle, Hogs, Goats, or any other Stock, and dispose of the Produce or Increase of the said Commodities to the Inhabitants of this Island. Provided always, That when they bring the said Commodities to Market, they shall apply first to the Custos, or any other Magistrate of the respective Parishes where they expose their Goods to Sale, for Licence to vend the same.

5thly, That Captain Cudjoe, and all the Captain's Adherents, and people not in Subjection to him, shall all live together within the Bounds of Trelawney Town; and that they have Liberty to hunt where they shall think fit, except within three Miles of any Settlement, Crawl or Pen. Provided always, That in case the Hunters of Captain Cudjoe, and those of other Settlements meet, then the Hogs to be equally divided between both Parties.

6thly, That the said Captain Cudjoe, and his Successors, do use their best Endeavours to take, kill, suppress or destroy, either by themselves or jointly, with any other Number of Men commanded on that Service by his Excellency the Governor or Commander in Chief for the Time being, all Rebels wheresoever they be throughout this Island, unless they submit to the same Terms of Accommodation granted to Captain Cudjoe, and his Successors.

7thly, That in case this Island be invaded by any foreign Enemy, the said Captain Cudjoe, and his Successors herein after named, or to be appointed, shall then, upon Notice given, immediately repair to any Place the Governor for the Time being shall appoint, in order to repel the said Invaders with his or their utmost Force; and to submit to the Orders of the Commander in Chief on that Occasion.

8thly, That if any white Man shall do any Manner of Injury to Captain Cudjoe, his Successors, or any of his or their People, they shall apply to any commanding Officer or Magistrate in the Neighbourhood for Justice; and in case Captain Cudjoe, or any of his People, shall do any Injury to any white Person, he shall submit himself or deliver up such Offenders to Justice.

9thly, That if any Negroes shall hereafter run away from their Masters or Owners, and fall into Captain Cudjoe's Hands, they shall immediately be sent back to the Chief Magistrate of the next Parish where they are taken; and those that bring them are to be satisfied for their Trouble, as the Legislature shall appoint.

10thly, That all Negroes taken since the raising of this Party by Captain Cudjoe's People, shall immediately be returned.

11thly, That Captain Cudjoe, and his Successors, shall wait on his Excellency, or the Commander in Chief for the Time being, every Year, if thereunto required.

12th, That Captain Cudjoe, during his Life, and the Captains succeeding him, shall have full Power to inflict any Punishment they think proper for Crimes committed by their Men among themselves (Death only excepted) in which Case, if the Captain thinks they deserve Death, he shall be obliged to bring them before any Justice of the Peace, who shall order Proceedings on their Trial equal to those of other free Negroes.

13th, That Captain Cudjoe with his People shall cut, clear, and keep open, large, and convenient Roads from Trelawney Town to Westmoreland and St. James's, and if possible to St. Elizabeth's.

14th, That Two white Men to be nominated by his Excellency, or the Commander in Chief for the Time being, shall constantly live and reside with Captain Cudjoe and his Successors, in order to maintain a friendly Correspondence with the Inhabitants of this Island.

15th, That Captain Cudjoe shall, during his Life, be Chief Commander in Trelawney Town, after his Decease the Command to devolve on his Brother Captain Accompong; and in case of his Decease, on his next Brother Captain Johnny; and, failing him, Captain Cuffee shall succeed, who is to be succeeded by Captain Quaco, and after all their Demises, the Governor or Commander in Chief for the Time being, shall appoint from Time to Time whom he thinks fit for that Command.

In Testimony of the above Presents, we have hereunto set our Hands and Seals the Day and Date above written.

John Guthrie. (L.S.)

Francis Sadler. (L.S.)

The Mark X of Captain Cudjoe. (L.S.)[1]

This treaty with the leeward Maroons — referred to in the official documents variously as "Agreement with Captain Cudjoe Vera Copia" or as "Articles of Pacification with the Maroons of Trelawney Town" or as "Articles of Agrement betwixt Coll. Guthrie Lieu. Sadler and Capt. Cajoe signed March 1 1738/9" — although not the first in the New World, is conceivably the best known. The Abbé Raynal, in his monumental work, *The Philosophical and Political History of the Establishments and Commerce of the Europeans in the Two Indies*, noted approvingly the "two colonies of fugitive negroes, whom treaties and power protect from assault. Those lightnings announce the thunder."[2] The thunder, as it turned out, was the great Toussaint Louverture who freed not just a section of his slave society but transformed the entire system from slavery to freedom. It was the Jamaican treaties and not the Mexican one of 1609 with Yanga that served as the model for the Dutch treaties with their Maroons in Surinam, in the 1760s.

The pious beginning, "In the name of God, Amen," no doubt has its antecedent in ancient Italian practice of opening contracts with *Dio la salvi, Amen!* But the ancient analogy cannot be pushed further, since as far the records go one can find no ancient precedents of rebel slaves and their ex-masters signing treaties conjointly. And it is in this sense that the Treaty is historically important, that it is a triumph for the Maroons. In practical terms, though, it is another matter, for the Treaty, in effect, represents more a victory for the colonial powers than for the Maroons, who were never defeated in battle by the British. It represents the triumph of diplomacy over warfare, demonstrating that what the British could not gain on the battlefield, they now gained in full measure over the negotiating table.

In trying to understand why Cudjoe signed the Treaty with all the "offensive" clauses which led one recent scholar to declare it "a completely unnecessary sell-out,"[3] there are certain propositions that may be considered. To begin with, we have no record to show whether Cudjoe and his captains could read and write; even if they had any such capability it would, in all probability, be merely rudimentary, not geared toward the understanding of the fairly technical language of the document Cudjoe had perforce to sign. To be noted is the fact that Cudjoe's "signature" was the mark of the cross legally accepted then as the signatory of the unlettered. In this regard, Cudjoe was even more at a disadvantage because the evidence suggests that the Treaty — or its essentials — were drawn up beforehand, possibly by the Board of Trade or by the Colonial Office, only to be refined by the governor, the Council and the Assembly in Jamaica. Even Bevil Granville in 1735, out on his foolhardy mission, had with him "proper Instructions, to treat with them, upon the terms of Ffredom, and having land allotted them for their Settlement."

Another proposition that could be considered is that it can be assumed that the terms were read to Cudjoe but it cannot be assumed that they were read truthfully. All this implies that Cudjoe might not have consented to the Treaty had he full understanding of the implications of all the terms.

The "offending" clauses, from the standpoint of those who see the Maroon struggle as a just one against inequity, are especially numbers six and nine, which obliged Cudjoe and his men to "take, kill, suppress or destroy either by themselves or jointly ... all rebels wheresoever they may be throughout the island ..."; and worse, they were to return runaway slaves to the nearest magistrate, for which task they would be reimbursed by the legislature. The question, then, is to what extent was Cudjoe voluntarily in congruence with these clauses. Cudjoe was clearly an intelligent man, possessing the natural suspicion and the acuity of mind forged out of precarious living constantly on the edge of danger throughout his life. Guthrie and Sadler both mentioned a second conference with him, the latter resulting in a solution of "our differences." This would seem to suggest hard bargaining. But if the available evidence is accurate, then the bargaining was certainly not over the suppression of rebels and the return of runaways.

It was clearly over guarantees from Guthrie that they would not attack Cudjoe's community. The Maroon leader, now aging and tired, was adamant on this point, necessitating Guthrie to "tye" himself by a "Solemn Oath" not to fight against them unless they infringed the Treaty. Another point over which there may have been some hard bargaining is that with respect to recent arrivals to Cudjoe's community. It must be noted that in Trelawny's "Thoughts," the governor had great difficulties in recommending freedom to those who had fled from their masters, irrespective of the length of time they were out. He thought they should be returned and all that he could "yet think proper to promise them is, that they shall be treated with humanity." Should they object to return, then they should be employed as slaves in the public service. But the Council, with more understanding of the reality of the situation, had cautiously suggested the return of those who had not been away from their masters "above two years." It is clear that Cudjoe scored a point here when clause two gave those who had fled their masters "within two years last past" two options. They could either return to their owners with full pardon and indemnity or remain under Cudjoe's jurisdiction "in friendship" with the authorities. This clause certainly favored both Cudjoe and the authorities. It protected Cudjoe from the potential machinations of the newly arrived to his community, not yet seasoned to his authority and who might thus have a strong propensity to challenge him or even to break away and form new bands. With the treaty, Cudjoe could now hold over their heads the big stick of returning them to their masters. Whatever the choice made by this group it bids fair to the authorities: should they remain with Cudjoe it would be "in friendship" with the government; should they return to their former owners, they thus become a part of the property of the land — albeit a troublesome species of property. It may be noted here that Yanga of Mexico had agreed to return only those who escaped slavery less than six months before his treaty.

Guthrie stated quite explicitly that at the first conference "they [the Maroons] offered to assist against any foreign Enemy and to take up for the future all Runaway Negroes . . . ," while Sadler said that they "of their own accord offered to be assisting on the first command against the Spaniards or any other foreign Enemy . . . ." It may be that Guthrie and Sadler should have said that they "agreed" rather than that they "offered" to so assist the authorities. From the documents, every mention of peace treaties with the Maroons had, as one of the specifications, their aid in returning runaways. Guthrie and Sadler may have forgotten that *they* had made the suggestion. Yet the promptness with which Cudjoe assisted in dealing with runaways, as will be noted later, does not suggest a man with any great compunction against doing so. If the Spanish documents are correct, then Yanga too, upon the occasion of his treaty in 1609, the model of the British colonial authorities, promised, for a fee, to aid the viceroy in capturing fugitive slaves. There does not appear to have been any coercion or twisting of the arm here for it is said that Yanga himself was responsible for the eleven conditions stipulated in the treaty. This aspect of the Maroon story, which is so universal, must be one of the most perplexing.

Another approach may well take the view that there was a lack of any general philosophy of freedom — or, more particularly of a pan-African or black solidarity concept — among the Maroons. The tendency then was toward ethnic exclusivity; in addition, the Maroons, over time, had developed an inordinate sense of their own importance and a marked feeling of superiority over the other blacks of the island, present to this day. They see these blacks as people supine enough to have continued to be slaves of the whites — working for them — while they, for their part, successfully *fought* them. The combination of ethnic particularity and earned superiority, as they perceived it, did not make for a feeling of black solidarity — which would view as anathema the notion of defeating the efforts of blacks who wished to gain their freedom.

Clause by clause, the Treaty favored the colonial authority and the local plantocracy. The doubtful exceptions are clauses one, two, and three, which ended hostilities, granted them "a perfect state of freedom and liberty," and granted them lands. The windwards, for instance, might not have seen the ending of hostilities as contributing to the cause of freedom. It conferred a negative benefit in so far as they could now live in "peace" — but still within a slave society. It was the colonial powers who gained markedly from the cessation of hostilities, as will be demonstrated shortly. In looking at clause two, we must recall that in 1663 the authorities had offered Juan de Serras "lands" and "freedom" to settle with his group as peaceful members of the community. But the redoubtable Juan scoffed at the offer. They were well satisfied with the more capacious range of land they possessed in the woods where their hunting could be unrestricted. Admittedly, the granting of the fifteen hundred acres of land to the leeward Maroons encouraged their perpetuation as a separate group with their own identity; their own quasi-government, free to act out their own cultural imperatives. In conducting field studies among the Maroons today, it soon becomes clear that the possession of these lands is as sacrosanct to them as the Treaty. Indeed they see the two things as inseparable. And the leaders will relate with spirit that the most common dispute they must adjudicate is that involving lands, whether among themselves or with local citizens or with the government. Any government of the island today that would wish to abrogate the Treaty by the fact of a new political situation arising out of Jamaica's independence would be heading toward a sea of troubles.

Yet, viewed historically, to be so corralled denied the Maroons their hitherto very expansive hunting grounds and their choice of extensive fertile lands to cultivate, and curtailed their predilection to splinter off and form new communities, separate, but with ethnic ties reflecting Akan practice, as mentioned above. The long-term sociological effect, too, of a group of people corralled into a "reservation" situation and isolated from the mainstream society may be of doubtful benefit. The comparison that can be made with the Maroons of Jamaica and those who finally went to Sierra Leone and were thrown into the wider community may give some useful insights into the relative value of a "closed" and an "open" society. However, it became clear, in the years following the Treaty, that many Maroons simply refused to confine themselves to their stipulated boundaries.

All the evidence would seem to suggest that Cudjoe's overriding consideration was security, and perhaps the reason for this predisposition is not difficult to find. With the hindsight of time, we now know from Edward Long that Cudjoe was under tremendous pressure arising from the more sustained attacks from the parties, resulting in the destruction of their provision grounds, limitations on their movements, leading to famine and, perhaps worst of all, evidence that some of his people were defecting at this time. Some of these defectors were to become informants to government parties. With his options greatly narrowed to starvation or surrender, Cudjoe must have welcomed peace offers — but with studied caution. Nevertheless, the trained guerrilla fighter should be accustomed to, and be prepared to deal with such extremities. Juan de Serras in the 1660s found himself in a similar situation and used subterfuge and diplomacy to get out of it. So did the windwards in 1732 who made their march to Cudjoe's town when cornered. It is known that these groups suffered tremendous hardships, especially after the capture of Nanny Town on two occasions. Yet there was no sign of surrender or coming to terms on their part. The fact is that the leewards under Cudjoe had not the long experience of sustained hardships arising from the constant pursuit of parties as had the windwards, who had been fighting with varying degrees of intensity since the 1690s. Relatively secure as they were in the Cockpits in the southwest of the island with Cudjoe's policy of consolidation, the leewards were out of practice. Had they been in constant practice, they probably would have managed to maintain a low profile for a period and then refurbished for further combat.

The economic impulse behind the Treaty is reflected throughout, but particularly in clauses four, five, six, seven, nine, ten, and thirteen. Clause four stipulated what they were to plant, with the conspicuous absence of the sugar cane, depicting the plantocracy's abhorrence of small farmers' interfering with this commodity, the export crop par excellence, and the planters' monopoly. It is interesting that in the Windward Treaty, they would not allow absence alone to be a policy, but stated explicitly that the sugar cane was "excepted" from the enumerated crops. In enumerating crops to be planted, the planters no doubt felt they were protecting themselves from the likelihood of the Maroons' developing into a "lazy and indolent" group and thus becoming a nuisance to the plantations or a charge on society. Equally, the authorities were well aware of the importance of these domestic items of food for the island. The slaves themselves had developed a network of markets throughout the country, where they would sell commodities from their provision grounds, and it was well known that the Maroons would intermingle freely with them, buying and selling provisions or livestock. This was a main source of food for the island, especially in periods of droughts and other natural disasters creating scarcity.

It was left to be seen whether the Maroons would adhere to the stipulation of clause four, binding them to apply for licenses from Custodes before bringing their goods for sale to the marketplace.

Clause five, in attempting to keep the Maroons within bounds (three miles of any settlement, crawl, or pen), represents the plantocracy's nervousness of Maroon presence at this time. And in asking the Maroons to share equally the hunters' game if there is a meeting with hunters from settlements, it clearly places the advantage on the planters' side, since the Maroons were invariably the better hunters — the result of long experience.

The "offensive" clause six spelled doom for the indomitable windwards, because only another Maroon group could conceivably succeed in taking, killing, suppressing, or destroying them. Clauses seven, nine, and ten together, requiring the Maroons to assist in foreign wars and to return runaways, would thus enable the planters to pursue the plantation economy with more confidence. Clause thirteen, in asking them to cut, clear, and keep open large and convenient roads from Trelawney Town (their community) to Westmoreland and St. James, and if possible to St. Elizabeth, was no more than asking them to create a necessary economic infrastructure in the form of communication. This would assuredly be of more benefit to the plantocracy than to the Maroons, who were adept at traveling along mountain passes on narrow tracks. More important, such roads would also make entrance to their communities very convenient in the event of an uprising that would necessitate troop or militia participation. Clause eight was also based on security considerations. The authorities were nervous that the Maroons might not respect the Treaty but would continue to make incursions on the plantations. Thus clause eight's stipulation of protection against attacks on either side was a reciprocity that favored the plantocracy because in all probability no one would dare attack the generally feared Maroons.

Clauses eleven, fourteen, and fifteen represent an inchoate form of the indirect rule the British were to practice so successfully in Africa. The yearly visitations of the Maroons on the governor soon became a grandiose spectacle, serving no other purpose than enabling the authorities to exercise their control exemplified by the governor's largesse in distributing presents of all descriptions to the grateful Maroons. This way, the governor, no doubt, saw himself as some latter-day feudal lord. Edward Long, writing in 1774, seems to bear this out. In the years following the Treaty the Maroon captains were decked out, by the government, each with a silver chain and medal inscribed with his name, and cockades to boot, and thus spuriously attired, they would descend on the governor at his sumptuous residence. Here he would confer, said Long, "some mark of favour, such as an old laced coat or waistcoat, a hat, sword, fusee, or any other articles of the like nature, which seem most acceptable. They are pleased with these distinctions, and a trifling douceur of this sort bestowed annually, accompanied with expressions of favour, wins their hearts, and strengthens their dutiful attachment."[4]

Clause fourteen, requiring the Maroons to have two white men, nominated by the governor, to reside in the Maroon community, was the most blatant attempt of the authorities to control Maroon destiny. In a sense, this clause and its relationship with clause fifteen could be seen as the most humiliating of the clauses that they accepted, and it is inconceivable that Juan de Serras or Yanga of Mexico would have consented to clauses they would have seen as an infringement on their hegemony. Yanga, it is true, did stipulate that his *palenque* be given the status of a free town with a government structured along the lines of other Spanish towns, conceding only to have a Spaniard as *justicia mayor*, but allowing no other Spaniard to live in the town, although they could visit on market days. The divisive effect of the white residents among them would certainly be made more effective when the latter half of clause fifteen's stipulation became effective. That the authorities, after the death of the succession line of the leaders named, could now appoint Maroon leaders must represent the greatest of British diplomatic successes, with respect to the Treaty. The resident whites would presumably have a good idea of the "well-disposed" — in the parlance of the period — who would certainly be recommended for leadership. The British propensity to divide and rule could thus be monitored and carefully implemented, theoretically, at least.

Clause twelve is no more than a continuation of the judiciary system the Maroons had practiced among themselves, but in excluding cases deserving death from their jurisdiction, the authorities curtailed a part of their traditional juridical function — and thus the actual powers of their leaders — since the Maroons had hitherto carried out their own sentences of death.

Let us now take a look at the Windward Treaty. In looking at this document, we remind ourselves that there are many who speak of one Maroon Treaty of Jamaica in the eighteenth century, but in fact two Treaties were signed with two distinct Maroon groups. Thicknesse, for one, who saw himself as an important participant to the second Treaty, has clearly taken umbrage to this unitreaty approach. He upbraided "the ingenious author of the history of Jamaica" [Bryan Edwards, no doubt] for not mentioning that it was "two distinct acts, and with two separate bodies of men, under different leaders, and quite unconnected, but as if it had been one act of grace; to one body of people . . . ."[5] The Windward Treaty, then, was signed in June 1739, only three months after Cudjoe's, but the dating system then placed it in the following year, and this has continued to confuse many.

Without the pious beginning of the Leewards', the second document said:

> Whereas his Excellency Edward Trelawney, Esquire; Governor and Commander in Chief of the Island aforesaid, hath given Power and Authority to Colonel Robert Bennett to treat with the rebellious Negroes, this Day, being the Twenty-third Day of June, One thousand seven hundred and thirty-nine, Captain Quao, and several others of them under his Command, surrendered under the following Terms, viz.
>
> First, That all Hostilities shall cease on both Sides for ever, Amen;
>
> Second, That the said Captain Quao and his People shall have a certain Quantity of Land given to them, in order to raise Provisions, Hogs, Fowls, Goats, or whatsoever Stock they may think proper, Sugar-Canes excepted, saving for their Hogs, and to have Liberty to sell the same;
>
> Third, That Four White Men shall constantly live and reside with them in their Town, in order to keep a good Correspondence with the Inhabitants of this Island;

Fourth, That the said Captain Quao and his People shall be ready on all Commands the Governor or the Commander in chief for the Time being shall send him, to suppress and destroy all other Party and Parties of rebellious Negroes, that now are or shall from Time to Time gather together or settle in any Part of this Island, and shall bring in such other Negroes as shall from Time to Time run away from their respective Owners, from the Date of these Articles;

Fifth, That the said Captain Quao and his People shall also be ready to assist his Excellency the Governor for the Time being, in case of any Invasion, and shall put himself, with all his People that are able to bear Arms, under the Command of the General or Commander of such Forces, appointed by his Excellency to defend the Island from the said Invasion;

Sixth, That the said Captain Quao and all his People shall be in Subjection to his Excellency the Governor for the Time being, and the said Captain Quao shall once every Year, or oftener, appear before the Governor, if thereunto required;

Seventh, That in case any of the Hunters belonging to the Inhabitants of this Island, and the Hunters belonging to Captain Quao, should meet, in order to hinder all Disputes, Captain Quao will order his People to let the Inhabitants Hunters have the Hog;

Eighth, That in case Captain Quao or his People shall take up any runaway Negroes that shall abscond from their respective Owners, he or they shall carry them to their respective Masters or Owners, and shall be paid for so doing, as the Legislature shall appoint;

Ninth, That in case Captain Quao and his People should be disturbed by a greater Number of Rebels than he is able to fight, that then he shall be assisted by as many White People as the Governor for the Time being shall think proper;

Tenth, That in case any of the Negroes belonging to Captain Quao shall be guilty of any Crime or Crimes that may deserve Death, he shall deliver him up to the next Magistrate, in order to be tried as other Negroes are; but small Crimes he may punish himself;

Eleventh, That in case any White Man, or other the Inhabitants of this Islands, shall disturb or annoy any of the People, Hogs, Stock, or whatsoever Goods may belong to the said Captain Quao, or any of his People, when they come down to the Settlements to vend the same, upon due Complaint made to a Magistrate he or they shall have Justice done them;

Twelfth, That neither Captain Quao, nor any of his People shall bring any Hogs, Fowls, or any other kind of Stock or Provisions to sell to the Inhabitants, without a Ticket from under the Hand of one or more of the White Men residing within their Town;

Thirteenth, That Captain Quao, nor any of his People, shall hunt within Three Miles of any Settlement;

Fourteenth, That in case Captain Quao should dye, that then the Command of his People shall descend to Captain Thomboy, and at his Death to descend to Captain Apong, and at his Death Captain Blackwall shall succeed, and at his Death Captain Clash shall succeed; and when he dies, the Governor or Commander in chief for the Time being shall appoint whom he thinks proper.

In Witness to these Articles, the above named Colonel Robert Bennett and Captain Quao have set their Hands and Seals the Day and Year above written,

Robert Bennet (L.S.)

The Mark X of Captain Quao[6]

In reporting on this Treaty to Newcastle, June 30, 1739, Trelawny said, with his usual terminological inexactitude, that the rebels submitted "upon pretty much the same terms as the leewards only that they are obliged to deliver up the slaves that have not been with them above three years and receive a garrison of soldiers that can command them."[7] To the Board of Trade, just under two weeks later, he dropped the "pretty much" to say they have submitted "upon the same terms as those which the others lately agreed upon," reiterating again the two items of difference above.[8]

The fact is, though, that a close study of the Treaties will reveal fundamental differences both in tone and in substance. It should be noted here that both Treaties were later ratified — Cudjoe's a few months after the event, and Quao's in 1740. This was done by the island's legislature in cooperation with the law officers of the Crown. All this was constitutional orthodoxy. But in this case many new words and clauses — all convenient to the authorities — were inserted in both Treaties. Even before ratification, the tone of Quao's Treaty was most haughty and imperious, lacking the more deferential approach of Cudjoe's. This, doubtless, suggested an awareness of a stronger bargaining position. The authorities were undoubtedly buoyed up by Cudjoe's willingness to cooperate with them to impose a treaty on Quao. Whatever were Quao's thoughts about making treaties with the slavocracy, he, in fact, had no more than Hobson's choice in the matter. Of Quao, we know next to nothing apart from the fact that his is an Ashanti name, suggesting a male child born on a Thursday, and he was probably a creole.

The terse preamble to Quao's Treaty stated unabashedly that the Maroon "surrendered" to the government. This must be contrasted with Cudjoe's elaborate preamble, concluding a treaty of peace and friendship amicably *agreed* upon. This was certainly more in line with the termination of hostilities between contending parties. There was no mention here of having surrendered. This, however, was to wait for its ratification.

Both Treaties affirmed the ending of hostilities on both sides. Quao's original treaty, before its ratification, had fourteen clauses and not in the same order as Cudjoe's fifteen clauses. Both Treaties granted lands to the Maroons, clause two of Quao's and clause three of Cudjoe's. But whereas Cudjoe's gave a specified number of acres (1500), Quao's imprecisely said he and his people were to be given a certain quantity of land to raise the same enumerated cash crops as stipulated in Cudjoe's, again explicitly exempting the sugar cane.

This vague land grant was to cause many a conflict between Maroons and planters and between themselves and the government. Equally, its imprecise nature was to lend itself to flexible interpretations both by the Maroons and by the authorities. Both Treaties required the presence of white men in their midst, clause three of Quao's, clause fourteen of Cudjoe's. Upon the signing of Cudjoe's, the stipulation was for two white men to reside among them to maintain a friendly relationship with the wider society. But four are stipulated for Quao's town. However, upon the ratification of Cudjoe's, it was enacted that Cudjoe's group, which had "lately *surrendered and submitted themselves to the government*," should also have four whites among them, to "receive and communicate such *orders* as shall be sent by His Excellency the Governor" to them (emphasis added). Each white resident was to be paid at the rate of £200 per year.

Such, then, was the beginning of the perfidy of the authorities toward the Maroon Treaties. Cudjoe is now characterized as having surrendered and submitted, and the white residents were to give orders to him and his people. As far as we know Cudjoe was never apprised of these inaccurate and highly charged terms that crept into his Treaty. As for the addition of the white presence, we have no record of Cudjoe's reactions to this. Indeed, as the years passed, we shall note the radically different interpretations given in law to the documents, and soon all these laws were made equally applicable to *all* the Maroon communities.

Both Treaties bound the Maroons to destroy all other rebel communities, clause four of Quao's; clause six of Cudjoe's. While the latter Treaty rather vaguely said that Cudjoe and his successor should use their best endeavors "to take, kill, suppress or destroy," either by themselves or jointly with the government, all rebels wherever they might be throughout the island, Quao's veered toward some sort of structured mechanism. They were required to be ready "on all commands" the governor might institute for the destruction of rebel hideouts or for the return of runaways. The question whether the Maroons could legally refuse any such commands is more than academic, but it was never put to the test, although it came close to it during the Trelawny Town War. The issue of readiness from a militaristic point of view is also not clear in Quao's Treaty.

Clause five of Quao's and clause seven of Cudjoe's, each binding them to assist the government in case of foreign invasion, are the closest in wording, as clause six of Quao's is miles apart from clause eleven of Cudjoe's, desiring them to wait upon the governor. Cudjoe's was just a simple statement requiring the captain and his "successors" to "wait" upon the governor "every year" if requested to do so. In the case of Quao's, the analogy with the feudal lord made above could not be more apposite. Imperiously, the article reminded Quao and his people that they were in "subjection to his Excellency the Governor" and the said Quao (no mention of his successors), "shall once very year, or oftener, appear before the Governor," if required. It is unlikely that Quao, viewed as hardly more than just a mere seneschal in the eyes of the government, would be expected to refuse.

Clause seven of Quao's, in relation to clause five of Cudjoe's, provides another intriguing comparison. Here, should the hunters of Cudjoe's people meet with those of the plantations, then the hogs should be equally divided between the two groups. Quao's hunters were not to be so fortunate. Upon any such meeting, "in order to hinder disputes," Captain Quao must order his people to let the white hunters have the hog or hogs.

Both groups were required to return runaways, clauses eight and nine of Quao's and Cudjoe's, respectively. Cudjoe was to return them to the chief magistrate of the parish, while Quao's group must return them to their owners, each group to be reimbursed for each returnee. Returning them to their owners would constitute a much more onerous task, since the owners might be miles away from where the runaways were taken. At this period they were not yet paid for mileage also.

Clause nine of Quao's has no parallel with Cudjoe's. It is protective to Quao's group, offering government assistance to them in the event they should be disturbed by a greater number of rebels than they were able to fight. This clause is somewhat puzzling. It could be that the authorities had some knowledge that the windward groups, consisting as they were of different towns with a more democratic ordering of power than was the case with Cudjoe, was potentially divisive. The clause could thus be seen as anticipating rivalries within Quao's group — which in fact, was to be the case soon after the Treaty was signed.

The wording of clause ten of Quao's Treaty, matched with Cudjoe's twelfth, relating to jurisdiction over their communities, is markedly different in tone. Quao's, in banal terms, simply stated that if any of his people should be guilty of any crime deserving the death penalty, he should deliver them up to the "next magistrate," to be tried as other blacks, but Quao (no mention again of his successors) might punish small crimes. In

Cudjoe's, the elaborate and formal wording suggests a polity with a large degree of autonomy and with expectations of permanence which the government was prepared to respect. "Captain Cudjoe, during his life and captains succeeding him, shall have full power to inflict" any punishment for crimes committed within his community, death only excepted; that is, if the captains so adjudged the case.

Clause eleven of Quao's, which matches clause eight of Cudjoe's, again presents some difficulties. Both clauses made provisions in case any white person or other inhabitants of the island should disturb or annoy any of Cudjoe's or Quao's people. But Cudjoe's Treaty went on to make provisions should Cudjoe or any of his people commit any injury against any white person. The lack of reciprocity in Quao's clause is certainly unclear. Even when we take into consideration the great sense of security and confidence the administration was experiencing when dealing with Quao, it is still puzzling — perhaps foolhardy — that no provisions were made for Maroons of the windwards who might injure or molest whites. There is no doubt that Trelawny's influence was stronger in this Treaty than in Cudjoe's. We saw in the governor's "Thoughts" how he would have taken a more insensitive line with the leewards than would the Council and Assembly, but nevertheless conceded to them finally. Trelawny, as said earlier, had never really taken the Maroon threat seriously and had, on occasion, treated the situation almost cavalierly. Again, by the time of Quao's Treaty, the country was so overwhelmingly grateful to him that his views could carry without much difficulty. We saw his self-assurance, in writing to Newcastle on the Windward Treaty (which was more the result of ignorance of the situation than of real strength at the time), when he observed that they would never revolt again, since they gained great advantages from the Treaty.

Clause twelve of Quao's Treaty is comparable to Cudjoe's fourth, requiring them to apply for permission before taking their commodities to market. Cudjoe must apply to the proper legal authority, a Custos or a magistrate, for a "licence," while Quao must apply for a "ticket" from one of the white residents of his town. These differences should not be overlooked. It was the intention of the executive to impress upon Quao as much as possible that he and his group were at the sufferance of the government, and in this regard, the white residents' position was strengthened by this clause — and was to become increasingly strengthened for all groups by the law of the land, especially from 1751 onwards. The same kind of difference, subtle at times, may be noted with Quao's clause fourteen, which compares with Cudjoe's fifteenth, naming the line of succession in each case. After the last person named, thereafter, the governor for the time being would appoint for Quao "whom he thinks proper," while for Cudjoe it was "whom he thinks fit for the command," reflecting an implied respect for the

Maroons' command, while in Quao's case, it is the governor's choice that mattered.

After the signature of Robert Bennett and the mark of Quao, we find some additional clauses appended to the ratified Treaty without any explanation.

The first addition deals with what Trelawny had already reported, "[t]hat all Negroes that have gone to them, or been taken by them, within Three Years, shall be pardoned their Offence and restored to their Masters, who shall be obliged to use them well." This compares with Cudjoe's clauses two and ten, with the vast difference that those who were taken by his community within two years had the option either to remain with him or to return, fully pardoned and indemnified, to their owners. The only category Cudjoe was to return unconditionally, was that which was taken by him since the raising of the final party against him before the Treaty. The second additional clause, not in Cudjoe's, states "that if hereafter, any of their Negroes shall endeavour to entice, or should entice, any Negroes from any Plantation, the free Negro shall be punished capitally." The third clause again showed some rudimentary procedure through which the Maroons were to be used as an auxiliary to the military component of the island. It states "that the Negroes shall be formed into Companies, to be commanded in chief by a White Man each, and when ordered out upon Service, they shall receive Pay." Like Cudjoe's thirteenth clause, this last addition states "that they shall be obliged to cut such Roads as the Governor shall order and that they immediately cut a Road, so as to be rideable, the nearest Way possible to a Plantation."[9] The infrastructural purpose of the road system was thus more explicitly spelled out here.

All these additional clauses were made in the interest of the plantocracy, and they reflected the thinking behind Trelawny's "Thoughts." Like the ratification of Cudjoe's Treaty, it can also be assumed that Quao was not consulted on the additional clauses.

In summary therefore, the Treaties as ratified favored even more substantially the authorities. They were predicated, from the slavocracy's point of view, upon the necessity for security within the island the better to deal with external threats. But more important, the *leitmotif* must be seen as arising out of economic considerations, although both factors are intimately interrelated.

To begin with, the cost in time and money in attempting to suppress their intestine enemies must have been well nigh incalculable. One source said that the Assembly passed forty-four acts dealing with the enemies, "and at least £240,000 [was] expended for their suppression."[10] But this is a rather modest sum even when it took into consideration only the suppression efforts since 1693, without regard for the fact that efforts had been made against them since 1655, when the British captured the island. It is not clear also whether or not the numerous successful claims made by private individuals to the government are included.[11] It is true that the greatest expenditure as well as the proliferation of acts of the Assembly must have been from Hunter's administration in 1729 to the time of the Treaty. The heavy expenditure of paying for defense, most of which fell on the British government, would now be over. The new local expenses in salaries to white resident representatives and for reimbursing Maroons who brought in runaways, and who served in parties, would be far less, in terms of effectiveness to security on the island — at least, from a cost/benefit point of view.

But there were wider economic considerations which had a profound influence on the Colonial Office and the merchant class in England interested in the planting economy of Jamaica. The fact that the Maroons had been occupying some of the most fertile areas in the colony and, by their presence, were preventing settlement of adjacent lands was to become a critical decision-making factor. Soldiers out in parties had noticed this. They reported on their discovery of great tracts of fertile land, in some instances, with lush Maroon cultivation, "unknown before" to the authorities. We have already noted the number of estates that were abandoned during Hunter's administration, and Trelawny, too, reported that almost all the "Small Settlements" were thrown up and for the most part overrun with "Trees and Bushes." He conjectured that "perhaps" more than two-thirds of Jamaica had uncultivated lands.[12]

These points soon became compelling to the Board of Trade. When they were told repeatedly that Jamaica "is very fertile and produces Sugar, Molasses, Rum, Indigo, Cotton, Ginger, Pimento, Fustick, Ebony, Lignum Vitae, Mahogony and Several other Sort of valuable Timber, and of late Coffee and if the island is improved, land uncultivated sufficient to make Sugar to Serve all Europe,"[13] it made them take stock of the island. Important capacious and secure coastal towns such as Manchionael and especially Titchfield, in the parishes of St. George and Portland respectively, despite the government barracks to protect them, remained undeveloped because of the Maroons. Titchfield was characterized to the Board of Trade by Hunter as "in embryo," consisting chiefly of "Hutts . . . and very few Houses." Yet, to Hunter, it was a natural, "strong and commodious situation for trade," with the best harbor in the island, and could become a thriving place, but only "when the Rebellious Negroes (whose chief Residence is but about twelve miles distance from it) shall be destroyed or taken."[14] Anything that adversely affected British trading would be taken seriously by the Board of Trade, with its unimaginative if honest title. The decrease in trade meant decrease in British shipping and the number of sea-faring men. These seafaring men from Britain were important to the island, as they helped to augment the declining white population, which was considered essential for security reasons. Hunter had reported to the Board that around 1710, as he was "credibly informed, there were upwards of 1500 Seafaring men Actuall Inhabitants of the Island and now [1730] the Number does not exceed 200."[15]

The efforts that were made in the early 1730s to develop Bath in St. Thomas only succeeded after the Treaty, and this resort, with its now-famous thermal springs, has become a modern tourist attraction.

By the mid-1730s the merchants of London, Bristol, and Liverpool, and others "Trading to and interested in" Jamaica petitioned the king to represent the alarming state of things, affecting the trade of the colony. They pointed out, *inter alia*, the great potential of the island's trade — "capable of producing double the quantity of Sugar and other commodities ... were it fully settled." One reason for its sparse population was the great tracts of uncultivated lands, the most fertile and best situated. The situation required that immediate steps be taken to secure the island from external as well as intestine enemies. Among the remedies the traders recommended were laws to encourage new settlement, the enforcement of existing deficiency laws, and discouragement of martial law to fight against such a "small Number of Rebellious Negroes" — some 300, they heard. Peopling the island, they argued, would so increase the strength of the white population that they alone could defend themselves against the rebels and the external enemies, and all this would increase the trade and the navigation of Great Britain. These were compelling arguments to a trading nation.[16]

In conjunction with the above factors, there was the real fear, as perceived by the authorities, of a Spanish invasion of the island with the Maroons in cooperation with them. From the 1720s this fear was expressed, but it became more insistent as the Maroon crisis developed. It was first suspected that from "the vast number of Arms, and Quantity of Ammunition, it is past doubt that the Rebels have a secret Correspondence within the Island, or from abroad, perhaps both ...."[17] The Spaniards were thought to be those from "abroad." In June 1730, Hunter received depositions from one John Tello and from Captain William Quarrell, attesting to Spanish-Maroon collusion. Tello, aged about 27 "or there abouts," obviously a trader on the Spanish coast, in his deposition stated that at Panama he was informed of the presence of 30,000 rebellious Negroes in Jamaica. Upon inquiring of the governor of Panama if this were so, the governor confirmed it and further stated that the said rebels had sent a letter to the governor of Carcas [Caracas?], desiring this governor to let the king of Spain know that should he, the king, guarantee them their liberty, they would put Jamaica into his possession. The governor of Carcas [?], not knowing by what means the letter came, consulted his Council to which there came an "East Indian Negro Man," who was finally sent to find out the source of the letter, but apparently nothing came of this.[18]

Quarrell, aged "about 50" (who therefore could not be the same William Quarrell who later figured in the 1795 Trelawny Town War) swore that "around May" 1730, he was on a trading voyage at Santa Maria in Cuba (apparently for cattle), and he happened to have said to some Spanish merchants that in seven years' time, Jamaica would have no more occasion for their use since she would breed her own. But they said that in less than half that time, the island would be theirs, and when the deponent asked them to explain — since there was peace between Britain and Spain — the reply was that the rebellious Negroes of Jamaica "had wrote" to the governor of Cracas (*sic*) that they would assist the king of Spain to take Jamaica. Later, at another destination, an "Eminent Spanish Merchant" and some other Spaniards told the deponent, when questioned about the veracity of the story, "that it was in the Mouth of every one at Porto Prince . . . ."[19] The British government was so alarmed by the Spanish threat to the island that Hunter, as noted already, was told by Newcastle to place the colony in a state of readiness because of the "fresh intelligence" Whitehall had received of Spanish designs on Jamaica. The Board of Trade also wrote to Newcastle, impressing on him the importance of Tello's and Quarrell's depositions, remarking that "the Spaniards had grounded their hopes of Success upon the strength of the Rebellious Negroes . . . ."[20] There is no doubt that both the Board of Trade and the local government were alarmed by the news of Spanish and Maroon collusion, and when this was "confirmed" by a captured Maroon the alarm grew. This captured rebel stated that one of their captains had gone to the Spaniards (where, we are not told) and had told them of their great numbers and that if the Spaniards invaded Jamaica "today," the Maroons would join them.[21] These rumors (for so they must be called, since there is no evidence one way or another) continued up to the time of the Treaty, and perhaps Trelawny's glee in coming to terms with the Maroons (so that the Spanish question could be dealt with) can be more readily understood — although there were other factors that made for his and Newcastle's bellicosity toward the Spaniards.

These, then, were the compelling arguments that made the Board of Trade finally decide to take the necessary measures, in this case, that of first dealing with the Maroon question, in order to place this Caribbean island, then the most important to British trade, back on her feet.

The Treaty's economic effect on the island was immediate and positive. There was first the psychological release from the fear of years of uncertainty. This is necessarily intangible and cannot be quantified, but this new sanguinity expressed itself in different ways. One of its first manifestations was the new and lively interest that developed in mining in Jamaica. Whether this was encouraged by the deposition of a captured Maroon, who maintained that they had "as much Gold and Silver as two Negroes can carry"[22] in their camp, is not clear. Nor is it clear whether this was so or not. In a reply to queries on mining in Jamaica, Trelawny told the Lords Commissioners that the island had two copper mines and one of lead, but the planters had not yet developed them fully.[23] The minerals for which the entrepreneurs wished to prospect included gold and silver. These, they thought, were to be found in the mountainous parts of St. Andrew and St. George — areas which the Maroons had occupied and which were not then safe for the colonists. Immediately after the Treaties, petitions from one Mathias Philip and one William Perrin, among others, repeatedly went to the governor asking for permission to dig the Royal Mines and to investigate further for other sources of mineral.[24] Nothing more has been heard of this, but there does not appear any evidence to suggest that the island had any mineral deposits of enough consequence to have been of commercial feasibility. Its importance here lay in the fact that the Maroon settlement unleashed energies of all kinds and opened possibilities to the white settlers which would not have been contemplated before the Treaties. Edward Long mentioned, without giving any dates, that "two or three principal gentlemen of the island" had applied for and obtained patents to prospect for gold and silver, but the venture failed and brought very heavy expenses upon them. Philip and Perrin may have been among these men.[25]

But the most spectacular economic effect of the Treaties was soon to be seen in the development of plantations. Trelawny could barely report to the Lords Commissioners on the leeward Treaty before he embarked on its economic importance. "The chief reason," he said, "of this Island's being so thinly inhabited, is because there is hardly any Good Land which has been hitherto safe from the Incursions of those Rebels unoccupied, at least unpatented: there is enough and upon all Accounts as good as that already patented which has remained desert for fear of those Incursions, and many who have began Plantations expos'd to that danger have been forced to abandon them upon that account. As these fears are now diminished and in a fair way to be soon entirely removed, I think it a critical conjecture to settle this Island better than it ever yet has been, and consequently to render it more beneficial to our Mother Country."[26] The governor then mentioned writing to Newcastle to represent to the King the importance of his consent to the island's having from parliament a sum of money for a settlement scheme. He thought that one-third or one-fourth of the money granted to Georgia — a favorite theme of Trelawny's — should be given to Jamaica to encourage newcomers with provisions and other necessaries, as well as tools to prepare lands and build conveniences till they could provide for themselves.[27]

The first response to this came from the Leeward and the Virgin Islands. By November 1741, Trelawny was reporting that since the "submission" of the rebels, "about sixteen families with servants and slaves have come from the Leeward Islands to Manchioneal," and he expected this trend to develop,[28] as others from the Virgins were expressing their desire to come. This should be compared with the earlier offers mentioned above, when the Maroon issue was at its height and no settler from these islands would venture forth despite the inducements. The inducements in this case consisted of fifty acres of land to the husband, fifty to the wife, to each child twenty, to each white servant fifteen, and to each slave ten acres, the whole not to exceed three hundred acres to any one family. The transportation cost for each family was also to be paid, and they should be supplied with provisions for one year.[29] By August 1752, Trelawny reported that ninety-seven families came to Jamaica under this scheme. However, the response was not as impressive as had been expected, and Trelawny soon discovered that the scheme was only "[e]ffectual with Men who had Slaves or Mony, but they will not do for very poor People."[30]

Nevertheless, the effect of the Treaties was to be seen in the eastern and northeastern parishes, which were almost without settlements. Edward Long wrote that "we may date the flourishing state of [the colony] from the ratification of the treaty; ever since which, the island has been increasing in plantations and opulence."[31] The roads that were cut from time to time (possibly with Maroon aid) facilitated the new settlers. Long remarked that the Treaty gave security to young settlers in the remote parts "even against any machinations of their own slaves,"[32] thus reversing the effects of having Maroon settlements contiguous to plantations, before the Treaties. Long pointed out how Moore Town (to be dealt with later) was so situated that it gave "speedy protection to the estates on each side the Rio Grande."[33] Manchioneal, in the parish of Portland, with its former uncultivated lands — some 15,000 acres vested in the Crown because of the hitherto Maroon presence — is now "well settled and promised to become very populous." The parish of Portland, first to be settled by Maroons, which had no plantation in 1739, despite the fact that it is one of the most fertile areas of Jamaica to this day, could boast of settlements "between 80 and 90," soon after the Treaty under the land settlement scheme. But, as Long knew, this number was "few in proportion to its extent."[34] The new settlement should be seen against the background that this parish had no plantations before. All the northern and northeastern parishes had more or less the same experience. To mention one more example, there was St. George, bounded on the east by Portland, on the north by the sea, and on the west by St. Mary.

The Maroons were so dominant in this parish that despite Hunter's efforts at settlement, by 1739 it possessed only four small sugar plantations, producing together 38 hogsheads of sugar.[35] Twenty years after the Treaty, if Long is correct, it had established sixty plantations, but greater development was much hampered because of the lack of roads.[36] Again, a parish like this, with some "65,000 acres of wilderness," was certainly not anywhere developed to capacity; but the new settlements should be seen in terms of what had been there, or not there, since 1655, when Britain took over the island and was raring to plant (unlike the Spaniards, who had hoped for gold) but could not because the Maroon presence, from the days of the Karmahalys, would not allow them to do so.

Altogether, it is estimated that Jamaica spent nearly £18,000 between 1739 and 1752 in the attempt to have a larger poor white population in the colony.[37] But it was the slave population that increased dramatically, depicting the new spirit of sanguinity among the large planters. The number of the slaves increased by 35,000, while that of the whites increased by only 1,500, during the above period.[38]

Meanwhile, let us return to the slave population immediately following the Treaties. It should not be difficult to understand that the slaves on the plantations did not take kindly to the Treaties. It has already been hinted that Guthrie's suspicious death, allegedly by poisoning, may have been done by disgruntled rebels, who, under the Treaty, were to be returned to their owners. This, if really done by them, would have been their first form of protest. From the slaves' point of view, there was a philosophical question. They could make the argument, as mentioned in the last chapter, that they were the loyal slaves who did not disobey rules and regulations but remained steadfast with their owners. The Maroons were the ones who not only fled the plantations but committed numerous atrocities against the plantocracy, incurring great expenses to the country. Yet the Treaties, giving them lands and quasi-independence, would seem to indicate no more and no less than recompensed disobedience. Second, from a more practical point of view, they saw the Treaties as denying them a haven of retreat from the brutality of slavery. Not only were the Maroon communities now free and semi-autonomous, but these erstwhile havens now became the most effective watchdogs against the slaves' propensity to run away. Then there is that category of slaves that could be designated perpetual truants. These would just simply take off into the woods, usually singly, and stay away without joining any existing Maroon bands, later returning to their owners. It appears that such slaves regarded these periods of respite as their well-earned and justified periodic furloughs — not unlike the vacation periods under a free system of labor. These truant slaves may well have anticipated modern labor unions with their rules and regulations of work and leisure.

Some of the slaves who repined on the injustice of the situation took matters into their hands and "met in great Bodies to consider of Mutinying."[39] It appears that one of their first rendezvous was at Spanish Town — then the capital city of the island — where "they openly and very insolently met several nights and began to form companys and name commanders amongst themselves."[40] But the cabal was soon discovered and a "troop of horse" was sent against them successfully. The most notorious were exemplarily executed,[41] and some were sent away to be sold as slaves, possibly to French or Spanish territories.

But a more ominous situation developed in 1742, involving both Maroons from Trelawny Town and slaves from an adjoining plantation belonging to one Colonel Foster. One source described these Maroons as some of Captain Cudjoe's "Head men who were disatisfied with the Treaty," and these were primarily from the Akan speaking group — as were the slaves from Foster's plantation, "of the same kind."[42] This was clearly another instance of an Akan-inspired rebellion — but with a difference. The plan between the two groups of the Coromantees — as the authorities would continue to designate them — was "to cut off all those there that were born in the woods, or came from other countries" and when this was accomplished, Foster's slaves were "to destroy the white people," presumably on the plantation, and then join their allies in the woods to become "masters" of it.[43] The difference here was that the "Coromantees" of Trelawny Town were prepared to destroy even their own kind, Cudjoe and apparently Accompong also included. This smacks of a coup d'état, and the schism might have been based on ideological grounds with a generational cleavage, Cudjoe and Accompong appearing senescent and rather conservative and overly accommodating to the plantocracy.

In the event, however, Cudjoe and Accompong soon had knowledge of the plot, "and immediately armed a sufficient number of the most faithful of their people, attacked the rebels, killed some, took others, and chased the rest home to their plantations."[44] Those they took, Maroons as well as slaves, they delivered up to justice. That Cudjoe delivered some Maroons to the island's jurisdiction meant that he thought their action deserving of the death sentence. They were accordingly tried, two of them did receive the death sentence, and two were ordered to be transported. The governor, however, exercised mercy and pardoned them, since it was their first offence. But with Cudjoe it was a different matter. On the contrary, he thought an example should be made of them, and insisted, "upon his own authority" — a manuscript source said — that they should be returned to him, whereupon he hanged the two condemned to death and returned the other two to town to be transported according to the sentence. It is said that "several" of the plantation slaves who were involved in the conspiracy were also tried and "some" were executed, the others, transported.[45]

The above incidents give telling insights into the degree to which Cudjoe was prepared to collaborate with the authorities. It would seem that Cudjoe was becoming just what the Council had predicted of the post-Treaty Maroons — that is, they would become the government's most faithful "Friends and Assistants;" in Trelawny's words, "a great addition of strength and the most useful people we can have in going after any slaves that may rise in rebellion hereafter." Governor Knowles, fourteen years after the Treaties, after visiting their towns, had asseverated: "I verily believe [the Maroons] will prove of more service to the country, then they ever were of prejudice."[46] It is no wonder that after Cudjoe's treatment of the rebels in his group and after the execution and transportation of the slaves who participated, the whole affair struck terror in the minds of the plantation slaves. We have already noted the efficiency of slave grapevines. But in this case it can also be safely assumed that the planters themselves would not have been tardy in disseminating information of this kind. If Cudjoe really did effect the execution of his men, it is a moot point whether, within the terms of the Treaty, his action would have been legal. But certainly the authorities would not quibble over a matter of this nature when Cudjoe's "justice" could be so exemplary to the slaves as well as to disgruntled Maroons. A quick glance at the pre-Treaty slave population will remind us how from the planters' perspective, the Jamaican slaves of the 1730s needed exemplary punishment of this sort. We may note the audacity of the slaves during this period, some hardly doing any work at all, some taking over and occupying plantations, and the cowed owners not daring to rebuke them. From among these we had made the acquaintance of Sam. Among the first protestors of the Treaty in Spanish Town, some of the leaders were definitely of Sam's class, described as belonging to the principal men of the island. These were considered by the authorities most "arrogant" and "insolent," insulting the whites, as had become the practice since the early 1730s, who were sent to reprove them. But the halcyon days of Sam and his fellows were now over. They were summarily crushed, and the ringleaders were executed or transported. A report mentioned that after these incidents the slaves became "more tractable than they had been for many years; since They met with no Encouragement to desert, being immediately taken up and sent to their respective Masters, agreeable to the Treaty."[47]

It need hardly be said that the planter class was delighted with Cudjoe and his assistants. A committee of the Assembly "[could] not help observing the great fidelity of the major part of the Negroes in the woods [the Maroons], shewn upon this occasion, and the use such an example must be in preventing, other Negroes, for the future, from running away in bodies, in hopes of being protected by them; this instance has also convinced the most numerous and governing body in the woods, that the Coromantees are their enemies, and would destroy them if they could, and the Coromantee slaves, the most turbulent nation of the Negroes are convinced by it, that they have nothing to trust to from them, but to be delivered up, and put to death, if they make any efforts for their liberty"[48] — a sad commentary on the post-Treaty Maroons.

The political authority, always in the advantageous position of being able to administer the ethic of reward and punishment, saw the importance of requiting acts of this kind, and looked around for "such methods . . . to be fallen upon as may effectually secure the fidelity of those negroes, who are in so good a disposition towards us."[49] Most opportunely, they had heard that the Trelawny Town Maroons were desirous of having a few cattle "to begin a breed," so they fell upon the method of indulging this wish. Two cows were allocated for Colonel Cudjoe (apparently Cudjoe was now promoted to the rank of colonel); two for Captain Accompong; one for Captain Johnny; one for Captain "Cuffie" (*sic*) "one for Quaco" (*sic*); one for "Bumbager" [?], and one for Captain Quao. [50] Of these personalities, we know all but two to have been captains under Cudjoe, during the time of the Treaty. Bumbager and Quaco might have been two new and loyal assistants in Cudjoe's group. Two bulls were also apportioned, one for Trelawny Town, the other for Accompong Town, as also a calf for each captain in Accompong Town. The apportionment of these gifts seems to suggest that the authorities continued to see Accompong Town as a sort of satellite of Cudjoe's Trelawny Town. Both leaders, too, seem to have been cooperating thus far, but with new leadership over time, this fraternal relationship clearly came to an end, and by 1795 the two communities were fighting on opposite sides. The Assembly congratulated itself for the nature of the reward it offered, observing that it was much better than giving them money, "for when that is spent, the benefit is forgot; but these will be a lasting advantage to them; and, if they increase in any great degree, they will be a pledge for their fidelity."[51]

It was at this time, too, that the yearly gift of clothes was instituted: "if a little clothes were annually allowed the several Negroes now in alliance with us, it might be a better means of securing them to us, than any other method that could be fallen upon; for that would be in the nature of an annual renewing our league with them, and the hopes and expectance of it would prevent their falling into rebellion; when, by that, they would be reduced to go naked." Ten yards of cloth were allowed to each officer and five to every other member of each community, the expense, the Assembly reckoned, would be "somewhat less than £300 per annum, which your committee think a trifling sum, in respect to the benefit that must arise to the country from the doing of it." The house also felt that every member of Cudjoe's and

Accompong's towns should receive, as a special reward, separate and apart from the yearly gifts, five yards of osnaburgh (a rough and coarse type of calico that derived its name, no doubt, from Augsburg in Germany, whence it was bought) for their recent display of loyalty to the government.[52] There is no doubt that the British understood only too well the efficacy of such gifts as a means of control.

We may also examine here Cudjoe's attitude to external enemies immediately after the Treaties.

When we bear in mind that the Spanish question was one of the critical factors that hastened the event of the Treaty, from the British government's viewpoint, then it should not be too surprising that the Spaniards were the first external enemies that Jamaica contended with immediately after the Treaty. Quao's Treaty was signed June 1739. By September of the same year war was declared between England and Spain, Jamaica was placed in a posture of defense, martial law was declared, Admiral Edward Vernon arrived in the colony in October with his fleet, and Trelawny was anxiously awaiting his command from Newcastle, which he would "execute ... with chearfulness."[53] Cudjoe, too, would seem to have tackled the Spanish situation with much enthusiasm, for "upon hearing of the Declaration of War against Spain, [he] sent one of his Principal men to the Governour for Instructions how to Dispose of his People for the Defense of the island, in Case of an Invasion, and to know in what manner He and They could otherwise be of Service ...."[54] Cudjoe later came down from the hills at the governor's order, but regretted that he could not make the sea because his head could not bear it. However, he sent "several" of his men against the Spaniards and these had already sailed as volunteers on the British ship *Louisa*. Cudjoe also promised the governor to send another reinforcement. While in town Cudjoe was introduced to the rich and influential William Beckford, who took the Maroon leader sailing on his boat, the *Wheatly*, and as if to give proof to his claim about the sea, Cudjoe became thoroughly seasick on this outing.[55] The campaigns against Spain at Cartagena and Panama all ended in disaster for the British, but there is no record of the part played by Maroon reinforcements. The importance of the story is to show the readiness with which Cudjoe entered into the external defense of the island, conformable to clause seven of his Treaty. There is no record as to whether of Quao participated in this war. The next occasion, as far as we know, when the Maroons were again associated with the island's external defense was in 1779–1780. At that time, the colony was threatened by the French under Count D'Estaing, who aimed at joining forces with the Spanish to attack Jamaica. The Maroons had assembled in readiness against the invasion, but apparently their services were not required, for the invasion was repelled by Admiral Rodney.[56]

In dealing with Maroon cooperation with the internal enemies — the slaves — one may observe here that the topic has become a sensitive one in recent times. In conducting field research among the Maroons today, one finds that some of the leaders wish to deny or to underplay the role of the Maroons in this regard. But the evidence is overwhelming that they, especially the leewards under Cudjoe, and later the Accompongs, willingly and faithfully assisted the plantocracy in the control mechanism of the slave population.

William Beckford, a large-scale planter with vested interest in the Maroon Treaties, writing in 1740 and 1741, declared with satisfaction that the Treaties had "succeeded." He was gratified that Cudjoe and his people had much confidence in the government. They were doing everything to cultivate good understanding, and they were becoming the authorities' "fast friends," and were likely to "make very good subjects"; but above all, they were keeping the woods clear of runaways. If a slave tried to escape, they were sure to bring him or his head back.[57] Another source said that "the advantages of their submission [the term that is now used by the entire slavocracy] began to be found immediately for many Negroes who used to absent and conceal themselves for sometime in the woods," were brought home to the masters. [58] It should be noted that all the early encomiums went to Cudjoe, paying tribute to the man and recognizing his authority among his people. Another manuscript source, in commenting on Cudjoe's "Fidelity and Regard to the Treaty," compared him favorably with "some European Princes who seem to regard their Engagements no longer than it Suits with Their own Interests and Conveniency."[59] And one may be excused here for straddling time and mentioning the Earl of Balcarres, some fifty odd years later, who, after ratifying a treaty with the Trelawny Town Maroons, said, "I hold the Treaty . . . ratified by me absolutely as nothing.[60]

There can be no doubt that Cudjoe saw the tracking down of runaways a very serious obligation by the terms of the Treaty. It appears that his best trained men, those who were the most reliable soldiers, were the chief ones who would go out in parties roaming the mountainous areas that were most likely to harbor runaways and returning them alive or dead (that is, the head or the ears, as the slave masters had done with them not too long ago) to the authorities. This occupation soon became an important part of their economic livelihood, for they were paid for each one captured. But it also appears to have served, equally, a strategic purpose — strategic in the sense that Cudjoe may well have been delighted to see some of the great warriors among his men occupied in a manner befitting their training and inclination. It is not unlike the situation with modern guerrillas or with liberation armies, when, after independence is won from one colonial power or another, the question of what to do with a large soldier class on hand becomes a vexing one. Some such unemployed soldier class equipped with weapons can constitute a menacing threat to tranquility. Cudjoe's warriors, with no engagement to occupy them, might have turned their frustrations inward on their own communities.

The evidence suggests that Cudjoe's men had shown more than ordinary zeal in hunting down what to them were to all intents and purposes nothing more than so many preys to be hunted with impunity. But this would not do in a slave society. After all, a slave is both capital and labor, so the bloodthirsty zeal of the Maroons had to be crushed in the interest of economy. "Being careless," wrote Dallas, "whether they brought in a runaway live, or only his head, a law was passed, with great policy, allowing, besides the usual rewards, mile-money for every runaway *produced alive.*"[61] This law of 1741 made clear its intention. It stated: "And as it is justly to be apprehended, that from the different Encouragements given by the said Laws, Cudjo and Quaw [*sic*] and the several Negroes under their Command in Trelawny and Crawford Towns ... may be induced to kill all straggling and runaway Negroes that may fall in their Way, with Intention to receive the greater Reward of Ten Pounds ... rather than to bring them in alive, and receive the lesser Reward of Ten Shilling for them as Stragglers or Runaways ...." It was therefore enacted that the attractive sum of £3 plus mile money be paid to any Maroon who returned a live runaway.[62]

It is clear that the zeal and the expertise of the post-Treaty Maroons, especially those under Cudjoe, soon made it difficult or well-nigh impossible for those truants mentioned above to indulge their habits. Dallas observed how the Maroons' trained sense of smell stood them in good stead in tracking down runaways: "they have been known to trace parties of runaway Negroes to a great distance by the smell of their firewood."[63] Trelawny was soon to be proved correct when in reporting the Treaties he had said that the "skulkers in small bodies of ten or twelve ... we cannot now fail to reduce." However, the long-term effect was another matter, as will be discussed later. There appears to have been an unquenchable thirst for liberty among these African people of Jamaica even in the teeth of the most difficult conditions. For, despite Trelawny's confidence, slaves did continue to run away and to skulk about right up to emancipation.

But before dealing with this further, let us examine how the post-Treaty Maroons affected rebellions on plantations. The propensity to rebel has been a constant feature of the Caribbean slave system, with Jamaica certainly in the lead position of rebellions. But even a planter historian like Edward Long, the staunch defender of the slave system and the implacable enemy of the blacks, could report that after the pacification made with the Maroons, "no insurrection of moment occurred for many years. Some trifling disturbances happened, and some plots were detected, but they came to nothing; and indeed the seeds of rebellion were in a great measure rendered abortive, by the activity of the Maroons, who scoured the woods, and apprehended all straggling and vagabond slaves that from time to time deserted from their owners." [64] Dallas, too, supported the view that the Maroons exerted themselves successfully in curbing potential rebellions "when small bodies of slaves have committed outrages."[65]

The first large-scale rebellion after the pacification occurred in 1760. This was one of the most well-planned, well-organized and widespread slave rebellions of the island. It took the authorities unawares, they having become somewhat lax in their security measures because of the effectiveness of their new allies and friends, the Maroons. This 1760 uprising was a classical example of an ethnic movement, engineered by the slaves of the Akan-speaking group, although the authorities had their own appellations. From the evidence, it is clear that the uprising was planned over a long period of time, given the fact that it encompassed parishes as far apart as St. Mary and St. James, embracing also St. Johns, Kingston, Clarendon, St. Dorothy, and Westmoreland, despite the communication difficulties of the time. The plan was conducted with the most determined secrecy, where "almost all the Coromantin slaves throughout the island were privy to it, without any suspicion from the Whites." Long was outraged by this "culpable inattention" on the part of the planters who neglected to keep a "vigilant eye over the Coromantins in general . . . ."[66] The key to the well-guarded secrecy was the famous Akan oath that each of the participants took, swearing to inviolable secrecy, fidelity to their chiefs, and perpetual war against the enemy — precepts to which the Maroons themselves were no strangers. It appears that these "Coromantins" under their leader, Tackey, wanted to transform the island into a free society, divided into small principalities and governed along traditional African lines as among the Akan-speaking people. It is noteworthy that they were inspired by the Maroon situation. They saw the Maroons as exemplary in having fought successfully for their freedom, and they too were determined to do the same,[67] thus fulfilling the fears of the Assembly when, as late as 1736, they opposed the signing of any peace treaty with rebel slaves, which to them would set a bad precedent for others to follow.

The rebels struck their first blow in St. Mary, and the whites, although taken unexpectedly, soon mustered all the forces at their command, including Maroons from the windwards and the leewards. Here for the first time we are given the opportunity to examine explicitly the behavior of the windwards when called upon by the slavocracy to defend the country. So far we have had no firm knowledge of their participation in the Spanish wars or in the quelling of the small domestic uprisings, where it was Cudjoe who had been praised for his zeal and loyalty. There is no doubt that the windwards continued to demonstrate a perception of themselves with respect to the slavocracy which was persistently different from that of the leewards. These Maroons from Scotts Hall, under Captain Davy, were the first to arrive at the government's rendezvous. But, they "behaved extremely ill at this juncture; ... under pretence that some arrears were due to them, and that they had not been regularly paid their head-money allowed by law, for every run-away taken up they refused to proceed against the rebels, unless a collection was immediately made for them."[68] The planters, realizing the importance of Maroon expertise in a battle of this kind, complied with what Long called the "extraordinary demand, rather than delay the service." A collection from "several gentlemen present" was made, the Scotts Hall Maroons were paid, and then they all marched and soon had their first engagement with the rebels, where they killed "a few" in the parish of St. Mary.[69] This incident, apart from showing that the windwards lacked the spirit of enthusiasm we noted in Cudjoe when called upon to serve the slave masters, is also representative of the Assembly's tardiness in making payments not only to Maroons, but also to others who rendered service to the government.

Without going into all the details of the rebellion which spread throughout the island, involving the Akan-speaking group, suffice it to say that it was crushed within six months — in the first instance, because others of the same nature broke out in 1761, to be repeated in 1765 and 1766. The speedy reduction of the rebels was due to the traitor slaves — in modern parlance, the Uncle Toms — who divulged some of the plans of the conspirators; thanks to the Maroons, especially the leewards, who fought and routed the rebels unrelentingly, although Bryan Edwards disagreed with this general view[70]; thanks to the regular troops, the militia, the seamen, the white volunteers who all, apparently, displayed more zeal and courage in this rebellion than was the case during the pre-Treaty period. But perhaps the acting governor, Sir Henry Moore, himself a planter with a stake in the system, should be especially congratulated by the plantocracy for coordinating and deploying with alacrity and intelligence all the forces at his command.[71]

In recognition of the outstanding service performed by the leeward Maroons — the Accompong and Trelawny Town groups — in these rebellions, the Assembly voted them £450 in payment of their arrears and "to encourage their future service,"[72] while the windwards — Scotts Hall, Moore Town, and Charles Town (all these new towns to be dealt with later) — received £228.4.5 altogether for their part in party service.[73] This apparently included the subvention to Captain Davy of Scotts Hall who was responsible for killing Tackey, the rebel leader of the first of these rebellions. Even so, it does not appear that the windwards fought with the same tenacity as did the leewards. After the death of Tackey, many of his group committed mass suicide rather than have themselves captured to be brutally executed, or to be reconsigned to slavery after punishment, or to be transported and sold as slaves elsewhere. Once the authorities were in control, their revenge was horrendous and incredible to those they caught. Edward Long wrote of the treatment of two of the ringleaders from St. Mary, with the ironic names of "Fortune" and "Kingston." They were hung up alive in irons on a gibbet erected in the parade of the town of Kingston. Fortune died after seven days while Kingston survived to the ninth. The morning before Kingston's death it was noticed that he was convulsed from head to foot, and a post mortem revealed that "his lungs were found adhering to the back so tightly, that it required some force to disengage them." Long went on to say that "the murders and outrages they had committed were thought to justify this cruel punishment inflicted upon them *in terrorem* to others."[74] A slave master in his slave society certainly requires a flexible and an accommodating conscience — otherwise how could he survive? It is not only the slaves who must work out survival strategies, but the slave masters too. Fortune and Kingston, being of the Akan heritage, where they were taught not to cringe under pain, however excruciating, for their part bore the ordeal stoically, "behaving all the time with a degree of hardened insolence, and brutal insensibility," wrote Long.[75] Edwards, another slave master of the period, recounting another punishment, said, "the wretch that was burned at Ballards' Valley was made to sit on the ground, and his body being chained to an iron stake, the fire was applied to his feet. He uttered not a groan, and saw his legs reduced to ashes with the utmost firmness and composure; after which one of his arms by some means getting loose, he snatched a brand from the fire that was consuming him, and flung it in the face of the executioner." Edwards, too, thought it was necessary to make a few terrible examples of the most guilty.[76]

During this period, the Assembly passed a series of stringent laws aimed at tightening security against the slaves, and another attempt was made to curtail the importation into the island of "all Fantin [Fantis], Akim [Akan], and Ashantee [Ashanti] Negroes, and all others commonly called Coromantins . . . ." All these belong, correctly, to the Akan-speaking group, and Long was convinced that their outrages discouraged "the effectual settlement of the island."[77] But the bill was not passed. Although it had become a reflex action of the plantocracy to attempt the curtailment of importation of the Akans after slave rebellions led by them, nevertheless considerations of their usefulness to the plantation economy (in terms of agricultural and other skills, their hardiness and their leadership qualities) always took precedence over security.

In counting the cost of the 1760 rebellion to the colony, it was noted that "about" sixty whites were killed, while the number of blacks executed, transported, killed in battle, or who committed mass suicides, "was not less than one thousand; and the whole loss sustained by the country, in ruined buildings, cane-pieces, cattle, slaves and disbursements was at least 100,000 pounds to speak within compass."[78] The 1761 uprising among the same group added further costs, the most substantial of which arose from the construction of barracks, and Long, perhaps in a hyperbolic outburst, said that these two together (1760 and 1761), cost the island "not much less" than that expended on the reduction of the Maroons, which was £240,000. Long would have had his reasons for wishing to inflate the sum, because he was incensed with the Assembly for not passing the bill to curtail the importation of the Akans to the island, who, to him, were bent on destroying the slave society: "instead of their savage race, the island would have been supplied with Blacks of a more docile, tractable disposition, and better inclined to peace and agriculture; so that, in a few years, the island might in all likelihood have been effectually freed of all such dangerous combinations."[79]

Long may have felt justified for this position when, in 1765 and 1766, other "Coromantin" disturbances broke out. The former was soon quelled because it was precipitated by an overly anxious slave who would not wait for final arrangements, but that of 1766 was somewhat more difficult. Here thirty-three of the Akans, most of whom were newly imported, suddenly rose up, and in the space of an hour killed nineteen members of the slave-owning class on an estate in Westmoreland. This, however, was soon crushed and the ringleaders were summarily dealt with.[80]

In evaluating the impact of the post-Treaty Maroons on the discipline of the slave population in general, one may examine this in three categories: first, their impact on the slaves' propensity to run away and form communities along African lines in remote regions as the co-opted Maroons themselves had done; second, the behavior pattern of those slaves we have already designated habitual truants; and third, the slaves' propensity to rebel on plantations, up to the time of emancipation. Viewed hierarchically, it is safe to say that, from the evidence, the Treaty Maroons were much more successful in preventing the formation of other Maroon communities than they were with the other two categories. This is not to say that Maroon or runaway communities disappeared altogether from the Jamaican scene after the Treaties. It is true that in the short-run view of things the Treaties did seem to eliminate these communities, but as we take a longer view, we begin to see that the early fears of the slaves for the Maroons would seem to have dissipated somewhat and even with the much greater risks involved, some did form out-of-the-way communities. Dallas wrote, "It is very well known that notwithstanding the vigilance and activity with which fugitives were pursued by the Maroons, a small body of them did actually establish themselves in the mountains, where they raised huts, and made provision grounds, on which some had lived for upwards of twenty years."[81] This was only one body to which Dallas referred and the community was called the "Congo Settlement," in what location of Jamaica Dallas did not mention but it appears to have been the Congo band of about thirty-five, settled deep in the woods around Black River in St. Elizabeth discovered by a party of Maroons in 1795.[82] If they lived there for "upwards of twenty years," then they were there since the 1770s or possibly some might have been escapees since the disturbances of the 1760s. If these were from the Congo, then they would not have been part of the Akan uprising but they might have taken the opportunity offered during the general upheavals to run off and form their own communities. The Maroons (whether windwards or leewards, is not clear) of course did not leave them alone. They routed them, some returning to their former owners, and apparently some joined the Trelawny Maroons in the 1795 war to be dealt with later.

Some of the most daring and vexatious to the plantocracy are those who operated singly or with very small bands. Perhaps the best known of these in Jamaica was "Three Finger'd Jack," as Makandal was the most notorious of this category in Haiti. Jack was a terror to the island for nearly two years during the late 1770s and the early 1780s. Parties proved unavailing against him and so desperate was the Assembly that a reward of £200 was offered for "the apprehending, or bringing in the head of that daring rebel, called Three Finger Jack, who hath hitherto eluded every attempt against him."[83] He was eventually killed by parties from both Moore Town and Scotts Hall — and typically, despite numerous complaints to the Assembly, they were not reimbursed until December 22, 1781, when the House finally voted them the stipulated reward of £200. But Three Finger'd Jack's fame became so widespread that his activities occasioned a play later in the century, "performed with unbounded Applause at the Theatre- Royal, Haymarket," in London, [84] and his name even found its way on the Jamaican maps up to 1828. Quaco Venter was another operator of banditti notoriety to the planters. He and a small gang, including "one of" his wives, Beauty, were said to have committed much mischief involving "several murders" for many years, until they were finally caught.[85]

The early nineteenth century witnessed the discovery of other runaway communities. Gardner wrote that in 1819 there were 2,555 runaway slaves at large. Of these, a "considerable number" had located themselves in the wild mountainous region between Kingston and Old Harbour, where they built little villages under a leader called Scipio. From their community, they would descend on plantations to rob according to their needs, and in

August 1819, a party under Major-General Marshall of the militia, with another party of Maroons, were sent out against them, but Scipio and his gang escaped. It appears that Scipio's gang was a more peripatetic one than a sedentary community as such, with banditti notoriety, if Gardner is correct.[86] The roving nature may have been dictated by security considerations, since searching Maroon parties were always on the lookout for runaways. Typical of Gardner's writing, it is somewhat obscure whether or not the second party, under Marshall, was successful against Scipio. Another village in Trelawny, said to have been formed around 1812, with the arresting name of "Me-no-sen-you-no-Come" — still to be found on the map of Jamaica — suggests the impudent defiance of this group. Here they constructed houses that "were well built, shingled and floored," with a population of only nine men, eight women, and four children. They lasted from 1812 to 1824 when, after an incident in which two white men were shot — possibly these two white men visited, unannounced — a party was sent out against them. This party, against seventeen adult men and women and four children, consisted of six companies of the militia and a party of Maroons, altogether amounting to 270 armed men, attacked and routed the village.[87]

Thus, despite the bold efforts of these people, devoted to freedom, it does not appear that any of these villages survived up to emancipation, largely because of the co-opted Maroons' activities against them. But this should be seen as tentative, because the fact of not finding records of them for the next ten years prior to emancipation does not mean that they might not have existed — in great seclusion and secrecy, which would have been critical for their survival.

The situation seems somewhat different for the next category, the truant slaves. By "truancy" is to be understood those slaves who ran away *without any intention of staying away permanently*, who would return to their owners after a period which could be from a few days to a year or two. Their absence was generally for the purpose of visiting friends, relatives, spouse, or children, or, in some cases it was just to defy authority, or simply to take a break from the rigor of plantation life. Gardner's figure of 2,555 runaways in 1819 may have included truants who would eventually return to their owners, but what is certain is that the evidence is overwhelming that truancy continued up to emancipation. The only element that is mystifying about it all is the size of the truant population at large in 1834. It appears, too, that running away to fend for themselves permanently outside the slave masters' hold, like truancy, continued up to emancipation. From the evidence, it would appear that running and staying away, always a process requiring skills, became much more differentiated, involving more the urban and the skilled slaves, as emancipation approached. Some of these hovered about certain towns, passing for free, and eking out a precarious living according to their trades; some, especially the women, became higglers and hucksters, thus making themselves rather conspicuous.[88]

A few tentative suggestions may be offered for this new pattern in the runaway business. First, there is the obvious one that fear of the Maroons would make the runaway choose other options rather than making for the woods to set up new hegemonies. It is noteworthy that some of these potential runaways saw mass suicide as their option after the Treaty. This is not to say that suicide had not been an expression of protest or escape before the Treaties, but there is much evidence to suggest that it increased after the Maroons were co-opted into the slave masters' security mechanism. The large number of Tackey's adherents who committed suicide after the death of their leader, when they thought the odds were weighted too heavily against them, might not have done so before the Treaties. These, as happened with the Maroons, would most probably have disappeared in the fastness of the mountains, have lain low, and then have reappeared later. Now the woods were no longer the haven they used to be. The great number of laws passed throughout the 1770s, '80s, and '90s to prevent slaves from deserting and departing from the island, or to prevent the inveigling or enticing them away by captains of ships, or "by persons wickedly disposed," would seem to attest to the slaves' wider options.[89]

As said before, most of those enterprising slaves who took off in canoes tried to make their way to Cuba. In 1788, for instance, Richard Martin of St. Mary had eleven of his slaves — eight males and three females — elope to Cuba, and despite strenuous efforts to redeem them, he was unsuccessful. The Spanish officials maintained on such occasions that their Catholic religion saw to it that no slave eloping from Jamaica would be given up unless it could be certified on oath that he or she was guilty of murder. The following year John Wilcox McGregor of St. Ann had the same response from Cuba, when "several" of his slaves stole a canoe belonging to a pilot at St. Ann's Bay and paddled to freedom. In pursuing his slaves later, McGregor actually saw one of them in the house of the governor at St. Jago de Cuba, but the governor refused to release the ex (?) slave, on the same grounds, giving the Jamaican a copy of the said Spanish law. Both men lost not only their slaves but also what they considered large sums of money expended to retrieve them.[90]

Further, there appears to have been an increase in the number of female runaways after the abolition of the slave trade in 1808. The amelioration component that went with abolition gave the slaves generally, but especially the women, some rights, and in some way or another they became aware of them and were not reticent in making the slave masters aware of this. Then again, there was the factor of fertility. The women soon became aware of their special responsibility as procreators for the labor force of the plantations, because of the inelasticity of supply of slaves resulting from abolition. These two objective factors gave the women an overweening sense of their own importance, and officials, from governors down to overseers, complained bitterly of the feminine "tongue" — and their "impudence." Some of these women would now find running away less intimidating and some took off singly, others with their children.

Also, as emancipation approached, the runaways, men or women, were mostly creoles, in contrast to the African preponderance during the pre-abolition period. It was the newly arrived Africans who were more likely to run away and to set up hegemonies in the woods along African lines. The creole runaways, with their new skills applicable to the plantation regime, were more likely to try to edge their way into the wider society, utilizing these skills in the process. In addition to all these factors, there is the practical one that the urban runaway slaves would probably not adapt too well to the exigencies of the mountainous, pastoral life of the Maroon — even if the Maroons had not been bent on tracking them down.

The laws of the island from 1749 into the next century reflected the plantocracy's increasing concern over the attraction of the town for their runaways. St. Jago de la Vega, Port Royal, and Kingston had, apparently, a large number of improvised huts and houses, built on lots of land "detached and separate" from the houses of the owners, where slaves and all manner of undesirable persons, as perceived by the planters, were congregating. A law of 1770 tried to remedy the "inconvenience" that might arise from such huts and houses, which had become a "Refuge and receptacle for Thieves, loose, idle and runaway Negroes and other Slaves, belonging to the said Towns and other Parishes [giving] an Opportunity of forming Cabals and Conspiracies, dangerous to the public Peace and Security . . . ."[91] The law ordered owners to keep a constant check on these places, to curtail their erection, and to pull down those known to be occupied by undesirables. Other laws of a similar nature tried to inflict more severe punishments on runaway slaves, who "have taken Shelter in the Towns or other Places; and . . . by their long and frequent Desertion, great Encouragement is given to others to follow their Example, which may prove of dangerous Consequence to this Island, if not timely prevented." It was accordingly enacted that the death penalty be inflicted on every slave age eighteen and over, whether born on the island or imported and resident there for three years, who ran away for six months.[92]

When we look at the post-Treaty pattern of rebellions on plantations, then we must conclude that the Maroons were also not very effective in preventing them, over the long-term period. It was only the first twenty-odd years after the Treaty that saw the slaves at their most quiescent. That is, in terms of violent rebellions at any rate, because we must remember that the more passive and subtle resistance of untold types was a constant feature. We saw that the few outbursts that took place immediately after the Treaties were soon quashed with Maroon assistance. But a new generation was appearing on the plantations, to whom the Maroons were not the fearsome creatures they had been to their elders. Tackey, for instance, was described as "a young man of good stature, and well made,"[93] and whether he was creole or newly arrived, the argument would still stand, since, naturally, the newly imported would also have no knowledge of the Maroons. Thus between the new generation and the African-born, the latter being the very source and inspiration of slave rebellions, it would seem that the propensity to rebel had greatly increased with the approach of emancipation. Patterson has listed the numerous slave rebellions from 1760 to 1831, most of which were led by people from the Akan-speaking group, the last one being the exception.[94]

The 1831 rebellion in Jamaica, the most organized, the most widespread, embracing some 20,000 slaves "with a much larger number of sympathizers," and transcending ethnic particularities, the most damaging to the plantocracy, costing well over a million pounds to property and "over 161,570.0.0 pounds spent" to suppress it, the very last slave rebellion of Jamaica, as if by the logic of teleology, was led by creoles.[95] This rebellion was a critical factor in helping to bring about the demise of slavery in the British Caribbean. [96] And the demise of slavery was to lessen, dramatically, the importance of the Maroons to the property-holding class in the colony — although they were to continue to assist the authorities, under freedom, in quelling uprisings on the island. The most notable was in 1865 when they assisted the government in putting down a peasant uprising under the leadership of Paul Bogle, in Morant Bay, and Governor Eyre paid glowing tribute to them. "[T]o the fidelity and loyalty of the Maroons it is due that the negroes did not commit greater depredations, and that the rebellion has not been a more protracted one. It is owing to them also, under the able indefatigable former Captain, now Colonel Fyfe, that the chief rebel, Paul Bogle, was captured, and that the recesses of the mountain fastnesses were searched, and the insurgents captured, destroyed or driven from them."[97] However, a Royal Commission of the British government of the day and many writers of the period have all condemned the brutal means the Jamaican government employed in crushing what started out as a peaceful demonstration among an oppressed peasantry, despite Eyre's rhetoric.[98] This being so, the Maroons' collaboration in quelling this uprising is not easily forgotten by the wider Jamaican society. On occasion, it makes for feelings of hostility toward the Maroons to this day. This is especially so since Paul Bogle, upon independence of the island, has been made one of its national heroes, and his uprising of 1865 is seen by many Jamaicans today as a most courageous act by a peasantry with a long history of insensitive neglect by the ruling classes.

Chapter 6

Maroon Communities and the Colonial Government

From the last chapter we saw that both Treaties seemed uncertain about the names and number of Maroon settlements. The only town mentioned in Cudjoe's Treaty is Trelawny Town, which was the new appellation of Guthrie's. In Quao's Treaty no town is specifically named, but the word "town" is mentioned only once, in clause three, stipulating that four white persons were to reside in "their Town." Had Adair or Bennett renamed Quao's territory, then conceivably we would have had a capital name place in this Treaty also. We do not know, for instance, the name of the town where Quao signed his Treaty. Even Thicknesse, a hostage of this place, stuck stubbornly to the term "the town" or Captain Quao's "town" in his *Memoirs*. Official designations of specific windward towns did not commence until the ratification of Quao's Treaty in 1740. Additional clause four of this ratified document mentioned certain towns when stipulating that four white persons should reside "at *Crawford's Town* and *New Nanny Town*, who have lately surrendered and submitted themselves to the Government." But we still do not know which of these towns Quao occupied at the time of his Treaty — although we have circumstantial, and only circumstantial, evidence to suggest that it might have been Crawford Town; nor can we fully understand the term "New Nanny Town," since it soon practically disappeared from the official documents.

Prior to the Treaties, we know that the windwards had many towns, the most important being Nanny Town, and others — Guy's Town, Molly's Town, Diana's Town, among others. But at the time of Quao's Treaty we do not even know for certain if any of these old towns existed. We already knew that Nanny Town or "the Great Negro town" had a most turbulent existence in the early 1730s, being captured by the parties, retaken by the Maroons, only to be captured again by the government, who built barracks and other fortifications and encouraged new settlements there.[1] By the early 1740s the names of four towns for both communities emerged: Accompong or Accompong's and Trelawny Towns for the leewards, and Crawford's or Crawford and New Nanny Towns for the windwards. But later, other names began to appear, and Nanny Town or New Nanny Town ceased to exist for official purposes. The new names that came on the scene were: Scots or Scot's or Scotts or Scott's Hall, which will be rendered "Scotts Hall" in this work, in keeping with its present name; Moore or Moors or Mures Town, which, likewise, will be given its present usage, "Moore Town"; Charles Town and New Crawford Town, for the windwards, while Furry's or Furry's Town was added to those already existing for the leewards. Of these towns, only Accompong Town (of the leewards) and Moore Town and Scotts Hall (of the windwards) still exist today.

Now how did these new towns come about? Let us first deal with the windwards, whose situation is somewhat more complicated — and it may well be for this reason that Dallas did not even attempt to sort them out, although he tried his hand at the leewards.[2] We remind ourselves that their land grant was rather vague, clause two merely stating that "Captain Quao and his People shall have a certain Quantity of Land given to them . . . ." Neither amount nor location was specified, and the authorities may have wished to manipulate this flexibility to their own ends. These windwards were occupying some of the most fertile areas on the island, and white settlers were determined to obtain these lands for themselves. In addition to fertile lands, there was the irony that Maroon settlements were now seen as magnets attracting white settlers for security reasons, and these white settlers were pressing onto the windwards as they were doing with the leewards. It appears that some of these settlers, in establishing their estates in proximity to the Maroons, were not averse to squeezing them out from the more fertile areas, thus confining them to the less cultivable parts. And this could be more easily done with the windwards, who had no land boundary. "As we are now Settling Estates near their Towns, they must be drove away soon from their Settlement and kept in Subjection,"[3] was the remark of one white planter, a sentiment that may have been most representative. But the windward Maroons, for their part, perhaps realizing that they were the first settlers in these areas — the autochthons, as we called them elsewhere — were equally stubbornly determined about their concept of what and where the boundary lines should be. These two positions were to lead to disputes.

As anticipated, the windward groups soon began to experience dissension — or "disorders, tumults and disturbances," according to the authorities. And the colonial government saw this as an opportunity to pass laws with portentous titles, like that for the better regulating "such of the rebellious Negroes as submitted to terms,"[4] and so forth. But for our purposes, the first instance we have of the formation of a new town as a result of these dissensions was in 1751, twelve years after the Treaties.

In this year, a message from the governor to the House mentioned that "about" two years ago (1749?), dissension arose among the Crawford Town Maroons. Some twenty-six of them desired to live separately from the rest, and a St. Mary planter, one Mr. Peete, had given his consent for them to settle on some lands he possessed close to Scotts Hall. The governor was quick to approve, "believing that a settlement of those Negroes in that part of the country, would conduce to the public safety." A committee of the whole house met on the issue the same day — reflecting its perceived importance — and recommended favorably, reiterating to the governor that such a settlement would be "for the public good," and the accounts committee was empowered to treat with the proprietor. A motion was also passed recommending that the adjoining lands to Scotts Hall be used for the settling of white families, according to the new policy of treating Maroon settlements as a part of the security force of the island. By the following month, the accounts committee could report that an agreement was made to purchase "the land called Scotts Hall," some 500 acres, for £600. This was executed in November 1751, but apparently the land was not officially surveyed until 1775,[5] and not 1820, as some said.[6] The surveyor of 1775, William Smellie, charged the government £115.18.6, which payment he received in December of that year.[7] But this was not to end the question of land boundaries between the Maroons of this town and the white settlers, and it is certain that Scotts Hall is one of the most surveyed of Maroon communities, most of which surveys took place in the nineteenth century. In some instances the surveys were requested by the Maroons upon claims that white settlers were trespassing on their lands; in other instances, the opposite was the case.

The most notorious and sustained of these land disputes was that of 1862 — which had its antecedent in 1844. In this year, Edward McGeachy, then crown surveyor, "ran lines" — to employ the term of the period — and apparently encroached on the Hill Side settlement (white families) by some seven acres and twenty perches (about 110 yards). The proprietors of Hill Side objected to McGeachy's survey and this became a constant source of disputes and wranglings. Finally, Roger Swire, a proprietor, on behalf of the Hill Side settlement, employed Thomas Harrison, then crown surveyor, to try to settle the dispute by what they conceived as a compromise. Swire was prepared to give up a parcel of just over two acres, which the Maroons claimed, if they in turn would give up a parcel of just over four acres, which, according to Harrison, was really unsurveyed lands that the Maroons were occupying. But the Maroons would have none of this. The surveyor complained that he was "interrupted and prevented from completing the Survey by the Maroons."[8] And it was at this point that the Maroon leaders sent a petition to the governor.

They wondered what right had Mr. Harrison

> to take land from Scotts Hall and other of the Maroons to give over to Hill Side seeing that it was Mr. Harrison himself some 19 years ago in the presence of many of the Maroons who are still alive and can testify to the truth and notwithstanding the true lines have been pointed out and Mr. Harrison reminded of his own marks still they persisted (both Mr. Harrison and Swire) to encroach on Scotts Hall land which consequently induced us to take up the chains [claims?].
>
> We further beg to submit to your Excellency and beg to be informed by return of bearer if Mr. Harrison is instructed by the Government to survey and sell the remaining portion of the unsurveyed land of Scotts Hall land, the greatest portion of which are in cultivation and in possession of the Maroons, Mr. Harrison having told us that the Governor has authorized him to sell the whole remaining portion of Scotts Hall land.[9]

The uncompromising tone as well as the asperity of this petition is representative of the Maroon attitude to land throughout all the communities. Up to this period, 1862, the unsurveyed lands had not yet been fully patented and occupied by the whites as the Assembly intended. In looking at the diagram one sees, apart from the Hill Side settlement to the southwest, only two adjacent plots, one belonging to Thomas Hamith and family who obtained his legal title only in 1851 (but the Maroons claimed part of this) and the other patented by Patrick Stewart and family in 1844. That more whites had not taken the opportunity of settling here — a location with an easy access, very fertile, lacking the awesome acclivity of other settlements, and within easy reach of Kingston — must have been largely due to the bellicosity of the Maroons.

Another feature of this dispute, which we shall encounter again and again when dealing with similar cases, is the factor of having unsurveyed lands contiguous to Maroon settlements. This was surely asking for trouble. Accustomed as they were to roam in uncharted lands, setting up communities, abandoning them, out of necessity in some cases, out of choice at other times, with their expansive grazing pastures, unsurveyed land about them

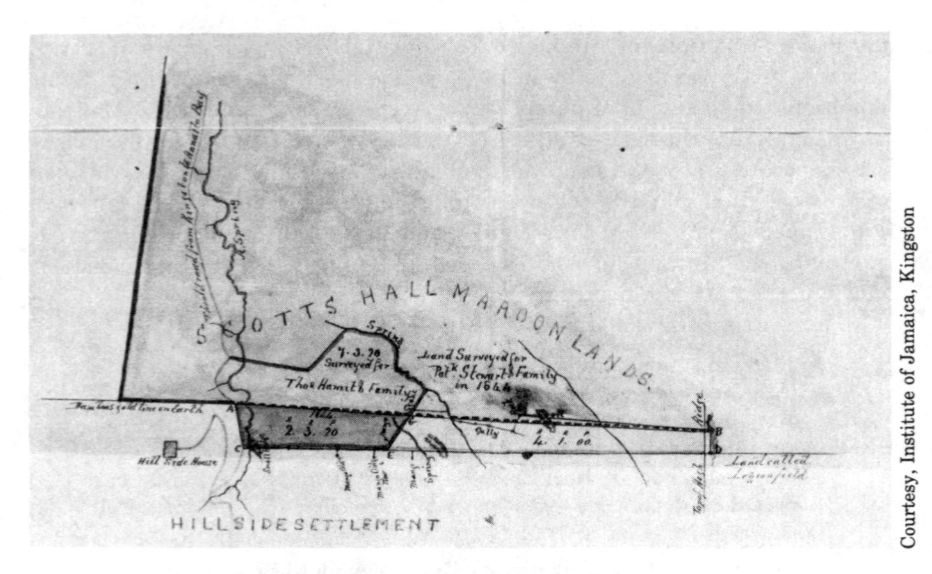

Courtesy, Institute of Jamaica, Kingston

The disputed Scotts Hall lands, surveyed 1862

was fair game. This attitude to such lands is well demonstrated in the last paragraph of their petition — "the unsurveyed land of Scotts Hall land, ... in cultivation and in possession of the Maroons." The years have not changed much their attitude to land. In conducting field work among the Scotts Hall Maroons, this author found the land question still a burning one. They still complain of illegal appropriation of their lands, and worse, of having to pay land taxes. For reasons not made clear, they are the only existing Maroons who pay a land tax. This was their insistent claim.

Charles Town also had its checkered history. Like Scotts Hall, this town also splintered from Crawford Town. Crawford Town, we may remind ourselves, is somewhat shadowy. We first encountered it upon the ratification of Quao's Treaty. We know that its location was in the parish of Portland, along the Buff Bay River. When Trelawny reported its population to have been 470, including men, women, and children, we cannot be certain that this was an accurate account, taken as it was by "notches on a stick," by a captain. And even if this number is accurate we do not know, if the Treaty town was Crawford Town and, if so, whether the number of 470 applied only to this one town. For there is every reason to believe — from a systematic perusal of maps and from surveyor's diagrams and comments, as well as from the legal documents — that there was more than one windward town at the time of Quao's Treaty. For instance, the legal documents ratifying Quao's Treaty made such vague references as "and all other Towns of rebellious Negroes" or "and any other of the rebellious Towns, who have submitted to Terms."[10] However it may be, we know that around 1754 Crawford Town was experiencing another state of tumult, and it appears that in this case the situation was much more violent than that which led to the formation of Scotts Hall. We have a rather fragmentary account of Crawford Town being burnt by the "rebellious Negroes," and one Edward Crawford was murdered. The identity of Edward Crawford, whether a Maroon or a white settler, is not clear. But apparently whites were also involved, for we find William Kennedy and Richard Godfrey, both whites, making claims for losses they sustained in this affray. The superintendent, too, John Kelly, swore that after the murder of Edward Crawford, when the town was burnt, he himself sustained losses to the tune of £63.4.6.[11] We have only this tantalizingly imprecise account of the fracas, but it is the consequence that is of importance to us for it is clear that it resulted in the formation of Charles Town.

In March 1754, even before the bloodshed in December of the same year, Governor Knowles approached one Colin McKenzie who had a parcel of land in St. George containing 146 acres. Knowles wanted the land "to settle thereon a Negrotown, for such of the Negroes that before belonged to Crawford Town." McKenzie agreed, the land was apparently bought, and a town was built there called Charles Town (also called New Crawford Town for a long time), three miles north of Crawford Town. Two years later we find McKenzie petitioning the Assembly for not having been recompensed. But in the meantime, the House received a petition from one Peter Woodhouse, claiming that the land which McKenzie thought he was selling, belonged to his brother, a minor, and as guardian he was demanding the sum to be paid for the land.[12] When a committee of the House looked into the matter, they found Woodhouse's allegations to be correct, and McKenzie soon admitted that he had no claim to the land. For one reason or another, the House did not pay the guardian, but resolved November 18, 1757 that the money, £292 (for 146 acres of land at 40/– per acre) was to be paid to Dally Woodhouse, the minor, upon his making a title to the land and that he should be paid interest on this sum from May 19, 1755.[13] Nothing more was heard of this complicated transaction until October 1770. Here we find another claimant to the land, one John Henderson. He stated that because of the minority of the true proprietor, "and on other accounts," the parcel of land in dispute was never purchased nor allotted to the use of the Maroons. What he probably should have said is that the Assembly, as usual, had not made good its resolution. It was soon discovered by the House that the minor had in fact sold the land to John Henderson since

March 1765, and when resurveyed, the "plat" contained 333 1/2 acres, of which 206 1/2 acres were occupied by the Maroons at Charles Town.

The House again resolved to purchase the latter amount at a "reasonable valuation," rather than suffer the Maroons to be removed again from their settlement. But the committee that treated with Henderson rather unjustly referred to the Maroons as having "encroached" upon the land, when in fact it was Governor Knowles who sent them there in 1755 — and they, for their part, had actually been complaining of trespassing on "their lands" since 1770. The House, with its multi-claimants in mind, demanded legal titles and "full and sufficient security against any other claimants," before the 206 acres were purchased at 40/– per acre for £412.[14] And the legal points must have been met, because we find William Smellie, crown surveyor, submitting to the House his costs, £122.17.5 1/2, for surveying Charles Town. It was at this time, 1775, that he had also submitted his costs for the same task done for Scotts Hall.[15]

But surveying Maroon lands did not mean the end of border disputes — largely because of the Maroon attitude to unsurveyed lands. One year after the official survey, we find George Gray, "and other the Maroon Negroes of Charles Town" petitioning the Assembly on the subject of land space. They claimed that when they were first settled "about 1756," there were no white settlers adjoining them, hence "they were able to raise large quantities of goats, hogs and other stock, so as to live very comfortably [but] within these few years past, several sugar works and other plantations have been settled in the neighbourhood of their town, and upon the lands where their stock formerly used to range; by which means, they cannot raise stock of any kind, without encroaching on the neighbouring plantations, as the land allotted for them is steep and hilly; this has occasioned many disputes between them and the white settlers, by their stock trespassing on the cane-pieces, and the cattle of the white settlers ruining their provision grounds."[16]

As with the Scotts Hall petition, Maroon attitude to land was even more clearly demonstrated in terms of nuance and conception. It has not changed since the 1670s when they were establishing their redoubts in these same parts and would not brook intruders, neither in the settled areas, with their houses, domestic gardens, and animals, nor in what they conceived as their purlieus. Regardless of surveyor's lines, they saw the environs of their towns as belonging to them as of right for hunting and grazing, or as possible retreats into which groups could splinter off, African fashion, to form new communities, as we shall see in the case of Trelawny Town. And now, as in the 1670s, planters were settling "in the neighbourhood of their town," and how could they live "comfortably" without expansive grazing areas? Before the Treaty they would have known exactly how to deal with the situation, successfully. Now they wrote petitions, continued to encroach, and, in this case, asked to be relocated. They did not wish to put the country to further expense but "a run of land" on either side of the Spanish River, about six miles from their present town, Charles Town, had been offered to them in exchange for their present settlement. Situated as it was, this land, they felt, would enable them to raise stock without inconvenience to themselves, and there would be no trespassing on their neighbors. They pointed out that this would remove every cause of murmurings and disputes "which is now too frequent between them and the white settlers in their neighbourhood."[17]

This request was not granted, and the apologetic beginning of their petition is well understood when it is borne in mind that just a year before, October 23, 1775, the government had rather generously granted these Charles Town Maroons some 670 acres of King's Land or Crown Land.[18] It appears that 600 acres were adjacent to their settlement, and the remaining seventy acres were closer to old Crawford Town. Thus, with their original 206 acres bought from John Henderson, they should now have had in their possession 876 acres. But a surveyor's note tells us that when the Henderson's land was later surveyed (always a troublesome plot), it contained only 173 acres, being covered by Prior Plats."[19] In any event, in Maroon land affairs no given acreage should be taken for granted, for when the 1794 survey of Charles Town was taken, it was discovered that they were occupying 94 acres of land belonging to the Kildair property. And from their long possession of it they were "unwilling to give [it] up, having their provisons chiefly upon that land; therefore," the superintendent wrote, "in order to pacify the Maroons, I was under the necessity of stoping Mr. Graham, the surveyor, from proceeding upon the lines, till a fair statement of their claims, should be laid before Your Honor."[20] The superintendent was certain that the Kildair proprietors had all the legal right on their side. It is not clear what became of this dispute, but it was probably "quietened down" through interpersonal persuasions and negotiations. We cannot say these boundary disputes were solved, because we continue to see claims from both Maroons and white settlers throughout the nineteenth century, not unlike those we have already encountered, but time and space will not allow us to mention them all. But it is interesting to note that Charles Town, as a Maroon community, was not named on the maps until 1832. Before this date the cartographers persistently identified Charles Town as "New Crawford Town."[21]

Let us now turn to Moore Town or Muretown, whose position Edward Long praised. Long observed that they first occupied "a place called Nanny Town; which they afterwards deserted."[22] He felt that their new location, as mentioned above, was much better situated for giving protection to estates on either side of the Rio Grande. Long wrote in 1776, but it is not clear when Moore Town came into existence. It seems clear though, that, like the Crawford Town Maroons, they occupied unpatented lands, which suggests that they existed as a group before the Treaties, and Long may well be correct in seeing them as an outflow of the old Nanny Town — as Crawford Town too may have been. We have official documents referring to Moore Town since the 1760s, but with respect to the usual land disputes endemic to Maroon communities, we did not hear of them until 1781. In this year, we find a petition from one John Cosens complaining that he is possessed of land and plantations in Portland contiguous to Moore Town and he was desirous to be certain about boundaries. To effect this, and not wishing to encroach on Maroon lands, he employed surveyors "at a considerable expence" to ascertain respective claims. But the Maroons "as often prevented the surveyors from proceeding upon this business," hence he was still "kept in the dark" with respect to the claims of the Maroons. He was of the opinion that 1,000 acres were "supposedly" set apart for the Maroons, but the lines were not known. Then, as should be expected, the petitioner said that the Maroons "set up a boundless and arbitrary claim to all lands situate in the neighbourhood of their town," in order, he was told, to discourage settlers coming close to them, so that they could have a "boundless range for the purpose of hunting."[23]

The petitioner gave it that the Moore Town Maroons were not a corporate body; they did not hold any legal title to any lands. This is an interesting observation which reflects the ambiguous nature of Moore Town, and the Assembly's reply to this petition will certainly cast some light on the relationship between Moore Town and the Nanny land grant to be dealt with below. The petitioner ended by requesting a surveyor to ascertain boundaries, and should the Maroons be seen to be occupying their lands, then they would be prepared to allow them to have its use for another fifteen months, a period they felt sufficient for planting and raising provisions.[24]

The House took the petition seriously, and a special committee was appointed, empowered to call for persons and papers; the committee was also instructed to look into the conduct of all the superintendents "and into the abuses committed by those negroes [the Maroons]."[25] In less than three weeks the committee reported.

It "appear[ed]" to the committee that the Moore Town Maroons were entitled to 1,000 acres of land, but only 500 acres "appear[ed]" to have been granted and laid out. This is a critical statement although even the committee does not seem certain about this 1,000 acres for the Moore Town Maroons. (This author has found no trace of this amount of land being granted to the Moore Town Maroons before this date.) But when it appeared to the committee that 500 acres were granted and laid out, then it seems a reasonable conjecture that they were referring to that intriguing grant of land to Nanny. This is the only piece of circumstantial evidence one finds that connects (not making them identical yet) Moore Town with Nanny's grant of land, despite the many undocumented affirmations that assume these two towns were identical from the beginning. The next statement of the committee would seem to confirm propinquity of the settlements but not sameness at this point, although we could posit kinship affiliation between the two communities granted the Akan/African heritage of the Maroons. The report mentioned a piece of land vested in the Crown lying between the land already laid out and the River "Grandee." And already the Maroons had settled upon part of this land, which Charles Douglas, a white settler, thought himself possessed of for "upwards of ten or twelve years." Douglas was willing to give up this piece of land if the Maroons would give him in return equal quantity to the northeast where he had another plot, and the Maroons agreed.[26]

The hypothesis (for so it must be called until further evidence) advanced here is that this arrangement with Charles Douglas made the original Nanny land grant of 500 acres contiguous to Moore Town, which had its own existence prior to the Nanny grant. This hypothesis accepts Edward Long's claim that Moore Town was formed after the great Nanny Town was deserted by the Maroons in the 1730s, thus receiving no official land grant, as Crawford Town would see itself entitled to, granted that it *was* Quao's Town at the time of the Treaty. When John Cosens mentioned that the Moore Town Maroons were not a corporate body and did not hold any legal title to any land, he may have known the true facts of the case.

The committee recommended that the governor appoint a surveyor to effectuate the exchange between Charles Douglas and the Maroons and to ascertain the boundaries of the "whole 1000 acres allowed the said Maroons by law at Moore town"[27] — but they did not mention the specific law and the date thereof. The committee may have been confusing Accompong's 1,000 acres with this situation. (Those of us who have perused the numerous official documents relating to Maroon affairs will know how careless or forgetful the authorities — or perhaps their amanuenses — can be in recording Maroon personal or place names.) Two surveyors were recommended, one to be appointed by the government and the other by the Maroons themselves, so as to allay their fears and suspicions. For this, the Maroons recommended Dougald or Dugall McPherson, who was apparently also accepted by the government. McPherson accordingly ran the lines, and his notes on the diagram should come as no surprise to us. In submitting this plan of "Muretown," July 31, 1782, to the governor, he said that the "above Platt contains 1270 Acres of Land, more than was granted by the Honourable House of Assembly for the use of the Maroons but as the present Survey cut off great part of their Provision Grounds it was out of my Powers and out of the Power of the Superintendents to [convince?] them to narrow their bounds without raising disputes of the most disagreeable Nature and it has been in their possession forty years and the survey now legally compleated without injuring any of the Neighbouring Settlers. I made my returns and hopes his Honour will take matters into his Considerations."[28] As usual, the House was tardy in reimbursing MacPherson the fees for surveying and his expenses for journeying to and from Moore Town, which he had computed at £370.4.11 1/2, as his petition of November 1782 explained.[29] The following month the Assembly paid him £310.4.7 1/2, charging that some deductions "ought to be made" for surveying 1,000 acres of land "allowed the Maroons of Moore town."[30] Thus there is a discrepancy between the diagram acreage and the Assembly's stated amount — as there is with MacPherson's petition and his very professional diagram with its 1,270 acres of surveyed lands. In his petition he would seem to be making every effort to stress the 1,000 acres the Assembly had in mind. He reminded the House of its request to appoint a surveyor for "Moore Town's 1,000 acres," and he, being appointed, ran the lines of the said 1000 acres.[31] It could be that he was trying to underemphasize the excess of land he found in Moore Town — no wonder the Maroons approved of him so readily.

However it was, if our hypothesis is correct, then MacPherson should have surveyed 1,500 acres and not 1,270, as is clearly shown and stated on the diagram. But, Maroon land figures never seem to agree. Perhaps the exchange with Charles Douglas went against them in acreage as they gained the continuous land face which they probably had been yearning for all these years and which probably was the primary factor that made them resist the surveying of their land for such a long time. All Maroon communities, at some time or another, were opposed to surveyors; Moore Town, however, seems unique in opposing them in such a sustained manner. We know that in some cases, in Scotts Hall and in Charles Town for instance, the Maroons themselves asked to have the lands surveyed to ascertain boundaries. It does not appear that Moore Town experienced the same constant border disputes as did the other Maroon towns, possibly because of their isolated position. There is some mention of some internal problem with Captain Clash in 1760, even before the community was surveyed. It appears that Clash and some followers lived at Bath for a period, but it is strange that at a time when there was a general willingness on the part of the government to form Maroon communities, Clash did not form one.[32]

And now we come to the most intriguing land grant of all. This was made to "a certain Negro woman called Nanny and the people now residing with her." Entered in the official book of patents, where records of land grants to white settlers are kept, and written in the elaborately formal language of the day reserved for such legal documents, with no attention paid to punctuation whatsoever, we find the document, beginning: "George the Second by the Grace of God of Great Britain France and Ireland King and of Jamaica Lord Defender of the faith and To all to whom these presents shall come Greetings Know Ye that We for and in consideration that a certain Negro woman called Nanny and the people residing with her have Transported themselves and their Servants and Slaves into our said Island in pursuance of a Proclamation made in the Reign of his late Majesty King Charles the Second of Blessed memory and for their encouragement to become our planters there and for divers other good Causes and Considerations ...," the document plods on. It then gave "unto the said Nanny and the people now residing with her and their heirs and assigns a certain parcel of Land containing five hundred acres in the parish of Portland bounding North South and East on Kings Land and West on Mr. John Stevenson ...." This land, the document said, was vested in the Crown by two acts of Jamaica passed in the 1720s encouraging "white people to come over and become settlers," especially in the north-east section of the island. It was in the north east, close to the town of Titchfield in the parish of Portland where the most speedy settlement was encouraged, that the land was laid out and allotted to Nanny and her people. Everything on the land — "Edifices Trees woods underwoods ways waters rents profits commodities Emoluments advantages Easements and heredits [hereditaments?]" — belonged to them, as well as all mines and minerals, gold and silver only excepted.

But the said Nanny and her people, "their heirs and assigns," must for evermore pay a "yearly and every year," rent of £1.0.10 current money of Jamaica on the feast day of St. Michael the Archangel and the annunciation of the Blessed Virgin Mary," in addition to a twentieth part of the clear yearly profits of all base mines that may be found on their allotted land. Also, Nanny and her people and their heirs "shall upon any insurrection mutiny rebellion or invasion which may happen in our said Island during her or their residence on the same be ready to Serve us and shall actually serve us ...in arms upon the Command of our Governor or Commander in Chief ...." Nanny and her people and their heirs must also "keep and maintain five white men" on their land, in conformity with the acts for increasing the number of whites on the island. It was also pointed out that this was a legal document, made good, firm and valid after enrollment in the chief court of administration, within six months of the undermentioned date (August 5, 1740). The land grant received the Governor's signature on August 5, 1740, was surveyed on December 22 1740, certified by the commissioners of surveys on December 23 of the same year, and enrolled in the patents on April 20, 1741.[33]

This fascinating document naturally raises many questions, but before we deal with them, let us first compare it with similar grants to white planters. The comparison must be done with those of identical dates, since a difference in time could also mean different land policies. The presentation for the white planters — that of Thomas Mathew, for instance, entered in the patents on the same date, April 20, 1741, as that of Nanny's — is more or less the same, with the automatic difference in gender and number. But there are also two other interesting differences that could be interpreted as discriminating in favor of the white settlers. The first is to be noticed where the document is citing the laws of the 1720s encouraging whites to settle in the island. In Nanny's case, the document said, "an act to encourage white people to come over and become setlers," while Mather's said, "an act for introducing of white People unto this Island for subsisting them for a certain time and providing — [sic] Land that they may become Setlers." Mather's document definitely holds out promise of assistance for a period, and the space between the words "providing" and "Land" permitted flexibility for dividing lands according to family size. Nanny was proffered no such assistance. Second, Nanny and her people — how many, we do not know — had to pay a land tax of £1.10 for 500 acres of land, while Mather was asked to pay 8/9 on 210 acres, thus making the latter proportionately better off.

We have already mentioned the subject of Nanny in this study and have admitted the difficulty of giving an accurate perspective to this legendary character, recognizing that historically, myths and legends are not woven around nonentities. With this document in hand it seems necessary to take a closer look at Nanny — or at the Nannies, because we may well be dealing with more than one. To return to the 1730s when "the great Negro Town" or "Nanny Town" was the cockpit of the Maroon battles, we may safely assert that no mediocre person, within the context of Maroon tradition, could give his or her name to a town. The Maroons are a people with a dramatic history forged out of constant warfare, hardships, and cruelty, and the accepted leader must prove strength, cunning, ability to command and to hold the community together, and, naturally, skill in warfare. Furthermore, from the web of evidence garnered from documents and from field studies, it appears that Maroons also required their leaders to possess profound understanding of the supernatural — its manipulation for good or evil for the benefit of the community. In this case, the Ashanti-inspired system of belief practiced by the Maroons was *obeah* or *obi* — according to the Jamaican authorities — but for the Maroons, they simply prefer the term "science." Most leaders of Maroon communities today will speak with awed reverence of Nanny's science.

Nanny, then, must have possessed science in full measure in the perception of her people. In addition, she is celebrated as a great warrior, leading her people into battles and repulsing the British soldiers — in some cases, applying her science for the purpose. We know that her community was one of the most aggressive against the slave masters, and we also have suggestive evidence that she was against signing treaties with them. Thus, we can feel confident that there existed a historical personage called Nanny. How then do we account for this character's accepting lands from the plantocratic government under the same conditions as any white settler who "hath transported himself with his Servants and Slaves into our said Island," and not as a victor in warfare, as the other Maroons?

In pursuing this question we may assume two things: one, that it was a different Nanny who received the land grant; the other, that it was the same Nanny with all the attributes mentioned above. In assuming an "other" Nanny, let us examine the evidence that may lead to this conclusion. We may remind ourselves that we have no clear picture of Nanny herself, although this has not prevented photographs of her from floating around in recent times. We are not even certain of the time when she was active. The descriptions we have of her town came from captured Maroons, the most important being that of one Sarra, alias Ned. Ned's deposition was taken October 1, 1733, and at this time Nanny Town, with its 300 men (and with women and children exceeding this number) had a headman called Cudjoe. Ned did not mention Nanny. In January 1734/5, a defector from the windwards, an Ebo called Cupid, said that he saw three white male prisoners "carried" to the "Negro Town," and there all three were "put to death by Nanny." Cupid saw Nanny as the wife of one Adou, a leader, but to Cupid, Nanny was a greater man than Adou though she never went in their battles.[34] However, the most intriguing reference to Nanny in the documents is undoubtedly that of March 29 and 30, 1733 in the Journal of the Assembly of Jamaica. Here a grateful Assembly rewarded those loyal slaves for their "resolution, bravery and fidelity" under the command of Captain Sambo (whom we have met before) in fighting against the Maroons. Among these slaves was William Cuffee, "a very good party Negro, having killed Nanny, the rebels old obeah woman." For this public service, Cuffee and the others were rewarded (in addition to the standard recompence of £10 and £8, respectively, for each Maroon male or female killed or taken alive) £5 each and "a common silver laced hat, a good blue baize coat, with a red cross upon the right breast, and ten yards of oznaburghs . . . [and] such coat and hat with ten shillings, should be given each of them on the 20th December yearly."[35] There is no evidence to show that they were freed. But if Cuffee did kill the Nanny of our quest, then Cupid could not have seen her nearly a year later.

Altogether, then, we find Nanny killing three white men: Nanny greater than her husband but not going into battle; and Nanny, the rebels' *obeah* woman, killed. But there is yet another reference which many, rushing headlong, have designated Nanny. This is the formidable "old Hagg" of Thicknesse's *Memoirs.* There is no doubt that this old woman, or the "obea Woman" — of no specific given name — possessed authority in Quao's Town at the time of the Treaty, June 1739. She could countermand Quao's decision and impose her own. Is this the historical Nanny? If so, then she should have been mentioned in Quao's Treaty. But there again, by 1739 Cuffee was strutting with his new fineries for killing Nanny, the *obeah* woman of the rebels.

From field research in Maroon communities in Jamaica, both the Moore Town and Accompong groups have claimed Nanny, some holding that she was the "sister," others the "wife," of Cudjoe — which would shatter the generally held view that she was of the windward's. Equally confusing is the fact that both these communities have burial places for Nanny. In Accompong Town this place is so sacred, that, ironically, the author was not permitted a visit, on the grounds that no woman is allowed there.

It is also somewhat strange that Dallas, the historian of the Maroons, and others, like Long and Edwards, have not mentioned the startling account that Nanny was given lands separately from the other Maroons and under terms similar to those of white settlers. The manuscript sources, too, are all silent on the matter.

If, on the other hand, we assume the grant to have been given to the historical Nanny, then we are called upon to explain how she came, with all her reputation, to accept lands apparently so tamely from the authorities. We would also have to assume that the Nanny who lost her life by Cuffee's hand was a different Nanny from the historical one, or that Cuffee, knowing the importance of the subject, may have made it up, or that, if he did kill a Maroon woman, he may have essayed to call her "Nanny the rebel's obeah woman" in order to receive a handsome reward. We have no record of any application made by her for such lands. One proposition could take the view that the "old Hagg" of Thicknesse's *Memoirs* was our Nanny, and that she was so disgusted with Quao for signing the Treaty that she was determined to break away with her followers to live an independent existence. Before the Treaties, this solution would have been most practicable. Afterwards there were problems. Lands were being patented all around them, and white settlers were already pressing upon them for more lands. Maroon presence was no longer a danger, but now a kind of police protection. In these circumstances, Nanny's choice was limited. Then again, should she decide to splinter off, and even if practicable, clause nine of Quao's Treaty could well see her as a renegade or as rebellious. We have already puzzled over this clause which is not in Cudjoe's Treaty. It said, "That in case Captain Quao and his People should be disturbed by a greater Number of Rebels than he is able to fight, that then he shall be assisted by as many White People as the Governor for the Time being shall think proper." This clause may have been inspired by the authorities' knowledge of the schism within Quao's Town. It should not be assumed that black people of the Caribbean were entitled to land grants. On the contrary, the political economy of race was such that even the indigines had their land wrested from them. Even the planters' own illegitimate children — the mulattos — could not inherit lands from their white fathers over and above a certain amount in many of the territories.

How then did Nanny become eligible under the Jamaican land acts? The answer folds back upon the same Maroon saga, specifically upon Nanny Town. During the burgeoning of the Maroon battles in the 1730s, when "the great Negro Town" or Nanny Town was being taken by the parties and retaken by the rebels, and when in April of 1732 the government held it, they hastily recommended that barracks should be built immediately and settlements be established there. All lands adjacent to the town were forfeited and vested in the Crown and were to be "granted to any person that will settle thereon, without any charge whatever; and to be exempted from all taxes for a certain time."[36] All this was within orthodoxy. But then they went on to say that encouragement should also be given to free blacks and mulattos who would settle, and this was new. Those loyal "Negroes," including Captain Sambo and others who were lately freed for good behavior, should all be encouraged to settle around the Nanny Town area. Most interestingly, the encouragement was particularly given "to any person of distinction" who would supervise the undertaking.[37] Nanny might have known of these new developments through the very effective Maroon grapevine. If the Nanny who received the land grant is the historical Nanny, then ironically, she would thus have availed herself of an act for which she and her kind were responsible. We have no record of her application for lands, but were this so, one could see her act as the very acme of sophisticated cynicism, and thereafter she must have planned her strategy with great care.

In choosing the site which, from a study of both her official diagram and "Muretown's," would seem to have been north of where Moore Town already existed, Nanny may have done so because of her good relations with that settlement. (In conducting field studies among the Moore Town Maroons, one finds, on occasion, vague references to a "Women's Town," situated "somewhere" adjacent to Moore Town. Could this have been in reference to Nanny's 500 acre town?) Between Nanny's land and Moore Town, initially, there were some unpatented lands, including a part of the river, but from around the 1760s, only Charles Douglas's plot and the river stood between them, as the surveyors discovered. This was due to two processes taking place simultaneously; the encroachings of both Maroon towns and the movement of white settlers into the area. Having thus settled, Nanny, most probably, quite consciously was determined to keep a very low profile. For one, she would not have viewed the paying of taxes favorably, and second, the idea of maintaining five white men on her land would certainly have been anathema to her. By the terms of the Maroon Treaties, four white persons must reside in each community, but these were at government's expense. The white settlers were obliged, on the necessity of security in having a reasonable ratio between whites and blacks, to keep and maintain five white men on their estates. Although more honored in the breach than in the observance, nevertheless, some estates, especially the more prosperous ones, would have at least two or three whites working as overseers or bookkeepers. The more Nanny's land and Moore Town appear to be one and the same thing, the more it would have suited Nanny — for certainly she would not have wished to lose her Maroon identity. Equally, if Moore Town had satisfied the requirements of having four white residents, then these would probably have been associated with her land also, and again, she would not have been required to pay land taxes if seen to be identified with Moore Town. Search as one may, one can find no more reference to this land grant "to a certain Negro woman called Nanny and the people residing with her," apart from the piece of indirect evidence we saw when it appeared to the Assembly that 500 acres of land were "granted" and "laid out" around the Moore Town area. Nanny must have died by this time, 1781. Nonetheless, this survey, culminating in Douglas' sale of the intervening land, probably represents the final and successful denouement of her carefully contrived strategy to merge with Moore Town.[38] It is interesting to note that later Charles Douglas became the superintendent of Moore Town.

Yet, one nagging question remains. The absence of evidence could also be construed to mean that Nanny and her people simply merged with the other free black and mulatto population who might have availed themselves of the 1733 offer, in the process losing their Maroon identity completely. The situation would not be unlike that of Lubolo and his people, who, with their special land grants in the 1660s, merged into the larger society, thereby losing their identity as a group. This proposition, however, would not appear to match the profile of the indomitable Nanny, who, in all probability, would consider it much beneath her dignity to settle down as just another free black — a category that won its freedom by fighting on the side of the slave master — without her special Maroon status. We simply do not know one way or another, for we do not have enough data on Nanny, although we feel confident that such a historical figure, who gave her name to a Maroon town — with all the connotations — did exist. If we are frustrated in the quest, we may remind ourselves, or console ourselves, that there are many important personalities in history whose backgrounds are as mystifying.[39]

So far as the leeward communities are concerned, the situation is somewhat less complicated than that of the windwards. Two towns were identified at the time of the Treaty: Cudjoe's, renamed Trelawny Town, and Accompong Town. It is not clear when Accompong Town was formed, but it clearly derived its name from one of Cudjoe's captains, Accompong, who apparently was made to found a new town during the period of intense government hostilities against them immediately before the first Treaty. This splintering off was presumably to facilitate the raiding parties Cudjoe had instituted during this period, both for attacking plantations and for decoying parties from the central town, Cudjoe's *sanctum sanctorum.* From the ratification of Cudjoe's Treaty, it is clear that the authorities had some vague notion that Accompong had a "Party of Rebels under his Command," and this was apparently construed by them as constituting a separate entity, although it is also clear that they understood Cudjoe to have had command over both towns with the authority to make Accompong accept the terms of the Treaty.

Accompong Town was first officially mentioned, almost *en passant*, when Venus, the quisling, was manumitted by the government after "having deserted from *Accompong's Town.*" But what has not been made clear is the land grant which gave Cudjoe "all the lands situate and lying between Trelawny Town and the Cockpits ... bearing North-west from the said Trelawny Town." It soon became a matter of concern whether Accompong Town was included or not. In 1756, around the time when Charles Town and Scotts Hall were already involved with their land question, the Assembly appointed a committee to look into the situation of Accompong and Trelawny Towns. It is not clear whether this initiative was inspired by the interest generated by the activities of the windwards or whether the leewards had requested an investigation. The committee was charged with three things: first, to ascertain if the Trelawny Town land grant of 1500 acres "to be enjoyed and possessed" by them and their posterity had been "run out" (surveyed); second, to ascertain if Accompong Town and the adjacent lands possessed by this town were included in the Trelawny Town grant; and third, to recommend measures necessary to prevent surveyors or other persons from disturbing the Maroons at both towns.[40] This latter function would seem to suggest that the leewards had registered complaints. The following month the committee reported and found that Trelawny Town lines had not been run, that the 1,500 acres would not include Accompong Town "or any of its settlements"; that Accompong Town and its provision grounds and the different parcels of planted and open lands comprised altogether 400 acres; and that Governor Knowles, before leaving the island, had assured this town "of their having a quantity of land laid out," but so far none had been given them.

It "appeared," further, to the committee, that surveyors had run out lands "very near Accompong's Town and their provision grounds" and had lately been surveying lands between the two towns, thus making Accompong Town particularly "uneasy and under great apprehension from the present uncertainty of their title"; every day they were liable to be disturbed by surveyors "and others." The committee warned that without some interposition in favor of the Maroons, the surveyors "may cover all their settlement, and leave them destitute of the means of getting a livelihood for themselves and families." They recommended that the 1,500 acres should be run out and that 1,000 acres be allocated to Accompong Town, in St. Elizabeth, and that the surveyors to be appointed should refrain from running out any lands or laying any orders for private persons, "within a due distance of the said town," until the lands were run out and until a grant of the 1,000 acres "hath passed the broad seal." The governor should also instruct the superintendents of the two towns as well as the other whites residing there and all the Maroons themselves to assist the surveyors, and to help with "marking fair lines and corner trees according to law."[41]

The tone of the committee suggests much good will towards the Maroons and a willingness to grant them lands — and this policy continued at least until the 1780s; thereafter we begin to see a marked change in this regard. The extent to which the white settlers were pressing in on the leewards, as they did with the windwards, is reflected in the committee's concern over the aggressive surveyors "and others" who seemed bent on covering Maroon settlements. Again, most of these areas adjacent to Maroon lands were thought to be fertile. Alexander Forbes, for instance, found the lands in the neighborhood of Accompong fertile and well suited for coffee, pens or penns, and provisions — areas which "formerly [were] the haunts of runaway and rebellious Negroes."[42] Thus it should be no surprise that by the time Accompong Town was surveyed there were settlers on all sides. It appears that the Assembly was perfectly confused by the many patented lands and other claims just merely marked out. They rather higgledy-piggledy said that 1,000 acres were "binding to the eastward and southward on the lands belonging to George Roxstead, Samuel Smith, George Currie and Alexander Stanhope, and such other lands as are now taken up."[43] But by 1791 the boundaries became more precise: to the east, on lands patented by James Smith and George Roxstead (both of whom, incidentally, had acquired their lands since October and May 1740, respectively, according to the patents); south, on land patented by Alexander Stanhope and partly on land laid out for George Currie; west and southwest, by rocky mountains and cockpits, and southeasterly, on land patented by Edward and Francis Smith.

Both towns were now (1758) surveyed for the first time despite the fact that Trelawny Town lands had been granted since 1738. William Wallace, the surveyor, had the usual problem with the Assembly's tardiness in paying its debts, and we find him petitioning for his fees in June and October of 1758.[44] When in October the House finally decided to pay him (£250), they found that Accompong Town was trespassing on the lands of Francis Smith, James Smith, and Edward Smith to the extent of 430 acres. James Smith, Jr., petitioned the Assembly the same month, complaining that Accompong's land covered fifty-nine acres of his property, "some of the best and most easy part of the said land," thus the value of the remainder was much diminished.[45] But the whole affair ended amicably. James Smith, after being called in by the House, decided to sell the said fifty-nine acres and was willing to make title "to His Majesty, his heirs, and successors for the use of the said Negroes."[46] But there appears to be a difference in the title arrangement of this piece of land. Usually the land is vested in the Maroons and their heirs in perpetuity. Here it is vested in the Crown for Accompong Town's use — which would seem to suggest a usufructurary relationship rather than one of fee simple. We do not know whether this was just another careless error or whether a proprietorial difference was meant to be established in this instance.

Between Trelawny Town and Accompong Town, they now had conjointly, just over 2,500 acres of land. This should be seen as the "official" figure, because we will hear of more trespassing later. We have no more record, for instance, of the remaining 371 acres of trespassed lands, after Smith's fifty-nine acres had been bought for the Accompongs. Yet even if each acre was entirely fertile, population pressure would soon place a great strain on land space. Dallas has characterized a third of the original Trelawny Town allottment as "merely rocks ... overun with a species of fern and Foxtail grass, which are certain indications of a poor soil,"[47] and recent field research has revealed this to be the case to this day. This allows for just "about 100" arable acres, with a population in 1739 of approximately 470 persons, including women and children. It is not clear whether this computation included Accompong Town.

Meanwhile, Trelawny Town had experienced some internal altercation that led one of the leaders, a Captain Furry, to betake himself off with some followers and form a new community. This was revealed to the government through a petition from one Dr. Mark Hardyman. Hardyman had obtained his 300 acres in the neighborhood of Trelawny Town in St. James, since 1755, and his intention was to have a sugar plantation with mills under the same unit, having already trained some seventy slaves "together with a competent number of mules and steers" for the undertaking. But upon resurveying his land, he discovered that "a negro named Furry, belonging to Trelawny Town, had separated himself from [the] said town, and built houses, and planted provisions, on the petitioner's said land, in the place where the works must have been erected." This trespass, Hardyman computed, was three miles beyond the Trelawny Town boundary. The petitioner had no other freehold, but this plot of land, yet he was prevented from settling it. He therefore asked the government to order Furry and his people to return within their boundaries and rather generously suggested later that he was willing to make a pecuniary recompense of £50 to Furry, for the improvement he made on the land and "to prevent any inconvenience" to him and his people.[48]

In less than two weeks the House deliberated on Hardyman's petition, found the allegation correct, and recommended that Furry be returned within the Trelawny Town border.[49] Up to this period Maroon affairs were treated with great promptitude, care and concern. The House advised the governor to give instructions to the proper officer in Trelawny Town, "to fall, settle and plant, thirty acres of provisions, in as effectual a manner as a certain quantity of land, now possessed by Furry, belonging to Dr. Mark Hardyman is, and also to assist the Negroes living with the said Negro Furry, on the land of Dr. Hardyman, to build houses, and make a town, as good as what he shall be dispossessed of ... and the expence to be incurred by this service, shall be supported by the public."[50] As we saw in the formation of Scotts Hall and Charles Town, there is no doubt that up to this period, the 1750s, the government supported the proliferation of Maroon towns, partly for security reasons and partly for the fund of good will that was still felt towards the Maroons generally. This resolution, for example, was passed on the same day they were purchasing the fifty-nine acres of land from James Smith for Accompong Town.

As usual, the Assembly's largesse did not match its performance. Twelve years later (November, 1770) we find the superintendent of Trelawny Town petitioning on behalf of Furry's group, who had returned within the boundary of Trelawny Town, had "fallen, cleared, and planted at their own expence thirty acres of land, and have erected and built fourteen houses, within the 1500 acres granted them ...." Yet Furry had never received any pay or allowance as promised.[51] The superintendent general of the Maroons, William Ross, in submitting his report, October 1770, also said that the Furry Town group "think it hard, that the money voted them by the honourable Assembly, some time past," had not been paid, although they planted "a great quantity of provisions, as well as building many houses thereon." Thus pressed, the House responded and in December of the same year voted £150 for Furry and his people, who had cleared the thirty acres of land.[52]

Despite the surveys conducted within the windward and leeward communities, boundary disputes continued. Both Charles Town and Trelawny Town, for instance, complained in 1770 of encroachments on their lands and requested new surveys to ascertain boundaries.[53] Whereas Charles Town appeared satisfied with the resulting survey, Trelawny Town was most dissatisfied. They complained that very little of their provision grounds were contained in the new lines and that a "great part of that which was run out for them, is rocks and cockpits."[54] Apparently the dispute was temporarily settled by the intervention of the custos of St. James, John Palmer, and some other gentlemen,[55] but there is no doubt, as yet another survey of 1787 shows, that the Maroon provision grounds as well as their grazing areas were encroaching on neighboring lands — in line with Maroon philosophy toward their agricultural lands and grazing pastures.

As the 1780s pass, we find a new official policy toward Maroon lands. One of the reasonings behind this was that many of the Maroons were moving too freely, in some cases living outside their boundaries. This became a great source of concern to the authorities, especially from the 1750s, and some stringent laws were passed from this date with a view to curtailing their mobility. The 1751 law maintained that several of the Maroons "have frequently left their several Towns, and continued absent therefrom a considerable Time without the Leave of their Commanding-Officer, or, having had such Leave, have not returned back by the Time prescribed to them, but have rambled about in the several Parishes of this Island, and been harboured and concealed in divers Places ...." To prevent all this, the law decreed that if any Maroon absented himself from his town without leave of the commanding officer, or, if he obtained leave, continued to absent himself for seven days after the expiration of such leave, then, upon complaint made to any magistrate of the parish where the truant was found, he was to be sent to the jail of St. Jago de la Vega in order to be brought to trial for the offence. The trial would be conducted in the same form and manner as free blacks were tried, that is, before two justices and three freeholders. If convicted — even if the trial was before one justice and one freeholder — then they were "required to deprieve the said Offender of his Freedom, and order him or her to be transported off this Island by the receiver-general and sold ...."[56] This was drastic indeed, and it foreshadowed the new policy that was to be developed in the 1790s.

Finding that the Maroons did not pay much attention to the act but continued to "ramble" about and to be away from their communities for long periods, the Assembly passed the 1791 law. By this date, the overall population of all the Maroon communities had increased markedly and was still increasing, and the government conceded that a consequence of this increase was that "the lands granted to them will soon be unable to provide for their support and maintenance."[57] So a rather radical decision was taken by the lawmakers — which could well have had serious consequences for the Maroons as a group, had it not been for their stubborn sense of solidarity. The Assembly ruled "That it shall be lawful for any maroon negro or negroes to appear in person before the justices of their precinct, ... and there and then publicly and solemnly to declare, that he, she, or they, are desirous and willing to give up any right he, she, or they, may have to any part of the lands which have been granted to the maroon negroes, and that he, she, or they, are desirous and willing to reside in any other part of the island, except in any of the maroon-towns." Should they make such a declaration then they would be "entitled to every right and privilege of a free person of colour, and shall no longer be subject to the command or control of any superintendent or maroon officer in the island ...."[58]

The grandiose declaration of entitlement to every right and privilege of the free people of color should, however, be seen in context. Free people, blacks and mulattos, were, within the slave system, incapacitated by numerous sociolegal, not to mention economic, restrictions too numerous to mention here.[59] Not many freed people at that period would have had access to the land each Maroon was free to cultivate, and they would now be subject to militia duty and to any tax the government might impose on them. So long as it was a slave society, the Maroons who abrogated their status were in fact exchanging their earned security for uncertainty and deracination. It is not difficult, therefore, to understand that not many availed themselves of the act. And the majority of those who did — or at least of those for whom we have records — consisted of the offspring of Maroon women and white men — the mulattos produced within the Maroon ethos. Again, almost all these official renouncements were made from Trelawny Town during the time of the government war with this group, when the war had gone badly for them and they were being deported against their will. Thus we find at the St. James Quarter Sessions, July 26, 1796, the undersigned personally appearing before the custos of this parish and his associates, who "did then and there in open Court publicly and solemnly severally declare that they were severally desirous and willing to give up any right that they respectively might have to any part of the Lands which have been granted to the Maroon Negroes, And that each of them was desirous and willing to reside in any other part of this Island except in any of the Maroon Towns." These were the names, all "descendants from some of the Maroon of Trelawny Town":

A Maroon Negro woman named Nimba

A Maroon Negro woman named Mary Morris
A Maroon Negro woman named Mary Simpson
A Maroon Negro woman named Sarah Saunders
A Maroon Negro woman named Susanna Palmer
Elanor Palpera Mulatto Girl Daughter of said Susanna Palmer
John Pendrill a Mulatto Boy Daughter [sic] of said Susanna Palmer
Emily Mountague a Mulatto Girl Daughter of said Susanna Palmer
A Maroon Negroe woman named Elizabeth Palmer
Sarah McSherry a Mulatto woman Daughter of said Elizabeth Palmer
Eleanor McSherry a Mulatto Girl Daughter of said Elizabeth Palmer
A Maroon Negroe woman named Lilly Allen
John Mostyn a Mulatto man Son of said Lilly Allen
Ann McLaughlan a Mulatto woman Daughter of said Lilly Allen
Rosanna Scarlett a Mulatto woman Daughter of said Lilly Allen
John Quick a Mulatto boy Son of said Rosanna Scarlett
William Scarlett Erle a Zuadroon boy son of said Rosanna Scarlett
Elizabeth Zuick a Zuadroon Girl Daughter of said Rosanna Scarlett
John Anglin Erle a Zuadroon boy son of said Rosanna Scarlett
Elizabeth Borthwick a Mulatto woman Daughter of said Lilly Allen
Mary Sharpe a Zuadroon Girl Daughter of said Elizabeth Borthwick
James Allen a Mulatto Boy son of said Negroe woman Lilly Allen.[60]

In this list of twenty-two people, all are of mixed blood with the exception of seven, all Maroon women, and of these seven, three had liaised with white men and were actively producing mulatto children. It is probable that the other four may have been living outside the Maroon community, and they may also have had similar liaisons.

In October of the same year in the same parish, and also in Trelawny Town, we find two more mulattos renouncing their Maroon status in the open courts: "Elizabeth Sewell Walcott, a mulatto woman," and "Martin Sewell, a mulatto man," each a descendant from one of the Maroons of Trelawny Town.[61]

It does not appear that many more Maroons availed themselves of the act. During the Trelawny Maroon war, a group of mainly old people, not wishing to be deported, appealed to the act successfully. We have evidence to show that at least two persons from Charles Town "took the benefit of the act," in 1798,[62] and in the 1833 report, we also note that two people, Tom Tough and Ann Giscome, were "sworn out," presumably under the 1791 act.[63] It is not clear if it is these four people that permitted one source to say, without giving evidence, "We know that some Maroons at Charles Town officially took this option."[64] From a study of the superintendent's reports, from 1791 up to emancipation in 1834, we discover that some Maroons did continue to live outside their communities without giving up their Maroon status, one of the most outstanding of these, in the period under study, being Captain Smith, who figured prominently in the 1795–96 war and in Ross's *Journal*.[65] They continued to live, unofficially, outside their communities into the nineteenth century and those who are living outside today, within mainstream Jamaican society or overseas, without giving up their status, may not know that they are breaking the 1791 law. Many of the women affiliated with white men as partners or as relatives also lived outside their communities, without giving up their Maroon status. From the reports, it appears that most of the women living apart with white males were from Moore Town; and at least two women from this town, in the 1798 report, lived in Port Antonio "for pleasure" (*fille de joie*)?[66] As usual, it is the mulatto progeny that was more likely to give up the Maroon status. We note also that almost every superintendent's report shows some intercommunity living.

As if to put the 1791 law to the test, the Trelawny Town Maroons petitioned the House a few months after the act, March 7, 1792, implying that they were in need of more lands. The petition came from Maroon officers Colonel Montague James, who also figured prominently in the 1795–96 war and in Ross's *Journal*, Captain Zachary Bayly, and Captain James Lawrence who claimed that it was written on behalf of themselves and their community. They complained that a great part of their allotted 1,500 acres consisted of "very high rocky mountains totally unfit for cultivation, that the rest had been under cultivation since 1739, and, the soil, being of a light texture, had become exhausted as to be totally insufficient and inadequate to the support of the present number of the Maroons, who, in the meantime, are greatly increased." And then, with much candor, they openly admitted that the consequence was that "trespasses are made on the lands of adjoining proprietors, and a scene of great distress and confusion must ensue, unless measures are taken to prevent it."[67] Nine months later, the House deliberated on this petition. The days when Maroon affairs were treated with promptitude and concern were over. It is true that the committee charged to look into the allegations of the petition said that they visited the Maroon "towns in Trelawny" — a nonsensical formulation since Trelawny, the parish, had no Maroon towns. At Trelawny Town, they found that only the officers who signed the petition "were acquainted with the contents," and that there were no previous meetings for the purpose of registering grievances. They did, however, find a general wish among the Maroons to have more lands, but the committee felt that such a wish should not be satisfied, for the following reasons: first, because the land they held was still uncultivated, although the soil was exactly the same as that of the adjoining proprietors, and many of these estates were in a high state of cultivation; second, because there was a very rapid settlement and cultivation taking place in that part of the country; third, because the provision made in the "late law" permitted them "to acquire what land they want as private property on leaving the town"; and fourth, because they did not depend on cultivation for their supply of clothing or other necessaries that they required.[68]

This negative reply reflects the new policy to the Maroons, but it is significant that, even when land hunger was so general among the Maroons and even when the authorities seemed adamant about not granting them more lands, the Maroons still did not opt to leave their community under the 1791 act. Even if they had chosen to leave, nowhere in the act has it been mentioned where they would find alternative places to reside. They were not entitled to land grants, not being white, and land prices would probably have been out of their financial reach. We have already noted the unique nature of the Nanny grant. Thus the committee's claim that the 1791 act permitted them to acquire what lands they required as private property is totally unfounded. The Trelawny Town Maroons who submitted to Balcarres's Proclamation of August 8, 1795 and appealed to the 1791 act were well aware of the predicament in which they were to find themselves when they reminded the governor that in doing so they would be "without any means of support." The uncultivated lands the committee saw may well have been due to the Maroon/African practice of leaving lands fallow for a time, only to be replanted later — a system which, as we shall see, befuddled Bryan Edwards. And second, as Dallas noted, much of their land, being rocky and of low energy content, was not cultivable. All in all, the committee seemed determined to support the white settlers who were apparently still rapidly settling adjoining lands to the Maroons — and the slave plantations' economy should not be disturbed by any means.

Land disputes continued in all the Maroon communities and so far as the Trelawny Town group is concerned their land question was put to rest after the 1795 war between them and the government (to be dealt with in the next chapter) terminated in their deportation. They were accordingly to be "deprived of and be barred from all and all manner of claim, or pretence to claim, of, in, to, or upon the hereintofore mentioned one thousand five hundred acres of land, or any part, or parts thereof."[69] David Schaw, for one, was probably not unhappy about this drastic measure, for just a few years before, he had complained to the Assembly that the Maroons of Trelawny Town were "continually trespassing" on his plantation as well as on his slaves' provision grounds, which they had "totally destroyed." Apparently the Assembly had not, up to the time of the outbreak, attended to Schaw's complaints. But with the deportation of this community Schaw may have returned to those parts of his property he had to "throw up . . . to the material injury of himself and slaves."[70]

Meanwhile let us take a look at the economic life of the Maroons in their different communities before we deal with the Trelawny Town situation. From the evidence, it is clear that their economic activities became more differentiated after the Treaty. Pre-Treaty economy was based on planting provision grounds, on the rearing of some livestock, and on hunting and fishing. These activities did not cease but continued alongside other activities that helped to supplement their earnings. So far as agriculture goes in Jamaica, the Maroons can claim to be the first domestic agriculturalists following the British occupation. In contrast, the white planters were bent on their export-oriented cash crop, sugar. The Maroon women, the cultivators, as we noted before, continued to grow plantains, coffee, cocoa, cassava, corn, yam, papaw, pineapples — citrus, avocado, and pears. Their diversified crops lent variety to the island's culinary needs.

Their allotted land, then as now, was held in common, and no Maroon might alienate any portion of it to an outsider, following African practice. Again, in line with African custom, they cleared their land by the "slash-and-burn" method — a very effective means of clearing among preindustrial peoples. It involved the placing of fire around the trunks of trees which soon fell to the ground, at which stage, wrote Gosse, "it now presents a very unprepossessing aspect; the large charred and blackened stumps stand as thick as tombstones in a churchyard; the bare ground is strewn with half calcined stones, unrelieved by a green leaf; and great heaps of ashes lie here and there with fragments of burned wood, the only remains of the giant trunks that once reared their verdant crowns to the skies."[71] Edwards did not seem impressed by the method. He thought it a "service of danger," being performed by the women at that, "but the Maroons, like all other savage nations, regarded their wives as so many beasts of burden; and felt no more concern at the loss of one of them, than a white planter would have felt at the loss of a bullock."[72] Edwards, the slave master, may have forgotten how prevalent it was for his countrymen to sell both their half-white children by slave women and their slave concubines into slavery. However, Dallas, his compatriot, was to point out the misrepresentation of this allegation.[73]

Typically, Edwards did not think much of their agricultural skills in general. He observed that they showed no disposition toward industry but in fact, pilfered or purchased most of their provisions from the plantations. He did, however, notice "small patches of Indian corn and yams, and perhaps a few straggling plaintain [*sic*] trees, near their habitation; but the ground was always in a shocking state of neglect and ruin."[74] Again, Dallas, acting as a disclaimer to Edwards's misunderstanding — in this case — was to point out that what appeared to have been ruinous to the casual visitor was in fact the Maroon/African practice of leaving the land to lie fallow for a season or two. But even during this period, Dallas observed, nutritive roots were growing, which invariably came to the support of the country, especially during periods of protracted droughts.[75] The fallow system is indeed deemed necessary in tropical agriculture which usually suffers from shallow topsoil and from a low level energy content. To this day the Maroons graze their cattle on communal pastures, and it does not appear that the historical trespassing is a feature today. In conducting fieldwork among them, one finds that there is also a laudable lack of theft or of disputes arising from misidentification of the communal cattle.[76]

It is clear that their commercial activities increased after the Treaties. Prior to this we know that they would disguise themselves as free blacks and descend upon the marketplaces to sell their produce and livestock and buy necessities, including gunpowder, under the strictest secrecy. Now their commercial activities could be conducted in the open, having regard to the fact that the Treaties actually identified the goods they were expected to produce for their own consumption as well as for commerce within the island. There is no evidence to suggest that the Maroons paid any attention whatever to the Treaty clauses that obliged them to apply for license or "tickets" from officials before transporting their goods to market; nor does it appear that the authorities made any attempt to enforce the law. Both men and women could be seen attending the marketplaces laden with ground provision and fruit, often carried on their heads, and not infrequently the women particularly would be leading, in addition, a pig or a kid or carrying fowl tucked under their arms and a baby tied to their backs, African fashion. Market day, then as now, was an important social outlet of the black peasantry of the island.

It appears that the pre-Treaty Maroons, particularly those of Trelawny Town, did develop a degree of technical skills — a situation which is not widely known. Even Dallas, always sympathetic, said, "They were none of them mechanics, all their knowledge of that kind was confined to the art of erecting a house, and repairing a gun."[77] In collecting material for his manuscript after the Treaties, James Knight was informed — possibly by soldiers in parties — that the Maroons' partiality for pewter plates and shots when they plundered plantations was due to the fact that they recycled these items into cannon balls.[78] Another letter to Knight from one J. Lewis, dated December 20, 1743, mentioned that "[t]he Maroons forged their own Iron works, making Knives, Cutlasses, Heads of Lances, Bracelets, Rings and a variety of other kinds of necessaries; they have Bellows, made of wood, about 6 feet high and 16 inches wide through which they make hollow and a hole at the Bottom through which the air passes."[79] We also know that they made the *abeng* from a combination of the horn of the cow and leather, which they used to communicate complicated messages for long distances. It would clearly be unrealistic to have expected too much creativity leading to the higher satisfaction of the luxuries of life from a people inured to warfare and precarious living. A people constantly on the defensive, furtively on their guard for invaders, cannot build a lasting "civilization." Civilization requires a sense of permanence and leisure for its development. We do not know if all the Maroon groups made articles like those mentioned above. Lewis' letter seems to have concentrated on Cudjoe's Town, and the probabilities are that Cudjoe's group, having had a longer period of peace and tranquility, would thus have had the leisure to manufacture some articles, even items of luxury, bracelets and rings. If the windwards did not make any such articles, it should not be too surprising, considering that they were always on the run, often leaving behind some of their possessions.

Dallas observed that they derived a considerable income from the "manufacturing" of tobacco after the Treaties.[80] Tobacco, a native plant of the Amerindians, from which they made intoxicating drinks and which they inhaled for hallucinatory purposes, soon became an important cash crop for the planters of the Caribbean to export to Europe. It does not appear that the Maroons cultivated tobacco themselves but they did help to satisfy a domestic demand for the manufactured product. According to Dallas, they bought the leaves of the plant from the planters, "which their women and children assisted them in carrying home, each loaded with a weight proportioned to the strength of the carrier."[81] The leaves were then dried, after which they were twisted into a kind of rope, of about one-third of an inch in diameter, and thus, having added their labor and skill to the commodity, they were now ready to sell the end product to the estates as well as to others within the society, including slaves. This kind of tobacco, thus prepared, was then finely sliced for use in pipes. How extensive was this occupation of the Maroons and what income they derived from it is not clear.

The Maroons also supplemented their economic wherewithal by selling the results of their hunting activities, which the men usually performed for pleasure as well as for food and perhaps to keep them in good shooting form. The main item, which was then sold especially in the eastern and southeastern sectors of the country, was the jerked pork. This has now become a main commercial dish sold all over the island, mainly by non-Maroons, many of whom have no knowledge of the historical origin of this delicacy. The vendors now sell the "jerk pork" as well as "jerk" chicken, which is even more prevalent, especially in the urban areas. The original jerk pork was a spicy, carefully prepared delicacy, apparently barbecued over selected woods and reminiscent of the Buccaneers in their manner of preparing or "boucaning" their meat. Edwards said that the Maroons cured their flesh without salting it,[82] while another source said that after

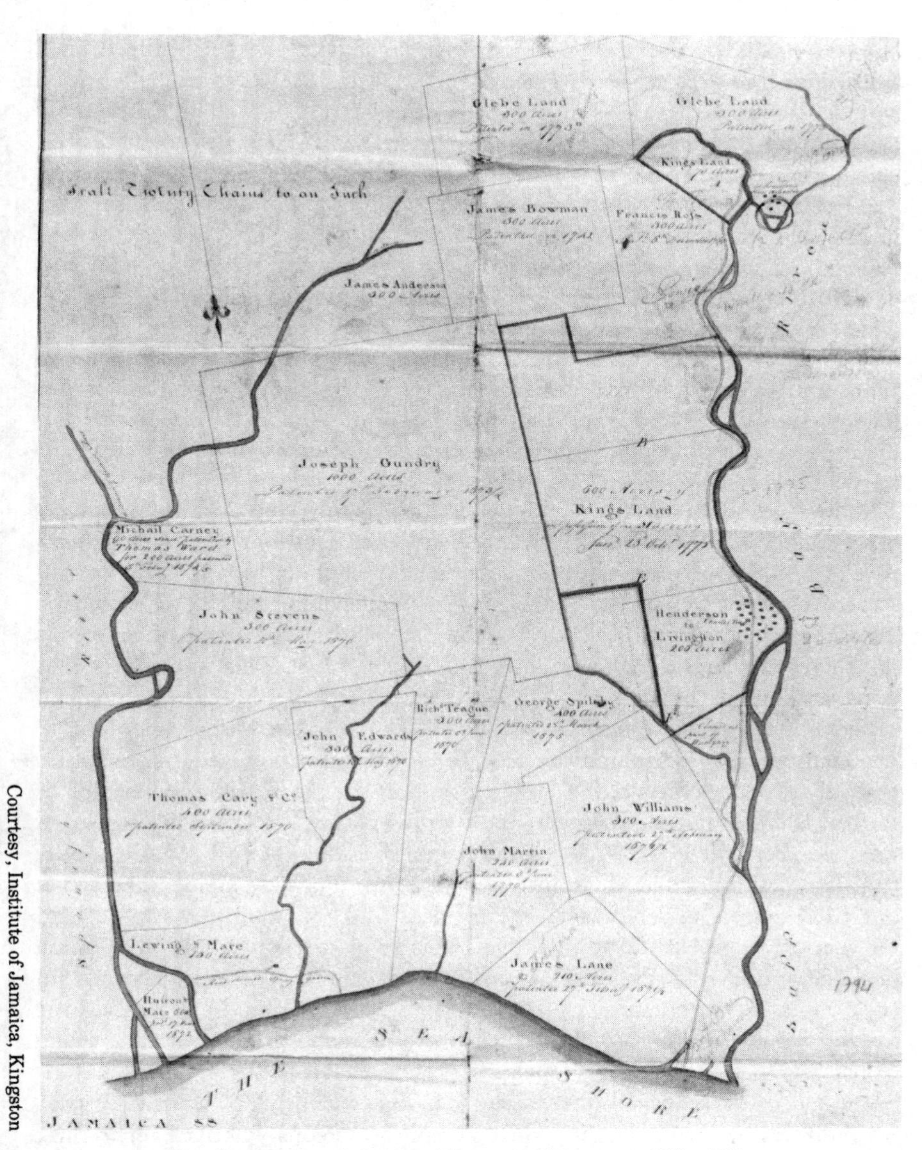

Courtesy, Institute of Jamaica, Kingston

Charles Town, in 1794 (discussed on pp. 168 - 71)

the boar was shot or pierced through with lances it was cut open, the bones taken out, and "the flesh ... gashed on the inside into the skin, filled with salt, and exposed to the sun, which is called jerking."[83] It is conceivable that during periods of salt shortage the Maroons may have substituted spices, including hot chili peppers, for salt. The jerked meat was a delicacy, "and eats much as bacon if broiled on coals," and the Maroon selling this item was a picturesque figure in post-Treaty Jamaica. "On his back, braced round his shoulders, and suspended by a bandage over the forehead, was generally seen the wicker cradle, that held inclosed a side of jerked hog, which he sold passing along, in measured slices, to ready customers, as an especial delicacy for the breakfast table. The accoutred Maroon, with this vendible commodity, was altogether a striking and characteristic figure in our streets,"[84] Gosse reported. The origin of this practice is uncertain, because this accoutrement for a vender was not unknown in Scotland, up to the Edwardian period, among fishwives.

The Charles Town Maroons particularly seem to have gained economically from the American War of Independence. This war meant the cessation of important estate supplies such as staves, shingles, and boards from America, about which the planters complained bitterly. But the Charles Town community, with its lush woodlands, could supply some of the needs of the estates by manufacturing and selling lumber. This apparently was done at the price of their hunting and also of the flourishing arrowroot and coffee trade they had hitherto conducted, at least during the war years.[85]

Commerce, as is so often the case, tends to lead to a greater appreciation not only of the luxuries of life, but it also makes for a greater appreciation of capital and accumulated wealth, and it appears that the Maroon experience was no exception to this. They soon began to look around for more opportunities to supplement their incomes. Some did this by hiring themselves out to "planters and new settlers, to clear and plant large tracts of land for certain wages."[86] It appears that this soon developed into a common practice and like any other relationship involving wages for workers within the context of an exploitative slave system, abuses soon crept in. In large measure, they arose from the reluctance or refusal of some estate owners to pay the workers. This became so prevalent that the law openly acknowledged dishonest practices against the Maroons when in 1791 it enacted that "it shall not be lawful for any white person or persons whomsoever to hire, work, or employ in his, her, or their service, ... any maroon ... without first entering into a written agreement with such maroon or maroons, two parts of which shall be signed by both parties ... and such agreement to be signed and subscribed by one credible white person as witness, one of which shall be delivered to the Maroon[s] ... and the other kept by the person or persons so hiring or employing him, her, or them" — all this because "it often happens that maroon negroes are hired or employed by white people and find great difficulty in recovering their just demands, for want of sufficient legal evidence."[87] Edwards, writing in 1796, said that a planter, one Mr. Gowdie, adjacent to the Trelawny Town Maroons, had hired "one of their chief men" as overseer on his plantation, showing no differential in the wage rates he would have paid to the white overseer.[88] There does not appear any body of evidence to conclude that this was a common or even an occasional practice. It may have been an isolated situation. Another source has mentioned what appears to have been the same case; he identified a Maroon chief as an overseer to one Mr. Gowdie, an "affectionate and indulgent master," close to Trelawny Town.[89]

The Maroons could also supplement their income by working on the roads. Although this was one of the clauses in their Treaties and although Trelawny had suggested in his "Thoughts" that they be paid for this service, nevertheless it was not ratified in law. The importance of roads to a plantation economy is obvious, and Long, the planter historian, was well aware that without suitable roads not much progress would be made in the development of estates in parishes such as St. George's for instance, with its wide tracts of uncultivated lands. "The first step towards further improvements here," he wrote, "will therefore naturally commence with opening new roads of communication which may allure the proprietors of plats on each side to begin settlements. It cannot be expected, that individuals will undertake this task or incur so much expense .... It must be executed at the public cost ...."[90]

In 1771 and 1780 laws were passed, possibly through the influence of resident planters like Long, authorizing the receiver general to pay the Maroons who worked on roads. Presumably with a view to making it appear more attractive to the Maroons themselves, the law said in its preamble that

> [W]hereas, the Roads leading to many of the Negro Towns are great Part of the Year very bad, and sometimes almost impassable: Be it enacted ... That the Negroes belonging to each of the Negro Towns shall once every Year repair the Roads leading to their respective Towns and Settlements, when they shall be so ordered by their Superintendent: And as an Encouragement to the said Negroes to amend and keep the said Roads in Repair, the Receiver-General ... shall pay to each Negro Man ... who shall be employed in making and repairing the Roads leading to the said towns, One Ryal per Day, Oath being first made by the Superintendent ... residing in the Towns, of the Number of Negroes actually employed, and the Time they worked on the said Roads: Provided always, that such Pay do not exceed the Sum of Ten Pounds to each Negro Town in each Year.[91]

There are a few points to be noticed in these acts. First is the increased and increasing power of the superintendent, which transcended the law of the Treaties. Second, it is not clear why the lawmakers set a limit to the earnings of each town unless it is that it would not sit too well with them to see the Maroon communities too affluent. In any case, this legal limit was regarded as ridiculous by the Maroons, and naturally roads remained impassable, especially in the more mountainous communities like Trelawny Town and Accompong Town. Superintendent-General Robert Brereton reported in 1773 that he gave directions to these two leeward towns to "go upon the roads," but they grumbled and asked "what was £10 per year to go on such roads?"[92] A committee of the House in 1781 agreed that the legal limit was "much too small"[93] for repairing the numerous and difficult roads about their towns, and by 1791 the maximum limit for each town was raised to £50; by 1835 it was £100 p.a., according to the superintendent's report.[94]

Another service to the state for which the Maroons were paid was that of hunting down and returning runaways to their owners. In this case the payment was stipulated in the ratified Treaties, although the amount was to be changed from time to time. Ironically, this occupation soon became a most — perhaps the single most — important source of income to the Maroons. It is important to note a correlation between hunting for runaways and hunting for food — each of which had the distinction, to the Maroons, of constituting a source of income as well as a source of pleasurable activity. It has been observed that the Maroons pursued "their business of hog-hunting far remote from the settlements, building huts 'in the places where swine came to feed on the fruits,' and where they remained marooning for several days."[95] It could be added that should a runaway chance by, then he, too, would have been hunted, and his chances of being returned to an owner alive would be minimal — especially before mile money was paid for each live returnee instead of his ears. The gruesome practice of returning the ears of runaways was not new to the plantocratic society, for the white soldiers, too, had been paid for the ears of pre-Treaty Maroons. Throughout the Maroon Wars, from the seventeenth century onward, the awards for killing or returning live runaways varied in accordance with the degree of fear generated by the Maroons. Immediately before the Treaties, when this fear was intense, the Assembly allowed £70 "*for every pair of wild Negroes ears which were brought in*," Thicknesse emphasized with moral horror. Inasmuch as the white soldiers of the colony had seen this bounty as a source of livelihood, now the Maroons, for their part, saw it no differently. Thicknesse, if he is to be believed, was probably an exception. A newly arrived soldier on the island, "qualified" for receiving such an award, he however said, "I thank God ... in that business, [supplying ears] I was fortunate; for I never gathered a single pair ...."[96] Although the payment to Maroons for capturing runaways did vary, at no time did it equal the sum paid to the white soldiers for similar service.

In addition to the prize money for each runaway returned, each Maroon party member was paid for the duration of the search in the woods, as the pre-treaty soldiers too were paid for party service. From 1741, the law stipulated 2/6 per day for Maroon officers and 7 1/2^d per day for volunteers, and to encourage new recruits, 6/3 was given as a lump sum to those who had not served before. The law was revised in 1780, and its intent was uncompromising. It stated that

> [W]hereas, the sending out Parties of Negroes belonging to the several Negro Towns, to scour the Woods and take up runaway Slaves, will be of great Ease and Advantage to the Planters and white Inhabitants of the Island; Be it enacted by Authority aforesaid, That as an Encouragement to the said Parties to be diligent in the said Service, there shall be paid by the Receiver General ... to the Officer among the Negroes in each Party in the Rank of Captain, Two shillings and six Pence per Day, to a lieutenant, One Shilling and Three Pence per Day, and to every common Man, One Ryal per Day, when on actual Duty, and no longer; and that each party ordered out shall be supplied with a proportionate Quantity of Provisions and Ammunitions requisite for the Service they shall be sent on, to be approved by the Commissary; and that no party shall consist of more than six Men, including Officers, except on particular Occasions.[97]

By 1791 certain changes were made in this law. One reflected yet another addition to the powers given to the superintendents. They were now responsible for sending out parties, as they were to order the Maroons out for road services, and the 1791 act raised the number of parties from six to twelve.[98]

As Maroon payments were not forthcoming when they hired themselves out to planters, so also did they have difficulties in receiving pay regularly for runaway services from the government. We have already noted the Scotts Hall group, who, when called upon to suppress the "Coromantee" rebellion in 1760, would not budge until paid their arrears. And this was not an isolated case. It is just as well that this particular Scotts Hall group, Long notwithstanding, demanded its payment at a strategic moment, for an officer of this town, Colonel George Gray, was not paid for similar services until thirty-one years later. In December 1791 we find a petition from the superintendent of Scotts Hall, pointing out that Colonel Gray, a Maroon, who was commanding officer of Scotts Hall, Charles Town, and Moore Town during the 1760 war, was frequently sent out with parties, for which services he was entitled to £70, certified by the superintendent at the time.

Following the post-Treaty Maroon custom of having confidants among the planters, Gray had placed the affair in the hands of one William Gray, who, up to the time of his death, continued to give the Maroon assurances that the House was making provisions to pay him.[99] This particular confidant was either a knave or a most ineffectual person, for with the superintendent's petition thirty-one years later, Colonel Gray received his payment from the Assembly in less than a week.[100]

As with earnings from road service, the colonial state also legislated to limit their earnings for party duties. In this case they legislated that £500 p.a. was to be the maximum for any one community. But this limit was not easy to maintain on a yearly basis since during times of turbulence it became expedient to call on Maroon service, and in such cases they could be handsomely rewarded — especially if they insisted on their payment. A perusal of the documents will show that party expenditures usually exceeded the stipulated sum, amounting to over a thousand pounds in each case for the most part. In very few instances the target of £500 was met. And it was for this reason that the Assembly made rules to ease the heavy public expenditure. In 1787, a committee of the House, examining party accounts, decided that they were "considerable" and ruled that no superintendent should order out parties at the request of any one person alone unless there was an affidavit stating that there were runaway slaves establishing quarters in the neighborhood.[101] Five years later the House went further. It requested the governor to give instructions to all the superintendents of Maroon towns "not to send out in future parties on the requisition of any private individual, unless the person desiring such party engage to make good all the expence of pay and subsistence of said party."[102] Thereafter, we begin to see superintendents' reports listing requests from individuals for Maroon services. But it does not appear that the Maroons lost revenue by this means. In fact, it appears that individual planters were already employing Maroons to go out in parties for which they were presumably well paid. That a committee of the House discovered this a year before the act would seem to suggest that the practice inspired the law — as is so often the case.[103]

Whether the Maroons did possess gold and silver enough for "two Negroes to carry," as a Maroon deponent had testified before the Treaties, or whether it is to be understood that they themselves had mined for these minerals, has not been made clear by the documents. But since Jamaica did not produce any mineral to any great extent, it would be difficult to assume that the Maroons had enriched themselves through mining. In conducting field studies in the different communities one did not find the Maroons aware of any mineral deposits historically or currently in their locations.

But it is certain that the Maroons did keep slaves among themselves, though not on a large scale, to be sure. Now what is to be said of a people who fought their way successfully out of slavery, just to turn around and to commence enslaving others? Without attempting a moralistic reply, we can only remind ourselves that in almost all known slave societies, from antiquity to modern, slaves have been known to keep slaves. Furthermore, in most slave revolts, in antiquity, for instance — Spartacus's being the most outstanding — the rebels' aim was invariably to reverse the system and not to overthrow slavery as such. This puts into relief the Haitian Revolution, the only one known to history which toppled the society from one of servitude to freedom.

Vic Reid, in *The Jamaicans*[104] — the second, and a most welcome, historical novel on the Maroons of Jamaica — may have used artistic license when he describes a captured British soldier who soon became a slave of the Maroon hierarchy. A captive of warfare, taken to the community to become property of the leader, was a classical and most prevalent means by which people came to be enslaved throughout history. We know that at least one of the windward pre-Treaty groups had at least two white captives in its midst. These were the two white boys who were made the group's amanuenses, performing the important service of writing passes for peripatetic Maroons engaged in the dangerous business of buying gunpowder, which was prohibited by law.

Post-Treaty Maroons also kept slaves, and this was the case in all their communities. The first official reference we have of this was just five years after the Treaties. Here a motion was made in the Assembly that several merchants were selling slaves to the Maroons. The House was against this and moved that a committee — which was already in existence, empowered to bring in a bill for the better ordering and government of the Maroons — should also include a clause to prevent them from keeping slaves. Soon "An act for the better order and government of the Negroes belonging to the several Negro towns, and for preventing them from purchasing of slaves" emerged and was duly passed.[105] It cannot be thought that the authorities were against slavery on moral or humanitarian grounds; thus once more it would seem that they were placing obstacles in the way of the Maroons' accumulating property. In addition to the economic grounds, their objection in this case could also have been based on security considerations, not wishing the communities to hold too many slaves, who might constitute an addition to Maroon strength in the event of a war.

How then did the Maroons obtain slaves? It is not easy to get a clear picture of slave holding among them because they tried as much as possible to conceal the practice by numerous devices. One of the commonest of these was to have a merchant or factor sell a slave to a third person (non-Maroon, free black, free mulatto, or white) in trust for the use of a Maroon.

This way, the title to the property — the slave — was not in the hands of the purchasing Maroon. As would be expected, this sale-by-proxy practice could lead to litigation when the person with the title claimed the slave. Yet it is somewhat puzzling that we do not have many instances of this kind of dispute. There is one indirect reference that could be interpreted as arising from this type of arrangement: John Hylton, superintendent of Accompong Town, reported in 1829 that some of the slaves "nominally" belonging to a deceased Maroon leader were being claimed by a mulatto woman. The superintendent said that the subject was still in dispute when he wrote. But, he opined, rather lugubriously, "It is a matter of doubt if all the slaves are not fraudulently possessed in the first instance."[106] In 1751 the Assembly reenacted the 1744 act, and by this date it was clearly cognizant of these devious practices. The law stated that

> Whereas some of the Negroes lately in Rebellion have purchased Slaves, and it is apprehended that more may be by them bought, which may be of ill Consequence to the Island, if not prevented; be it therefore enacted by the Authority aforesaid, That no Negroe, belonging to any of the Negroe Towns, shall purchase or buy any Slave whatsoever, under the Penalty of forfeiting the said Slave to his Majesty; and if any Merchant, Factor, or other Person whatsoever, shall sell any Slave or Slaves to any of the said Negroes, or to any other Person in Trust for or to the Use of the aforesaid Negroes, every such Merchant, Factor, or other Person shall, for every Negroe so sold, forfeit the Sum of One Hundred Pounds, and every Person who shall purchase or be concerned in the Purchase of any Slave in trust for any of the said Negroes, belonging to the said Towns, shall forfeit the like Sum of One Hundred Pounds.[107]

This law was reenacted in 1780 and 1791, but it was clearly not effective. In some cases the slaves were simply bought through the marketplaces or by proxy; others were hired from slave owners.

In cohabiting with slave women, Maroon men would also produce slave children, the progeny taking the status of the mother. But it appears that most of these Maroon slave children remained on the plantations where they were born, as the slave master's property. This shocked Dallas. The Maroons, he said, valued the freedom they possessed, yet "were totally indifferent to that of their children born slaves."[108] But Dallas, always honest, unlike Edwards, went on to state another parallel practice, which was much more prevalent in all New World plantation societies. He observed that "in this deficiency of nature they are not singular; for, as I have before told you, the white people on estates have as many sable wives as they please, and change them as often as they please; and there are few properties in the West Indies on which families of mulattoes have not been left by each succedding overseer and book-keeper. A father parts for life with his children, whom in its very birth he consignes to slavery, with as much indifference as with his old shoes."[109]

Despite the law forbidding Maroons to hold slaves, it appears that attempts at enforcement were rather perfunctory and chaotic. Indeed, the superintendents were expected to report quite routinely on slave holding, and in 1797 the governor found himself annoyed with Accompong's superintendent for not reporting on the town's slave holding. The report appeared "to his honour to be incomplete, in not setting forth if any and what number of slaves were in the possession of the Maroons, of that town."[110] However, not wishing to occasion any delay, the governor sent all the reports to the Assembly, and James Anderson's comments on slave holding at Charles Town could well be seen as representative. He said, "There are a few slaves in the town, but cannot ascertain the number; I understand that they have no title to them, being made out in other people's names; others staying with them for a certain time, for past favours . . . ."[111] The meaning of this last sentence is not clear. But it could be that a planter might, on occasion, lend a slave or two to a Maroon in lieu of payment for some favors or service rendered. It appears that under such an arrangement, the Maroon would be designated the slave's "guardian" for the time being. Anderson ended his report by saying, "No children that I have seen," but in other communities children were held as slaves. Moore Town, for instance, had at least ten slave children in 1797.[112]

The first official returns traced, that of 1770, has no mention of slaves, while the second, that of 1773, shows Robert Brereton, the superintendent-general of all the towns, as perplexed about slave holding as Anderson was to be twenty-four years later. Brereton, lumping all the towns together, said, "I find there are about twenty slaves in all the towns, belonging to the Maroon officers, which they do not care to acknowledge or give me an account of; but they have purchased none lately."[113] There must have been other reports in the '70s and '80s, but they have not been traced; apparently they were made "to lie on the table." But it is clear that from 1796 onwards the Assembly insisted on yearly reports, each of which was accordingly sent to the committee of the whole house for discussion. In 1781 the House received complaints that the Maroons were purchasing slaves, apparently on the open market, but when a committee investigated the matter they found the complaints "groundless."[114] By the early nineteenth century the House became alarmed over what it perceived as an increase in Maroon slave holding. This period is outside our study, but it is difficult to determine whether there was indeed a substantive increase or whether it may not have been for the simple reason that the superintendent's reports on the slaves in the different communities became less vague and much more explicit. The House's alarm expressed itself in a message to the Governor in 1805, requesting him to instruct the superintendents to give him the "earliest information of any purchase of slaves which may hereafter be made by the Maroons in order that a stop may be put to an evil of so alarming a nature."[115]

The laws notwithstanding, the fact is that the Maroons continued to own slaves up to emancipation, and they, too, like the white planters, were compensated under the Emancipation Act of 1834[116]; after August of that year, their slaves, too, assumed the new title of "apprentices." In 1832 they held, among the communities, 112 slaves altogether, while in 1833, a year before the Emancipation Act became effective, they held 121: Moore Town, always the largest slave holder, possessed sixty-six, out of a population of 565; Charles Town, forty, with a population of 365; Accompong Town, fourteen, with 400 inhabitants; and, as usual, Scotts Hall holding only one. It was only in 1773 that Scotts Hall, the smallest of the Maroon communities, held five slaves; three in 1798, and two in 1799. Thereafter, it held only one, with a population between forty-two in 1770 and ninety-three in 1833. It is not clear why Scotts Hall's slave holding was so small in relation to the other communities. So far as the Trelawny Town Maroons are concerned, their slaves (number not specified) were sold and disposed of after the 1795–1796 war by commissioners appointed by government, and the revenue was supposed to have been returned to the Maroon owners.[117]

Let us now take a closer look at government encroachments on Maroon Treaty rights up to 1795. We have already noted that the law of 1791 gave them the option to remain in their communities or to relinquish their Maroon status. Regulations were made, as we saw, restricting the number that could go out in parties, restricting the length of time they could remain out in parties, limiting the amount of money any one community could earn from runaway duties or from road works, preventing them from owning slaves, and forbidding slaves from plantations to have "a large concourse" with them, although they could, in their dances among themselves, invite "a small number of slaves, provided it be between sun-rise and sun-set."[118] The area in which the post-Treaty laws affected them most intimately was that involving the power of the white superintendents. We may remember that their duties as stipulated in the Treaties were rather ill-defined and vague and subject to different interpretations. The authorities could thus, with impunity, extend their functions in a manner that impinged on the power of the Maroon leaders. As early as 1744, the act already mentioned, for the better order and government of the Maroons, saw the need for more power in the hands of the superintendents.

It was the superintendent who had to discipline them within their towns, to order them to repair roads, to go out in parties, to prevent slaves' visiting their towns, to see that Maroons did not keep slaves, and the like. To make matters worse, their very courts were now to be under the jurisdiction of the superintendents. The 1751 law explicitly states,

> Whereas Disorders frequently happen in the several Negroe Towns, for Want of Authority in the Chiefs or Commanding Officers, of the Negroes to keep a proper Command over the rest; and because the White Men who reside amongst them are not vested with legal Power to punish them; and it being necessary for the retaining those Negroes in their Duty and Obedience, that an exact Discipline be observed, that all Disorders, Tumults, and Disturbance amongst them be suppressed on their first Appearances, and the Authors and Abetters of them brought to speedy Punishment; ... [it is enacted that] every Negroe being resident in, or belonging to any of the Negroe Towns, who shall disobey ... the Governor's Orders, or excite others to do the same; or shall excite, cause or join in any Disorder, Tumult, or Disturbance, tending to break the Peace and good Order of the said Towns or any of them, shall suffer such Punishment as shall be inflicted *by the White Men residing in the Town* [emphasis added] to which the Offender belongs, and Four of the Negroes of the said Town, of which the Chief or Commanding Officer shall be one, not extending to life.[119]

Thus the traditional custom of the Maroons to try their own cases was gradually whittled away; first, by denying them the right to pass sentences of death among themselves; second, by having the white superintendents presiding with full power to try and to punish (also not extending to life). This law was reenacted at intervals without any substantive changes until 1791, when the law added transportation of Maroon offenders to life and limb as exempted from the superintendent's range of punishment.[120]

New restrictions as well as added duties were also placed on each superintendent. He was to report to the governor all his court proceedings within thirty days after each hearing, under penalty of £20 for each neglect; he was to reside in his town and "on no pretence whatsoever, [should] he be absent therefrom for a longer time than a fortnight," without the governor's leave.[121] However, despite the imperious demands on the superintendents to reside in their towns, it soon became clear that no provisions whatsoever were made for their accommodation, and this was to be a vexing question for every superintendent of each town. In some cases, after repeated petitions from these men, the House would grant the sum of £50 as lodging money for a year; invariably the superintendents would have to petition at least twice again to receive a similar sum for the following year, and so on.[122]

In some cases officers, not finding any accommodation in the town, would, like John James of Trelwany Town, simply live outside the community, thus breaking the law; in other cases, they rented houses or boarded with, presumably, the more affluent Maroons in the community; in a few cases, as in Charles Town, they rented houses from Maroon women. A few of these white officials viewed living with local Maroons as tending to impair their authority with the community. Despite the repeated petitions from all the superintendents, it was not until 1784 that the House rather half-heartedly voted the paltry sum of £100 for a residence to be erected at Moore Town, and two years later the same was voted for Trelawny Town, but up until 1791 no house was yet built.[123] It is not clear if a similar sum was voted for the other towns, nor is it clear if the two voted for were ever built at all, for superintendents of all the towns continued to complain about accommodation well into the nineteenth century. The superintendent was now also asked to make a return every three months, on oath, to the governor, of the number of Maroons residing in each town, "setting forth particularly the Number of Men capable of bearing Arms," also those unfit for duty, the number of women and children, their increase and decrease, the condition of the superintendent's house, the quality of the roads leading from the towns and to the estates, and by the 1790s he was to report on slave holding in the towns. It appears, however, that the reports remained yearly instead of quarterly. Both superintendents and Maroon chiefs, if guilty of neglect of duty or of "improper favour or partiality towards the offender or offenders to be tried," were liable to punishment. This was to be executed by a court-martial convened by the governor, and the punishment should not exceed six months' imprisonment "or loss of commission."[124]

But perhaps the most galling regulation to Maroon pride was the act that admitted the evidence of slaves against them. It has been noted elsewhere that the Maroons had a robust contempt for slaves — a category that "chose" to remain slaves and not to fight successfully against the master class as they had done. The fact that the Maroons were now a primary deterrent to the slave's propensity to run away, to rebel, to set up Maroon communities, or to break the system generally, did not appear to have affected the underlying assumption on which their contempt for the slave was based. By means of slave evidence or any other evidence deemed valid, if sufficient in substance, a Maroon might be sentenced to death "without benefit of clergy," to transportation, to public whipping, or to confinement at hard labor for a period not exceeding twelve months.[125] Maroon women were equally subject to all these laws; women with children were temporarily excepted from execution "until a reasonable time after delivery."[126] The nature of the execution of Maroons should serve as a key to the new way the Maroons were being viewed by the authorities by the 1790s. The execution, without any distinction between men and women, should "be performed in a public part of the parish, and with due solemnity; and care shall be taken by the gaoler or deputy-marshall that the criminal is free from intoxication at the time of his trial, and from thense to and at the time of his execution, under penalty of five pounds; and the mode of such execution shall be hanging by the neck, and no other . . . ."[127]

It is clear that the colonial state was determined to treat the Maroons like any other free blacks. Both the mode of trial, before two justices and three freeholders in the public courts, and the punishment testify further to this. A clause of the 1791 law suggests that slaves were chained while in jail. And this clause is granting a concession to the incarcerated Maroon. It states that where they were confined to hard labor in a public workhouse, it would not be lawful to cause a Maroon "to be chained to a slave," but he should be confined to work within doors with other free blacks.[128]

How did the Maroons abide all these new laws? Naturally they did not sit too well with them, and the 1795 outbreak was a direct result of the authorities' new attitude to them. Dallas said that "to some of these laws very little attention was paid. The Maroons bought slaves without any notice being taken of it. Parties of them were suffered to wander about the island, and many of them formed temporary connexions with the female slaves on the different plantations in the country. Whole families of them left their towns, and were permitted to establish themselves on the back settlements of the planters without complying with the forms required by the law respecting such removals."[129]

But even before the 1795 outbreak there were several incidents that reflected the tensions that had accrued in Maroon societies over government regulations. Some of these involved incidents with government surveyors over land disputes between Maroons and government and between Maroons and white settlers. No other single issue could contribute so much to Maroon solidarity and intransigence as the land question. But we have seen that in some instances the disputes were settled by the intervention of certain planters in whom the Maroons confided. Indeed this became so prevalent that it could be seen as systematic, and not unlike the eighteenth-century European system of patronage. And, as a form of settlement between Maroons and government, it was so effective that one wonders why it was not resorted to during the 1795 outbreak.

An incident which took place in 1774 was even more symptomatic of things to come. This incident also continues to give us more insights into the windwards' cognitive view of themselves in remaining decidedly more aggressive than the leewards in relation to the plantocratic society. In April 1774 a scouting party of windward Maroons, under Captain Davy, of Scotts Hall, apprehended a slave they thought was a runaway. The slave resisted, pointing to his owner, one Mr. Thompson, who soon came on the scene and fired at Davy; another slave, a passerby, was killed. The Maroon, Sam Grant, who had shot this slave accidentally, ran away from the scene, and in the melee which followed he was pursued by one Captain Townshend — obviously a newcomer to the island — "of a Bristol ship, an active young man [who carried] a loaded whip."[130] Whatever may be the nature of a loaded whip, Townshend soon blocked the way of Grant, who requested him to let him pass, adding that he did not wish to hurt him; when Townshend refused, Grant shot him fatally. Meanwhile, Captain Davy, realizing that an unsavory situation had developed, retreated to his town and from thence to Crawford (Charles Town) and Moore Towns for support in anticipation of the authorities' response. What is important here — and must have been quite frightening to the colonial state — was that three Maroon communities now stood together in readiness against the authorities. All this, naturally, created much alarm and excitement in the country "as if the Maroons had revolted, and many weak and wicked reports were raised on the occasion."[131]

As was expected, the island's officials soon arrived where the Maroons were encamped, under arms, near Charles Town, and report had it that they received the officials with great haughtiness; and Cudjoe (not to be confused with old Cudjoe of the Treaty), their headman, had the "insolence" to address them thus: "You see, it is true Gentlemen, but a handful of Men here, but dont' expect to treat us ill on that account. Tho' we take up rebels and runaways, we know how to make use of them, and if you persist, we can bring twenty blacks to one white."[132] The situation was threatening. But once again it was saved by the intervention of "some Gentlemen," who carried much weight with the Maroons, and it was agreed that Sam Grant should be brought to justice. Grant took his trial before two justices and three freeholders, and, intriguingly, was acquitted on the grounds that both killings were done in self-defence. This leniency was due to the urbane and diplomatic Sir Basil Keith, who was always willing to "consult the welfare of the Colony ... [and] the inclination of the Inhabitants."[133] The Maroons, for their part, had their own kind of test to determine the man's innocence. In situations of this sort, by a kind of gentleman's agreement among the soldier class, the accused was expected to take his own life, if he knew that he was guilty. Grant was thus reminded by the captain of his town what in honor bound he must do should he be guilty: "[G]o this instant into the wood and shoot yourself." But Grant pointed out that the first killing was accidental and was done to protect his superior, who was being shot at, while the second was done for his own self-defence.[134] He was equally "acquitted" by the Maroons, and Dallas wrote, "Sam Grant is at this time [the work was published in 1803] Major of Maroons, and Chief Commander at Charles Town."[135]

This incident created a great deal of alarm in the country, and it led a manuscript source to speculate on the likelihood of a war with the Maroons: "It would be a very unequal warfare ... with a parcel of savages who have nothing to lose; and what might still be worse it is to be feared, that if we had the fortune to extirpate them, our great wilderness which occupies the middle range of the Island, would soon be filled again by another set of Banditti more Savage than these ...." Making a virtue of necessity, the manuscript then gave it that "the best course to be pursued with any prospect of success, is a uniform adherence to justice in all our dealings with them ...."[136] This attitude is not unlike that which characterized the relationship with the Buccaneers in the seventeenth century, that is, a balancing of fear among the slavocracy: fear of the Buccaneers despite the friendly relations and fear of the Maroons despite the Treaties; but a greater fear of the consequence should they cease to be friends of government. The conciliatory Sir Basil Keith voiced it officially when he wrote to the Earl of Dartmouth about the trial, hoping that his leniency would serve "His Majesty better ... than by directly sending Troops against them and making a body of people desperate, who might do us infinite Mischief in the Country, and who are living amoung us under the Sanction of a Treaty we found convenient to make after a very long War with them ...."[137] He was to have the same conciliatory attitude to the Miskito Indians.[138]

The general suspicion the incident generated may have been the reason for some rather frenzied resolutions the House passed a few months later. It instructed the governor to issue orders "forthwith" to the superintendents of the Maroons "not to permit or suffer on any pretence whatever, the Maroons, or any of them, in their several departments, to fire guns or any fire arms, or to blow horns, on any occasion, after sun-set till sun-rise, unless when actual duty may render their firing necessary." The Maroons were semiautonomous in their communities, and the terms of the Treaties did not forbid them from doing the above. It was well known to the authorities that they possessed firearms used for tracking down slaves and for hunting. And as for not blowing on their horns — the *abeng* — this was surely unrealistic, as it was part and parcel of the Maroons' cultural tradition, transmitted from Africa. The House also ruled that the superintendents should be ordered to muster together the Maroons severally, "in the most public place in such towns," once every three months, "and then and there to read openly to them, the articles of pacification concluded and agreed upon between Colonel John Guthrie, Lieutenant Francis Sadler, and Cudjoe, and the articles of pacification" between Bennet and Quao, as well as the laws subsequently passed with respect to the Maroons. The superintendents were also to explain as carefully as possible all the articles and laws to the Maroons, obliging them strictly to adhere to and observe "all and every clause, article, matter and thing, therein contained, which to them relate."[139]

One can find no more reference to these imperial injunctions, but it can be safely conjectured that the Maroons paid no attention to them whatever — as it can also be assumed that the authorities made no attempt at enforcing them.

If the situation between government and Maroons did not reach breaking point by the 1780s, it was largely due to three factors: the patronage system which worked well in settling disputes; the character of the superintendents in any given town; and the type of governor on the island. Most of the governors from 1752 demonstrated much sensitivity to Maroon affairs. Governor Charles Knowles, for instance, who administered the colony from 1752 to 1756, showed a great deal of willingness to grant the Maroons new lands, and Charles Town may well have been named after him, while a governor like Sir Basil Keith was always anxious to maintain good relations with the Maroons. But a governor unmindful of, or hostile to, the special situation of the Maroons could easily exacerbate a relationship which was always a tenuous one, to say the least, and this was exactly what happened during the administration of the Earl of Balcarres.

Chapter 7

The Trewlawny Town War, 1795–1796

Lord Balcarres arrived in Jamaica as lieutenant governor in April 1795, when the Haitian (St. Domingue) revolution was in full swing. He, in fact, succeeded Sir Adam Williamson, who was sent by William Pitt and his war secretary on a commission "to such parts of St. Domingo, as are now or may hereafter be in our possession," with a corps of black slaves included in His Majesty's service.[1] Balcarres, for his part, after a month on the island, was writing home, May 11, 1795, to say, "This island seems in a state of perfect internal Tranquility," but by May 30, he was reporting an attempt to burn Kingston, and characteristically, he blamed it on the French emigrés on the island.[2] The governor was surprised that, "Although there is every appearance of Happiness and Contentment among the slaves, it did not deter the agents who were introducing persons of various descriptions, particularly mulattos and blacks from St. Domingo into the interior of the island." But Balcarres pledged not to allow any foreigner to remain "unless I know what he is and where he is."[3] However, he was certain that despite the assiduity of the French to introduce their "Principles" into Jamaica, he did not think they made any impression, but he would, all the same, "suffer no Inlet whatsoever for their doctrines."[4]

Balcarres's letter to the Duke of Portland, the then Secretary of states for the colonies, gives a fitting background to the situation now in contemplation. To begin with, Balcarres was an unyielding enemy of French revolutionary ideas, and he saw himself as especially destined to crush such doctrines wherever they might appear. A scion of an ancient Scottish family of great ferocity, one of whom was called the Tiger Earl or the "hirsute barbarian," Balcarres at fifteen purchased his ensigncy in the 53rd Regiment of Foot; served in Gibraltar, Germany, and in the United States War of Independence under General Burgoyne; and in 1784 became one of the sixteen representative Scottish peers in the House of Lords. [5] We have already mentioned his unsuccessful attempts in assisting England to place Louis XVII of France on the French throne and his penchant for a sword. He quite clearly had a strong sense of destiny, especially with respect to crushing revolutionaries: "Should the King of France regain his throne by the assistance of England," Balcarres said, "it must not be forgotten that the idea was mine, and that I have pinned my glory to it, and I think the young King will owe me the best sword in his arsenal!"[6] Both his zeal for suppressing revolutions and his penchant for swords were to follow him to Jamaica. Balcarres sailed from England with his brother, General Lindsay, who was sent out to quell a rebellion in Grenada, "then in a dangerous state." That rebellion had been instigated by free blacks and mulattos, and Lindsay soon dealt with it successfully; Balcarres may have taken his cue from his brother on how to deal with insurgents in the area. In this year, the Caribs were also defeated in Grenada, and British naval supremacy was being solidly established.

It was an era of revolutions with its beginning in Europe, but spilling over into the West Indies. The principles of the French Revolution had reached the area by different routes and with many results, the most dramatic being the Haitian Revolution. War was declared between England and France in 1793, and the Caribbean, as usual, became a part of these combatants' cockpit. Any mention of "French Principles" or of French persons in Jamaica was viewed by the planter class as nervewracking. Balcarres, on the island at this time, was determined that French enthusiastic ideas — in the parlance of the period — should not besmirch Jamaica, and he was probably responsible for deporting more Frenchmen from the island than any other governor.

When therefore an altercation took place between the Trelawny Town Maroons and the local government of Montego Bay in the parish of St. James, in July 1795, Balcarres was certain that French revolutionary ideas were behind it. Although, he said, "It is probable that this Insurrection is owing to private disputes [and] hatred to their Superintendant and such causes, ... your grace knows how very jealous I am of everything that has the tendency to Insurrection, and if the minds of these mountaineers have been poisoned by Emisseries, it may prove very fatal to the Country."[7] Later, he was to assert more unambiguously the French influence on the Trelawny Town Maroons. This, of course, was nonsense.

What, then, led to the insurrection of the Trelawny Town Maroons in July 1795? In situations of this sort, there is usually the immediate, objective "cause" as well as the more cumulative ones that had been festering for some time. We have already discussed the latter — the tension that was building up between government and Maroons generally. But the fact that the situation took place with the Trelawny Town Maroons can be traced to the seemingly trivial affair where two from this town were convicted "by the evidence of two white people, of killing tame hogs," for which they were punished by flogging in the common workhouse by a slave they had previously taken up and lodged for punishment in that institution. This delighted the other slaves. To them, it was an opportunity for triumph and revenge over the Maroons, whom they hated. But to the Maroons, with their inbred contempt for slaves, it registered the very depth of humiliation, and it was, indeed, an egregious error on the part of the local authorities. The two chastized Maroons left the scene in a rage and as they "went through the town and plantations they were laughed at, hissed, and hooted by the slaves."[8] Even if the Trelawny Town group did not have grievances already on their minds, this by itself would have been cause enough for the greatest excitement and posturing. Their first and immediate response was to expel their superintendent, Thomas Craskell, who was already a part of their grievance. Craskell had succeeded Major John James, whom the Maroons practically worshipped and wished to have returned to them.[9]

Major John James was appointed superintendent of Trelawny Town in 1767 and, having performed his duties with undisputed energy and diligence, was appointed major-commandant of all Maroons in the colony in 1779 (not 1791, according to Dallas). [10] This extended his functions and sent him traveling constantly to the other Maroon communities to settle disputes between them and neighboring whites as well as among themselves, in addition to going out with Maroon parties in search of runaways. In some cases James even found himself saddled with the task of going to sea against enterprising slaves who took off in boats in search of a Spanish colony, usually Cuba, whence they would be certain that they would not be extradited — and some may well have thought that they were on their way back to Africa. Richard Martin, for instance, mentioned above, had employed James's services to pursue his eleven slaves who took off to Cuba in a canoe. James's merits and abilities were fully appreciated by the Assembly, and in 1782 this body granted him £250 as recompence for his "extraordinary service" to the country, and for his good conduct and success in "keeping under proper subjection" the Maroons in their towns. Despite the House's appreciation of his abilities, however, it was characteristically tardy in reimbursing him on a regular basis, and for this he petitioned this body constantly, not only for himself but also for his son, who served under him for some time.[11]

The lack of a superintendent's accommodation, peculiar to all the towns, soon found James living illegally outside the community. The Maroons missed having him around, and, with a view to having him returned, they complained to the Assembly that he had not been residing in Trelawny Town. It came as a surprise to them, and was completely contrary to their objective, when the House dismissed James for negligence in 1792, one year after the 1791 act, and at a time, as we saw above, when Maroon affairs were treated rather cavalierly.

James possessed all the qualities the Maroons respected. He was tough and fearless and could scale a mountain path as lithely as any one of them: "Nature," wrote Dallas, "never produced a form more calculated for vigour and activity. Barefoot, he equalled the speed of the hardiest Maroon over rocks and precipices, darting on with an agility peculiar to himself. He was indefatigable in every pursuit to which the Maroons were accustomed, and nothing that he pursued escaped him. Hunting the wild boar had been his earliest amusement and employment .... When dreadful disputes took place among the Maroons, their cutlasses brandished against one another and serious mischief likely to ensue, he would run among the thickest of them, knock down the most refractory, put them into irons, and afterwards punish them .... They loved, venerated and feared him. He arranged and settled their accounts for their labour, adjusted differences, and neither suffered them to be imposed upon, nor to impose upon others. Had he been born a Maroon, he could not have been better acquainted with their character, disposition, and prejudices."[12] It was thus not easy to succeed a man like James within the Maroon context, and Thomas Craskell was certainly no James. The son of the island's engineer, he was an officer in the regular service and, from all accounts, a rather conventional and nondescript young man with no knowledge whatever of Maroon affairs, least of all Maroon character. Naturally, he soon fell foul of them, and their contempt for him was immense. They resented his presence and complained bitterly; thus he was an easy target for their wrath.

In the meantime the magistrates had written to Balcarres "that a very serious disturbance is likely to break out immediately with the Maroons of Trelawny Town"; they were threatening the destruction of the two plantations nearest them and of all the whites residing there; they had sent their women into the woods, and would soon be killing their children and cattle, which could be an encumbrance; the magistrates, as a precaution, had recommended the calling out of the troops; while Colonel James had ordered out two companies of militia for the immediate protection of the plantations in the neighborhood. They also proposed, in line with the patronage system we have mentioned, that four magistrates should meet some chosen Maroons "to settle all differences."[13] To this the Maroons sent a very bellicose but thoroughly confused reply.

> The Maroons wishes nothing else from the country but battle; and they desires not to see Mr. Craskell up here at all. So they are waiting every moment for the above on Monday.
>
> Colonel Mountague, and all the rest. Mr. David Schaw will see you on Sunday morning, for an answer.
>
> They will wait till Monday, nine o'clock; and if they dont come up, they will come down themselves.[14]

It is easy to believe Dallas when he said, "This curious epistle, it was afterwards well known, was dictated by a few drunken Maroons, to a poor ignorant white man without the concurrence of old Montague, who was then sick and absent; nor was it known to one-tenth part of the people."[15] The following week, Craskell's assistant, John Merody, who was not dismissed by the Maroons, sent another letter as if a message from the irate Maroons to Craskell: "The Maroons inform you that they do not want anything, for they have got plenty of powder and ball; for it is too late to do anything that is good. They have received an answer from the bay, by Mr. David Schaw, and he has taken all the business upon himself; for there will be four magistrates from the bay today, at Mr. Schaw's property; they do not want any more letters from you, except it is from the bay ...." Merody ended by saying he was prevented from leaving by the Maroons, but they might let him go soon; in the meantime they were "very severe" with him.[16]

Those acquainted with the Maroons would know that such strong language did not necessarily mean very much. In this case it was more a ploy to rivet attention to their demands. Men like John James, General Reid, and John Mowat of St. James knew this and did not hesitate to proceed to Trelawny Town to confer with them on their own accord. The Maroons too had sent a messenger to the militia, now stationed but three miles from their town, requiring Custos John Tharp and three other gentlemen to visit them. This they did, only to find that James and his group had already mitigated much of their anger, although the gathering of the armed men that they met still displayed in their "countenances and manners ... a spirit of violence."[17] These were critical meetings, and with another kind of governor, the whole affair could well have ended here. With the visitors, the Maroons set forth their grievances under three headings. First, they complained of the whipping of the two Maroons at Montego Bay by a slave, declaring it to have been an infringement of the Treaty. Second, they pointed out that their original land grant was worn out, and they therefore were asking for an additional quantity, citing the adjoining properties of Vaughn and David Schaw, as well as the lands commonly called and known as Crews or Robert Kenyon, that would be convenient to them. Third, as would be expected, they complained against the conduct of Thomas

Craskell, arguing that he was not qualified for the office of superintendent of their town; that he lacked authority, "for when young men quarrel and fight, instead of interfering with his authority to adjust their differences, he appears frightened, and runs to his house for safety; and as they have experienced the disposition and abilities of captain John James (their late superintendent), they are desirous of his reappointment to the office, and are adverse to the appointment of any other person."[18]

James himself, who stayed overnight in the town, may have helped to frame the last grievance, but there is no doubt that the Maroons independently held no brief for the likes of Craskell. They saw the James family, as Dallas rightly said, as of hereditary right to the superintendency over them, the father before having served to be followed by Major James and his son — all of whom were successful in their relations with the proud and difficult Maroons. As for their request for more lands, we saw, in the last chapter, their 1792 petition for lands refused, and it is interesting that they now asked for the property of David Schaw, who had petitioned the Assembly against their trespass. As for the flogging of the two Maroons, many felt that, had they been transferred to the town for punishment, they would have been dealt with much more severely. But their grievance was not about severity; it was the humiliation of a Maroon — any Maroon — being punished by a slave: "Do not subject us to insult and humiliation from the very people to whom we are set in opposition," complained a Maroon representative to some officials.[19]

Balcarres, we know, was a man who saw things straight and with simplistic clarity. He had no doubt at all of French influence on the Maroons, and to him, the remedy was to take "every vigorous measure to reduce them by Force."[20] The magistrates, too, and other gentlemen of Trelawny and Montego Bay, aware of the large number of French aliens in the country and at a time when their "long boats [were] daily captured by the French privateers composed of motley crews," saw the likelihood of a French threat to the island, but they did not see any evidence of Maroon/French collusion. They could not therefore share Balcarres's view as to remedy. On the contrary, because of the French presence, they rather counselled temporizing with the Maroons, especially since their claims were not unreasonable. Should hostilities break out, then, to them it would present a fine opportunity for the French brigands to intervene and execute their favorite plan of destroying British property. Furthermore, although the Maroons at arms might not have exceeded 300 men, yet "the fastnessess they possess[ed]," and their control of the mountain provision, coupled to the fact that they could at pleasure receive aid from the slaves, were forceful reasoning to recommend acceptance of their demands.[21]

Balcarres did not and possibly could not understand this reasoning. He was not unaware that the Maroons could do some damage to the island, but he was convinced that with all the force at his command he could reduce them in no time. It should be pointed out that Balcarres was not around during the long-drawn-out Maroon war which led to the Treaties, and therefore knew nothing of Maroon warfare. But he was not to remain ignorant for long.

Apart from the militia and the regular troops, Balcarres, like every other governor contemplating the defense of the island from either intestine or external enemies, saw the importance of raising a corps of black troops, and with characteristic energy he wrote to Portland: "It is not time for waiting for orders, I may be obliged to judge, decide, and execute in an Instant Should any disturbance happen in this Island it can only be saved by raising Negro Corps."[22] This recommendation presented no problem to Portland because he had all along suggested the efficacy of black troops. As time progressed, Balcarres began to see himself and not John James, as the magistrates thought, as the only man who could "save" Jamaica from the savages — for so he saw the Maroons. Energy and vigor became the *leitmotif* of all his actions, and his dispatches home are replete with these forceful words. He now "had Intelligence that Emissaries from the French had been in that country of the Maroons," which he traced and found them to have been men of the most "dangerous description." He wrote that it was "the opinion of the Council that the French have been at the bottom of this Business, but that there has been no concert with the ... Slaves." He treated with contempt the temporizing policy of the Montego Bay magistrates, considering that the island possessed a force capable of reducing the Maroons "in two days." He was therefore stoutly against acceding to their three-point demands, declaring that "the giving way to any one of them is sowing the seeds of future Mischief."[23]

Martial law was declared August 2, and, heartened by the "manly and energetic" advice of the Council not to temporize, Balcarres himself advanced near the scene of battle.[24] At this point he had two major aims: the one of course was to crush the Maroons, but he was also well aware how critical the situation would become should the slaves join in a general insurrection. To this end he hoped the great show of force to be mustered would put them in a state of awe and apprehension. But in looking around for the most expeditious manner of deploying his large troops from Kingston to Montego Bay — which was by sea — he soon discovered that he had already dispatched all his ships with troops to Sir Adam Williamson, who was doing his bit for the empire in St. Domingue. A man of action, Balcarres soon sent orders to divert them back for his own use in Jamaica, before turning to the slaves. He ordered, "secretly and confidentially," custodes and other officials of all parishes to assemble their militia and to make a search in the huts of every slave for concealed arms and the like. Also, he dispatched an open boat to intercept any craft that sailed. Convinced that the slaves were now under check, the governor positioned himself at Vaughansfield, within a mile and a half of Trelawny Town. His strategy was to blockade the Maroon town by having a military presence at every entrance despite the inhospitable terrain of the area — "the most rugged and mountainous country in the universe."[25] He boasted of having perfect knowledge of every road, path, or track of Trelawny Town, and this, in all probability, was no idle boast, since he had the Accompong Maroons allied to him and providing him with necessary strategic information. However, as the war progressed, Balcarres was to find that there were Maroon bulwarks that remained unknown to him and his auxiliaries.

His force was impressive. It consisted of some 1,500 British troops trained in the best tradition of military science, supported by "several thousands of militia." By December this formidable force was joined by some one hundred fierce bloodhounds from Cuba. All this outfit was to fight against just a little over 500 uneducated, untrained, "uncivilized" Maroons, consisting of men, women, children, and old people, only 167 of whom were men able to bear arms; Balcarres himself mentioned later that of these, only about thirty were really "stout boys."[26] And it cannot be overemphasized here that the Maroons must have been nonplussed and must have wondered what occasioned the gargantuan mustering of force against them. Be the cause what it may, having deployed his forces to cut the Trelawnys off at every point, and having sent a battalion under George Walpole to St. Elizabeth around the Accompong Town area, the governor should be excused if he felt that victory was just around the corner. It was with the confidence, then, of a man who felt himself in control, that he issued his proclamation on August 8, inviting the Maroons to surrender on or before August 12 and offering rewards to anyone capturing a Maroon after this date. Balcarres also promised that if they surrendered, their lives would be spared, and that was all he was prepared to offer.[27]

The Maroons, for their part, reconnoitered and found that they were indeed blockaded. This created a division in their ranks. The older ones recommended surrender, while the younger refused, arguing that they could repair to the sanctum of the cockpits and wage guerrilla warfare. At "about" two p.m. on the eleventh day — a day before the expiration of the time — some thirty or thirty-one of the older Maroons, including their chief, Montague James, surrendered, and laid down their arms "at my feet," Balcarres told Portland. But the energetic governor had already clapped in irons, "secured," as he termed it, a small deputation of six, on its way to surrender directly to him. The governor was pleased with this beginning, pointing out that he now had in his possession more than a third of the

Maroons' men of arms.[28] This slight exaggeration is certainly a reflection of his sanguinity at this point.

It is clear that the treatment of the six deputies and of the thirty or so under Montague was to give a new turn to the course of events. In all probability others might have joined their old and beloved chief, were he and his companions not so savagely treated upon surrender, before any hostilities took place. "They were all," wrote Dallas, "old Montague excepted, bound with their hands behind, and on the 13th sent into confinement at Montego Bay; one of them, exasperated at this disappointment, ... put an end to his existence by ripping out his bowels."[29] Another source said that old Montague was not excluded: "All, not excluding the white-haired veteran Montague, had been put in irons and hurried off to prison — perhaps to death ...."[30] It should be noted that Balcarres's dispatches home are silent on all this, only mentioning that he had "secured" the six men and that the others had surrendered. As we have mentioned throughout this study, Maroon spies during warfare were everywhere, and very effective, commanding, as they did, the plains below from their eminence. So they saw the reception their venerable chief and the others received, and they could not be certain that their kinsmen were not to be put to death as Gardner observed. A sense of intense distrust, which loomed like one of the dramatis personae in this encounter, had began, and Walpole was to have much problem with it later. The younger component of the Maroons — "the wild and impetuous young savages," in the words of Balcarres — were now even more determined to resist at any cost and began by applying the scorched earth policy. They burnt both the old town and the new — Furry's — three-quarters of a mile away, and tried initially to push their way west toward Hanover out of their encirclement.[31]

But the earl was ready for the situation. He sent a strong company of mulattos from the St. James' Regiment against them, and the mulattos, fighting with vigor and determination, repulsed the Maroons, who sustained "considerable loss." The extent of this loss is not clear, but it is the only one we know of throughout the war. When the situation developed into a regular guerrilla warfare, we have no evidence of any Maroon casualities. This early success satisfied the governor, who saw in it the beginning of the end of the conflict. He thus ordered Colonel Sandford with forty-five of his 20th Dragoons to mount the hill and attack the town from the rear with the intent of driving the Maroons into the government's strong line of defense. Sandford took the new part of the town, and, flushed with his first success, he recklessly galloped on toward the old town, contrary to orders. The Maroons were delighted because the colonel became ensnared in an ambush, where nearly half his troops, including himself, were killed, and not a Maroon was lost. The rest of the Dragoons, under Captain Butler,

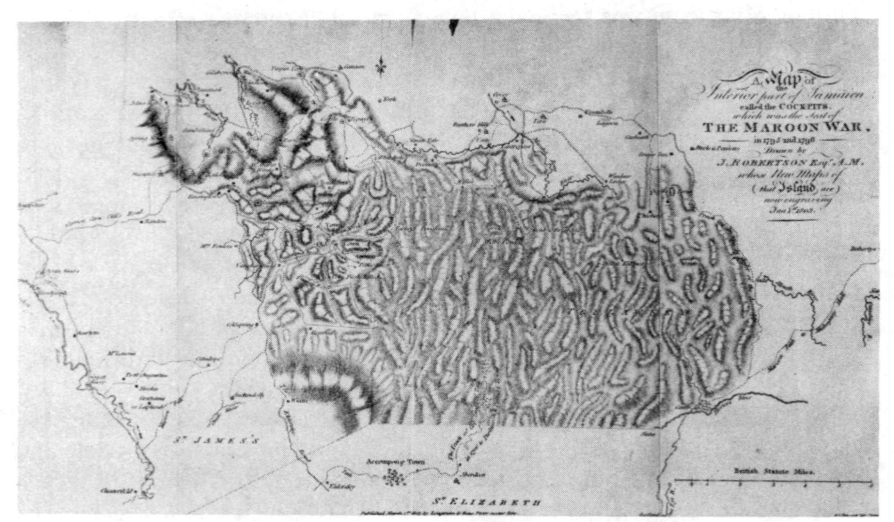

Courtesy, Institute of Jamaica, Kingston

The Cockpits, at the time of the Maroon War, 1795–96

by the most daring feat, galloped their way through the Maroons into a country almost inaccessible, and joined Balcarres at Vaughansfield.[32]

Balcarres began now to understand something of the nature of Maroon warfare and of the terrain on which it was conducted, and he was soon to change his views that they could soon be defeated. He assessed the situation in different dispatches to Portland at the end of August. He, himself, was personally involved in getting provisions and supplies to the troops. But the labor of effecting this service in so rugged a country was beyond description. His outposts and his convoys were daily attacked by the enemies. He, however, attacked the new town successfully on August 19, and on the 23rd the old town was also taken after an assault by three separate columns, with only three soldiers killed. But as we saw during the 1730 conflicts, taking a Maroon town did not mean the end of hostilities. In fact, in dispersion they could now become more formidable and more brutal in their attacks. Balcarres wrote that "the Maroons retreated into a Country of Rocks [the Cockpits] beyond description — wild and barren into which no white person has ever entered."[33] He hoped that they would either starve in these redoubts or that famine might drive them out. In the meantime, he would send parties of militia against them, but more important, he had in service armed and confidential blacks — the Black Shots, as adept as the Maroons at ranging the woods — to send after them. He discovered that the enemies had a country of "considerable strength," a district abounding in ground provision: should they be joined by other Maroons, they would make a formidable force; and as potential allies of the slaves, "the properties and liberties of every Person in this Island were at their disposal and under their dominion," and the example of St. Domingue pointed to them the dominion of this country. Thus there could be no turning back, no appeasement.

As in the early conflicts culminating in the Peace Treaties, the government policy was to destroy all known Maroon provision grounds so as to starve them into surrender. This was done with much persistence; when it became more dangerous, the slaves of the militia were made to do it, often being shot at, but covered by troops. Trelawny Town, never to be regained by the Maroons, was, by August 25, possessed by His Majesty's forces and militia parties, while armed "confidential" blacks and His Majesty's troops and the Accompong Maroons were pursuing the "rebels." Balcarres observed that they would be attacking in small numbers as a "Band of Robbers" but never to be considered "as an Enemy capable of endangering the Security of this Island." And not missing a chance to congratulate himself, he ended by saying, "I have accomplished every object that I had in view when I undertook the ardous task of giving a Severe and sudden check to the Trelawny Maroons."[34] Nevertheless, the conflict dragged on. And the situation developed into a classical guerrilla warfare. The Maroons were able to make their attacks at night, and Balcarres, who was in the field, was badly injured after a fall from his horse, whereupon Colonel Fitch took over his command. But Fitch soon met the same fate as Sandford, when he too was ambushed and later killed along with a militia captain, two Accompong Maroons, and some privates from his own 83rd regiment, again without a Maroon casuality. This was a great blow to the country, for Fitch was universally admired, and morale slumped.[35]

The Accompong Maroons fought faithfully and steadily on the side of the government. This, perhaps, requires some explanation, given the fact that Accompong Town was really an extension of Trelawny Town from the days of old Cudjoe, and both towns up to this period — as far as we know — had worked closely together. The rumor at the beginning of the outbreak that Accompong was about to join the Trelawnys, though false, is understandable. We do not know why the two towns became such implacable enemies. Dallas mentioned that the Trelawny Maroons "had long manifested their discontent against the Accompongs, for not yielding to them the original treaty made with Cudjoe, which they claimed the right of keeping."[36] This seems clear enough, but then Dallas went on to say: "About this time it was again sent for, to be shown if necessary, and was given by the Accompongs, but never returned to them."[37] So apparently the Trelawnys had the original Treaty during the war. If this is correct, it is not clear what its fate was since they were finally deported from the island. It seems unlikely, though, that this alone could have created rancor enough for the Accompongs to have fought with the plantocracy against their former allies. However it may be, the Accompong's fidelity to the government was immediately expressed, upon the outbreak of the war, in a formal compact. And to give symbolic point to the compact with government, the Accompongs held a solemn ceremony baptizing all the younger Maroons. The authorities were appreciative and the families of those, for example, who fell with Colonel Fitch were recompensed. The superintendent of Accompong Town, Alexander Forbes, reported to the Assembly that the bereaved families seemed reconciled to their fate and were impressed by the attention shown them by the authorities. These families were the children of Captain Reid and the wife of Edward Badnedge. Captain Reid, for his part, had seventeen children, nine with his wife Jenny and eight with his other wife, Lucinda. Badnedge had no issue but was survived by his wife Tabia. The Assembly voted £500 for "providing for and rewarding the Accompong Town Maroons for their good conduct," and particularly the families of those who suffered in action with Fitch.[38]

As far as we know — and if Dallas is correct — only one Trelawny Town Maroon defected to the side of government. This was one Captain Thomas, not mentioned in the official documents. He fought under Colonel Sandford and was one of the few survivors after Sandford's debacle. Dallas reported that he was offered protection and reward for his services, but he refused, and felt hurt that rewards should be thought necessary. It is not clear why Thomas fought with the authorities against his people.[39]

The attitude of the windwards — the Maroons of Moore Town, Charles Town, and Scotts Hall — to the war, should now be considered. Repeatedly we have seen that the windwards, especially the Moore Town set, displayed a more independent and aggressive attitude towards the planter class. Balcarres complained, two months after the outbreak, that the windwards refused to obey his orders to "come in." He was not sure whether the refusal was based on fear or "something else." As for those of Moore Town, "who are a very warlike Tribe of them," they declared that not only would they not "come in" but they asserted that if Charles Town joined the rebellion, they too would follow suit. Balcarres felt that the situation was tricky, and even he saw the necessity to temporize under the circumstances — at least for the time being, because he had not enough force to take them on, too. He viewed the 13th Regiment as "useless," and the island's stores were also exhausted. Of those ordered to come in, only six from Charles Town, out of sixty-two arms-bearing men, attended the governor, and to these he gave presents and used flattering words to remove their fears. He also showed them the remaining presents that he had for the others, should they also come in. But Balcarres admitted that they were "a bold hardy looking people and seem by their Deportment to have a much greater portion of Contempt than Fear in their Constitution." He felt that his best hope of their continuing quiet was that from the evidence he acquired, the French had only gained "a part of the Maroons," but he did not say which part; perhaps the Trelawnys. He reflected that the collective force of the windwards would amount to that of the Trelawnys and Accompongs together, and the windwards, too, could "fly" at a moment's notice to their fastnesses — in this case the Blue Mountains.

All in all, Balcarres summed up the situation, when he said that the windwards were in a state of "inactive rebellion," having refused to obey any of his orders. They also established sentinels at strategic points to reconnoitre the situation; they were stopping people on the roads; they had bought new supplies of gun powder, and even more ominous, they had built huts in the heart of the Blue Mountains — as if in a state of preparedness. But the governor felt reassured when it became his understanding that if the troops did not attack them then they, too, would not attack the government forces.[40]

Meanwhile, the position of the slaves on the plantations with respect to the rebellion was rather complex. Soon after the outbreak, some of the plantations in the neighborhood of Trelawny Town had complaints against overseers submitted by slaves.[41] These were bold actions, apparently concerted, and even if these slaves did not intend to join the Maroons, they nevertheless might have taken advantage of the plight of the planters. We are not clear about the result of their complaints, but it was at this time that the energetic Balcarres was sending troops in the area to keep the slaves on neighboring plantations in awe. As the war developed the generalized fear of the whites that the slaves would join the Maroons in a wholesale insurrection receded. This is not to say that some did not join; some did. We have already seen from this study that there were always slaves waiting for the opportune moment to rise against their oppressors. Some even took the occasion to fight on their own and committed ravages on plantations without actually joining the Trelawnys. There were reports of slaves, ranging from 400 to forty, who were said to have joined the Maroons. At the termination of the war, Balcarres insisted on saying that some 400 altogether joined, while Dallas was of the opinion that they did not amount, "in the whole, men, women, and children to a hundred, and of these many had been forced away."[42] Even if Balcarres's number is inflated, Dallas's is most certainly too low. At the termination of the war Balcarres actually had 123 runaways in custody, and this figure clearly had not taken into consideration those who had escaped upon finding out that the Maroons would betray their identity to the authorities. Of the 123, the governor expected "the most notorious offenders" to be tried for their lives, and he had "pitched upon 11 only to be made Examples of," while the others were to be sold to the Spaniards. [43]

Nevertheless, there appears the need to explain why more slaves did not join the Trelawnys. To begin with, the slaves in general both feared and disliked the Maroons, since the Treaties. They could not forget that the Maroons placed great constraints on their propensity to run away or to rebel. Those well-organized slave rebellions of the 1760s, especially that led by Tacky, might have been successful had it not been for the part played by the Maroons in quelling them. Dallas reminded us that in the rebellion of 1766 the Maroons brought in the head or the person of practically every slave in rebellion in the space of one month.[44] All this was bound to leave the slaves frustrated and resentful against the Maroons. Again, some slaves who joined the war simply returned to their plantations upon finding that the Maroons were experiencing tremendous difficulties, especially with respect to food, when the authorities burnt their provision grounds. Some of those who returned from the war were savagely dealt with by their fellow slaves, demonstrating their hostility toward the Maroons. Furthermore, some also resented being conscripted for the war as Black Shots or as baggage slaves, and these were invariably made to do the most arduous and dangerous tasks. Very important, too, was the fact that the slaves' provision grounds during the war were either trodden upon by the troops or raided by the Maroons themselves. With their own grounds being destroyed by government, often it was the provision grounds of the slaves that rescued the Maroons from starvation.

It is interesting to note that it was chiefly the Maroon women who would collect the provisions from the slaves' grounds, while being covered by the men — as the militia slaves were covered when destroying Maroon grounds. The pillaging of their provision grounds rankled with the slaves, who valued these grounds[45] as much as a means of retreat from the nearness of slave masters, as they were a source of food. In addition, they were a source of revenue when they sold their surplus at the marketplaces. In having to pillage the slaves' provision grounds, then, the Maroons were adversely affecting them in important psychological, nutritional, and economic areas. Balcarres would seem to have understood this, and soon treated it as a part of the war strategy. "So long as the Maroon holds out the charm of Food and Freedom," he maintained, so long will the slave look up to him. But the matter is entirely changed when the Maroon throws himself on the slave to be fed. It was upon this "principle" that Balcarres attacked and took their town and destroyed their provision grounds. "I have thrown them upon the lands of the slaves for subsistence," he declared.[46]

There is no doubt that the Maroon encroachments on slaves' provision grounds was a part of the slaves' hostility to the Maroons, and the governor was convinced that it was attended with the "happiest effects." He cited the case of a slave belonging to Pembroke estate, who "seized" a runaway who had joined the Maroons but left them, and "with the greatest difficulty the other Slaves have been prevented from tearing him to pieces."[47] But Balcarres has not given us evidence to show that their hostility to the runaway was based solely on the provision-ground issue. A fascinating facet of this war, too, was the apparent lack of deserters — whether Black Shots or baggage slaves — who could have joined the Maroons, as happened in the 1730s. But the lack of records on this category should not lead us to conclude too readily that they did not desert. What appears to have happened is that those who did desert, went on their own and established their own communities, independent of the Maroon groups. All this is suggested by the number of runaways in the woods, who became a source of great irritation to the authorities soon after the Trelawnys were deported.

Balcarres was also convinced that a large proportion of slaves joining the Maroons would have an inverse effect upon Maroon chances of success. Thus when, in October 1795, he heard that forty more slaves were missing from one estate and they were thought to have joined the Maroons, he gave it as his opinion that they would weaken instead of strengthen the Maroons; the less numerous they were, "the more trouble they will give us." In another dispatch he pointed out that many of the slaves who had joined were returning. Some of these were said to have been forced by Maroons to join, and it is just as well that they returned because, upon the termination of the war, the Maroons did not scruple to give them up to the authorities, as we shall see. If 400 instead of 200 slaves joined them, it would not give the governor "a moment's uneasiness," and the end of the business would be nearer than if fewer joined them.[48] Apparently a part of Balcarres's reasoning was based on the fact that slaves deserting from Maroon citadels were an invaluable source of strategic information as to the Maroons' whereabouts. This was in addition to his favorite provision-ground thesis: the more Maroon mouths to feed, arising from the destruction of their plantations, the greater the raids on slaves' provision grounds; the greater the raids on these provision grounds, the greater the slaves' hostility to the Maroons.

Meanwhile, the war continued. After the death of Colonel Fitch at the end of August, a real guerrilla situation developed. At this point Colonel George Walpole became most prominent in the war. Aided by the Accompongs, he was already commanding the troops in the south, and had occupied a "most judicious post," when Balcarres made him commander of all operations against the Maroons after Fitch's death, and gave him the rank of colonel, and later that of major-general (in each case, subject to His Majesty's pleasure).[49]

Walpole's task was not easy, because from mid-August to December, the dispersed Maroons were wreaking vengeance on plantations. Throughout the island, they were burning, killing, and confiscating cattle, taking and killing slaves, burning houses, offices, stores, and horses, taking the lives of some proprietors and threatening others, forcing many to evacuate their plantations, and each day brought new depressing news. In September news came from the Westmoreland militia, appointed to cover some slaves who were ordered to destroy Maroon provision grounds, that the Maroons had fired from an ambush, killing one officer and wounding another, while three privates were killed and four wounded. The following day, they set fire to one George Gordon's dwelling and to the house of his slaves; and within the week, the dwelling houses, works, slave barracks, and a coffee plantation of one Jacob Graham were burnt, and thirty of his slaves were missing. The experience of the Troughts was among the worst. This family owned the Catadupa and Mocha coffee estates in St. James, and here the Trelawnys came "in considerable numbers ... and burnt and destroyed all the houses, stores, and buildings ... on the 17th September, 1795." They also threatened the life of Joseph Tucker, the overseer, and the slaves, necessitating overseer and slaves to abandon the said property from September 17, 1795, until March 1796. The result was that a great part of the coffee crop was lost, and the Maroons also killed some of the cattle, forced or enticed away one of the slaves, and plundered and destroyed all the provisions, together with that which was destroyed by order of the general commanding in that quarter. Thus was the petition of Alma Maria Trought to the Assembly, asking for relief to the tune of some £4,755. Jacob Graham, too, was among the others who had perforce to leave his estate from September 1795 to February of the next year. His losses were computed at £4,830.[50] The House was faced with many other claims of this nature, too numerous to mention here. Yet, according to Dallas, not one of the Maroons was known to have been killed while they were spreading "devastation around the country, and had slain many fine fellows."[51]

And in the face of all these difficulties Balcarres found the St. James planters and those of the parish of Trelawny more a hindrance than a help — rather reminiscent of the problem Governor Hunter had had with the leading men of the day in the 1730s. Balcarres considered these two parishes an *Imperium in Imperio* in Jamaica, for the men opposed and thwarted everything he recommended. In fact, he found that most of them had connections with the Maroons, "and almost the whole of them pay contributions to those Fellows to induce them not to injure their properties"[52] — as had also been alleged during the 1730s.

But, to Balcarres, the most dangerous man in all this was Major James, ex-superintendent of Trelawny Town. James, he said, had a network of relationships within these two parishes based on blood and marriage, and his influence was great: his niece of twenty, for instance, was married to the octogenarian custos of St. James, who was the major-general of the militia before Balcarres superseded him with Walpole. The second major-general was one Mr. Reid, hated by the militia, but equally under the thumb of Major James and having close relations with the Maroons. The speaker of the house, who resided in Trelawny, was the brother-in-law of General Reid, and all these men disapproved strongly of Walpole's appointment to major-general.[53] It should be remembered that from the outset there was a basic disagreement between Balcarres and these gentlemen over the way to approach Maroon complaints — the latter enjoining temporizing, while Balcarres was always for showing some muscle. The incompetent performance of the militia of these two parishes — Trelawny and St. James — was no doubt the result of resentment over Balcarres and Walpole. It may have been due also to the relative sense of security these planters were enjoying, if Balcarres was correct when he accused them of paying the Maroons not to attack their properties. By the end of the war, however, these same men were to become supportive of Balcarres.

It is highly probable that Walpole had Guthrie of Cudjoe's Treaty as his model when he developed his military strategy against the Trelawnys. Like Guthrie, he made use of blacks — the Accompong Maroons or runaways from Trelawny Town, as well as his "confidential" slaves, the Black Shots — to acquaint him with the whereabouts of the enemy, and by October 1795 he thought he knew their "citadels" with certainty. He knew they were divided into two main bodies, one of which was situated in the Cockpits at heights that were surrounded by perpendicular precipices. He knew what they were doing and even what some were saying, some of his scouts being within yards of their posts. Walpole first strengthened the forces around the Cockpits to ensure that the Maroons would be prevented from obtaining food from plantations or from slaves' provision grounds, and even — borrowing a page from the Maroons — set up ambushes near provision grounds which the Maroons would most likely invade. Having a bird's-eye view of the Maroons' redoubts, Walpole then "by the most unremitting Exertions, possessed himself of the difficult Tracts and Paths of communication into those cockpits," and, like Guthrie, pressed on into Maroon territory, and all the while the Maroons, too, could see every movement of the major-general and his force.[54] In this instance, the Maroons abandoned their post rather than risk a combat with Walpole. But this was definitely a part of the strategy to lure the party further into the fastnesses of the Cockpits. Walpole, of course, was wrong, as he was to discover later, when he thought he knew all the Maroons' strongholds. The grounds he covered, however, could only be done by one with great courage and pertinacity. He reported later that it took seven hours to march only five miles up those steep precipices, and along this route, there was no water save that which could be obtained from the wild pine.[55]

The other body of Maroons situated "upon the border of Westmoreland" had just had a confrontation with the militia where seven of the latter were killed. Even with the efficient handling of the war by Walpole, who, by the last months of 1795, was apparently accepted by the country and recognized for his abilities, the situation had reached a deadlock, and the governor was in a quandary. "As it is impossible to get up with the Savages, without first receiving the fire of their Ambush, our loss in every affair is constantly from 8 to 12 men killed and wounded," he grieved.[56]

The "savages" were for the most part led by a few indomitable Maroons, outstanding for their valor. Among these were Johnson and Smith. These two men were living, with their families, "on the back lands in the parish of Westmoreland" close to certain estates "where they lived very peaceably and engaged in useful employments."[57] As far as we know they did not invoke the 1791 act and were thus living outside their community illegally. However, they must have kept in touch with Trelawny Town and must have been highly regarded individuals, for upon the imprisonment of the deputies by Balcarres, the Maroons, perceiving that the Rubicon was crossed, had sent intelligence to these outlying Maroons but particularly to Johnson and Smith. Fortunately for them, before they repaired to Trelawny Town, they had removed their women and children "into the woods," taking with them nine "active and enterprizing fellows."

Intriguingly, Johnson and Smith recommended peaceable measures to their fellow Trelawnys, who appeared to have agreed, for it was after their departure that Montague and the others surrendered. Upon returning to their settlements in Westmoreland, they found them destroyed by a party of the Westmoreland militia, their houses burned and their provision grounds "laid waste," and what was more, some of their people who were left behind were clapped into prison by the tough governor. These were not released until after the war.[58] Johnson and Smith were outraged, and so far as they were concerned, it was at this moment that *their* Rubicon was crossed. They saw bad faith on the part of government in all its actions: the high-handed treatment of the six, now the destruction of their property, and the imprisonment of their people living outside Trelawny Town and having no part with the war, and soon they were to hear of Montague's treatment. So they returned with their families, pledging vengeance and retribution on the perpetrators. On the way, Johnson and his sons inveigled away some plantation slaves they encountered, but these soon made good their escape and promptly communicated to the magistrates of Westmoreland the threats they heard the Maroons make against the whites.[59]

Johnson and Smith soon became the bane of the planter class, from the end of August up to December. Johnson, described as influential and distinguished for his ferocious disposition, was undoubtedly more the fighter than Smith, who soon capitulated and was to become a confidant of government. Indeed, Smith was to carry the suspicion of "traitor" with him to Nova Scotia and Sierra Leone. It was in Johnson that the Maroons placed the greatest confidence. They submitted to his command, and he gave regularity and effectiveness to the whole enterprise. His ultimate strategy was to force the government to advantageous terms, but the dogs were to change this. Johnson's sortie consisted of a few slaves he trained with an iron hand. Added to these were two of his sons, and these did not escape the father's rigorous discipline. His little group was largely responsible for the ravages committed on the Mocha and Catadupa estates, as well as on many more in St. James and Westmoreland. As the war progressed he was splendidly decked out with a spyglass — the result of plunder, doubtless — and he must have cut an impressive figure with the slaves.[60] Unfortunately though, Johnson's and Smith's treachery to the slaves cannot be overlooked. Each had separately promised the slaves fighting with them that they would be included in any peace treaty as *Maroons* and not as runaways, but this promise was not kept.

Two other intrepid Maroon leaders — among others — were Palmer and Parkinson, the latter immortalized by a print on the outer cover of Bryan Edwards's *Proceedings*. Palmer and Parkinson became famous when they too surrendered with Montague, but were sent back to Trelawny Town to try to persuade the others to surrender — some of whom, as we saw, were not antithetical to this way of thinking. The two men, probably glad of the opportunity never to return, reported in detail the rough treatment they had received from the officials, joined in the burning of the towns, and were to become two of the outstanding leaders of the war, with their activities repeatedly mentioned in the official documents. Among these was one of Balcarres's numerous proclamations, that of August 13, offering rewards, *inter alia*, for the capture of these two freedom fighters: "And whereas one particular Maroon Negro man named James Palmer, and one other named Leonard Parkinson, have behaved in a manner singularly atrocious; I hereby further offer an additional reward of eighty pounds amounting in the whole

LEONARD PARKINSON, a Captain of MAROONS
taken from the Life.

to one hundred pounds; in like manner for apprehending or killing the said James Palmer; an additional reward of thirty pounds, amounting ... to fifty pounds, for apprehending or killing the said Leonard Parkinson."[61]

Parkinson, with his small sortie of some twenty men, followed by four women and three girls, wreaked vengeance on plantations. At Amity Hall, for instance, they killed a bookkeeper, plundered the house, took three muskets, two pounds of powder, cartridges, and the like; and carried away three barrels of beef and pork. In the process, Parkinson tried to persuade the slaves to join the Maroons, using a kind of inchoate pan-African argument, claiming that they were fighting the whites as a common enemy and his purpose was to make them free.[62] But the slaves were not impressed, most certainly remembering Maroons' collaboration with the whites to frustrate the thrust for freedom of those in servitude. Parkinson wisely did not try to force them to join, but gave them that part of the plunder which he could not carry — perhaps a more effective means of gaining support, in this case, than verbal persuasion. From Amity Hall this small group went off to other plantations and pens, plundering and burning. All this demonstrated the destruction a few Maroons could wreak in no time. Palmer, for his part, was engaged in similar activities — and it was later learned that some enterprising slaves, singly, were also busily engaged in destruction. The plan of the Maroons was to advance further afield, throughout the island, thus making it more difficult for the unwieldy troops to deploy on different fronts. The country was nonplussed, and the Maroon leaders continued to hold out hopes of reaching advantageous terms with the government.

This might have happened if a new dimension had not entered the war — the Cuban bloodhounds. Soon after the rebellion, Balcarres said that he had deemed it necessary to send to Cuba to procure a number of large dogs of the bloodhound breed, which were used to hunt down runaways in that country. This apparently was first suggested to Balcarres by Walpole. To procure the dogs, W. D. Quarrell, a planter from Hanover and Dallas's main source for his work on the Maroons, was commissioned by the government to proceed to Cuba for the animals, and "near 100" dogs and forty-three keepers, *chausseurs*, arrived in Jamaica, December 17, 1795.[63] Balcarres was delighted. "The Negroe all over this Island has been struck with Horror at hearing of this measure, and these Doggs have most opportunely arrived," and the bloodthirsty earl went on to describe their horrendous characteristics.

The dogs had the appearance of the greatest ferocity, and soon gave some demonstrations of this trait before actually going for the Maroons: there was an old black woman cooking in the open, and one of the dogs attempted to seize a piece of her meat, whereupon she struck it and was instantly killed by the bloodhound; on another occasion a soldier of the 83rd Regiment, having seized one, was severely torn in the arm and only with great difficulty saved; again, two of the dogs went into fighting, and the keeper was forced to kill one of them, since they never let go of their hold; further, four more were let loose at a steer that was difficult to catch, and they killed it and tore it to pieces "in a minute." The keepers of the dogs had so much confidence in them that they were prepared to go out with them against the "Enemy," armed only with lances. The dogs were very large, with a greyhound head and a mastiff body, and not being of the best scent, excepting where there was blood, they were attended by "a small little black dog of a very nice scent," who would find the game — the Maroons in the ambushes — and the bloodhounds would then take over. The governor would certainly endeavor to preserve the breed, should they have the full effect of "reducing the Enemy" — which was clearly another way of saying exterminating them. He was elated that "the Savages [the Maroons] have the utmost dread of a large Dog," as did the slaves, and the governor looked further forward and said that if the dogs did esssential service in Jamaica, then they should also be used against the Brigands of St. Domingue — that is, the slaves fighting in that country, for their freedom.

George III, however, did not share Balcarres's enthusiasm for the "hellish brutes," as one writer terms them. He had Portland reply immediately to express his "Abhorrence of the mode of warfare" pursued in Jamaica, and to direct the governor "to remove forthwith, and to extirpate from the Island, the whole Race of those tremendous Animals, of whose ungovernable ferocity you have already seen a very shocking effect."[64] As communications go at that period, this dispatch, which was written March 3, 1796, would not have arrived in Jamaica until sometime around the end of May or even early June of that, year depending on the trade winds.

Let us therefore see what effect the canine creatures had on the war. There is no doubt that the dogs had an immediate impact on the Maroons. On December 20 — three days after their arrival — we find Walpole writing a private letter to Balcarres announcing that Colonel Hull had something of a success with the Cockpit Maroons and something of a truce was arranged. In this private letter to the governor, Walpole confessed a dislike for the truce: "This is the only part which, *entre nous*, I dislike: But, however, for the sake of public faith, I shall keep it." Walpole's preference was to give them terms, "but by no means to suspend hostilities until they should first lay down their arms." The terms of the proposals of the Maroons were formally signed by Walpole and Montague James at Guard Hill, December 21, 1795, and they were ratified by Balcarres, with his signature and other names added, on December 28. These terms were, first, that they [the Maroons] would, "on their knees," beg his majesty's pardon; second, that they would go to the Old Town, Montego Bay, or any other place that might be pointed out, and would settle on whatever lands the governor, Council, and Assembly might think proper to allot; third, that they would give up all runaways. In the process, Walpole himself had entered into a secret article with the Maroons. He told Balcarres that he "was obliged to accede on [his] oath ... that they should not be sent off the island," and this was soon to be the occasion of a major disagreement between the major-general and the governor.[65]

In ratifying the treaty, Balcarres set January 1, that is, only three days later, for the Trelawny Town Maroons "to come in body" by ten o'clock — a.m. presumably — to him at Spanish Town.[66]

But this process was to be a protracted one. In his letter to Balcarres on December 25, Walpole observed that "Old Montague is, as far as I can guess, the obstacle to peace, as much as he dares: Some of the Maroons were heard to tell him, that they would have peace, whether he would or not." Old Montague's participation in the Treaty requires explanation, since we saw him surrending to the government at the outset of hostilities. Like Palmer and Parkinson, who were sent to persuade the other Maroons to submit, so also was Montague, as well as Dunbar and Harvey. They were sent on a mission, just before Colonel Fitch's disaster, to enjoin their people to surrender. At this point some of the Maroons had called for a ceasefire only as a ploy to position their men in strategic places, and we have already seen the result. Montague remained with his people and became more adamant against the authorities than even some of the younger ones. He could not forget the treatment he had received. Up to the time of the introduction of the dogs there were reports that he was prepared to die in the woods, rather than surrender. Thus it is clear that in signing the truce the cunning old Montague James — reminiscent of another Maroon leader, Juan de Serras, in the 1670s — was merely playing for time. This created a schism again among them. On December 24 Smith, along with Dunbar — two of the leaders — gave themselves up to Walpole, who assured them that the governor had promised that whatever might be the future disposal of them they would be a free people, and the ominous implication could not have escaped them.

To assist the process, the Assembly offered £500 to those who surrendered. But although Walpole reported on the 30th that sixteen were with him, these must have returned to their redoubts, for on January 1, the final date, obviously frustrated, he said, "I now give the matter up," for only five surrendered: three adults — Smith, Dunbar, and Williams — and two boys.[67] Balcarres, a master of duplicity himself, was not surprised. "The farce has ended as I expected," he told Portland, and he was now prepared to employ his canine friends to extirpate the enemies, if possible.[68] Indeed, it was a farce, but orchestrated by Balcarres, for he could not possibly have expected all the Maroons to come in within that short period of time. "If this was the record," wrote Gardner, "of a great continental war, instead of a conflict with three hundred black woodsmen, the question would long be earnestly discussed whether Balcarres did not really design, when he signed the treaty, to occasion the embarrassment which followed. The Maroons were accused soon after of breach of faith, and on this plea were sent from the island."[69]

It is clear that by January 5, the canine threat was having the desired effect, from the viewpoint of the government. By this date thirty Maroons came in, including the determined Montague, and Walpole reported that they were daily increasing. He reminded Balcarres that this number was far beyond what two battles could give him in slain Maroons. He was convinced that more would have come in but for distrustfulness. "Each is desirous that his neighbour should try the white faith first; and when one is satisfied, the way is, that he returns and brings back most of his family."[70] Smith, for instance, finding that he could repose some trust in Walpole, had returned to the Cockpits for his family, which consisted of a wife and twelve children.

Even if Walpole had agreed with Balcarres after January 1 that force was the answer to the impasse, by this time he now conceived that a show of force would, without a doubt, be counterproductive. To Walpole, trust should be a critical factor in the entire operation, for the Maroons had a great deal to be distrustful about, as we saw above. There is no doubt that at this point they were between the devil and the deep blue sea. It is not for nothing that G. W. Bridges wondered at what was more perilous for the Maroons — the bloodthirsty earl or his bloodhounds. And Balcarres had candidly admitted that he had "more faith in the Dogs than in the Maroons."[71] Yet, had they the earl alone to contend with, it is certain that these hardy mountaineers, who traveled light, would have fanned themselves out over the island — as Juan de Serras had done in the seventeenth century — and settled anew. There were reports that "it was their intention, when pressed too closely by the troops, to cross over to Clarendon ... where they had many friends [possibly descendants of the remnants of the earlier De Serras group], and so compel the army to break up its camp and recommence operations in another part of the colony, which, with their accoutrements, they could only reach by a tedious march or by sea"[72] — by which time their depredations on plantations would have been felt.

Pressed by Balcarres to proceed against the "rebels" with a great force including the canine auxilliaries, Walpole temporized as much as he dared, for he was obviously against using the bloodhounds. He reported to Balcarres that there was a problem with respect to the dogs and the lack of a supply of water. There was none during seven hours' march in the awesome Cockpits, but "if the dogs cannot be got through want of water, we must leave them behind." This infuriated Balcarres. "Surely a very few breakers," he replied, "will serve to carry water for the dogs. Ten are procured here, and I dare say some more may be picked up .... I sincerely hope and trust, that no column shall proceed against the enemy without the dogs, until their inefficacy is proved," whereupon Walpole reminded the earl of the impracticability of carrying "water enough in breakers for so many men and dogs," in the almost inaccessible terrain they must negotiate.[73] On January 12 Walpole began his march with the dogs in the rear of the column, and had "scarcely moved two-hundred yards" when he again heard from Johnson, who had not surrendered with his former partner, Smith. Johnson had first sent word to Walpole to say he was not able to prevail on the women to come in and that "several" of them were lost in the woods, and he would like to know what the general had to say on the matter. Walpole replied that he would march against him unless twenty more men should arrive by the next day. Johnson asked for four o'clock, but Walpole was to march at 2 p.m., when it was still daylight.

Balcarres would have none of Johnson's prevarication. "The Maroons, with Johnson at their head, are either serious or they are not serious," he wrote, and ordered Walpole to give them until 2 p.m. the following day to surrender and then proceed against them and the others if they did not, as he was "for pushing them hard."[74] Johnson might have been sincere about the women, because it soon became clear that some were sick in the woods and some might have been lost, but he was also most certainly playing for time, waiting to see how the others who surrendered fared with perfidious Albion, before he gave himself up. By the 15th, however, most, including Johnson, had surrendered. The total at this date consisted of ninety-one men, 111 women, and 124 children.

A few stout-hearted ones were still at large, Parkinson and Palmer included. Although Balcarres was happy with this result, he felt that the embers of rebellion still remained as long as Parkinson and others were still abroad. He gave Walpole *carte blanche* to "extinguish" them, and congratulated the general, assuring him that his conduct would be highly approved by his majesty. Those that remained were scattered in different bodies and had retreated deep into the woods when their spies discovered that those who surrendered had been sent off to Montego Bay. They construed this as another treachery, convinced that they, too, were to be put on board a ship for subsequent deportation. Walpole reported that some of these had actually come to surrender, but returned to the woods, certain that treachery was afoot. But the threat of the dogs still held, and by January 16 Balcarres was reporting to the Assembly that he had in his possession "upwards of 400 persons, of whom, I count about 130 men," and although a few of the young ones were still out, he was hopeful that the rebellion was coming to an end. He asked that the "pleasing event" be speedily announded in the Spanish Town papers. It was not until March, however, that they finally trickled in — and were tricked — to surrender, Palmer and Parkinson being among the very last.[75]

Smith and Johnson had become great friends and assistants to Walpole, acting like couriers in going out to persuade others to come in. Walpole was so pleased with them that he had requested permission of the governor for them to remain with him before the final surrender. This had alarmed Balcarres, but he nevertheless allowed it, permitting Walpole to have only ten with him at any given time. Without the efforts of these Maroons, the completion of the surrender would have taken a much longer time — if at all. Not only did they know the terrain, but they could use themselves as examples to show good faith on the part of Walpole. All these Maroons laid down their arms feeling confident that they were doing so under the terms of the treaty signed by Walpole and Montague, including the secret clause stipulating that they would not be deported. This was an aspect of the trust they had in the major general.

Walpole asserted that the dogs had nothing to do with the surrender, claiming that the introduction of the beasts was not known to the Maroons when the first group sued for peace.[76] This is an odd claim to make and can only be due to the general's overweening sense of his own importance. The claim is odd not only because of the effective Maroon grapevine we have discussed repeatedly, but also because of the near invincibility of the Maroons, which Walpole himself had recognized. He had reminded Balcarres of "the impossibility of penetrating [Maroon] country" and even if the troops could get to the redoubts, enough for them to destroy the enemy, they would increase by runaways, "and if you destroy them to five, those five will be a rallying point for more runaways to resort to, and thus the wars be perpetuated by years." He pointed out what even a single runaway, like Bowman, for instance, could do. Bowman had conducted a one-man vendetta on plantations and did infinite mischief over a wide area. More to the point, having been in the field against them in some of the most remote areas, Walpole could speak authoritatively on the nature and conduct of the "Internal Enemy ... [who] had manifested great Fortitude, great Generalship and has preserved a secrecy in their manoeuvres unparralled among European Soldiers ..., the Velocity of their Movements and the knowledge of the Grounds was so superior to ours as to make them be considered as almost unconquerable."

Walpole marvelled, as one must, that during the war the Maroons had concealed their women and children — contrary to the authorities' claim that they had murdered them, viewing them as encumbrances to warfare — in retreats so impenetrable that not a soldier had heard a child cry. It showed Walpole that many of their haunts were still totally unknown to the whites. And as for the provision-ground strategy, he discovered this to have succeeded only partially, for, in some of these retreats, the Maroons were not deficient in provision, and in ammunition as well. Indeed, it was Walpole's opinion that if Palmer and Parkinson alone had decided not to cooperate with the authorities, the country could not defeat them. On another level, he addressed the question of foreign — or French — intervention. They knew of the country's internal problems and could thus exploit the situation to their benefit, if the war were prolonged.[77]

Even Balcarres — who, having observed his vast force at the beginning of hostilities, had confidently asserted that the war could end in two days — was soon of a totally different opinion. He discovered that the Trelawny Maroons, being centrical to the sugar plantations, could descend with ease and set fire to canefields; their power of doing mischief was "almost unbounded, and I do not see that an army of 20,000 men can prevent it." Peace, to the earl was desirable, "but nothing," he thought, was "more remote from the Intentions" of the Maroons. He recalled that they held out proposals twice, only when they were in some momentary difficulty, only to extricate themselves and to remove to some new place of concealment.[78] But the awesome bloodhounds were to change this.

Beyond his every expectation, Balcarres could now write to Portland: "I have the gratification to inform your Grace of the termination of the Maroon War," March 16, 1796. "Thus has ended the Nation of the Trelawny Maroons, a People which Historians (X) [*sic*] assert, were not to be overcome, but would ultimately acquire the Dominion of this Island," Balcarres boasted.[79] He reported that the most perfect internal tranquility was restored to Jamaica, and "the slaves on every Plantation are obedient, contented, and happy." But this was mere poetic excess and wishful thinking, for even at this time these same bucolic creatures — as he would seem to perceive them — were up in arms against their slave masters, again committing "considerable outrages," as hinted earlier. And the governor himself had already reported that the success against the Trelawnys "was not without its alloy," for some 150 runaways were still in the woods, armed and with some ammunition. He felt that their reduction might take some time and was fearful of the further expenses that would cause.[80]

As with the cessation of the earlier Maroon wars, credit on the island soon became more buoyant, and even those who had been denied access to it because of the colony's uncertainties were immediately successful in this respect. Balcarres, in a euphoric mood, felt that, with credit restored, property acquired a degree of security never before held on the island. Mr. Shirley, for instance, who had applied for credit from the House of Manning in London, had his application stopped with the beginning of the rebellion, but upon the last batch of the Maroons' coming in, he had his £40,000 loan.[81]

Meanwhile, Balcarres had no doubt whatever as to the policy to be pursued with respect to the Maroons who surrendered. In ratifying the treaty and in allowing the Maroons a mere three clear days to come in, as mentioned before, Balcarres was merely "show[ing] the Maroons up," as he himself admitted, since, even with the best of intentions, they could not possibly have surrendered with their womenfolk and children, who were scattered in remote places, in such a short time. He thus engineered for his own benefit the pretext of deporting them on the grounds of having broken the treaty. To him, the final solution to the Trelawny Town Maroon was deportation, and it was at this time that he flatly stated that he held the Treaty "signed by Major General Walpole on the one part, Colonel Montague James, the Chief of the Maroons on the other part and ratified by me absolutely as nothing."[82] And yet it was something to him in so far as he used it as a pretext to betray the Trelawnys on two counts: one, that they did not surrender at the time prescribed; two, that they did not deliver up their runaways.

Balcarres had ample support for his policy of deportation. This came from the island's legislature, from the principal men, some of whom, according to Balcarres (if his word can be trusted on this matter) recommended "the extirpation of the Trelawny Maroons,"[83] and from the Colonial Office. The speaker of the Jamaica Assembly, William Blake, saw trickery a valid weapon to be used when force could not subdue an enemy. Further, he considered the Maroons as having forfeited their claim to the terms of the treaty when they did not surrender by January 1, according to Balcarres's unilateral condition. The Duke of Portland had written to Balcarres in a most obtuse and roundabout manner and, after much hedging, said that the safety and security of the island would be best served "first by not restoring to them their District, and secondly, by placing them in such a situation within the Island (if it cannot be done out of it, which was preferable) as will from its nature incapacitate them from contriving further mischief."[84] Balcarres also repeated time and time again that he had a secret communication from Portland apprising him of the policy to be pursued toward the "rebels," which clearly was deportation. It gave the governor a sense of "pecular satisfaction" to find that the duke had anticipated both the wishes and the policy of the island, in that they had already adopted the measure of sending them off to another country.[85]

Balcarres had also set up a secret committee of twelve, three from the Council and nine from the Assembly, to look into the "disposal" of the Maroons. They reported that all free people who joined the rebels should be dealt with according to the law, and, incredibly, they recommended that those Maroons who surrendered under the first proclamation, and the six deputies who were taken up at St. Ann en route to see the governor, having surrendered before any hostilities, were to be sent off the island to another country. In fact, all, with the exception of Smith, Dunbar, and Williams with their wives and children and the two boys who came in on January 1, and a few others who served the country, were to be deported. Walpole thought all this outrageous. A series of letters on this disagreement passed between the governor and Walpole, the first of which established the latter's position:

> I must trouble your lordship with a few words in privacy and confidence. For some days past I have been in a state of considerable uneasiness at a Report which seems to gain ground, that the Legislature mean to Infringe the Capitulation accepted by me and Ratified by your Lordship.

> My Lord, to be plain with you it was thro my means alone that the Maroons were Induced to Surrender from a Reliance which they had in my word; from a Conviction impressed upon them by me that the white people would never break their faith. All these things strongly call upon me as the Instrumental Agent in this business to see a due observance of the Terms or in case of Violation to resign my Command and if that should not be accepted to declare the facts to the world and to leave them to judge how far I ought or ought not to be Implicated in the Guilt and Infamy of such a proceeding. So much the more strong is this call upon me, as there was no occasion to Ratify the Terms. Your Lordship will well Recollect what I told you ... that the time appointed by me for fulfilling them was expired and the Terms therefore null and void, but your Lordship then thought that there was so much of Advantage to the Country in these Terms that it would be best not to give them up. As the great object of the war is now declared to be accomplished, I shall shortly solicit your Lordship for permission to return to England with an Intention to Retire from the Service.[86]

Balcarres was not deficient in acknowledging Walpole's skill and courage in this war, pointing out also the major general's additional merit of going unarmed — like Dr. Russel of Cudjoe's Treaty — into the woods to confer with the Maroons on the Treaty. He understood Walpole's sense of "delicacy" but his public duty could not support it.[87]

Walpole's anger was genuine. He felt that he had been placed in the dual position of being made a cat's paw by the legislature, who also made use of his special skills to deceive the Maroons. This rankled with a man not only with a strong sense of conventional honor but also with a strong supposal of his worth. He could not conceive the Maroons' delay in coming in a breach of the treaty, and he rightly pointed out that the delay was due to fear of treachery, and that it thus took him some time by a show of humanity and strength (threatening them with dogs when necessary) to allay their fears before succeeding in gaining their confidence. He might also have pointed out the impracticability — perhaps the impossibility — of their coming in within the stipulated time. Reviewing the charge of not returning runaways, Walpole considered this even more insidious, noting that the Maroon leaders dealt with this issue with tact and finesse, all to the advantage of government. They first confiscated the runaways' firearms, then allowed them to surrender as Maroons, only to point out their identity afterwards. This duplicity was said to have been suggested by Smith, to prevent their escaping — as many did when they discovered that the Maroons would betray them. Walpole finally resigned from the army, refused a sword for 500 guineas the Assembly voted him for his great service to the country, and returned to England to contest a seat for the House of Commons to declare the facts of the betrayal of the Maroons "to the world."

But even before he contested his seat, successfully, the matter was debated in the Commons on October 21, 1796. The discussion considered the issue of bad faith on the part of the Jamaican authorities in deporting the Maroons despite the treaty stipulations. Some members were obviously disturbed by this. But Bryan Edwards, then a member of the Commons, was on hand to represent the Jamaican case, and his performance is extraordinary even by his known anti-Maroon standards. All in all, he portrayed the Assembly as humane and just to the Maroons, a group of "ignorant savages," who not only entered into an "unprovoked" war, but also violated the treaty stipulations made with Balcarres. One member observed that it was indeed a most damaging reflection on the island's establishment to have kept the Maroons so devoid of moral sentiments and so ignorant as depicted by Edwards. They were British subjects and had been in the colony for over 140 years. Yet, he had not heard from Edwards that any steps had ever been taken to instruct them or to introduce them to the "blessings of Christianity." Thus cornered, Edwards overreached himself. He said that it would have been "absurd" to baptize such "savages," and as for sending clergymen among them he did not know of any who would risk going. To his "certain knowledge, the Maroons were Cannibals — and were such men proper to send Clergymen among? He was sure if a Clergyman was to be sent to them, instead of listening to his [the Clergyman's] doctrines, they would *eat him up*." Credit should be given to the House that the few members who participated in the debate did not take Edwards's indelicate slander seriously. On the contrary, it was decided that the matter should be brought to the House again with the hope that His Majesty's ministers would vindicate the propriety of deporting the Maroons against treaty stipulations. We need not, however, be detained by any further debate on the issue, since the Maroons *were* deported. And, as a recent writer pointed out, those members of the British legislature with interests in the slave economy of the West Indies "did not normally want them discussed in Parliament."[88]

When all is said of Walpole's position, however, it can hardly be considered as one based on general humanity or on any special love for the Maroons. It was a punctilio of his honor that he sought to defend. It should not be forgotten that he had approved Balcarres's zeal in crushing the Maroons, arguing that Jamaica could never be safe so long as a rebellious and petty republic remained in its midst. Nor should it be forgotten that it was he who first suggested the use of the dogs to Balcarres — although when they did arrive he showed great reluctance in using them in the forefront of battle, only making the utmost strategic use of them. Furthermore, he was known to have spoken disparagingly of Wilberforce's efforts for the slaves. But most important of all, he had recommended to Balcarres (in a letter of December 24, 1795) that the Maroons should be settled near Spanish Town or adjacent to some other of the large towns in the lowlands where they would have more than ample access to liquor. "The access to spirits," he proposed, "will soon decrease their numbers, and destroy that hardy constitution which is nourished by an healthy mountainous situation"[89] — a recommendation reminiscent of what some of his countrymen were to practice successfully in China in the 1840s, thus leading to the "Opium Wars" that eventually defeated the Chinese. Walpole's policy was much more cynical and insidious than deportation *qua* deportation. No doubt, had Balcarres not been so bent on deporting the Maroons, this scheme might well have found favor with him, but he was determined to "save Jamaica," as he claimed repeatedly, by ridding the country of them forever.

Let us take another look at the windward Maroons, now that the war has gone against the Trelawnys with the introduction of the dogs. The Moore Town group had continued stoutly to refuse the governor's order to attend him, either as a body or in small groups. They also sullenly refused the presents the governor had for them, and also maintained the huts they built since the war in the deep seclusion of the Blue Mountains, "a country of immense strength, as if preparing for Hostilities," Balcarres observed. The governor bristled with anger over this group but was unable to do anything about them. In his impotent hostility, he devised a scheme with the purpose of ensnaring them: he would ask one Mr. Shirley to have all the windwards attend him, Shirley making certain conciliatory promises to them, but at the same time insisting that his (Shirley's) was not the final word — the governor's was. This way, the Moore Town group would come down and then "fall into the snare," and Balcarres, glad of the occasion, would "secure them, and they [should] share exactly the fate of the Trelawny Maroons."[90] It was therefore just as well the Moore Town group disobeyed this ferocious earl, who offended the sensibilities of Lady Nugent: "I wish Lord B. would wash his hands, and use a nail-brush, for the black edges of the nails make me sick. He has, besides, an extraordinary propensity to dip his fingers into every dish. Yesterday he absolutely helped himself to some fricassee with his dirty finger and thumb,"[91] the exasperated first lady, wife of Governor Nugent complained.

We have one piece of evidence from a slave who deserted the Maroons (how reliable, it is difficult to say), suggesting that the Moore Town group was in touch with the influential Johnson. This deserter said that about nine members of the Moore Town community visited Johnson, and advised him not to surrender, stating that they too would join but they did not have sufficient powder. These nine were young men armed with guns and "macheats."[92]

The Charles Town group, too, disobeyed the orders for the most part, but a few, as we saw, did attend the governor, and other small and detached parties did attend later. Balcarres praised this group of Maroons, finding them "infinitely more docile and softer people than those of Trelawny Town." One of Balcarres's arguments for deporting the Trelawnys was that should they be resettled on the island; then, in the event of a rupture with them again, the windwards would join them and the country would thus achieve little or nothing after all the heavy expenditure of the war. We do not know how he arrived at this conclusion because it is indeed startling that the Trelawnys fought alone, with one Maroon group, their neighbors and kinship brothers, actually fighting against them. The Scotts Hall group apparently remained neutral throughout. But by March 21, when all the Trelawnys had surrendered, Balcarres could now employ his iron hand against the windwards, who had shown "a most refractory and disobedient spirit," he wrote to Portland. He chose Charles Town as an example to the others to submit on their knees — possibly because Charles Town's population was larger, possibly because the governor had viewed them as "docile" and could thus see them an easy prey to deal with. Whatever the reason, he appointed a commission of three to visit Charles Town "for the purpose of receiving their submission upon their knees, together with a solemn declaration that their disobedience proceeded from no evil design, but solely upon fear and apprehension."

The commissioners carried with them a lengthy rigamarole from Balcarres. The trumped-up document declared that the superintendent of Charles Town had convinced the governor that the Maroons of this town had manifested every symptom of concern and uneasiness at having incurred his honor's displeasure. His honor had therefore taken the matter into his most serious consideration and thought it probable that the disobedience of the Maroons "was occasioned by the alarming reports of evil designing persons operating upon their minds . . . ." His honor was thus disposed to forgive them upon their solemnly declaring allegiance to King George III, that they were ready to defend him against all his enemies, that they would, on all occasions, obey with great readiness the orders of the governor and the laws of the country, and that they would faithfully fulfill the treaty made with Governor Trelawny. The commissioners proceeded to Charles Town where they found the Maroons "drawn up in a line" and under arms, and there, in a semicircle formation, the Maroons, "on their knees," repeated the declaration of submission and loyalty, whereupon they received pardon for their offence and assurances of protection of their persons and property from the government.[93]

At this point Balcarres was receiving the highest approbation both from the Duke of Portland and the Jamaican legislature for the termination of the war. He was voted a sword for 700 guineas by the Assembly, which the governor received with enthusiasm, considering his penchant for swords. A soldier's honor, to him, is placed in his sword, and he promised to transmit the precious gift to his posterity.[94] It appears that Balcarres wished to receive the high military honor of Order of Bath, too, from home. He hinted at it in a private letter to John King, March 26, at the end of the war. He told King that the ceremony accompanying the honor, at this time, would enhance its value one hundred fold. However, it was just a "hint" arising from something King had previously said to him.[95] A pencil notation, at the margin of this letter, obviously by King, said, "this something is more than I know anything of." It cannot be overemphasized that Balcarres had no doubt at all that he had saved Jamaica from Maroon savagery or from French anarchy and confusion, according to his mood. "I thought the saving of Jamaica," he wrote the Countess of Hardwicke, "and seventy million sterling of British capital was rather a good service." On another occasion he said that he was engaged "in a nasty, ugly war," which he had "reduced ... from a Rebellion affecting the Empire at large and one hundred million sterling of Property to a local disturbance ...." When the French were foremost in his mind, he would insist that the daring and "unprovoked Rebellion ... had long been premeditated and at the Instigation of the Convention of France, whose object it undoubtedly is to throw this Island into a state of Anarchy and Confusion," and certainly not in the "killing of a pig" and the punishment of two Maroons. If he did not receive the Order of Bath, he nevertheless drew extra salary — some £5,000 more, it was said, during the period of martial law.[96]

The Maroons of Trelawny Town, for their part, were now placed on transport ships, some 568, of whom 401 were old men, women, and children, 167, arms-bearing men, ready to be deported to a destination, which, ironically, was not clear up to the last moment. Sierra Leone? Although the Maroons were finally sent there, the suggestion at this time was greeted with horror, apparently by W. D. Quarrell and others. "No punishment was intended them beyond their transportation much less a banishment to that dreary, barren and inhospitable spot, to which Death by the hands of the Executioner is Mercy."[97] Balcarres did not want to take the full responsibility of sending them — somewhere — but the British government was equally deficient of ideas on this matter. The governor mentioned New Brunswick but complained that he could not possibly "divine your Grace's [Portland's] sentiments, nor Resources as to the future fixing of this People."[98]

The island's legislature finally decided to send the Trelawny Maroons to

Nova Scotia and appropriated £25,000 for their expenses. They sailed on June 6, 1796, with Colonel Quarrell, who was appointed commissary general of the enterprise, charged with the task of supervising Maroon settlement in Nova Scotia until they could provide for themselves. Balcarres reported that once on board, the Maroons were anxious to leave, because they were aware that sentiments in the country were violently hostile toward them. In a petition to Balcarres for the King, before their destination was known, they wrote:

> Being sensible that our stay in this Island is impossible from the resentment shown against us by the whites and people of colour [mulattos] and also that the Legislature has declared it a capital crime for us to reland in Jamaica after we are transported we beg that your Lordship will be pleased to settle us in any Country under H.M. Government and if that cannot be effected we humbly offer ourselves to serve His Majesty as Soldiers in any of his Governments to defend and protect the same as dutyfull and loyal subjects provided our old Men and Women, our Wives and Children who are numerous may receive such protection and support from Government as may enable them to live comfortably ....[99]

Bryan Edwards notwithstanding, the Maroons have always — even to the extent of risking their strategic positions — been most protective of their old, their womenfolk, and their children.

A very telling example of Maroon attachment to family ties was further demonstrated with respect to those who were entitled to remain in the island — Smith, Dunbar, Williams, and the two boys who surrendered before January 1. But the Assembly had also ruled, upon the end of hostilities, that a few, "by their Repentance, Service and good Behaviour since their Surrender," albeit after the time limit, could remain. Among these was the enterprising Johnson. Smith was the first to begin making demands about family connections. He would only remain if all his family — a real extended one, African fashion — were allowed to stay, too. These included cousins, "other distant relations," some married to those who must leave, and so on. Johnson, too, began to make similar claims. He would not budge unless his three sons — known warriors already, being chips of the old block — could remain with him. But the authorities protested against these scions of Johnson remaining on the island, claiming that they would create the greatest alarm in Westmoreland, where Johnson and his family had been residing without giving up their Maroon status. In the event, both categories of Maroons petitioned finally to be allowed to accompany the others, and some fifty of them joined the fate of exile with their kinsmen.[100]

Even the legal instrument deporting the Maroons gave no precise indication of their destination. The law said, in part, that the return of the

Maroons to the island would "be productive of the most dangerous and evil consequence, not only to the government thereof, but to the lives and properties of individual inhabitants ... [and enacted that] from and after the passing of this act, the said rebellious Maroons shall, with all convenient speed, be transported off this island, into any of his majesty's dominions in North America or elsewhere, there to remain and not to return, ... and if any of the said Maroons ... shall be found to have escaped, or attempting to escape, from their present confinement, or shall, after being so transported off the island, be found to have returned thereto, or to any part or place thereto belonging, every such Maroons shall be therefore apprehended," and tried. If found guilty, the court should find the Maroon guilty of felony, and he should therefore "suffer death, without benefit of clergy."[101]

Their 1,500 acres of Treaty lands were confiscated. Ever since the war and the discovery of flourishing Maroon provision grounds, as well as what the authorities perceived as extensive tracts of uncultivated lands, with soil well adapted to the cultivation of sugar cane, guinea grass, and coffee, the whites had an eye on these lands. The earlier push in the area had slackened largely because of Maroon intransigence. When, in October 1795, Balcarres sent a series of questions to leading men of the island for their opinions on the best procedure for the war, W. Blake, for instance, reflected on the great fertility of the locale of the Trelawnys. Any terms, to him, which could "secure the possession of such a District to the Whites, would greatly contribute to internal security and enhance the value of the property in it."[102] With opinions of this sort, the task of deportation was easy for Balcarres, and the Assembly, too, experienced no difficulty in passing an act — even before it decided on an alternative site — to deprive the Trelawnys and their posterity forever from all claim on the 1,500 acres of land vested in them by treaty. The land was to be sold either as a whole or in lots not exceeding 100 acres each. But "at least" 300 acres were to be reserved for the use of troops. By mid-nineteenth century, barracks were built on the site, and the area was designated Maroon Town, and is still so identified on the maps.

It was now left to the authorities to count the costs of this most expensive war. The official figure gave it at £350,000, but even when this was an early estimate, it was an understatement.[103] It did not take into consideration the lavish rewards the Assembly was dispensing — even recommending a monument to be built for those who fell in the war, but it is clear that this was not implemented. Seven hundred guineas were voted for Balcarres's sword; 500 for Walpole's, although he refused it; £700 currency or £500 sterling to W. D. Quarrell for effecting the transport of the Cuban dogs to Jamaica; then $7,000 as well as £2,500 are mentioned together for rewarding the *chasseurs*, and the list continued.[104] All this does not take into consideration damages to property — claims for which found their way to the Assembly long after the termination of the war. Edwards's delineation of the war expenses would seem to be closer to the mark. He thought the country had expended £500,000, "exclusive of the loss which was sustained by individual proprietors; consequent on the removal from their plantation of all the white servants, to attend military duty. In the meanwhile, cultivation was suspended, the courts of law had long been shut up; and the island at large seemed more like a garrison, under the power of law-martial, than a country of agriculture and commerce, of civil judicature and increasing prosperity."[105] And all this was, it should be remembered, to quell just over 150 arms-bearing Maroons.

The Assembly tried numerous means of becoming solvent, including excessive borrowing, 200,000 guineas being mentioned on one occasion, and the imposition of higher and new taxes — on absentees, on certain wheel carriages, on trades, on supercargoes, on masters of vessels, on offices and houses and the like — but exactly how effective these were is not clear.[106]

The costs accrued to the country in terms of compensation to "faithful" slaves, blacks and mulattos, were also not computed in the official figures. Cudjoe, for instance, who commanded an army of Black Shots, behaved so "meritoriously" — from the plantocracy's viewpoint — that he was manumitted, his price paid to his owner, presented with a badge of distinction, and granted an annuity of £20 during his natural life. In fact, his whole company behaved so meritoriously that £500 was also granted by the Assembly to be distributed among them. A mulatto "man slave" named Billy of St. James and Jonathan of Hanover were also freed for their meritorious service "whereby the public . . . was greatly benefited in the efforts to subdue the said rebellion." Cato, too, the faithful — in this case, also a good soldier — evinced great fidelity, when employed as a guide against the Maroons. "He has," said Walpole, recommending him to Balcarres, "during the whole campaign, been a most faithful guide; it was by his means that we discovered the retreat of the rebels, and he behaved, by every account, with singular bravery during the action," but was killed in battle.[107] The Assembly awarded Cato's sons, William and Francois, £10 and a yearly grant of £10 throughout their natural lives — apparently for each. All this was to be "an encouragement for slaves in future to conduct themselves in a manner tending to the public advantage."[108] Similar acts were passed, freeing a mulatto slave named Benjamin Blake (Ben), the property of John Rogers of Westmoreland, a black slave called Bacchus, of the same parish, another called Garrick of St. James, and another called Cornwall of the same parish. Cornwall was a guide to parties, and his great knowledge of the woods served to rescue one of the militia men from a very perilous situation. All these were not only set free but were also to receive £10 each for the duration of their lives. Ben and Bacchus were also, like Cudjoe, to receive silver badges, and it is interesting that Cudjoe's annuity, £20, was twice as much as the others — doubtless because, like Sambo in the 1730s, his service was outstanding.[109]

About this time, too (March 24, 1796), the Assembly passed an act granting certain privileges to mulattos and blacks "of free condition and Christians," because, "during the present rebellion of the Trelawny Town Maroons, essential services have been rendered to the Island by the zeal and prompt obedience of the free persons of colour and free Negroes, serving in the militia, who thereby manifested their faithful attachment to His Majesty's Government." By this act, they could now give evidence against whites in certain criminal cases, such as assault or battery, on condition that they were in possession of their baptismal certificate. This was an important step toward the extension of freedom to these categories of persons who, though "free," were incapacitated by local laws.[110]

If there is anything that this war proved, it is the extent to which the Maroons had become distanced from the slaves, so much so that relatively few joined, and even those who did either soon returned to the plantations of their own volition or conducted their own warfare against the slave system without joining the Maroons. This, perhaps, registered the final *denouement* of the divide and rule intent of the Treaties, on the part of the plantocracy. There is no doubt that there were more slaves — at least proportionately — loyal to government during this war than during the 1730s, as demonstrated by the large number of rewards to such slaves. There was also the relatively conspicuous absence of deserters — as far as the records go. Indeed, we have more evidence of slave deserters from the Maroons, especially those who were coerced into joining them, than from the government forces.

From the point of view of Maroon attitude, too, this war represented their nemesis. Their ethnic exclusivity married to their overweening sense of their own importance and their feeling of superiority to the other blacks finally backfired. There is also another perspective that recent scholarship has pointed out, namely, that by the late eighteenth century, ethnic particularity among the slaves and free blacks of the island would seem to have been yielding place to a kind of pan-Africanism, embracing the concerns of all blacks.[111] This was to be exemplified in the very next slave rebellion, that of 1798, which saw a mix of ethnicity fighting the common enemy, although the leader, Cuffy, from his name, was of the Akan group. But the greatest demonstration of the pan-ethnic rebellion in Jamaica was that of 1831–1832.

It is difficult to defend the Trelawny war, and this, ironically, is written at a time when we are under the shadow of the Falkland Islands situation where some would see a parallel with the contending parties. Even when the background of Balcarres's war (for so it should be called) is considered — the French threat in the area and the constant deportations of French "agents" from the island, the nearness of St. Domingue in turmoil, the loss of a British governor in Grenada to revolutionary forces, and, internally, the political activities of the mulattos and the general restiveness of the slaves — it would not be easy to defend, given the "causes" discussed above and given the usefulness of the Maroons to the planters. But if justification is based on the principle that any means will justify a desirable end, then this, despite its questionable morality, is more easily understood. For there can be no doubt that from the long-term point of view of the plantocracy, this war was a success in terms of its effect on the other Maroons. The leading men of the island, even those from St. James and Trelawny, including the influential custos, John Tharp, soon openly acknowledged their gratitude to Balcarres.

Robert Renny, writing his *History of Jamaica* soon after the war, enthusiastically dedicated the work to Balcarres, comparing him with Governors D'oyley (of the Lubolo treaty in 1662/3) and Trelawny (of the 1738/9 Treaties). "Your Lordship," he wrote, "is regarded, not unjustly, as one of their [the colonists'] greatest benefactors; and you are already classed by them, among the D'oyleys and Trelawnys, who, by their wise and patriotic administrations, were equally an honour and an advantage, to the mother country and the colony." The planters' gratitude should be seen in context. After all, the Maroons were loyal auxiliaries to the colonial policing force, and repeatedly the island's legislature, or individuals singly, testified to their service in quelling rebellions on plantations, in policing the woods, and in returning runaways. And now this auxiliary force, the largest of the Maroon communities, was being deported, and the planters, whose estates were formerly protected by them, demonstrated gratitude for this extreme act. The answer to the paradox revolves around the tenuous nature of the relationship between Maroons and colonials. We have made it analogous earlier to that between Buccaneers and government in the seventeenth century, which was characterized by fear. Despite the Maroons' usefulness they were basically perceived by the whites as proud, temperamental, and potentially unreliable, but better to have as "friends" than as enemies.

Many of the whites had deplored the Treaty arrangements, giving them their own communities. This, to them, constituted a threat to the security of the island: "[T]ime," to Edwards, writing after the 1795–1796 war, "has abundantly proved that it was an ill-judged and a fatal regulation. The Maroons, instead of being established into separate hordes or communities, in the strongest parts of the interior country, should have been encouraged by all possible means to frequent the towns and to intermix with the Negroes at large. All distinctions between the Maroons and the other free blacks would soon have been lost; the greater number would have prevailed over the less: whereas the policy of keeping them a distinct people, continually inured to arms, introduced among them what the French call an *esprit de corps*, or a community of settlements and interests: and concealing from them the powers and resources of the whites, taught them to feel, and at the same time highly to overvalue, their own relative strength and importance." And, like Long, Edwards also said they should have been socialized within Western norms by education and christianity.[112] But Dallas did not share this view and rightly argued that even if the Treaty Maroons had disappeared as a distinct group, other Maroon societies would have been formed, and they, too, would have been as difficult to be subdued as the former.[113]

There is no doubt that the fate of the Trelawnys had a tremendous impact on the other Maroon communities on the island. Even apart from the formal submissions of Charles Town, the fact of deportation was a traumatic experience to the others. This, too, should be viewed contextually. Curiously, the word "deportation" in all New World slave societies had a very evil and sinister connotation, both to slaves and to the freed — perhaps based on the reckoning that it was better to deal with the known devil than with the unknown. Slaves were terrified of being deported or transported, and so were the "free" mulattos. In one of their petitions of the same period, the mulattos considered the punishment of deportation for certain crimes, "superior to death." The Maroons were no exception in their attitude to deportation, and this is indicated when they made Walpole, on his oath, swear not to send them off the island. It should be recalled that it was at this stage that some Trelawny Town Maroons, chiefly mulattos, appealed to the 1791 act to relinquish their Maroon status, as mentioned above. Still another group from this town, consisting of fourteen women and one man, at the end of the war appealed successfully to the 1791 act in order to remain on the island. They informed the Assembly that they had "always been faithful to their King and country, and obedient to the laws. That they have never joined in any rebellion or rebellious conspiracy; on the contrary they detest and abhor all treasons and treasonable practices." Most of these women, like those we mentioned earlier, may have been liaised with white men, and producing mulatto children, while some might have been related to whites. In their petition they pointed out that many of them were "totally dependent on the goodness of the white inhabitants; that many have children, and have it not in their power to procure a settlement," and were thus praying for relief — as did the group we mentioned above who appealed to the act after Balcarres's proclamation of August 8, 1795.[114]

But the most dramatic impact of the deportation must have been on the Moore Town group. Definitely the most self-conscious and aggressive of Maroon communities, they, however, appeared psychologically traumatized by the extreme act and were soon to be economically affected by it. This brought about their final capitulation, and their petition to the House in 1804 must have been a difficult undertaking. They pointed out that "they were desirous of enjoying the full confidence of the white inhabitants of this country, and will always obey the orders of the Governor ... and of their superintendent, and also conform themselves to any law which the legislature shall think proper to make for their regulation and government; that they are very willing to fight in defence of the country, and to march under the command of their superintendent to any part thereof where their services may be required, but hoped to be excused from serving at sea. That they are willing to bring in runaways as they did formerly, and most humbly solicit the house to place them on the same footing as they were before the rebellion of the Trelawny Maroons, and they promise faithfully so to conduct themselves as to merit the approbation of the house."[115]

This must have been humiliating for a proud people. But this obsequiousness was clearly induced by economic necessity. At the end of the Trelawny War, the House had passed a special act to employ the Accompong Maroons for "the internal defence and security of the island," without a mention of, and therefore excluding, all the windwards.[116] This was an economic blow to these communities, because we have already noted that fees for securing runaways and for going out in parties constituted the main, if not the greatest, source of income to the Maroons generally. Moore Town, with a population of 266 in 1798, consisting of fifty-four able men, eighty-two women, twenty boys, nine girls, and 101 children, in addition to twenty-five slaves,[117] was clearly feeling the effect of the nonreceipt of such fees, as the planters in the area were also suffering from its effect, in another way. On the same date of the Moore Town petition (and the two may have been planned to coincide) the magistrates, vestry, freeholders, and other inhabitants of Portland also sent a petition to the House. They complained that in consequence of the Moore Town Maroons' not being sanctioned by law to go out on parties in search of runaways, "as formerly ... several bodies of the latter are secreted in the woods, and have in consequence become a great annoyance to the back settlers of the said parish." And they gave it as their opinion that the fate of the Trelawny Town Maroons "will effectually deter those in the country from having a thought of entering into rebellion." Therefore, they did not understand why the Moore Town group should not "be rendered a very useful body of men, in defence of the country," especially when it was well known that they possessed firearms and could procure as much gunpowder as they wished.[118]

Even the superintendents of the windwards were affected economically by the discontinuance of party service. Two years after the Trelawnys were deported, the superintendents of Moore Town, Charles Town, and Scotts Hall also petitioned the House, reminding this body of the growing inflation, rendered more severe since they were "deprieved of the perquisities which formerly arose from the setting out of parties," by the operation of "recent laws."[119]

It cannot be doubted that the deportation of the Trelawnys soon acted as a constraint on the propensity of the other Maroon groups to rebel, as much for economic reasons as for the fear of deportation. And perhaps a testing case of Maroon fidelity to the colonial government came with the Morant Bay "Rebellion," in 1865, the peasant riot led by Paul Bogle in an attempt to rectify long standing injustice. We know that Paul Bogle had actually sought help from the windwards and apparently had a favorable response, for he is known to have said "the Maroons is our back,"[120] but this was a false hope. The windwards, in fact, became staunch allies of government and they were, ironically, responsible for the capture of Bogle.

Chapter 8

Conclusion

In a study of the Maroons of Jamaica from 1655 to 1796, we may be reminded of Dallas's observation that "although wars be necessarily attended with horror; yet the account of them affords, in the perusal of truth, a pleasure similar to that of a well-told tale; expectation is kept alive by uncertainty, and by the interest we naturally take in the fate of contending parties, in the efforts of courage, and in the exercise of talents."[1] Yet this study, although one of constant warfare and not without its horror, its courage, and talents, was more besides. In the social relationships that emerged after the *rapprochements* (such as that with Lubolo in 1662/3) and the treaty arrangements that were instituted between rebel slaves and their masters, we find ourselves bewildered by behavior we perceive as paradoxical or contradictory and even embarrassing. Our modern minds have difficulties in permitting us to comprehend or accept the fact that the Maroons, who fought so courageously for their freedom, could in turn be a major stumbling block to others who also wished to wrest freedom from the slavocracy. But there is no way that we can explain away or gloss over this pervasive phenomenon, when the evidence is overwhelming: the Maroons under the terms of the Treaties cooperated and collaborated[2] fully with the slave society in apprehending and returning runaways. Yet, despite this collaboration, the colonial state did betray them with deportation.

In searching for an explanation for the collaboration of the post-Treaty Maroons, we are bound to recognize those who would say that movements of this kind did not really provide an agenda, any sustained organizational structure, a program, and, perhaps, most important, an ideology. Equally, we cannot ignore the line of reasoning that would require us to confront the issue of the Maroon/African worldview — then and, to some extent, today.

We have mentioned before that the Africans who were transported to the New World did not constitute a culture bloc. They encompassed a multiplicity of ethnicities, from different parts of the continent of Africa, with distinct linguistic affinities. Each ethnic group viewed itself as exclusive — as a "nation" — despite certain commonalities. The notion of a pan-African solidarity was alien to their contemporary way of thinking, and judged by the current problems of the Organization of African Unity, the situation would hardly seem to have changed. We must recognize, however, that this is a particularistic argument and not one based on any universalistic concept of freedom. And to the extent that most of the Maroon leadership was in the hands of the Akan-speaking group, this made for even greater exclusivity.

The failure of Akan exclusivity was dramatically demonstrated in the 1795 Trelawny Town War. In the first instance, relatively few slaves deserted from the government parties, and most of those who did established their own Maroon communities to harass the plantation society, even after the Trelawnys were deported. This is in contrast to the early wars, especially to those from the 1720s up to the time of the Treaties, when desertion was legion. Here the deserters swelled the ranks of the Maroons, fortifying them with much-needed supplies — ammunition, gunpowder, and the like — gave them useful strategic information, and acted as guides to recently departed plantations for the purposes of plunder. And even when certain slaves did not join them, these would supply, from their plantations, all of the above, in addition to shelter and entertainment. Perhaps the most telling point to the slaves' distrust and dislike for the Maroons was demonstrated when some slaves were actually manhandled by other slaves for having participated on the side of the Maroons. The Maroons had reaped their nemesis by the 1790s.

Another aspect of the fissiparousness among the different black groups is the fact that no other Maroon community joined the Trelawnys in their battle against the slavocracy, but in fact their closest neighbors, in consanguinity and in circumstances, aligned themselves with the authorities against them. This is most perplexing. The notion of a dispute between the two groups over the control of their (leeward) Treaty seems neither satisfactory nor sufficient to have created such an irrevocable rift. And even if the vigorous Balcarres had practiced the divide-and-rule strategy it still should not be sufficient to explain how they could be so easily induced. It is true that, by 1795, we can assume that both Cudjoe and Accompong were no longer alive. We cease to hear of them in the documents after the 1750s. Unfortunately, we have no record of the succession line of Accompong Town since this town was, at the time of the Treaty, rather in the position of a satellite of Cudjoe's Town. But the friendly relations between Accompong and Cudjoe might not have continued in the two communities after their expiration. Indeed, there might well have been much tension. We remind ourselves of the 1742 situation, when Cudjoe had some Maroons along with some "Coramantine" slaves, executed for their attempted coup against him and Accompong because of the Treaty. We saw in this case a probable generational/ideological schism. We do not know what proportion of Maroons from Accompong Town was executed or given over to the authorities by Cudjoe. It is likely, given the authoritarian rule of Cudjoe, that most of this dissent against the Treaty came from Accompong's group. But we do know that those Maroons of Accompong who supported the attempted coup would never allow themselves to forget Cudjoe's "treachery." And they would have told their children. The Trelawnys' outbreak with government in 1795 might thus have been seen by Accompong Town as their opportunity for revenge. We may also note here that, in conducting field studies among the different communities in Jamaica, we found no strong sense of cooperation or even of empathy among them. Indeed, in some cases, even some of the leaders displayed indifference to the other groups.

The position the windwards assumed during the war is more easily understood. To be sure, they did not join the Trelawnys in the fight against a "common enemy," but throughout the hostilities they did maintain a state of intransigent neutrality, Moore Town specifically refusing Balcarres's order to attend him and his proffer of gifts — a useful means of imperial control.

In making treaties with the Maroons, the British government and the local colonial authorities, for their part, had very limited objectives, initially, all bearing on economic considerations. Maroon activities were deleterious to the mercantile interest in the metropole, and a cessation under a peace treaty would enable the planters to get on with the plantation economy. This was the case whether the arrangement was made with Lubolo in the seventeenth century, with Juan de Serras later in the same century, or with Cudjoe and Quao in the eighteenth. As an auxiliary force against internal and external enemies, the Maroons would help to stabilize the economy. And if the local planters, at the outset, had doubts about the efficacy of this proposition, the colonial authorities felt that they knew better. Did they not have their model from the free communities of ex-*cimarrones* in Mexico, Panama, Peru, and the "whole continent of the West Indies" now loyal to Spain? Domestically, pacification was attractive not only for the obvious police/military function the Maroons would now perform, but also for the long-term political benefit it would serve in creating a division between them and the other blacks under slavery.

The Dutch, in making their treaties with their Maroons in Surinam in the 1670s and who modelled theirs on the Jamaicans', were even more unambiguous in their divisive intent. They planned to "respect the peace with those who had been set apart by the Peace ... and persecute those outside the scope of this Peace ... [and] divide them, and, if possible, sow dissension among them."[3]

But British colonial objectives were decidedly more complex. How, for one, did the idea of establishing quasi-states within the colonial polity — a slave society at that — sit with the authorities? They could not have been unaware of the potential consequences attendant on any system of political pluralism, consequences that could be inimical to stability. In fact, up to the time of the last Treaties, the authorities had hardly more than Hobson's choice in the matter of negotiating terms with their "rebels." But as soon as the Treaties were instituted, the relative positions of the parties shifted dramatically. The official position could thus be characterized as one that underwent a configuration based on the order of progression from one of embarrassed helplessness (1655–1739) to that of condescending, albeit urbane, protectiveness (1740s to late 1770s) to that of cavalier disregard for the concerns of Maroon affairs, eventually culminating in that of arrogant control (by the 1790s). But even in designing the Treaties within the context of their weak position, there can be no doubt that the authorities had an awareness that they would, sooner or later, be in a commanding position with respect to Maroon hegemonies. The eventual success was the result of a conjunction of circumstances: the presence and the personalities of the white residents among the Maroons; the social dynamics within the Maroon communities; their relationship — formal or perceived — to government, and to the other blacks, and the implications of the economic relations between these communities and the wider society. All of these, one way or another, were under the control of the colonial state.

In the final analysis, therefore, the Maroon story is a study of colonial power. And it is in this sense that we can see a parallel with the proposed "indirect rule thesis" as practiced by Britain in colonial Africa.[4] If this thesis is to be maintained, though, we would need to be precise about the meaning or meanings of indirect rule, specifically because in many cases it soon came to have a different meaning for the ruler and for the ruled. To the British officials articulating (if not practicing) this policy, indirect rule was indigenous local self-government conducted primarily by local chiefs *in situ*, where "the function of the British administrator is rather to guide by influence and advice than to rule by direct commmand."[5] Historically, ruling indirectly came about as a result of conquest, and though the tendency is to view this system as peculiarly British, the Dutch, the French and the Germans had also practiced it in Africa to some extent. And even further back, ancient imperial Rome may have conducted some of its colonial administration by some version of this mode of government.

Different African principalities soon had a completely different version of a system the British officials thought fair, just, reasonable, beneficial to the governed, as it was convenient to the ruler. One such official sanctimoniously exclaimed that it was "not often in history that a virtue has been consciously made of this necessity [indirect rule], and a system dictated by the convenience of the ruler prolonged in the interests of the ruled."[6]

But this is jingoistic reasoning, for even when the system could be defended on grounds of efficiency, it was still an alien intrusion conducted primarily with a view to catering to alien interests. The very efficiency, too, has its obverse side, for all too often this serves to inculcate a feeling of helplessness among the "natives," leading them to negate their own cultural values and spawning in its wake a cadre of "mimic men" with an excess of reverence for the ruler. And this, it seems to me, is the worst aspect of colonialism. To strip a person, a "tribe," or a race of its self-confidence is to leave its members starkly vulnerable.

The Maroon case would seem to conform to the indirect rule practiced under King Aggrey of Cape Coast in what was then a part of the Gold Coast (Ghana today). In 1865, Aggrey complained that he was "compelled to observe that in the days of Governor Maclean, the Governor in a very peculiar, imperceptible and unheard of manner wrested from the hands of our Kings, Chiefs, and headmen their power to govern their own subjects."[7] Montague James, by the 1790s, could, if he had essayed to think things through, have lamented similarly; but with the difference that the whittling away of Maroon customary powers and jurisdiction, as we saw in this study, was not "imperceptible"; rather, it was done in a bold, open manner and under the rubric of legality, by acts of the Assembly.

Just as, one could suggest, Frederick D. Lugard, the dynamic British administrator, has come to be peculiarly associated with Britain's indirect rule in Nigeria, so could John James, the forceful, vain, courageous, and successful generalissimo of Maroon affairs, be associated with this intrusive, external, alien rule. James's very success or efficiency nearly spelled doom for Maroon hegemony. Maroon officials under James's rule soon lapsed into a state of lethargy, so that by the time of the termination of his tenure the Trelawnys seemed to have lost their fierce independent spirit and their reliance on their own initiative. The colonial-dependency syndrome had begun.

Their attitude to Thomas Craskell, James's successor, is instructive. Here was a young man, weak and ineffective, who should, in fact, have been the perfect choice for the Maroons had they had the same pre-Treaty robust confidence in their ability to conduct their own affairs. But in fact, they found him unacceptable precisely because he was too weak and not able to govern them as did James. James's influence on the Maroons —

earned, perhaps — practically transformed some into gratuitous emulation, inclining some to reject their proud cultural heritage.

An important point to mention in this regard is the fact that by the time of the Trelawny War, most of the Maroons had chosen Anglo-Saxon names — elitist, too — for they adopted the names of men of the first rank in society, men of substance and influence — all slave masters, it should be remembered. Montague James himself, their chief, most probably adopted his surname from the James dynasty, and his aristocratic first name should not go unnoticed. A roll call of the Maroons would find them answering to appellations like Captain John Tharp, Captain Robert Jackson, Captain James Lawrence, Captain Samuel Shaw, Captain James Williams, and so on among the Trelawny officeholders. Any random assortment among the rank and file, among which was one John James, would reveal the same. A similar pattern, more or less, existed in the other communities, although among the windwards, a sprinkling of African names still remained, chiefly among the oldest. Thus Charles Town at this time (1796) had one officer with an African name, Lieutenant Colonel Afee Cudjoe, aged eighty; Moore Town, also about this time, had a sole surviving African cognomen among its officers, Lieutenant Yeaon, aged seventy; and Lieutenant John Sambo could be considered as having half of his name still African. Like Trelawny Town, all of the officers of Accompong Town, as would be expected, had assumed Anglo-Saxon names. Scotts Hall's officers have not been identified at this time, but its listing for the previous year had only a few African names. If one is to be guided by names alone in a discussion of cultural contact, then it appears that the women were more resistant to change, judged by the larger proportion of African names still existing (Nanny, for instance) among all the communities.

The declining importance of African names with Akan/Ashanti predominating earlier, is certainly a departure from the pre-Treaty days, and indeed up until the early 1770s. What's in a name? Well, this change represented to Bryan Edwards [8] — who for the first time recognized a redeeming feature in Maroon psyche — an upward movement on civilization's ladder. From an opposite view, however, it could represent the mimicry than can come about when a person or a collective has lost its confidence in its cultural values. There are those who might say that this name-changing procedure was merely an African practice. Africans very often (to this day) would simply choose the name of an authority figure or that of an individual they respect and admire. But in the case of the Maroons, it cannot be forgotten, within the context of their history, that these names that they *chose* were those of prominent slave masters. There are others, too, who may read into the Maroons' practice of changing their names nothing more than part of the creoleization process of the Caribbean. [9]

John James's influence on public policy was no less substantial. It is true that he was not himself a member of the assembly initiating those acts that wrested traditional pre-Treaty as well as post-Treaty powers away from the Maroons, but we have already noted his influence on this male-oriented hierarchial colonial society. And, in so "influencing" the leaders by his conscious and well-orchestrated "indispensibility" to them, he helped to create the conditions that made it even more possible for the direct legal framework of government to bear. Equally, although his influence was more long-lasting, more direct on, first the Trelawnys, and, next in line, the Accompongs, his impact on all the other Maroon communities should not be seen as negligible. James's fame as the major domo of the Trelawnys soon spread to the other groups, and like a veritable ombudsman, he was invariably called upon by them to settle disputes among themselves as well as between them and white settlers. The colonial state, with its overarching power, soon recognized James's juridical as well as his social engineering qualities and promptly formalized the position by appointing him major-commandant of all the Maroons in 1779, for his good conduct "in keeping under proper subjection" — in the words of Governor Dalling — the Maroons of Trelawny Town. James was very conscious of his role, and the Maroons, for their part, played into his hands by being overly enamored of his forceful and efficient qualities, and, as a man of overweening conceit, he enjoyed every moment of his power over them and used it in the grand manner of a latter-day seigneur. He boasted that, under his care, the Maroons had "behaved and demeaned themselves well . . . [and] have rendered very great services and benefits to many of the planters and other settlers in the island."[10] James thus did to Maroon morale — especially to that of leadership — what Walpole had recommended rum's function to be.

When the Trelawnys therefore importuned the colonial state for social welfare in the form of medical care, they, in effect, gave validity to their client status in the local system. It was also an aspect of the new dependency syndrome and the creoleization process. In the pre-Treaty days, they would have relied on their own local "doctors" or "medicine" men and women, with their African knowledge of herbs and "science." Now they requested Western doctors. This was done in 1770 and was granted two years later when Dr. Robert Barland was appointed to attend them; for fourteen months he visited them regularly, in addition to extraordinary visits arising from gunshot wounds, fractures, and other accidents. As would be expected, the doctor was not reimbursed, and after petitioning the Assembly on several occasions, he finally sued the superintendent, John James, for the sum of £186.10 with costs. The judgment went against James in 1776, and the outcome is not clear; nor is it clear whether or not Barland's service continued.[11]

But the irony is that it was Balcarres, and not John James, who rescued Montague James and his people from lethargy. Dallas characterized Montague as having lapsed into a "pathetic figure of fun" who had lost authority over his councils by 1795. To Dallas, he was "considered in no better light than as an old woman, but to whom the shadow of respect was to be paid, as he bore the title of chief."[12] This should be seen against the background of Montague's appointment by John James as his assistant from around 1781 to 1792. This appointment is unique. No other Maroon leader was so appointed, and perhaps only a John James could have effected this. Montague, although still called captain of the Maroons, was now, in addition, officially called "assistant superintendent of Trelawny Town." His appointment was under a special commission, and he was paid a salary, although, as would be expected, he had problems collecting it from the Assembly.

Dallas's characterization of Montague might be overdrawn. Nevertheless, we cannot forget how submissively and quickly he surrendered to Balcarres's first proclamation, when he and his Maroons had, in fact committed no wrong against the colonial state. This behavior is not in line with the traditional character of the Maroons. It was only when he was so callously treated by Balcarres and then sent back to treat with his people that he became a real Maroon leader again, and no longer James's stooge. It is interesting to note that Montague continued to be the Maroons' chief in Nova Scotia, where they complained bitterly of the injustice of sending West Indians to live in such a climate — a place fit only for "bears"; a place where the pineapple could not grow. Their final journey to Sierra Leone came about largely because of their own energetic and sustained representations to the British government, and Montague continued to be their leader until his death in Sierra Leone.[13]

Balcarres's insensitivity had a similar impact on all the other Maroon leaders, including Johnson, Smith, Dunbar, Shaw, and Harding, to name a few. Some of these had actually advised Montague to surrender, but Balcarres's excesses brought them back to their former fighting spirit, and they soon became the main force in the war. As with Montague, they never lost their old spirit again, as they traveled first to Nova Scotia and then to Sierra Leone. The ancestors of these brave men and women were soon to become a part of the very foundation of the Creole society in Freetown, distinguishing themselves in leadership positions, in government, in business, and in the professions.

We could also note that the Maroons never lost their implacable hatred for Balcarres, who betrayed them. In one of their numerous engaging petitions from Nova Scotia, they begged the British monarch never to send "any of dem poor cotch Lord for Gubner again."[14]

All in all, we would like to suggest a reexamination of the indirect rule thesis as applied to Maroon government in Jamaica. Historically, and everywhere that this mode of government was utilized, it was applied by the fact of conquest. It was applied to a people who had been conquered or taken over by an alien power. The Maroons of Jamaica were never conquered by military action. Indeed, their special relationship with government came about precisely because they were never conquered. Thus the system resorted to after the eighteenth-century treaties by the colonial state was indirect rule turned upside down. It was direct rule brought about by the overarching power of the whole colonial apparatus. It was direct rule by the presence of the white residents in their midst, by their obligation to wait on governor when so commanded, and even more important, by the governor's authority to appoint their leaders after the demise of those named in the documents. This was the cutting edge of real direct control — a point that has not escaped even some vendors of popular literature.[15] Again, what real power, what social control could a post-Treaty Maroon leader wield, given the nature of his society, nurtured as it was in warfare and cruel courage, with the power of administering the death sentence wrested from him, and how effective could he be when his people could now appeal over his head to white resident officials of the local government?

Furthermore, with respect to the indirect rule practiced in colonial Africa, it was the traditional rulers, kings, chiefs, and headmen, whose services were utilized — even if to carry out the orders of the alien administration. But at least, for the most part, the chief's people could continue to see their ruler (even if a legal fiction) conducting business — albeit never quite as usual. Cudjoe, perhaps, was the only chief after the Treaties who continued, seemingly, to possess some authority, although bereft of the ultimate power of punishment.

In all this we have dealt with the stipulations of the Treaties, which reduced Maroon power. But more power was further wrenched from their hands by the unilateral extralegal (in terms of the Treaties) activities of the colonial state. Even during the period we characterized as condescending protectiveness, the action of the government in facilitating different Maroon communities with land grants was one that favored colonial interests. Undoubtedly, the social dynamics, especially among the windwards (with the numerous wranglings — "disorders and tumults," to the officials —and the propensity to break away and form new groups), assisted government-aided fissiparousness. The smaller the units and the more dispersed they were, the easier they were to control and the more effective could be their policing role.

Outside of the specificities of the terms of the Treaties, we also saw the government legislating in a manner that placed constraints on Maroons' economic earnings, on their mobility, on their ability to intermingle with slaves, on their traditional juridical functions, so that by the 1790s they could be tried in the ordinary courts like any other black in the society, and, even more humiliating, white superintendents now presided over their courts. And the whittling away of the powers of the Maroon leaders bore an inverse relationship to the increased powers of the white superintendents. Not only could they now usurp the position of the chiefs by presiding at their courts and passing judgments (the death sentence continued to be exempted), they now supervised search parties, supervised road services, and made sure that the limits set on expenditure were satisfied. They kept a strict surveillance on the movements of Maroons by issuing passes to those who wished to leave the towns — and the litany of their new functions continued. But perhaps the most onerous to them, and most probably suffocating to the Maroons, was the requirement that obliged them to report regularly on the Maroon communities, noting their demographic profile, the number of arms-bearing men, the number of slaves and slave owners in their midst, the number living outside their communities — the sum total of which could be considered official espionage on Maroon affairs. All this was direct intrusion and can hardly be seen as indirect. It is in the area of consequences as a result of alien intrusion, direct or otherwise, that we can detect similarities.

The Trelawny Town War was the denouement of a process that began with the Treaties. That it happened among the Trelawnys is merely fortuitous, for it could have happened in any of the communities by the 1790s. Moreover, that a major uprising did not occur earlier was largely, as we saw, the result of the patronage system that worked well with influential men acting as arbiters in disputes, partly due to the character of the superintendents in the towns and partly due to the type of governor in the colony. That the accumulated tension finally exploded in Trelawny Town was due to the fortuitous conjunction of the presence of a governor like Balcarres, who exacerbated the situation, and the fact that Thomas Craskell and not John James was their superintendent. The ingredient of patronage would have been available with another superintendent (James, for instance) and with another governor (Sir Basil Keith, for example). Trelawny Town was in a state of disequilibrium, and there can be no doubt that it was a matter of supreme humiliation to them when two of their members were whipped by a "common slave." This can only be understood when viewed within the context of their perceived notion of themselves as a special people and of their perceived special relationship with government. But even this egregious error could have been rectified with the usual intervention of men of influence, under a different administration. The Maroons were betrayed; and as we trace them through to Nova Scotia and Sierra Leone, we find that the generation of the 1795 War never allowed themselves to forget it.

That some of the Maroon communities exist today (although they would seem to be disintegrating, and the author has not been able to ascertain an accurate picture of their population) is due to atavistic stubbornness. When in the 1840s the government tried to encompass them into the wider political system of the island, which, to official thinking, was the logical thing to do — considering how their powers had been whittled away — the Maroons stoutly refused. The Maroons have their own reality carved out of their history. It is the abstract notion of this history exemplified by their Treaties and lands, sacrosanct to them and inalienable, that has fed this stubbornness. It has given them a perception of themselves that borders on "the chosen."

NOTES

Chapter 1

1. Adapted from the title of a recent documentary film made by a professor of biology and an admission officer, both of Harvard University. "I shall moulder before I shall be taken."

2. See Richard Price, ed., *Maroon Societies* (New York: Anchor Books, 1973), pp. 1, 171, 172, and *passim.*

3. Ibid., p. 1, n. 1. Other views on its origin include that of Edward Long, to be repeated by many writers after him. Long felt that the word "Maroon" (which he rendered "Maron") is probably derived from the Spanish *Marrano,* a young hog of one year, which was also used to describe the hunter of wild hogs, to distinguish them from the *bucaniers* — hunters of wild cattle and horses. See Edward Long, *The History of Jamaica ...* (3 vols., London: Frank Cass, 1970), vol. 2, p. 338 n. (first published, 1774).

4. Price, *Maroon Societies,* p. 1; Eric Williams, *From Columbus to Castro: The History of the Caribbean, 1492–1969* (New York and Evanston: Harper & Row, 1970), pp. 66–68.

5. Ibid., p. 67.

6. See, among others, Price, *Maroon Societies, passim*; Vera Rubin and Arthur Tuden, eds., *Comparative Perspectives on Slavery in New World Plantation Societies* (New York: New York Academy of Sciences, 1976), pp. 389–480; Michael C. Meyer and William L. Sherman, *The Course of Mexican History* (New York: Oxford University Press, 1979), pp. 216–17.

7. Price, *Maroon Societies,* p. 195.

8. This center is to be found at Alamar, east of Havana, where young Jamaicans worked on the construction of housing and community facilities. See *The Daily Gleaner,* October 31, 1975.

9. Mavis C. Campbell, "Marronage in Jamaica: Its Origin in the Seventeenth Century," in Rubin and Tuden, eds., *Comparative Perspectives,* p. 392.

10. R. C. Dallas, *The History of the Maroons* (2 vols., London: T. N. Longman and O. Rees, 1803), vol. 1, pp. 122–23.

11. Williams, *From Columbus,* p. 68.

12. See The Municipal Council of Panama to the Spanish Crown, February 24, 1573. Document No. 21, in I. A. Wright, *Documents Concerning English Voyages to the Spanish Main, 1659–1689* (London: Hakluyt Society, 1932).

13. Kenneth R. Andrews, *The Spanish Caribbean: Trade and Plunder, 1530–1630* (New Haven: Yale University Press, 1978), p. 140.

14. Documents 68–73, in Wright, *Documents.*

15. Andrews, *Spanish Caribbean,* p. 145.

16. Meyer and Sherman, *Mexican History,* pp. 216–17; Colin S. Palmer, *Slaves of the White Gods: Blacks in Mexico, 1570–1650* (Cambridge: Harvard University Press, 1976), pp. 128–29; David M. Davidson, "Negro Slave Control and Resistance in Colonial Mexico, 1519–1650," *Hispanic American Review* 46 (1966): 235–53; for the connection of the "Bron nation" with a branch of the Akan stock,

see R. S. Rattray, *Ashanti* (Oxford: Clarendon Press of Oxford University Press, 1969), p. 113.

17. Sylvia W. DeGroot, *From Isolation towards Integration: The Surinam Maroons and Their Colonial Rulers* (The Hague: Martinus Nijhoff, 1977), p. 7.

18. See Dee Brown, *Bury My Heart at Wounded Knee* (New York: Bantam Books, 1979), *passim.*

19. See Robin W. Winks, *The Blacks in Canada: A History* (New Haven: Yale University Press, 1971), p. 78; Barbara Klamon Kopytoff, "The Maroons of Jamaica: An Ethnohistorical Study of Incomplete Polities, 1655–1905," (Ph.D. diss., University of Pennsylvania, 1973) pp. 18–19.

20. Colonial Office (C.O.) 137/47, *Some Consideration Relating to the Present State of Jamaica with Respect to Their Runaway Negroes*, October 26, 1734; see also Cyril Hamshere, *The British in the Caribbean* (Cambridge: Harvard University Press, 1972), pp. 45 and 171–79; *Lady Nugent's Journal* (Kingston: Institute of Jamaica, 1966), p. 279.

21. Bryan Edwards, *The History, Civil and Commercial, of the British Colonies in the West Indies*, 2 vols. (Dublin: Luke White, 1793), vol. 1, p. 131. (3 vols., 1801 edition; the 1793 edition is used throughout this work.)

22. Dallas, *History,* I, pp. xxvii–xxviii.

23. See Winks, *Blacks in Canada*, p. 78.

24. A. E. Furness, "The Maroon War of 1795," *Jamaica Historical Review*, 5, no. 2 (1965), p. 31.

25. Frank Cundall and Joseph Pietersz, *Jamaica under the Spaniards: Abstracted from the Archives of Seville* (Kingston: The Institute of Jamaica, 1919), p. 51.

26. See, for instance, Jean Fouchard, *The Haitian Maroons: Liberty or Death* (New York: Edward W. Blyden Press), Part 2.

27. Due to some predetermined fateful birth, the child of a Batomba would be "thrown away" and left to die, but if "found" by a member of the Fulbe tribe, would be enslaved by this group. See Bernd Baldus, "Social Structure and Ideology: Cognitive Responses to Servitude among the Machube of Northern Dahomey," *Canadian Journal of African Studies*, vol. 8, no. 2 (1974), pp. 355–88, who found, with interviews, no desire for change among the Machubes, although they have more than ample opportunity to run away and form alternative communities; they judge their situation fortunate since their fate could have been death.

28. Most of these are to be found in the Institute of Jamaica, Kingston. There are even pictures of Nanny here; how arrived at is not clear. Also, in a 1986 brochure of the Commonwealth Institute in London, focusing on the Caribbean, is a picture of Nanny, probably obtained from the Institute of Jamaica.

29. Frantz Fanon, *Black Skin, White Masks* (New York: Grove Press, 1967), p. 64.

30. See Peter Worsley, *The Third World* (Chicago: University of Chicago Press, 1977), p. xiii.

31. See A. D. Dridzo, "The Origin of the Second Maroon War, 1795–1796,"

Jamaica Journal, vol. 6, no. 1, March 1792, pp. 21–25. Dridzo contends that this war was a plot instigated by the plantocracy to advance their interest.

32. Eugene D. Genovese, *From Rebellion to Revolution: Afro-American Slave Revolt in the Making of the New World* (New York: Vintage Books, 1981), p. xiv. This brilliant Marxist scholar found much of the Maroon story maddening. "Relations" for instance, "between Maroons and slaves after promulgation of such treaties became maddeningly ambiguous," pp. 52–53.

33. E. J. Hobsbawm, *Primitive Rebels: Studies in Archaic Forms of Social Movement in the 19th and 20th Centuries* (New York: W. W. Norton, 1965), p. 3.

Chapter 2

1. Edwards, *History*, I, p. 146; Dallas, *History*, I, p. xxviii.

2. Ibid., p. 149 and xxviii, respectively; Long, *History*, I, pp. 238–39. However, the nervous governor, Don Juan Ramirez, who offered no resistance whatever to the inefficient British occupation force, wrote to his monarch upon the occasion of the invasion, that "[t]he Island, Sir, is most fertile in every description of provisions and cattle and tobacco, which is what the enemy [the British] wants." Ramirez also inflated the number of the British force, designating it as "composed of 53 ships of war, 11 small ones and more than 40 pinnaces, with 15,000 seamen and soldiers," arguing that "to such strength there was no resistance [and] the colonists abandoned the port and town and went to the mountains with the families," whereupon the enemy took possession of everything. See Cundall and Pietersz, *Jamaica*, pp. 51–52. The British ships really numbered thirty-eight and the soldiers, 7,000, with a sea regiment of 1,000. Ibid. And it should be remembered, as every school child knows, that it was a most ill-fed, ill-disciplined, factious, and bungling force that took Jamaica from the Spaniards.

3. S. A. G. Taylor, *The Western Design: An Account of Cromwell's Expedition to the Caribbean* (Kingston: The Institute of Jamaica, 1965), p. 48.

4. Edwards, *History*, I, p. 150.

5. Ibid., p. 149.

6. Cundall and Pietersz, *Jamaica*, p. 102. Ysassi landed in Cuba a frustrated man with bitter complaints about the way the Cuban governor took advantage of his situation in Jamaica, particularly in withholding his supplies: "I came empty-handed to this Island [Cuba]," he complained, "where eighty thousand pesos from Jamaica are lying in your royal chests, I was not assisted although I asked," p. 102; also p. 52.

7. Price, ed., *Maroon Societies*, p. 20.

8. Philip D. Curtin, *The Atlantic Slave Trade: A Census* (Madison: University of Wisconsin Press, 1970), pp. 95–116.

9. See, for example, Kopytoff, "The Maroons of Jamaica," p. 22.

10. Taylor, *Western Design*, said that the black hunters "were to prove their loyalty to the Spaniards and their aptitude as guerilla fighters," p. 48.

11. Charles Leslie, *A New and Exact Account of Jamaica* (Edinburgh: Fleming & Kincaid, 1739), pp. 71–72.

12. Ibid. This fellow was a slave with a beloved wife who bore him many children, but soon, "the old Fox, his Master, with brutal Fierceness tore the fond Creature from his Arms, and cruelly forced her to comply with his own sordid Desires." The Mozartian tragedy ended in his killing his wife first, before joining the British to avenge himself on his exmaster. He fought so courageously that D'Oyley gave him his own piece of land, on which he settled quietly in a state of melancholy. Ibid., pp. 75–76.

13. Taylor, *Western Design*, p. 61.

14. Edwards, *History*, I, p. 153.

15. Cundall and Pietersz, *Jamaica*, pp. 55, 62.

16. Taylor, *Western Design*, pp. 101, 107.

17. Cundall and Pietersz, *Jamaica*, p. 62.

18. John Thurloe, *A Collection of the State Papers* (London: n.p., 1742), vol. IV, p. 154.

19. Ibid., pp. 601–2.

20. Ibid., p. 605. It is intriguing that S. A. G. Taylor reechoed this sentiment even more emphatically: "To such men, [the slaves in the woods] living the kind of life that was natural and agreeable to them, the yoke of slavery would have seemed light," *Western Design*, p. 48.

21. Thurloe, *State Papers*, vol. IV, p. 749.

22. Ibid.

23. Cundall and Pietersz, *Jamaica*, p. 81.

24. Ibid., p. 90.

25. *Journal of the Assembly of Jamaica* (*JAJ*), October 28, 1662.

26. Thurloe, *State Papers*, vol. 4, p. 605.

27. Cundall and Pietersz, *Jamaica*, p. 81.

28. Dallas, *History*, I, p. 25.

29. *JAJ*, January 10, 1660; Appendix to First Volume.

30. Cundall and Pietersz, *Jamaica*, pp. 51–52; Taylor, *Western Design*, p. 55; H. Barham, "A Most Correct and Particular Account of the Island of Jamaica, From the Time of Spanish first Discovering, and Settling Upon it," (1722), British Museum (B.M.), Sl. Ms. 3918. The pagination of all the manuscript sources used in this study is either incomplete, imperfect, or inaccurate — in some cases two different numbers on the same page — thus no page numbers are given.

31. James Knight, "The Naturall, Morall and Political History of Jamaica ... From the Earlist [sic] Account of Time to the Year 1742," B.M. Ms. 12415.

32. Thurloe, *State Papers*, vol. 9, p. 137.

33. C.O. 140/1, Council meeting, February 1, 1662/3.

34. Cundall and Pietersz, *Jamaica*, p. 98.

35. Long, *History*, II, p. 339, and Edwards, "Observations on the Disposition, Character, ... of the Maroons of Jamaica ...." Appendix 2 to his *History* (1807), vol. I, reproduced in Richard Price, ed., *Maroon Societies*, p. 231.

36. Edwards, *History*, I, p. 153.

37. Ibid., p. 159.

38. Although it should be remembered that Kipling's "White Man's Burden"

(1899) was originally meant to instruct the Americans to adopt towards their new Philippine subjects what he believed to be self-sacrificing paternalism as displayed in the British Empire! The author is grateful to Christopher Fyfe for reminding her of the original meaning of this phrase. Christopher Fyfe to author, October 30, 1982.

39. C.O. 140/1, February 1, 1662/3.

40. Taylor, *Western Design*, pp. 185–86.

41. C.O. 140/1, Council meeting, October 23, 1663.

42. Ibid.

43. These various renderings may have been a corruption of the Spanish-named plateau in the interior of Jamaica, "Los Vermejales." Edward Long, for example, in his *History*, II, p. 339, referred to them as "Vermaholis Negroes."

44. Ibid.

45. Ibid.

46. Ibid.

47. Dallas, *History*, I, p. 26.

48. C.O. 140/1, Council meeting, October 23, 1663.

49. Ibid., August 15, 1665.

50. Ibid., September 1, 1665.

51. Ibid.

52. Ibid.

53. Ibid., February 29, 1667/8.

54. Ibid.

55. Ibid., March 28, 1668.

56. Ibid.

57. Price, ed., *Maroon Societies*, p. 20.

58. C.O. 140/1, Council meeting, May 2, 1670.

59. Ibid.

60. Ibid.

61. Ibid.

62. Orlando Patterson, *The Sociology of Slavery* ... (Rutherford, N. J.: Fairleigh Dickinson University Press, 1969), p. 267.

63. See Chapter 7 below.

64. Edward Long papers, Add. Ms. 12431.

65. For an account of the Buccaneers, see, among others, Edwards, *History*, I, pp. 160–61; Dallas, *History*, I, pp. xxxix–xliv; Leslie, *Account of Jamaica*, pp. 95–100.

66. Long, *History*, I, p. 300.

67. C.O. 140/1, Minutes of the Council, June 29, 1670.

68. Ibid., June 29, August 13 and 31, and September 1 and 28, 1670; also, Frank Wesley Pitman, *The Development of the British West Indies* (New Haven: Yale University Press, 1917), pp. 14–15.

69. C.O. 140/1, November 28, 1671.

70. For these rebellions on plantations, see Patterson, *Sociology*, pp. 267–68.

71. Leslie, *Account of Jamaica*, p. 250.

72. *Acts of the Assembly of Jamaica*, 1691–1737.
73. C.O. 140/3, January 23, 1675/6.
74. Edward Long Papers, Add. Ms. 12431.
75. Patterson, *Sociology*, p. 268; Frank Wesley Pitman mentioned that a few slaves from Madagascar were brought to the West Indies by interlopers. See *West Indies*, p. 76.
76. Dallas, *History*, I, pp. 31–32.
77. Leslie, *Account of Jamaica*, p. 21.
78. Edwards, *History*, I, p. 149.
79. Anon., *Jamaica: Enslaved and Free* (London: Religious Tract Society, 1799), p. 82.
80. Pitman, *West Indies*, p. 27.
81. C.O. 140/4, September 16, 1686.
82. Ibid.
83. Ibid., September 24, 1686.
84. CSF. 154/2, B.M., Acts of Assembly Passed In the Island of Jamaica from 1681 to 1733 Inclusive.
85. C.O. 140/4, September 24, 1686.
86. Ibid., September 29, 1686.
87. Ibid.
88. Ibid.
89. Ibid.
90. J. Stewart, *A View of the Past and Present State of the Island of Jamaica* .... (Edinburgh: Oliver & Boyd, 1823), p. 321.
91. C.O. 140/4, November–December, 1686.
92. Ibid.
93. Ibid.
94. C.O. 140/4, Council meeting, January–February, 1686/7.
95. Ibid., February 21, 1686/7.
96. Stewart, *A View*, pp. 316–17.
97. Ibid., p. 317.
98. C.O. 140/4, Council meetings, February–August, 1687.
99. Ibid.
100. Ibid., and C.O. 140/5.
101. Ibid.
102. Stewart, *A View*, p. 318. Although this statement was made in connection with the 1795 war, it is more or less true of most Maroon engagements.
103. C.O. 140/6, June 18, 1692.
104. Ibid.
105. Ibid., December 10, 1694.
106. Ibid.
107. Edward Long Papers, Add. Ms. 12431.
108. Dallas, *History*, I, p. 32.
109. Robert Renny, *History of Jamaica* (London: J. Cawthorn, 1807), pp. 52–53.
110. Dallas, *History*, I, pp. 28–29.

Chapter 3

1. Taken from Anon., *Jamaica*, p. 82.

2. Edward Long Papers, Add. Ms. 12431; see also Dallas, *History*, I, p. 31.

3. Patterson, *Sociology*, pp. 119, 276; Curtin, *The Atlantic Slave Trade*, p. 161.

4. Codrington to Council of Trade and Plantations, December 30, 1701, CSP, XIX; see also Sir Alan Burns, *History of the West Indies* (London: George Allen & Unwin, 1954), p. 55.

5. Edwards, *History*, II, pp. 58–59.

6. Long, *History*, II, pp. 473–75.

7. Edward Long Papers, Add. Ms. 12431.

8. Dallas, *History*, I, pp. 26–28; Long, *History*, II, p. 446; James Knight, "History," Add. Ms. 12415.

9. Ibid.

10. See, for example, Carey Robinson, *The Fighting Maroons of Jamaica* (Jamaica: William Collins & Sangster, 1969), p. 46.

11. *JAJ* 2, p. 683.

12. Dallas, *History*, I, p. 53.

13. For elaboration, see A. R. Radcliffe-Brown and Daryll Forde, eds., *African Systems of Kinship and Marriage* (London and New York: Oxford University Press, 1950), p. 260.

14. Letter to James Knight, n.d., in Add. Ms. 12431.

15. Ibid.

16. Ibid.; also C.O. 137/18, Examination of Nicholas Plysham before governor and Council, June 18, 1730.

17. James Knight, "History," Add. Ms. 12415; Edward Long Papers, Add. Ms. 12431.

18. James Lewis to James Knight, December 20, 1743. Add. Ms. 12431. Flimsy and unreliable as is this sole piece of evidence — coming as it does from one white officer — it has not prevented certain scholars from pontificating that it could be accepted "that there was some wife sharing, that it was regulated, and that the original husband retained primary rights in the wife and rights in the children." See Kopytoff, "The Maroons of Jamaica," p. 80; or another, who, from the same source, gave it that "[t]his system of wife-sharing should be seen as an outgrowth of the shortage of women in the Maroon camps and the desire to perpetrate their numbers." See Daniel Lee Schafer, "The Maroons of Jamaica: African Slave Rebels in the Caribbean," (Ph.D. diss., University of Minnesota, 1973), p. 67.

19. Edward Long Papers, Add. Ms. 12431.

20. C.O. 137/21, The Further Examination of Sarra alias Ned taken by order of His Excellency, October 1, 1733.

21. For further elaboration, see Radcliffe-Brown and Forde, *African Systems*, pp. 252–62; R. S. Rattray, *Ashanti Law and Constitution* (Oxford: Clarendon Press of Oxford University Press, 1929), chap. VIII.

22. C.O. 137/21, Examination of Sarra ..., October 1, 1733.

23. Ibid.

24. Ibid.

25. Robinson, *Fighting Maroons*, p. 53; for more on Nanny, see Chapter 6.

26. Chancellor Williams, *The Destruction of Black Civilization* (Chicago: Third World Press, 1974), pp. 273–74, 276–89.

27. Lord Lindsay, *Lives of the Lindsays; or, A Memoir of the Houses of Crawford and Balcarres* (3 vols., London: John Murray, 1849), vol. III, p. 4.

28. Dallas, *History*, I, p. 35.

29. For these acts, see the B.M. OPL, CSF. series, *Acts of Assembly passed in the Island of Jamaica from 1681 to 1737* inclusive (hereinafter referred to as *Acts*); see also C.O. 137/18–56.

30. CSF., 154/2, *Acts*, 1718, p. 164.

31. C.O. 137/21, Examination of Sarra . . . , October 1, 1733.

32. *JAJ* 2, p. 651.

33. Ibid., pp. 270–71.

34. Long, *History*, II, p. 85.

35. Ibid.

36. C.O. 137/13, Lawes to Board of Trade, August 24, 1720; H. Barham, "Account," Sl. Ms. 3918; James Knight, "History," Add. Ms. 12415.

37. H. Barham, "Account," Sl. Ms. 3918.

38. Ibid.

39. C.O. 137/19, Hunter to Lords Commissioners of Trade, November 13, 1731.

40. Long, *History*, II, pp. 343–44.

41. Bryan Edwards, *The Proceedings of the Governor and Assembly of Jamaica in Regard to the Maroon Negro . . .* (London: John Stockdale, 1796; reprinted, Negro Universities Press, 1970), pp. xii–xiii. Edwards's is a verbatim account of Long's, above.

42. For some of the land reform schemes, see, among others, H. Barham, "Account," Sl. Ms. 3918; CSF., 154/2, *Acts*, 1681–1733, pp. 149–58; C.O. 137/13, Lawes to Board of Trade, February 2, 1719; C.O. 137/19, Hunter to Board of Trade, December 24, 1730; for a good systematic account, see Pitman, *West Indies*, chap. 2.

43. Ibid.

44. C.O. 137/19, Hunter to the Board of Trade, December 24, 1730.

45. Barham, "Account," Sl. Ms. 3918; Knight, "History," Add. Ms. 12415; also, Pitman, *The British West Indies*, p. 111.

46. Ibid.

47. Ibid.

48. Barham, "Account," Sl. Ms. 3918.

49. Dallas, *History*, I, p. 35.

50. *Dictionary of National Biography (DNB)* (London: Smith, Elder & Co., 1885–1901), vol. 28, pp. 299–300; *Dictionary of American Biography (DAB)* (New York: Scribner's, 1928–1937), vol. 9, pp. 401–2; Cundall, *Governors of Jamaica*, pp. 130–55; Barham, "Account," Sl. Ms. 3918.

51. C.O. 137/47, Newcastle to Hunter, February 7, 1728/9; Board of Trade to Newcastle, February 29, 1729/30; C.O. 137/18, Hunter to Newcastle, May 8,

1729, etc.

52. See note 50 as well as George Metcalf, *Royal Government and Political Conflict in Jamaica 1729–1783* (London: Longmans, 1965), pp. 33–34.

53. The full extent of the abandoned estates was not made clear until after the treaty. See, for example, Trelawny to Newcastle, March 5, 1738/9, and Chapter 5 below; also, Edward Long Papers, Add. Ms. 12431.

54. C.O. 137/19, Hunter to Newcastle, January 28, 1730/1; by July 20, 1731, Hunter was so encouraged by the landing of extra troops — which, unfortunately for him, did not remain beyond six months in the colony — that he sold his slaves and abandoned the patents.

55. Barham, "Account," Sl. Ms. 3918.

56. C.O. 137/19, Petition to H.M. from Planters, Merchants and Traders, referred to Board of Trade, January 19, 1731/2.

57. For a systematic study of this, see Mavis C. Campbell, *The Dynamics of Change in a Slave Society: A Socio-political History of the Free Coloreds of Jamaica, 1800–1865* (London and Rutherford, N.J.: Fairleigh Dickinson University Press, 1976), especially chaps. 1–3.

58. Pitman, *West Indies*, p. 112; Thomas Attwood, *The History of the Island of Dominica* (London: n.p., 1791), p. 81.

59. Edward Long Papers, Add. Ms. 12431.

60. Ibid.

61. Ibid.

62. Ibid.; see also, C.O. 137/18-21.

63. Edward Long Papers, Add. Ms. 12431.

64. Ibid.

65. C.O. 137/19, Hunter to Board of Trade, April 21, 1731; CSF., 154/2, *Acts*, 1681–1737, p. 236.

66. C.O. 137/18, Hunter to Newcastle, May 8, 1729, February 11, 1730/1.

67. Ibid., Hunter's speech to Council and Assembly, March 12, 1729/30.

68. C.O. 137/19, Hunter to Lords Commissioners of Trade, November 7, 1730.

69. C.O. 137/18, The Humble Address and Representation of the Governor and Council of Jamaica to the Crown, November 27, 1730.

70. C.O. 137/18, Coll. Townsend to Walmesley, March 3, 1730/1.

71. Ibid., Coll. Hayes to Major Sowles, February 14, 1730/1.

72. Ibid., Coll. Townsend to Col. Cape, March 2, 1730/1; Coll. Townsend to Walmesley, March 3, 1730/1; Col. Cornwallis to Lord Cornwallis, March 5, 1730/1, Ibid. to Ibid., March 10, 1730/1, Ibid. to Ibid., March 15, 1730/1, Ibid. to Ibid., March 20, 1730/1.

73. Ibid., Extract of "a letter" (most certainly by a private) communicated to Lord Torrington, March 20, 1730/1.

74. C.O. 137/19, Newcastle to Board of Trade, July 12, 1731.

75. C.O. 137/19, Address of Governor and Council to King, November 27, 1730; C.O. 137/20, Hunter to Newcastle, January 16, 1731/2.

76. C.O. 137/19, Hunter to Lords Commissioners of Trade, November 13, 1731.

77. C.O. 137/19, Newcastle to Lords Commissioners ..., August 31, 1731. Memorial from Major Ayscough to [?] relating to the number of acres and other supplies to be given each soldier, August 10, 1731.

78. C.O. 137/20, Hunter to Newcastle, February 19, 1731/2; also, Frank Cundall, *The Governors of Jamaica in the First Half of the Eighteenth Century* (London: West India Committee, 1937), p. 142.

79. C.O. 137/23, Trelawny to Board of Trade, October 12, 1738.

80. C.O. 137/19, Hunter to Board of Trade, December 24, 1730.

81. C.O. 137/18, Hunter to Newcastle, March 12, 1729/30.

82. Ibid., July 4, 1730.

83. C.O. 137/19, Hunter to Lords Commissioners ..., November 7, 1730.

84. C.O. 137/19, Hunter to Lords Commissioners ..., November 13, 1731.

85. Ibid.

86. C.O. 137/20, Hunter to Newcastle, March 16, 1731/2; March 28, 1732, April 14, 1732.

87. Ibid., Hunter's Address to Council and Assembly, April 5, 1732.

88. Ibid.

89. For these attacks, see Hunter to Newcastle, June 1, 1732. For an account of the size of plantations about this time, see Edward Long, "Sugar Plantations in Jamaica with the Quantity of Sugars Made Generally for Some Years, Christmas, 1739," Add. Ms. 12434.

90. Edward Long, "Sugar Plantations ...," Add. Ms. 12434; C.O. 137/20, Memo. of June 24, 1732 from Clarendon, signed by John Moore, Sam Smith, and Thomas Rodon.

91. C.O. 137/20, Hunter to Lords Commissioners ..., September 20, 1732.

92. C.O. 137/20, Hunter to Council and Assembly, March 14, 1733. For an account of the depressed economic situation and the shortage of coins at this period, see, Pitman, *West Indies*, pp. 149–55.

93. C.O. 137/20, Hunter to Council and Assembly, March 14, 1733; Ibid., Hunter to Lords Commissioners, September 20, 1732; Ibid., Message from Assembly to Council, March 24, 1733.

94. C.O. 137/20, Hunter to Board of Trade, September 20, 1732, with enclosures.

95. Ibid.

96. Ibid.

97. C.O. 137/20, Hunter to Lords Commissioners ..., November 18, 1732.

98. C.O. 137/20, Draper to Titchfield, June 25, 1733; Henry William and Ebenezer Lambe's account, enclosed in Hunter to Newcastle, June 29, 1733.

99. Ibid.

100. C.O. 137/20, Ashworth to Hunter, June 27, 1733.

101. Ibid., and Draper's account of same date; see also, C.O. 137/54, Journal of Edward Creswell and Ebenezer Lambe, from February 27, 1732/3 to March 12.

102. C.O. 137/20, Copy of "Confession" of one "Cyrus" or "Seyrus," owned by George Taylor, in Hunter to Board of Trade, August 25, 1733.

103. Among the many such imprecise statements, see, for example, C.O.

137/20, Ashworth to Hunter, June 27, 1733.

104. Edward Long Papers, Add. Ms. 12431; also, C.O. 137/21, Hunter to Board of Trade with enclosures, November 11, 1733.

105. C.O. 137/20, Hunter's address to Council and Assembly enclosed in Hunter to Board of Trade, July 26, 1733, August 25, 1733.

106. C.O. 137/20, Hunter to Assembly, July 6, 1733.

107. Ibid., Address to Lords Commissioners from Council, August 17, 1733.

108. Ibid., Hunter's message to clerk of the Assembly, n.d., Hunter to Lords Commissioners, June 4, 1733, June 29, 1733.

109. For the constant squabbling between Council and Assembly, see C.O. 137/20, and George Metcalf, *Royal Government*, pp. 42–43.

110. C.O. 137/20, Hunter to Board of Trade with enclosure, August 17, 1733.

111. C.O. 137/20, Hunter to Board of Trade, August 18, 1733.

112. C.O. 137/20, Hunter to Board of Trade, September 8, 1733; Ibid., Swanton's Report, September 4, 1733; Ashworth's report, September 4, 1733; J. Draper's Report, September 4, 1733; Hunter to Popple, November 3, 1733, with enclosures. Extract from Swanton's Journal, September 8, 1733.

113. C.O. 137/20, Extract of letter from Mr. Hals to the Earl of Westmoreland, October 13, 1733.

114. C.O. 137/20, Hunter to Board of Trade, September 8, 1733.

115. For all these letters, see C.O. 137/21, September 20, 1733; October 13, 1733, September 10, 1733, February 15, 1733/4, March 18, 1733/4, March 23, 1733/4.

116. C.O. 137/21, John Gregory to Lords Commissioners, February 20, 1733/4.

117. C.O. 137/21, John Hoe[?] Loe[?] to Board of Trade, September 20, 1733.

118. Ibid., Hunter to Board of Trade, November 11, 1733.

119. See, Edward Long Papers, Add. Ms. 12431; also C.O. 137/21, Hunter to Board of Trade, March 11, 1733/4, December 24, 1733.

120. C.O. 137/21, John Gregory to Board of Trade, February 20, 1733/4, with enclosures.

121. C.O. 137/21, Representation of Council and Assembly to Lords Commissioners, March 11, 1733/4.

122. C.O. 137/21, Smith's Account enclosed in John Gregory to Board of Trade, February 20, 1733/4.

123. C.O. 137/21, Representation of Council and Assembly to Lords Commissioners, March 11, 1733/4.

124. Ibid.

125. C.O. 137/20, Hunter to Board of Trade, August 25, 1733; C.O. 137/21, Examination of Sarra . . . , October 1, 1733.

126. C.O. 137/21, Ayscough to Board of Trade, October 21, 1734, with enclosures.

127. *JAJ* 3, p. 210; see also Dallas, writing of the leewards: "Cudjoe was always apprized in time of the parties that were fitted out, and knowing the routes they must necessarily take, prepared his ambushes accordingly." I, p. 34.

128. C.O. 137/21, Extract of a letter dated September 10, 1733.

129. C.O. 137/54, Journal of Edward Creswell ..., February 27, 1732/3, March 12.

130. C.O. 137/21, Hunter's Address to Council and Assembly, August 17, 1733.

131. C.O. 137/20, Hunter's Address to Council and Assembly, April 5, 1732; Ibid., Hunter to Newcastle, June 1, 1732; Ibid., Hunter to Board of Trade, September 20, 1732; Ibid., Hunter to Ibid., June 29, 1733; also Cundall, *Governors of Jamaica*, p. 145; *JAJ* 3, p. 51.

132. For some account of Sambo, see C.O. 137/20, Hunter to Newcastle, June 1, 1732, telling the duke that he was "depending more on Sambo than on Peters"; C.O. 137/54, Journal of Edward Creswell ..., February 1732/3, March 12, where an entry mentioned how Sambo would "use his utmost endeavor to get [the other officers] to go forward and all to no purpose," and also reiterating Hunter's claim that they relied more on him than on Peters. Entry of March 10 saw Sambo frustrated over his men who refused to fight and were more "inclined to run away" from the rebels, obliging him to quit, thereby losing 2 whites, 2 blacks and "18 or 19 wounded." One of the white commanders, Ashworth, was later charged for refusing to support Sambo. See *JAJ* 3, p. 158.

133. C.O. 137/20, Message from Assembly to Council, March 24, 1733; see also, CSF., 154/2, *Acts*, 1681–1737, p. 258.

134. J. G. Stedman, *Narrative of an Expedition against the Revolted Negroes of Surinam* (Amherst: University of Massachusetts Press, 1971), in discussing the Rangers — as the Surinam slave soldiers were called — referred to them as a "corps of manumitted slaves, though in number they amounted but to three hundred, they indeed proved ultimately of as much service to the colony as all the others put together ... I have been an ocular witness to astonishing proofs of the fidelity of these *enfranchised* [emphasis added] slaves to the Europeans, and their valour against the rebel negroes ... [who each wore] a scarlet cap, the emblem of liberty, on which is their number ...." See pp. 47–48.

135. C.O. 137/21, Hunter to Board of Trade, December 24, 1733.

136. Ibid., see also, CSF., 154/2; *Acts*, pp. 267–75.

137. Ibid.

138. *JAJ* 3, p. 186.

139. Written by one Richard Hennigs, a member of the Jamaican Assembly, to his aunt in London, enclosed in C.O. 137/21, Samuel Williams to Alured Popple, December 9, 1734.

140. C.O. 137/19, Hunter to Board of Trade, April 21, 1731.

141. The Board of Trade even petitioned the King against the measure. See Board of Trade to Hunter, 28 July 1731 in C.O. 138/17. See also Metcalf, *Royal Government*, p. 42.

142. Ibid., C.O. 137/19, Hunter to Popple, July 20, 1731; C.O. 137/20, Hunter to Board of Trade, 16 March 1731/2.

143. Siding with the Assembly, in effect, Hunter told Newcastle that the taxes on slaves were justified; what with the exigencies of government, he himself had been behind in his salary; he was obliged to borrow money from local men for

the use of the parties. See C.O. 137/20, Hunter to Newcastle, March 16, 1731/2.

144. C.O. 137/19, Hunter to Board of Trade, April 31, 1731; CSF., 154/2, *Acts* p. 236. For the tax on Jews and their protests, see C.O. 137/22, The Humble Memorial and Proposals of the Merchants of London, Bristol, Liverpool and others, Trading to and interested in Yr. Majty's Island of Jamaica to the King Most Excellent Majesty, December 12, 1735. For some of the colonial discriminations against the Jews in Jamaica, see Campbell, *Dynamics*, pp. 24, 45, and 219. Pitman, *West Indies*, pp. 28–31.

145. C.O. 137/19, Hunter to Board of Trade, November 13, 1731.

146. C.O. 137/47, Unsigned Memo., Some Consideration Relating to the Present State of Jamaica ..., October 26, 1734.

147. Ibid., Hunter to Board of Trade, July 17, 1729.

148. C.O. 137/19, Hunter to Board of Trade, November 13, 1731.

149. As Britain was doing at the time — curtailing Catholic participation in public life and forbidding any British monarch to be of the Catholic faith. See, for instance, J. H. Plumb, *England in the Eighteenth Century* (New York: Penguin Books, 1981), pp. 50–51; C.O. 137/19, Hunter to Board of Trade, November 13, 1731.

150. But see Chapter 4 herein for a more sympathetic view.

151. C.O. 137/54, Board of Trade to Newcastle, October 8, 1730, with paper relating to the affairs of Jamaica.

152. Walter L. Dorn, *Competition for Empire, 1740–1763* (New York: Harper Brothers, 1940), p. 100.

153. C.O. 137/55, Newcastle to Ayscough, June 6, 1734; also Board of Trade to Newcastle, February 22, 1733/4, 22 August 1734.

Chapter 4

1. Metcalf, *Royal Government*, p. 50.

2. Ibid., p. 51; Frank Cundall, *Governors of Jamaica*, pp. 118–19.

3. C.O. 137/54, Hunter to Newcastle, 29 September 1733; taken from Metcalf, *Royal Government*, p. 51. This may have been a private dispatch. See also C.O. 137/20, Hunter to Board of Trade, September 8, 1733, where he remarked generally on the men in public life, "[i]ndustrious in getting themselves elected, some for protection of their persons, others with designs to embroil matters and perplex the administration from private resentments, or worse intentions."

4. C.O. 137/21, Ayscough to Board of Trade, April 4, 1734.

5. Ibid., May 11, 1734, with enclosure; see also Edward Long Papers, Add. Ms. 12431.

6. Ibid.

7. Robinson, *The Fighting Maroons*, p. 55. It should be noted that to this day Maroon folk version gave it that Stoddart was the officer in charge and does not admit that the party was successful against Nanny Town. (Field Study, January 1975).

8. Swanton's (also rendered Swarton in some secondary sources) list in C.O. 137/21, Ayscough to Board of Trade, May 11, 1734, with enclosures. Iron Polls

could "mean the flat side of an edged tool, so presumably it's used here meaning the tool itself." Christopher Fyfe to author, October 30, 1982.

9. C.O. 137/21, Ayscough to Board of Trade, May 11, 1734, Ibid. to Ibid., January 4, 1734/5. See also Chapter 6 herein for more on Nanny Town.

10. C.O. 137/21, Ayscough to Board of Trade, April 16, 1735.

11. Ibid., Ayscough's Address to Council and Assembly, April 11, 1735; Ibid., Ayscough to Board of Trade, April 15, 1735, and May 15, 1735.

12. Ibid., Ayscough to Board of Trade, January 4, 1735, and January 11, 1735.

13. Ibid., and Ayscough to same, February 27, 1735. It should be noted that Ayscough did not make use of the double dating; see also, Edward Long Papers, Add. Ms. 12431.

14. Ibid., and see C.O. 137/22, Ayscough to Board of Trade, August 16, 1735. In the dispatch to the Board of Trade of March 22, 1735, under C.O. 137/21, Ayscough had then given the figure of "40." Yet Cunningham, in December of the same year, reported that despite all the attempts against the rebels, not "above 10 of them have been taken or slain these two past years." See C.O. 137/22, Cunningham to Board of Trade, December 27, 1735.

15. C.O. 137/21, Ayscough to Board of Trade, February 27, 1735.

16. Ibid.

17. C.O. 137/22, Gregory to Board of Trade, October 23, 1735.

18. See Edward Long Papers, Add. Ms. 12431.

19. C.O. 137/21, Ayscough to Board of Trade, February 27, 1735, with enclosures.

20. Edward Long Papers, Add. Ms. 12431.

21. 137/21, Gersham Ely to Ayscough, April 9, 1735.

22. See *JAJ* vol. 3, and C.O. 137/21, Ayscough to Board of Trade, April 16, 1735; Ibid., Gersham Ely to Ayscough, April 9, 1735, among others.

23. C.O. 137/21, Ayscough to Board of Trade, October 21, 1734, with enclosures.

24. Ibid.

25. Ibid.

26. Ibid., Ayscough to Board of Trade, January 4 and 11, 1735; also C.O. 137/22, Gregory to Board of Trade, October 23, 1735.

27. For the "complaints" against Maroon surcease, see C.O. 137/21, Ayscough to Board of Trade, June 22, 1735; Ibid., Gregory to Board of Trade, October 23, 1735, June 2, and November 23, 1736.

28. Ibid. Exactly when the windwards returned to their original haunts is not clear, although we find Gregory reporting this, May 26, 1737.

29. C.O. 137/22, Cunningham to Board of Trade, December 27, 1735, and February 9, 1736.

30. Metcalf, *Royal Government*, p. 55; Cundall, *Governors of Jamaica*, pp. 156–70. It should be noted that Gregory Park was named after the governor.

31. C.O. 137/22, Gregory to Council and Assembly, March 9, 1736.

32. Ibid., Gregory to Board of Trade, June 2, 1736, November 23, 1736.

33. Ibid.

34. Ibid., Address of President and Council to King, November 23, 1736; Ibid., Gregory's address to Council and Assembly.

35. Metcalf, *Royal Government*, p. 57.

36. Ibid., pp. 58–59; Cundall, *Governors of Jamaica*, pp. 171–207.

37. Metcalf, *Royal Government*, p. 61. Metcalf made an obvious error when he said that "in September 1736 Newcastle instructed . . . Hunter to investigate the possibility of making a treaty" with the rebels. By September 1736, Hunter was already dead, and Metcalf seems unaware that Hunter had implanted the idea of a peace treaty onto the island's legislators since 1730.

38. Cundall, *Governors of Jamaica*, pp. 153–54.

39. Metcalf, *Royal Government*, p. 60.

40. Letter from Edward Trelawny to the Earl of Wilmington, April 22, 1739, in Ms. file 1739, NLJ.

41. See Chapter 7 herein.

42. C.O. 137/18, Hunter's speech to the Assembly, June 17, 1730; see also *Weekly Jamaica Courant*, June 24, 1730, with speech reported.

43. C.O. 137/20, Hunter's Address to Council and Assembly, January 4, 1731/2.

44. C.O. 137/47, Newcastle to Hunter, February 7, 1728/9.

45. Metcalf, *Royal Government*, p. 61.

46. C.O. 137/47, "Some Consideration Relating to the Present State of Jamaica with Respect to the Runaway Negroes," October 26, 1734.

47. Davidson, "Negro Slave Control," p. 247.

48. C.O. 137/47, Board of Trade to Newcastle, October 7, 1730, with Paper relating to the Affairs of Jamaica.

49. C.O. 137/21, Ayscough to Board of Trade, January 11, 1735.

50. Ibid.

51. C.O. 137/21, Bevill Granville to John Ayscough, February 6, 1735.

52. Davidson, "Negro Slave Control," p. 247; see also Palmer, *Slaves of the White God*, pp. 128–29.

53. C.O. 137/21, Ayscough to Board of Trade, February 27, 1735.

54. Ibid., Ayscough to Board of Trade, February 27, 1735.

55. C.O. 137/21, Journal of William Lamport and Thomas Williams, February 23, 24, and 25, 1735.

56. C.O. 137/22, Gregory to Board of Trade, March 9, 1735.

57. C.O. 137/22, Gregory to Council and Assembly, March 9, 1735; Gregory to Board of Trade, May 26, 1737; see also *JAJ* 3, p. 328–410.

58. Ibid.

59. Ibid.

60. C.O. 137/56, Trelawny to Newcastle, with Memorial enclosed before arriving in Jamaica, London, June 30, 1737.

61. Ibid.

62. C.O. 137/56, Trelawny to Newcastle, with enclosure, July 7, 1737.

63. Ibid.

64. Ibid.

65. A generosity which Governor Hunter did not show. Ibid.

66. Ibid.

67. Ibid., Trelawny to Newcastle, January 6, 1738/9.

68. It should be noted that one had to do detective work on these letters because the addressee was not identified, each letter beginning with "Sir." One therefore had to blend together specific points and specific references with the addressee; but the perfect piece of evidence, which closed the case, is a letter written by Gregory himself (addressee illegible) in Bristol, England, July 28, 1743, which says, in part, that the two letters from Col. Guthrie are to show "I had some little merit in the Treaty with the Rebels tho' Mr. Trelawny had the good fortune to complete it, the design was laid, and some steps taken before his arrival." See Edward Long Papers, Add. Ms. 12431.

69. Edward Long Papers, Add. Ms. 12431.

70. CSF., 154/4, *Acts*, 1681–1754, p. 231.

71. Edward Long Papers, Add. Ms. 12431.

72. Davidson, "Negro Slave Control," p. 247.

73. C.O. 137/56, Trelawny to Newcastle, March 5, 1738/9.

74. Edward Long Papers, Add. Ms. 12431.

75. C.O. 137/56, Guthrie to Trelawny, February 17, 1738/9.

76. Ibid.

77. Ibid., February 18, 1738/9.

78. Ibid., Sadler to Trelawny, February 17, 1738/9.

79. James Knight, "History," Add. Ms. 12415; also, Edward Long Papers, Add. Ms. 12431. This is not mentioned in Guthrie's or Sadler's account, nor in any other official source.

80. *JAJ* 3, April 12, 1740. Russel was highly praised by the Assembly as "careful and industrious to keep the minds of the Negroes easy, and to remove [their] jealousies, suspicions, and diffidence," his courage and conduct contributing to the "beneficial" treaty. Russel, immediately after the Treaty, was appointed as one of the superintendents for Trelawny Town. See Ibid., April 13, 1739.

81. C.O. 137/56, Trelawny to Guthrie, February 23, 1738/9.

82. Ibid., C.O. 137/22, Gregory to Board of Trade, November 23, 1736.

83. C.O. 137/56, Trelawny to Council and Assembly, March 30, 1739.

84. Ibid., Trelawny to Newcastle, March 5, 1738/9.

85. Edward Long Papers, Add. Ms. 12431.

86. C.O. 137/56, Trelawny to Guthrie, February 23, 1738/9.

87. Dallas, *History*, I, pp. 55–56.

88. See Guthrie to [Gregory], February 21, 1738/9, in Edward Long Papers, Add. Ms. 12431; also, James Knight, "History," Add. Ms. 12415.

89. Robinson, *The Fighting Maroons*, p. 49.

90. For more on Monck, see Thomas Gumble, *The Life of General Monck, Duke of Albemarle* (London: Thomas Basset, 1671), among others.

91. Long, *History*, II, p. 344.

92. Ibid., pp. 344–45.

93. Robinson, *Fighting Maroons*, p. 50.

94. The work is dedicated to Quarrell; see Dallas, *History*, I, pp. iii–v.

95. I do not wish to enter into the controversy over Dallas's sole portrayal of Cudjoe's behavior before Guthrie until I can find more evidence to prove it so. Kopytoff, for example, accepted it as a fact, seeing Cudjoe's action as "the reverence in which Maroons held representatives of the white government ... expressed on several occasions by their kissing the feet of the White men"; and "[w]hat Cudjoe did indicate by his act was that he considered the King, and the Governor, and the Governor's representative, Colonel Guthrie, to be the superior, the Lord, the 'parent,' in their relationship; but lower did not mean 'lowly' in this context, 'humbled' did not mean 'humiliated'; it meant that protection was expected and reverence due." See Kopytoff, "The Maroons of Jamaica," pp. 254–56. For another interpretation, see Orlando Patterson, "Slavery and Slave Revolts: A Sociohistorical Analysis of the First Maroon War, 1665–1740," in Richard Price, ed., *Maroon Societies*, pp. 272–78.

96. Ralph Korngold, *Citizen Toussaint* (New York: Hill & Wang, 1965), pp. 140–44.

97. C.O. 137/56, Assembly's Address to Trelawny, March 16, 1738/9.

98. Ibid., March 14, 1738/9, Council's Address to Trelawny.

99. Ibid., April 14, 1739.

100. Ibid., Newcastle to Trelawny, June 15, 1739 (private).

101. Ibid., Trelawny to Newcastle, June 30, 1739.

102. This quaint mode of computing was also used in England by the exchequer up until the eighteenth century; see Plumb, *England in the Eighteenth Century*, p. 48.

103. C.O. 137/56, Trelawny to Newcastle, June 30, 1739.

104. Ibid.

105. James Knight, "History," Add. Ms. 12415; Edward Long Papers, Add. Ms. 12431.

106. Philip Thicknesse, *Memoirs and Anecdotes of Philip Thicknesse Late Lieutenant Governor, Land Guard Fort, and Unfortunately Father to George Touchet, Baron Audley* (Dublin: William Jones, 1788), pp. 57–67.

107. Ibid., p. 69.

108. Ibid., pp. 70–73.

109. Ibid., p. 73.

110. Ibid., p. 74.

111. Ibid.

112. Ibid., pp. 74–75; see also Dallas, *History*, I, p. 75.

113. Thicknesse, *Memoirs*, p. 57.

114. CSF., 154/4, *Acts*, 1681–1754, p. 241.

115. C.O. 137/56, Trelawny to Newcastle, June 30, 1739.

116. Thicknesse, *Memoirs*, p. 56.

117. George Metcalf said that Trelawny's "methods of dealing with both the Home Government and with the colonists were of such subtlety and backhandedness as to be very nearly dishonest." But here Metcalf himself would seem to be too subtle. See Metcalf, *Royal Government*, p. 60.

118. C.O. 137/56, Newcastle to Trelawny, September 30, 1739.

119. Ibid., Trelawny to Newcastle, August 8, 1739.

Chapter 5

1. Copies of this Treaty are to be found at the Public Record Office, London, under C.O. 137/23; C.O. 137/56 (two copies) enclosed in Trelawny to Board of Trade, March 30, 1739, and Trelawny to Newcastle, March 5, 1738/9 respectively; also, at the British Library (British Museum), Add. Ms. 12431; CSF., 154/4, *Acts*, pp. 228–31; The National Library of Jamaica (Institute of Jamaica), *JAJ* 3, p. 457–58. It is thought that one of the existing Maroon communities has possession of a copy, but this author, in fieldwork, found Maroon officials somewhat elusive on this matter.

2. Quoted by C. L. R. James, *The Black Jacobins: Toussaint l'Ouverture and the San Domingo Revolution* (New York: Vintage Books, 1963), p. 25. It is interesting that Lord Balcarres knew of Raynal's appreciation of the Jamaican Maroons, see chapter 7, n. 79.

3. Patterson, "Slavery and Slave Revolts," p. 273.

4. Long, *History*, II, p. 347.

5. Thicknesse, *Memoirs*, p. 77.

6. C.O. 137/56, Trelawny to Newcastle, June 30, 1739; and CSF., 154/4, *Acts*, pp. 239–40.

7. Ibid.

8. C.O. 137/23, Trelawny to Board of Trade, July 12, 1739.

9. CSF., 154/4, *Acts*, pp. 240–41.

10. Long, *History*, II, p. 340.

11. Among the many, see *JAJ* vol. 3. These claims are numerous but have not been systematically studied by this author.

12. C.O. 137/23, Trelawny to Board of Trade, November 21, 1741.

13. C.O. 137/19, Hunter to Board of Trade, replying to a series of Questions from the Board, reflecting on trade, productivity, security, of the island *inter alia*, December 24, 1734 (in a special cylinder).

14. Ibid.

15. Ibid.

16. C.O. 137/22, Memorial and Proposals of the Merchants of London, Bristol and Liverpool and Others Trading to and Interested in Yr. Majty's Island of Jamaica, to the King, December 12, 1735.

17. C.O. 137/18, Hunter to Newcastle, July 4, 1730.

18. Ibid., Assembly to Hunter, with enclosure, June 19, 1730.

19. Ibid.

20. C.O. 137/47, Newcastle to Hunter, February 7, 1728/9; Ibid., Board of Trade to Newcastle, February 29, 1729/30.

21. Ibid., Extract of Col. Campbell's report on the Examination of "some" captured Runaways, n.d. but possibly enclosed in Hunter to Board of Trade, July 4, 1730.

22. Ibid.

23. C.O. 137/23, Trelawny to Board of Trade, November 21, 1741, February 10, 1741/2.
24. Ibid.
25. Long, *History*, II, p. 240.
26. C.O. 137/23, Trelawny to Board of Trade, March 30, 1739.
27. Ibid.
28. C.O. 137/23, Trelawny to Board of Trade, November 21, 1741.
29. Ibid.
30. Ibid., and C.O. 137/24, Trelawny to Board of Trade, December 19, 1743; see also Pitman, *West Indies*, pp. 108–26 for an account of Jamaica's attempts at settling the island with poor whites at this period.
31. Long, *History*, II, p. 348.
32. Ibid.
33. Ibid., p. 176.
34. Ibid.
35. Long, "Sugar Plantations" Add. Ms. 12434.
36. Long, *History*, II, p. 180.
37. Pitman, *West Indies*, p. 121.
38. Ibid.
39. Edward Long Papers, Add. Ms. 12431.
40. Ibid.
41. Ibid.
42. James Knight, "History," Add. Ms. 12415.
43. *JAJ* 3, May 1, 1742.
44. Ibid.
45. Ibid., and James Knight, "History," Add. Ms. 12415.
46. C.O. 137/25, Knowles to Board of Trade, March 26, 1753.
47. Ibid.
48. *JAJ* 3, May 1, 1742.
49. Ibid.
50. Ibid.
51. Ibid.
52. Ibid.
53. C.O. 137/56, Newcastle to Trelawny, September 30, 1739; Ibid., Trelawny to Newcastle, August 8, 1739; Trelawny to Newcastle, October 30, 1739, January 20, 1739/40, among others.
54. James Knight, "History," Add. Ms. 12415.
55. William Beckford to James Knight, October 11, 1740, Add. Ms. 12431.
56. Dallas, *History*, I, p. 104.
57. William Beckford to James Knight, October 11, 1740, and Ibid. to Ibid., August 19, 1741, Add. Ms. 12431.
58. Edward Long Papers, Add. Ms. 12431.
59. James Knight, "History," Add. Ms. 12415.
60. See chapter 7, n. 82.
61. Dallas, *History*, I, p. 97. In this instance, Edwards had his field day in

condemning the Maroons. "In their treatment of fugitive slaves, they manifest a bloodthirstiness of disposition, which is otherwise unaccountable; for, although their vigilance is stimulated by the prospect of reward, they can have no possible motives of revenge or malice towards the unfortunate objects of their pursuit: yet is it notoriously true, that they wish for nothing more than a pretence to put the poor wretches to death; frequently maiming them without provocation ..." Edwards, *Proceedings*, pp. xxxiv–xxxv.

62. CSF., 154/4, *Acts*, p. 251.

63. Dallas, *History*, I, p. 90.

64. Long, *History*, II, p. 447.

65. Dallas, *History*, I, p. 103.

66. Long, *History*, II, pp. 447 and 472.

67. Ibid., pp. 447–48.

68. Ibid., p. 451.

69. Ibid.

70. Edwards accused the Maroons (he did not stipulate which group) of collecting human ears from rebels already killed by the regular soldiers, in order to collect their payment. In another engagement he said not a Maroon was to be found, but it was later discovered "that immediately on the attack, the whole body of them had thrown themselves on the ground, and continued in that position until the rebels retreated, without firing or receiving a shot." See Edwards, *Proceedings*, pp. xxv–xxxvii. If this really happened, then this disinclination to fight their own kind for the slave masters could be assumed as coming from the windwards.

71. For more on the rebellions of the 1760s, see Patterson, *Sociology*, pp. 271–72; *JAJ* 5, pp. 181–210; Edwards, *History*, II, pp. 59–65, among others.

72. Long, *History*, II, p. 461; *JAJ* 5, p. 181.

73. *JAJ* 5, p. 226.

74. Long, *History*, II, p. 458n.

75. Ibid.

76. Edwards, *History*, II, pp. 61–62.

77. Long, *History*, II, p. 470.

78. Ibid., pp. 462, 471.

79. Ibid.

80. Ibid., p. 465.

81. Dallas, *History*, I, p. 101.

82. C.O. 137/96, Balcarres to Ricketts, December 31, 1795, with enclosure.

83. *JAJ* 7, December 18 and 22, 1781.

84. Anon., *The History of 3 Finger'd Jack, The Terror of Jamaica: Being the History on which is Founded the Pantomimical Drama of OBI or Three Finger'd Jack. Performed with Unbounded Applause at The Theatre Royal Haymarket* (London: S. Brown, Clare Market, n.d.), 4th edition.

85. *JAJ* 9, November 2 and 4, 1752.

86. W. J. Gardner, *A History of Jamaica* ... (London: Frank Cass & Co., 1971), p. 254. Gardner's work was first published 1873.

87. Patterson, *Sociology*, p. 264.

88. For more on running away up to emancipation, see B. W. Higman, *Slave Population and Economy in Jamaica, 1807–1834* (London and New York: Cambridge University Press, 1976), chap. 8; Edward Brathwaite, *The Development of Creole Society in Jamaica, 1770–1820* (Oxford: Clarendon Press of Oxford University Press, 1971), pp. 201–3; Patterson, *Sociology*, pp. 262–64.

89. Among them, see, for example, CSF., *Acts*, 167/2; 154/7.

90. *JAJ* 8, November 27, 1788; December 1, 1788.

91. CSF., 154/5, *Acts*; CSF., 167/2, p. 3.

92. Ibid.

93. Long, *History*, II, p. 457.

94. Patterson, *Sociology*, pp. 271–73.

95. Ibid.

96. It is sad that even in the 1980s the fact of the British Caribbean (French and Danish, too) slaves' participation in their own emancipation is not yet well known. Perhaps too much attention has been given to the Wilberforces by earlier historians. For a systematic account of this, see Williams, *From Columbus to Castro*, pp. 320–27; W. L. Burn, *Emancipation and Apprenticeship in the British West Indies* (London: Jonathan Cape, 1937), particularly pp. 95–97; Campbell, *Dynamics*, pp. 213–15, among others.

97. C.O. 137/398, Eyre to Cardwell, October 19 and 20, 1865.

98. Among those who condemned Eyre was John Stuart Mill. See Campbell, *Dynamics*, chapter 7.

Chapter 6

1. There is much curiosity over what has come to be called the Nanny Town Stonewall — a man-made structure some 1,900 feet above sea level, located on the north bank of the Stony River in Portland on a small flat plateau of about two acres. Alan Tuelon, a surveyor, led a group of botanists, geologists, etc., to identify the site, which they found to be in a dilapidated condition, but which could be identified as a dry-packed stonewall approximately two feet six inches thick by three feet four inches in height, rectangular in shape, with a three-foot "doorway." There is much speculation as to whether this structure was built by the Maroons themselves (and sacred) or a breastwork (but why only one such found?) or whether it was a part of the fortifications built by the soldiers. See "Report on Expedition to Nanny Town" by Alan Tuelon, July 1967, at the National Library of Jamaica (Institute of Jamaica), to be referred to as NLJ.

2. Dallas, *History*, I: "The people of the eastern towns were called Windward Maroons. I will not enter into a separate description of these places, but speak chiefly of Trelawny Town, as being the most considerable," p. 79.

3. Edward Long Papers, Add. Ms. 12431.

4. See *JAJ* 4, October 16, 1751; CSF., 154/4, *Acts*, p. 332.

5. *JAJ* 4, October 16, 1751; November 14, 1751; *JAJ* 6, December 8, 1775.

6. Kopytoff, "The Maroons of Jamaica," p. 142.

7. *JAJ* 4, December 19, 1775.

8. NLJ (uncatalogued), Notes of Thomas Harrison, Crown Surveyor, on diagram, December 24, 1862.

9. NLJ (uncatalogued), Maroon's Petition to Governor, December 18, 1862.

10. See, for example, CSF., 154/4, *Acts*, p. 251.

11. *JAJ* vol. 4. The incidents took place in December 1754, but, with the House in Christmas recess, it did not start its deliberations on the matter until April 19, 1755.

12. Ibid., March 3, 1755, and 5(November 11, 1757).

13. Ibid., November 18, 1757.

14. Ibid., 6(October 30, 31, 1770; November 1, 1770).

15. Ibid., (December 8 and 19, 1775).

16. Ibid., Petition of George Gray and others to Assembly, November 28, 1776.

17. Ibid.

18. NLJ (uncatalogued), Notes on Survey Diagram of Charles Town by William Frazer, n.d., but the survey was ordered May 6, 1794.

19. Ibid.

20. Ibid.

21. This was most puzzling to this author who therefore embarked on a thorough search of the available maps of Jamaica in the National Library, from mid-eighteenth century to the latter part of the nineteenth. This search was laborious — because relatively few of these maps are catalogued — but most interesting. Although Scotts Hall, for instance, was created in 1751 (surveyed 1775), search as one might one could find no trace of this town on subsequent maps. But there was one clue: most (not all) of the maps from the 1750s made mention of a site in St. Mary called "Negro Town." Suspecting this to be Scotts Hall, I pursued the search assiduously and was finally rewarded with the map of 1832. There was a false alarm when the Weimar Im Verlage des Geographischen Institute's map of 1805 mentioned a "Scot's Town," but this is situated in St. Andrews. The 1832 map, as if to give proof to my hypothesis, actually mentioned the site as "Scotts Hall or Negro Town" just at the border between the old parish of St. George and St. Mary, and north of Old Crawford Town. The puzzle of Charles Town was also solved on this map. Suspecting that what the cartographers consistently called New Crawford Town was really Charles Town, the search again proved the conjecture correct.

22. Long, *History*, II, p. 176.

23. *JAJ* vol. 7, Petition of John Cosens and others, November 30, 1781. The origin of the name "Moore Town" is not clear, but it possibly could have been named after Henry Moore. Born in Jamaica in 1713, educated at Eton and Leyden University, he inherited a large sugar plantation in Jamaica and served as lieutenant-governor twice, September 1756 through April 1759 and August 1759 through December 1761. See Metcalf, *Royal Government*, pp. 139–52. But in looking carefully at the diagrams of land patents in Portland, around the Rio Grande River where Moore Town is situated, one sees a host of Moores owning property here: John Moore, Daniel Moore, Ms. Francis Moore among them. Could they, or one of them, have sold lands to the Maroons, thus giving the name Moore to the

town? Or did the Maroons simply squat on a portion of their unoccupied land when regrouping after the fall of Nanny Town? A charming folk tale of Moore Town is that it was so named because the Maroons asked for more lands (field research).

24. *JAJ* vol. 7, Petition of John Cosens and others, November 30, 1781.

25. Ibid., November 30, 1781.

26. Ibid., December 18, 1781.

27. Ibid., December 22, 1781.

28. *Patents*, 35, Part 2, p. 214. This document is in a very poor condition, yellow with age, and torn at some of the edges, and along the fold lines. But fortunately the Survey Department has a copy in very good condition. I am grateful to Mrs. Silvia MacKenzie of this department, who very generously brought the other document to my notice.

29. *JAJ* 7, November 28, 1782.

30. Ibid., December 10, 1782; February 10, 1783.

31. Ibid., November 28, 1782.

32. In computing debts owing by the public of Jamaica to the superintendents of Maroon towns, up to 1774 there was a sum (£100) listed for the overseer of Bath Negroes. This may have been in reference to Clash's Town. See Ibid., December 9, 1774.

33. Land Patent to Nanny, April 20, 1741.

34. C.O. 137.21, Ayscough to Board of Trade, with enclosures.

35. *JAJ* 3, March 27, 29, and 30, 1733.

36. Ibid., April 20, 1732.

37. Ibid.

38. One is almost envious of those authors mentioned in this study who merely glossed over this puzzling piece of history without even bothering to question by what means a black woman named Nanny came to qualify for land under the Jamaica land scheme of the period. Most of these authors also simply referred to this land grant as the origin of Moore Town. See, for example, Kopytoff, "The Maroons of Jamaica," pp. 137–41 and n. 44, p. 160. See also Barbara Klamon Kopytoff, "The Early Political Development of Jamaica Maroon Societies," *William and Mary Quarterly*, vol. 35 no. 2(April 1978). Here again, Kopytoff "assumed" Thicknesse's "old Hagg" to be Nanny, and then simply continued to treat it as a "fact." "An unnamed obeah woman, *who must have been Nanny* [my italics], was described by an Englishman . . . ." "The Old Hagg," and then the article said that "Quao wanted to accept, but Nanny did not trust the whites to keep their part of the bargain . . . . Nanny stayed in the background, but her importance was recorded in the law ratifying that document — which named New Nanny Town as one of the two official Maroon settlements in the east — and shortly thereafter, in the grant of land for that settlement, which was made in her name," p. 300.

39. In conducting archival and fieldwork in Jamaica the author was constantly asked if Nanny's being made a national hero could be justified? Fragmentary as is the evidence, there appears to be no doubt that an important personage called Nanny did figure during the Maroon epoch, but like the Arthurian legend we may

never be able to put the pieces together.

40. *JAJ* 4, September 24, 1756.

41. Ibid., October 26, 1756.

42. *JAJ* 6, December 7, 1775.

43. Ibid., 4, October 26, 1756.

44. Ibid., 5, June 15 and October 20, 1758.

45. Ibid., October 21, 1758.

46. Ibid., October 24, 1758; October 31, 1758; Smith was accordingly paid £70.1.3 for the fifty-nine acres. Ibid., November 8 and 9, 1758.

47. Dallas, *History*, I, p. 84.

48. *JAJ* 5, September 29, 1758.

49. Ibid., October 13, 1758.

50. Ibid.

51. Ibid., 6; Petition of John James superintendent of Trelawny Town, on behalf of Furry and others, November 24, 1770.

52. Ibid., October 20, 1770 and December 20, 1770.

53. Ibid., and December 21, 1770.

54. Ibid., December 19, 1791.

55. Ibid.

56. CSF., 154/4, *Acts*, pp. 332–33.

57. CSF., 154/7, *Acts*, p. 482.

58. Ibid.

59. For a systematic account of these restrictions, see Campbell, *Dynamics. passim.*

60. File 1C/10, Kalender Book, 1793–1841, St. James' Court of Quarter Session, July 26, 1796.

61. Ibid., October 29, 1796.

62. Votes of the Assembly of Jamaica (*Votes*), Return of Maroons from July 1, 1797, to November 1, 1798.

63. *Votes*, Appendix, No. 58, Return of Maroons of Charles Town, October 23, 1833.

64. Kopytoff, "The Maroons of Jamaica," p. 156.

65. This author has edited, with added headnotes, a long Introduction and Appendices, George Ross's Diary. Ross, an employee of the Sierra Leone Company, was commissioned to supervise the transportation of the deported Trelawnys from Nova Scotia to Sierra Leone, and on this mission he kept a daily journal, a veritable vignette, and indeed, the closest to an ethnographic history of the Maroons.

66. *Votes*, Return ... of Moore Town, November 2, 1798.

67. *JAJ* vol. 9, Petition of Montague James ... to Assembly, March 7, 1792.

68. Ibid., December 6, 1792.

69. CSF., 154/8, *Acts*, pp. 270–72.

70. *JAJ* 9, November 21, 1791.

71. Philip Henry Gosse, *A Naturalist's Sojourn in Jamaica* (London: Longman, Brown, Green & Longmans, 1851), p. 151.

72. Edwards, *Proceedings*, p. xxx.

73. Dallas, *History*, I, pp. 108–9.
74. Edwards, *Proceedings*, p. xxx.
75. Dallas, *History*, I, pp. 107–8.
76. Mavis C. Campbell, "The Maroons of Jamaica: Imperium in Imperio?" *Pan African Journal*, vol. 6, no. 1(Spring 1973), pp. 43–55.
77. Dallas, *History*, I, p. 109.
78. Edward Long Papers, Add. Ms. 12431.
79. Ibid.
80. Dallas, *History*, I, p. 110.
81. Ibid.
82. Edwards, *Proceedings*, p. xxvii.
83. Gosse, *Naturalist's Sojourn*, p. 393.
84. Ibid., p. 396.
85. It is estimated that in 1818 and 1819 the sums of Charles Town's trade were £400 and £1,400, respectively. See Kopytoff "The Maroons of Jamaica," p. 164.
86. Dallas, *History*, I, p. 105.
87. CSF., 154/7, *Acts*, p. 480.
88. Edwards, *Proceedings*, p. lxi.
89. Lindsay, *Lives of the Lindsays*, III, p. 136.
90. Long, *History*, II, pp. 179–80.
91. CSF., 154/7, *Acts*, p. 204.
92. *JAJ* 6, November 26, 1773.
93. Ibid., 7, December 18, 1781.
94. *Votes*, Appendix, September 1, 1835.
95. Gosse, *Naturalist's Sojourn*, pp. 393–94.
96. Thicknesse, *Memoirs*, p. 50.
97. CSF., 154/7, *Acts*, p. 204.
98. Ibid., p. 482.
99. *JAJ* 9, December 2, 1791.
100. Ibid., December 7, 1791.
101. Ibid., 8, December 11, 1787.
102. Ibid., 9, December 12, 1792.
103. The committee found that "neighbouring white people" were in the habit of sending Maroons out in parties on hire. *JAJ* 7, December 18, 1781.
104. Victor Stafford Reid, *The Jamaicans* (Kingston: Institute of Jamaica, 1978). The first novel on the Maroons is Namba Roy, *Black Albino* (first published 1961; republished, Longman Group Ltd., London, 1986).
105. *JAJ* 3, May 12 and 17, 1744.
106. *Votes*, Appendix, No. 44, John Hylton's Return of Accompong Town, November 16, 1829.
107. CSF., 154/4, *Acts*, pp. 332–33.
108. Dallas, *History*, I, pp. 126–27.
109. Ibid.
110. *Votes*, Appendix (not numbered), November 1, 1797.

111. Ibid.

112. Ibid., Nelly Yeaw, for instance, had, as slaves, three women and two children; Betty Scott, two women and two children; Kay Cameron, one woman and one child; Nancy Harris and Hanne, one woman and two children; Lieutenant Yeaw, one man; James Philips, one woman and one child; John Sambo, one woman and one child; Quality [!] Quasheba, one girl, among the slaveholders of Moore Town, thus making a computation of ten children.

113. *JAJ* 6, November 26, 1773.

114. Ibid., 7, December 18, 1781.

115. Ibid., 11, December 14, 1805.

116. Higman, *Slave Population*, p. 47. Professor Higman has this information from R. E. P. Wastell, "The History of Slave Compensation, 1833 to 1865" (M.A. thesis, University of London, 1932), pp. 117–19. The author's attempts to get a copy of this thesis have been unsuccessful.

117. *Votes*, December 7 and 13, 1796. The House moved for a bill to name certain commissioners "[t]o sell and dispose of certain slaves, the supposed or reputed property of some of the late Trelawny Town Maroons for the benefit of the said Maroons." The outcome is not clear.

118. CSF., 154/7, *Acts*, p. 129.

119. Ibid., 154/4, *Acts*, p. 332.

120. Ibid., 154/7, *Acts*, p. 474.

121. Ibid., pp. 474–81; Ibid., 167/2, *Acts*, pp. 200–4.

122. Any random case could be cited, but Thomas Craskell's superintendency of Trelawny Town in the 1790s is typical. Craskell petitioned the House, November 12, 1793, stating "that the petitioner, immediately on his appointment as superintendent, repaired to the said town, but there be no government house there, he was for some time under the necessity of residing at a private property adjoining the said town. That, in order to dwell in the town, as required by law, the petitioner has since procured a tenement from one of the Maroons, at the rate of £35 per annum, and cannot at a less expense provide a residence therein." See *JAJ* 9, November 15, 1793. The House's Committee of Accounts responded, November 27, 1793, by recommending that £50 be paid to Craskell for a year's rent in Trelawny Town. The following year we find Craskell petitioning again, pointing out that he had "expended" the £50 for the previous year and was left "in the same predicament" for the next year. The Accounts Committee allowed him another £50, and this pattern was to continue well into the nineteenth century, not only for Trelawny Town but also for all the other towns.

123. *JAJ* 8, December 2, 1784; December 2, 1786. In this latter year, the superintendent of Trelawny Town reported that there was no residence "or even a place to shelter him from the inclemency of the weather," while William Broadbelt of Scotts Hall, with no official residence, was paying the wife of a Maroon "who keeps a tavern" six bits per night for lodgings. See Ibid., December 8, 1785. Peter Ingram of Charles Town, with the same problem, was paying Margaret, a Maroon woman of the town, £5 p.a., and having been so domiciled for a year and a half, was petitioning the assembly for £7.0. See *JAJ* vol. 9, and *Votes*, December 6,

1792.

124. CSF., 154/7, *Acts*, pp. 474–75.

125. Ibid., pp. 475–76.

126. Ibid., p. 476.

127. Ibid.

128. Ibid.

129. Dallas, *History*, I, p. 99.

130. Ibid., p. 130.

131. Bryan Edwards to Mark Davis of Bristol, April 18, 1774, Add. Ms. 12413; C.O. 137/69, Keith to Dartmouth, April 22, 1774.

132. Ibid.

133. Metcalf, *Royal Government*, p. 184.

134. Edward Long Papers, Add. Ms. 12413.

135. Dallas, *History*, I, p. 130; Ms. Kopytoff's account of this incident does not appear to square with the records, even including that of Bryan Edwards, who held no brief for the Maroons. See Kopytoff, "The Maroons of Jamaica," p. 251, for example, where it is given that "the Maroon Sam Grant tried to kill an Englishman and did kill a slave and the captain of a British ship," without mentioning the circumstances.

136. Edward Long Papers, Add. Ms. 12413.

137. C.O. 137/69, Keith to Dartmouth, April 22, 1774.

138. Metcalf, *Royal Government*, pp. 191–95.

139. *JAJ* 6, December 21, 1774.

Chapter 7

1. C.O. 137/94, Portland to Williamson, October 6, 1795; Williamson to Portland, December 20, 1795.

2. C.O. 137/95, Balcarres to Portland, May 11, 1795; Ibid, May 30, 1795.

3. Ibid.

4. Ibid.

5. Lindsay, *Lives of the Lindsays*, II, pp. 342–43.

6. Ibid., pp. 356–57.

7. C.O. 137/95, Balcarres to Portland, July 19, 1795.

8. Dallas, *History*, I, p. 145.

9. For all this, see, C.O. 137/95–97; *JAJ* vol. 9; Edwards, *Proceedings*, among the primary source material.

10. Dallas, *History*, I, p. 135; see, too, *JAJ* vol. 8, one of the numerous petitions of John James, November 29, 1786, to the Assembly, asking for reimbursement for services rendered, pointing out in the process that he was appointed major-commandant of all the Maroons since 1779.

11. Ibid., Assembly's Report, December 2, 1786, December 18, 1786, among others.

12. Dallas, *History*, I, pp. 133–34.

13. C.O. 137/95, Montego Bay Magistrates to Balcarres, July 18, 1795.

14. Ibid., July 10, 1795.

15. Dallas, *History*, I, pp. 147–48.
16. C.O. 137/95, July 11, 1795, Merody to Craskell; *JAJ* 9, July 19, 1795.
17. *JAJ* vol. 9, James Stewart, magistrate of Trelawny, to Balcarres, July 20, 1795, with enclosure.
18. Ibid.
19. C.O. 137/95, Balcarres to Portland, August 25, 1795, with enclosures.
20. Ibid., July 19, 1795.
21. *JAJ* vol. 9, J. Palmer, custos of St. James, to Balcarres, July 21 and 23, 1795; C.O. 137/95, John Tharp to Balcarres, July 25, 1795.
22. C.O. 137/95, Balcarres to Portland, July 21, 1795.
23. Ibid., Balcarres to Portland, July 23, 1795.
24. Ibid., Balcarres to Portland, August 11, 1795.
25. Ibid.
26. C.O. 137/96, Ibid., May 13, 1796.
27. C.O. 137/95, August 8, 1795 (Proclamation).
28. Ibid., Balcarres to Portland, August 14, 1795.
29. Dallas, *History*, I, p. 181.
30. Gardner, *History*, p. 228.
31. C.O. 137/95, Balcarres to Portland, August 14, 1795.
32. Ibid.
33. Ibid., Balcarres to Portland, August 24, 1795.
34. Ibid., Balcarres to Portland, August 25, 1795.
35. C.O. 137/95, Balcarres to Portland, September 27, 1795, with enclosures.
36. Dallas, *History*, I, p. 146.
37. Ibid.
38. *JAJ* 9, September 23 and 30, 1795, with enclosures; also, C.O. 137/95, Balcarres to Portland, August 25, 1795, with enclosures on Maroon renewed compact.
39. Dallas, *History*, I, pp. 186–87.
40. C.O. 137/95, Balcarres to Portland, September 29, 1795.
41. C.O. 137/95, Montego Bay Magistrates to Balcarres, July 18, 1795.
42. Dallas, *History*, I, p. 218; for Balcarres's, see C.O. 137/97, Balcarres to Foster-Barham, May 23, 1796.
43. C.O. 137/96, Balcarres to Portland, January 1, 1796.
44. Dallas, *History*, I, p. 158.
45. C.O. 137/96, Balcarres to Portland, October 25, 1795.
46. C.O. 137/96, Balcarres to Portland, November 16, 1795.
47. Ibid.
48. C.O. 137/95, Ibid., October 4, 1795; C.O. 137/96, Ibid., October 25, 1795; see also, *JAJ* vol. 9, Lewis to Balcarres, n.d.
49. C.O. 137/95, Balcarres to Portland, September 30, and October 8, 1795; C.O. 137/96, Ibid., October 25, 1795.
50. C.O. 137/95, Balcarres to Portland, September 27, 1795; *JAJ* 9, November 2, 1796.
51. Dallas, *History*, I, p. 236.

52. C.O. 137/96, Balcarres to Portland, October 27, 1795.

53. Ibid.

54. Ibid., Balcarres to Portland, November 16, 1796.

55. *JAJ* vol. 9, Walpole to Balcarres, December 8, 1795.

56. C.O. 137/96, Balcarres to Portland, November 16, 1795.

57. Dallas, *History*, I, pp. 177.

58. C.O. 137/96, Balcarres to Walpole, February 25, 1796.

59. *JAJ* vol. 9, Lewis to Balcarres, n.d.; Dallas, *History*, I, p. 180.

60. Ibid., pp. 199–200; C.O. 137/96, Balcarres to W. Ricketts, December 31, 1795.

61. *JAJ* vol. 9, Proclamation, August 13, 1795; also, Ibid.

62. C.O. 137/96, Balcarres to Portland, October 25, 1795.

63. C.O. 137/96, Ibid., December 29, 1795.

64. Ibid., and Portland to Balcarres, March 3, 1796.

65. C.O. 137/96, Walpole to Attorney General, December 26, 1795, stating that he received the Maroon proposals on 23 December, while the *JAJ* records gave it as December 20. See *JAJ* vol. 9, Walpole to Balcarres, December 20, 1795 (private), December 22, 1795.

66. Ibid., December 28, 1795.

67. Ibid., December 25, 1795; Ibid., Walpole to Balcarres, December 30, 1795, and January 1, 1796.

68. C.O. 137/96, Balcarres to Portland, January 1, 1796.

69. Gardner, *History*, p. 233.

70. *JAJ* vol. 9, Walpole to Balcarres, January 5, 1796.

71. C.O. 137/97, Balcarres to Attorney General, January 9, 1796.

72. Gardner, *History*, p. 231.

73. *JAJ* vol. 9, Walpole to Balcarres, January 8, 1796, Balcarres to Walpole, January 9, 1796; Walpole to Balcarres, January 12, 1796.

74. Ibid., Walpole to Balcarres, January 12, 1796, Balcarres to Walpole, January 13, 1796.

75. Ibid., Walpole to Balcarres, January 14, 15, 1796; Balcarres to Walpole, January 15, 16, 1796.

76. Ibid., Walpole to Balcarres, January 23, 1796.

77. *JAJ* vol. 9, Walpole to Balcarres, December 24, 1795; C.O. 137/96, Walpole to Balcarres, December 26, 1795, with enclosure.

78. C.O. 137/96, Balcarres to Portland, December 31, 1795.

79. It is clear that Balcarres is referring to the Abbé Raynal, as praising the Maroons for their successful fight for freedom. A pencil notation, barely decipherable, would seem to agree with this interpretation, for the scribble appears to read, "Abbe Raynal," in the margin of Balcarres's dispatch — most certainly from a Colonial Office official. See C.O. 137/96, Balcarres to Portland, March 26, 1796.

80. C.O. 137/98, Balcarres to Portland, March 3, April 30, 1798, and C.O. 138/96, Ibid., January 30, 1796.

81. C.O. 137/96, Balcarres to Portland, January 30, 1796.

82. Ibid.
83. C.O. 137/95, Balcarres to Portland, August 29, 1795.
84. C.O. 137/96, Portland to Balcarres.
85. C.O. 137/96, Balcarres to Portland, April 20, 1796 (private). Portland's private letter to Balcarres is not traced.
86. Ibid., Walpole to Balcarres, March 11, 1796 (private).
87. Ibid., Balcarres to Portland, April 20, 1796; January 1, 1796. For the series of these letters, see C.O. 137/96.
88. A. E. Furness, "The Maroon War of 1795," *Jamaican Historical Review*, 5, no. 2 (November 1965): 47–48. For the debate, see *The Senator: or Parliamentary Chronicle ... The Proceedings and Debates of the Houses of Lords and Commons*, vol. 16, London: 1796, pp. 103–8.
89. *JAJ* vol. 9, Walpole to Balcarres, December 24, 1795.
90. C.O. 137/96, Balcarres' memo, n.d.
91. Maria Nugent, *Lady Nugent's Journal: Of Her Residence in Jamaica from 1801–1805*, ed., Philip Wright (Kingston, Jamaica: Institute of Jamaica, 1966), p. 11, entry of July 30, 1801. It should be noted that Balcarres was a large slaveholder on the island, owning properties in St. Elizabeth and St. George, registered in 1801 as having, respectively, 242 slaves and 663 head of stock, and 204 slaves and 26 head of stock; p. 44n.
92. C.O. 137/96, Balcarres to Attorney General, December 31, 1795.
93. *JAJ* 9, March 31, 1796.
94. Ibid., April 22, 1796; C.O. 137/96, Balcarres to Portland, May 9, 1796.
95. C.O. 137/96, Balcarres to I. King, March 26, 1796.
96. C.O. 137/95, Balcarres to I. King, September 1, 1795; Balcarres's address to Council and Assembly, September 20, 1795; Gardner, *History*, p. 236.
97. C.O. 137/97, Extract of a letter from Quarrell to [?] n.n. June 26, 1796; Ibid., June 28, 1796. Ironically, Quarrell was to be instrumental in sending them to Sierra Leone later.
98. C.O. 137/96, Balcarres to Portland, April 20, 1796; Balcarres to Admiral Parker, May 3, 1796.
99. C.O. 137/96, Petition of Maroons, May 10, 1796.
100. Ibid., Balcarres to Portland, April 17, 1796; C.O. 137/97, Balcarres to William Quarrell, June 1, 1796, Quarrell to Balcarres, June 4, 1796; C.O. 137/97, Extract of a letter from Quarrell to n.n. June 26, 1796 on His Majesty's ship *Dover*; Dallas, *History*, II, pp. 182–83.
101. CSF., 154/7, *Acts*, pp. 48, 49; Ibid., 154/8, pp. 272–74.
102. C.O. 137/96, Blake to Balcarres, October 26, 1795.
103. Ibid., Balcarres to Portland, April 17, 1796.
104. *JAJ* 9, April 23, 26, 27, 29, 1796; Gardner, *History*, p. 236.
105. Edwards, *Proceedings*, p. lxxvi.
106. See, for example, *JAJ* 9, December 15, 1795.
107. Ibid., March 23, 1796.
108. *JAJ* 9, December 20, 1795.
109. CSF., 154/8, *Acts*, pp. 287–88; *JAJ* 9, December 17, 1795, where sub-

sistence was to be given to Dick's family of the Industry Estate, who was killed in battle, as a reward for his "attachment to his master, and for his exertions to give alarm to the neighbourhood at the approach of the Maroons."

110. CSF., 154/8, *Acts*, p. 233. For a systematic study of the "free" coloreds, see Campbell, *Dynamics, passim.*

111. See, for instance, Monica Schuler, *"Alas, Alas, Kongo"* (Baltimore: The Johns Hopkins University Press, 1980), pp. 33–34, particularly.

112. Edwards, *Proceedings*, pp. xxiv–xxv.

113. Dallas, *History*, I, pp. 99–100.

114. C.O. 137/97, A Petition of sundry ... Maroons, to Assembly, November 30, 1795; also *JAJ* vol. 9, same date.

115. *JAJ* 11, November 14, 1804.

116. Ibid., 10, June 18, 20, 1798; CSF., 154/8, *Acts*, June 23, 1798.

117. *JAJ* 11, November 20, 1798.

118. *JAJ* 11, November 14, 1804.

119. Ibid., 10. November 16, 1798.

120. Clinton V. Black, *History of Jamaica* (London and Glasgow: Collins Cleartype Press, 1976), pp. 199–204; Vincent John Marsala, *Sir John Peter Grant, Governor of Jamaica, 1866–1874* (Kingston: Institute of Jamaica, 1972), p. 22.

Conclusion

1. Dallas, *History*, I, pp. 22–23.

2. The phenomenon of collaboration, which is not new to history, has, however, been given much scholarly attention since World War II. It has even generated a new pejorative word "quisling." But the collaboration of the Jamaican Maroons would not fit well under the quisling model. Nor should it be seen as "servile" in Stanley Hoffman's terms. It was also not an act of submission, defeat, or resignation. Rather, it was "an active policy of cooperation and compromise" as Steinhart found when dealing with collaboration in Western Uganda. For an excellent theoretical approach to collaboration, see Stanley Hoffman, "Self-Ensnared: Collaboration with Nazi Germany" in his collection of essays, *Decline or Renewal? France Since the 1930s* (New York: Viking Press, 1974), pp. 26–44; Edward I. Steinhart, *Conflict and Collaboration: The Kingdoms of Western Uganda, 1890–1907* (Princeton: Princeton University Press, 1977) pp. vi–vii. See also John A. Petropoulos, "Forms of Collaboration with the Enemy during the First Greek War of Liberation" in Nikiforos P. Diamandouros et al., eds., *Hellenism and the First Greek War of Liberation 1821–1830: Continuity and Change* (Thessaloniki: Institute for Balkan Studies, 1976), pp. 131–43.

3. DeGroot, *From Isolation Towards Integration*, pp. 8–12.

4. This view was first proposed by George Cumper, although he did not develop it. See George Cumper, "The Maroons in the 18th Century: A Note on Indirect Rule in Jamaica," *Caribbean Quarterly* 8(1962):25–27. It was later adopted by Kopytoff, "The Maroons of Jamaica," pp. 350–57.

5. Charles Jeffries, *The Colonial Empire and Its Civil Service* (Cambridge: Cambridge University Press, 1938), p. 134.

6. Margery Perham, "A Restatement of Indirect Rule," *Africa* 7(1934):321.

7. Taken from Mary McCarthy, *Social Change and the Growth of British Power in the Gold Coast: The Fante States, 1807–1874* (Lanham, Md.: University Press of America, 1983), p. ix.

8. Edwards, *Proceedings*, p. xl n. After mentioning that Maroons attached themselves to "different families among the English; and desiring gentlemen of consideration to allow the Maroon children to bear their names," Edwards opined, "I think great advantages might be derived from it if properly improved."

9. But the comparison with the blacks of the United States or even with the non-Maroon Caribbean blacks is not a valid one. The blacks of the diaspora, on the plantations had *no choice* in the changing of their names. This was the slave master's/mistress' prerogative. After each deed of sale, the slave would undergo a change of name whether he/she wished it or not. For the chief exponent of the creolization concept, see Brathwaite, *Creole Society*, passim.

10. *JAJ* 8, November 29, 1786.

11. *JAJ* 6, December 8, 1770; December 2, 1774; December 5, 1775; December 6, 1776.

12. Dallas, *History*, p. 136.

13. In another volume, the author has a more complete biography of Montague James, tracing his activities in Nova Scotia, en route to Sierra Leone, and while in this country.

14. In translation, "any of those poor Scottish Lords as Governor again."

15. See Leslie Charteris, *The Saint on the Spanish Main* (New York: Charter Communications, Inc.), pp. 112–13, especially.

Index